D0770120

# Trust in Modern Societies

## The Search for the Bases of Social Order

Barbara A. Misztal

Polity Press

First published in 1996 by Polity Press in association with Blackwell
Publishers Ltd.

2 4 6 8 10 7 5 3 1

*Editorial office*:
Polity Press
65 Bridge Street
Cambridge CB2 1UR, UK

*Marketing and production*:
Blackwell Publishers Ltd
108 Cowley Road
Oxford OX4 1JF, UK

Blackwell Publishers Inc.
238 Main Street
Cambridge, MA 02142, USA

ISBN 0-7456-1248-2
ISBN 0-7456-1634-8 (pbk)

A CIP catalogue record for this book is available from the British
Library and the Library of Congress.

Typeset in 10/12pt Sabon
by Best-set Typesetter Ltd, Hong Kong
Printed in Great Britain by TJ Press Ltd, Padston, Cornwall

This book is printed on acid-free paper.

# Contents

# Acknowledgements

I am grateful to the Faculty of Humanities, Griffith University, which generously assisted my research project and enabled me to take a six-month period of leave in which I was able to make substantial progress in writing. I have greatly appreciated discussions with Constance Lever-Tracy and John A. Hall and their unfailing constructive support. My warmest thanks are also due to Jacqueline Limberger for the care she devoted to my text. Finally, I owe an immense debt to my family for their forbearance and love, without which this book would have not been finished.

The author and publishers are grateful to *The Observer* © for permission to reproduce an extract from M. Bracewell's 'Civil rites and wrongs'.

# Introduction

## Why the new interest in trust?

The rationality of trust within particular structures of social
and political relations is a pressing issue in political understanding in any society of the modern world.

Dunn 1984a: 281

The concept of trust entered sociological theory by way of philosophical
and political writings, never having been a central focus of sociological
theory. Although incorporated into many models of social relationships,
trust was seldom explicitly questioned or studied. Its silent presence can
be detected in all main sociological writings, starting with the assumptions of classical theory about changes in the basis of trust which occurred in the process of transition from pre-modern to modern society
(from those based on kinship, community and tradition to the impersonal trust of functionally interdependent modern society). Within the
following debate over the moral basis of the new industrial order two
positions on the role of trust can be distinguished. In the first strand, trust
was assumed to be a valued and scarce resource which could soften the
atomistic individualism of modern society. The other, more vocal, position in this debate argued that in modern society, with its complex
division of labour, there was a need to economize on trust in persons and
confide instead in institutions. When sociology abandoned its first
'moralistic' stand, notions of moral obligation, such as trust and solidarity, were rendered irrelevant. In fact, the structural functionalist and
Marxist phases ignored the issue of trust altogether.

Consequently, until recently, in both political theories (which debate
the means of creating and sustaining organizational structures to enable

cooperation between political agents) and sociological theories (which search for mechanisms of integration) the focus was 'the more or less rational pursuit of interests' (Dunn 1993: 641). Similarly, in economic theory, assumptions underlying the market process have rested on the perception of individual actors as rational egoists. Generally, it can be said that modern social sciences have not contributed significantly to our understanding of the concept of trust and the conditions under which trust relations thrive or struggle to survive. Fortunately, however, in the last decade the concept of trust has featured with growing frequency and prominence in theorization about modern society. Moreover, this time, the interest in trust has not been limited to disputes about how to confide in institutions but has related to debates as to how to project qualities of trust and cooperation on to the state and the market. Trust is no longer seen as a regulatory mechanism but rather as a public good; these theories do not dismiss interpersonal trust but investigate its changing role.

The most recent use of the term places trust in relation to changes in the conditions of modernity and presents the importance of trust in the context of the specific features of modern societies, such as their reflexivity, globalization and level of risk (Giddens 1990). It is argued that the rationality of modern society, which requires consideration of the possibility of future damage, as a consequence of our actions, and risk taking, as far as others are involved, demands trust (Beck 1992).

The notion of trust is also being increasingly used by social researchers in an attempt to explain the empirical differences in achieved levels of cooperation in various social and political environments. They investigate trust as a supplement to or substitute for contractual and bureaucratic bonds, arguing that trust lubricates cooperation and is thus in the collective interest (Gambetta 1988a). In a similar vein, many studies of successful economic regions emphasize the importance of the trust relationship between partners in economic activity. Trust is seen here not only as a necessary precondition for the development of flexibly specialized local economies but also as a product of this type of development (Sabel 1989: 45–52).

The concept of trust has also been entering sociological debate under the headline of civil society, albeit less explicitly (Wolfe 1989; Keane 1988; Bellah et al. 1991; Seligman 1992; Wolfe 1991). The search for ways in which the demands of individuality can be reconciled with those of community leads to the revitalization of the idea of civil society, at the centre of which trust and mutual obligations are placed. The same mood of debate resurfaces in contemporary political philosophy, with an entire new school claiming the necessity of attending to community, which is seen as based on mutual obligations and trust, alongside liberty and equality (Raz 1986; Walzer 1983; Sandel 1982; Kymlicka 1989; Mulhall and Swift 1992).

At the present time there is also a growing interest in the study of personalized trust, which is based on deliberately cultivated, face-to-face relationships with friends, lovers and family (Giddens 1991, 1992). Furthermore, the increase in research on motivation that goes beyond self-interest, in which the empirical and normative points of view are quite frequently mixed, has contributed to a new understanding of collective behaviour (Mansbridge 1990). The revision by psychologists and economists of the adversary model (and the rational choice strand within it) supports the need for a new approach incorporating values and norms (Margolis 1984; Ostrom 1990). Empirical answers to the question of whom we trust can also be found in numerous studies of social values and political cultures (Dalton 1988; Anderson 1993; Ashford and Timms 1992). In these types of studies, however, trust does not appear at a high level of conceptualization or abstraction.

Trust will never be a central topic of mainstream sociology. Nevertheless, even a quick survey of recent sociological literature provides convincing evidence of the popularity and increased topicality of the notion of trust in many sociological subdisciplines. These various investigations into the changing, renewed and continuing role of trust within modern society raise the question: why is the concept of trust becoming increasingly popular in so many areas of the social sciences?

The recent increase in the visibility of the issue of trust can be attributed to the emergence of a widespread consciousness that existing bases for social cooperation, solidarity and consensus have been eroded and that there is a need to search for new alternatives. It is often argued that we live in uncertain and confused times and that we have lost the symbols or ideologies able to represent the meaning of integration. Hence the current search for new bases of integration. This new need for a re-discussion of alternatives to the traditional bases of cooperation revives a concern with trust seen as a valuable asset, which develops in the mutually formative interplay of public institutions and individuals. The awareness of the transitional character of present Western society is widely acknowledged in the social sciences and is labelled in many different ways: some researchers write about post-modernity, others about post-industrial society and yet others about global society. Since '[t]rust is central to social life when neither traditional certainties nor modern probabilities hold' (Hart 1988: 191), the renewed significance of the issue of trust in recent studies can be explained by the transitional character of our present condition. It seems that the main characteristic of the present transitional stage is the trend towards 'the decentring of some of our most important institutions' (Wolfe 1991: 462).

One of the most important developments in modern Western societies in the twentieth century has been the expansion of citizenship rights – civil, political and social. The Keynesian welfare state in the West and the presence of centralized party states in Eastern and Central Europe ensured a low profile for issues of social cohesion in the post-war era. Moreover, national consensus at the time of the Cold War was facilitated by the perception of a mutual military threat and was sustained by favourable economic conditions. However, the decade of the 1980s, with its deregulation and privatization and its reliance on individualistic culture, showed not only that social citizenship was not firmly founded in civil and political rights (Marquand 1991), but also that the old consensus and solidarity no longer exist (Galbraith 1992). With decreasing resources and the ongoing process of globalization – and faced with the collapse of communism – modern industrial nations are being forced to redefine and articulate new collective values and aspirations. A similar process of decentring and a growing confusion of values has been affecting people's personal lives (Wolfe 1991b), demanding from them a redefinition of rules by which they structure their existence. Thus, until new patterns of normality emerge, which will restore confidence and predictability to our social, political and economic arrangements, 'things once taken for granted will increasingly be subject to complex and difficult negotiations' (Wolfe 1991a: 468). This collapse of traditional standards around such issues as family, work, discipline, the decline of industrial and class identities, the increase of culturally specific identities (ethnic, racial, territorial), the weakening of the welfare state and the decline and suppression of national boundaries, all raise a vital question for modern society: where are we to look for reliable bases for social solidarity, cooperation and consensus? Consequently, the questions of how social trust is produced and what kinds of social trust enhance economic and governmental performance increasingly become the central set of theoretical issues in social sciences (Levi 1993: 375).

The search for new bases of social cohesion and cooperation not only occupies social scientists but also animates public discussions, political debates and journalistic disputes. One of the best-known and most popular answers to the question of a new basis for integration points to the necessity for a restructuring of the micro-foundations of our lives. In particular, it emphasizes the need for a new cultural basis to support the economic system. This perspective begins by asking what are the causes of our main failures – that is, unemployment and slow economic growth. These economic problems, seen in the context of increased competitiveness and the impressive growth rates of east Asia – over the past twenty-five years, eight economies in this region have together raised their incomes per head by nearly 6 per cent, compared with the 2.3 per cent of the OECD countries (*The Economist*, 2 October 1993: 18) – cast a special light on the nature of difficulties experienced by the Western industrialized world. Practically all explanations of the economic success of east Asia emphasize the significance of their cultural context, which – it is assumed – facilitates its industrial expansion. For instance, comparisons between Japan and the United States or Western European countries, so often pursued not only in academic writing but also in many popular newspapers and magazines, bring to our attention the solidaristic structure of Japanese industry, whereby a relatively high level of trust exists between employees and managers. At the same time, the low-trust culture of Western management style (particularly British and American styles), the presence of conflict and a lack of mutual loyalty and responsibility between workers and bosses are stressed (Block 1991). Consequently, the growing concern over the failure of Western capitalism in the context of increased competition from east Asia results in calls for a national revival based on a recognition of the importance of mutual obligations and a more collectivistic culture. A proposed way forward is to embrace group solidarity, a more communal and unselfish orientation and the creation of bonds of trust between people (Dertouzos et al. 1989; Reich 1991; Clarke 1992). This stance not only echoes the way that political philosophy questions the relationship between rights and duties or between the individual and community but also the ways in which sociological writing perceives economic action as embedded in social relations and argues that social relations and the obligations inherent in them are mainly responsible for the production of trust, which in turn facilitates cooperation (Sabel 1989; Zetlin 1989).

With the collapse of communism, the debate about what kind of cultural characteristics are needed to sustain economic growth has been enriched and has gained in importance. The disintegration of the Soviet system, which proved that the weakness of undemocratic states lies in their lack of social trust, has brought forward an additional question about the role of political arrangements in securing economic development. Can an economic system based on distrust and disinformation sustain long-term economic growth? Again, this type of debate has been taken up by a wide range of publications, from daily newspapers to academic studies. As the majority of writers note, this new knowledge does not mean the 'end of history', but rather it initiates a new and confusing search for the proper mixture of culture, politics and economics, adequate for the new world. The different type of answer to the question of the bases of a new integration and social cohesion comes from two traditional ideological camps. Although the Left and the Right differ in their proposed alternatives to existing economic and political arrangements (more state or more market, respectively), both perspectives imply a crucial role for trust. Each of them recognizes the need for trust as public good or as social capital. According to the New Right, 'market order would depend upon certain public goods – civility, honesty, mutual trust, community even – which the market itself cannot supply' (Marquand 1991: 337). On the other hand, according to the critics of liberal democracy, who postulate the democratization not only of political but also of economic life, and thus recommend a powerful and interventionist state, the state-based solution should depend upon the legitimacy of government. This solution, consequently, leads to a need for 'still greater attention to the ways in which states' action can be made more democratically accountable' (Pierson 1993: 196). Central to this argument is the role of trust within the community and of governmental trustworthiness, both seen as an essential condition for effective, responsive representative institutions.

The tension between the moral and economic dimensions of the liberal solution, and the tension between the moral and political aspects of the socio-democratic approach, present the same kind of difficulties. In the past the valuable public good, such as trust, was supplied by common tradition, community and the Church. What are the sources of trust now? The answer to this question provided by the representatives of both perspectives points to the concept of civil society. Some argue that one vague and murky concept is simply replaced by another. Certainly, it does not solve the problem, but only pushes the question further: how can the problem of civil society – that is, the problem of 'the synthesis between collective solidarity and individualism and of reigning definitions of each' (Seligman 1992: 169) – be solved?

This way of approaching the problem of the bases of social cohesion brings sociological enquiry to centre stage. Placing civil society at the heart of the issue of integration presents a very interesting challenge for social theory. Sociologists make it clear that issues of civil society should be seen as the problem of constituting trust in society (Wolfe 1989; Seligman 1992). Thus, the revitalization of the idea of civil society is, in essence, nothing more than an attempt to theorize more concrete and meaningful criteria of trust in modern, rationalized and highly differentiated societies. The sociological search, initiated by the civil society's approach, for new bases of obligations and new relationships between members of a society, is an interesting continuation of the classical sociological belief in the progressive triumph of civil society over the state and the Church (Touraine 1992: 60). One of the consequences of this sociological preoccupation with civil society has been the decreasing significance of Marxism, which excluded trust and based social order on conflict, rejecting, by the same token, the importance of civil society. The understanding that not all forms of social relationships can be classified around conflict and calculative action, that people in interdependent relationships can sometimes renounce conflict and cooperate, that egoistic behaviour alone cannot account for social order – seem to be at the core of the new thinking. The re-invention of civil society, the renewal of the importance of personal bonds and the adaptation of the post-modern and post-industrial schemes as features of Western development relate to sociological attempts to find a balance between the competing nature of the different values. Sociology, thanks mostly to the Durkheimian and Weberian traditions, seems to be able to recognize the importance of particular affiliations without rejecting the formal rationality of our modern age. It seems that the majority of sociological strategies put strong emphasis on moderation, preferring the optimal solution, which in a rational way tries to combine positive elements of various perspectives. It rejects a zero-sum vision of society and aims at the minimalization of risk and increasing stability. This sober and balanced approach assumes that neither conflict nor liberation, but rather mutual adjustment and self-control, will secure a better future. Thus, a new critical politics, as Offe and Preuss (1991) and Cohen and Arato (1992) argue, will be a reflective politics of self-control and self-limitation.

This does not mean, of course, that sociological answers to the question of the basis of social integration are not confronted with many difficulties related to the properties of the notion of trust. Firstly, it is not always realized that, while the present changes have made trust a more explicitly valuable asset than it was previously, they have not made its attainment or maintenance any easier. The pressures exerted by global changes on the cohesion of national electorates, on the autonomy of national economies and on the extent of economic inequalities between both classes and regions make the production of trust increasingly problematic. Trust cannot be seen any more as an automatic by-product of macro-social or macro-economic processes, but rather it needs to be perceived as an active political accomplishment.

Secondly, any attempt to integrate society as a system of trust relationships is faced with new tensions between universalism and particularism, duties and rights, autonomy and community, market and state, integration and fragmentation, local and global. The search for a new balance between these tensions has re-opened debates about the fate of modernity and the meaning of progress, about the principles of integration, about individual freedom and collective responsibility, about the modern political identity and the construction of the modern self.

Thirdly, the sociological emphasis on civil society can be accused of relying on too many optimistic assumptions. It is impossible to believe that civil society, as the domain of solidarity and justice, can solve problems of limited resources and limited sympathies. Maybe it is even too Utopian for our sceptical world. However, if we agree with Habermas (1992: 26) that the exhaustion of a particular model of Utopia, based on the concept of self-realization through labour, does not mean that progress is not possible, we ought to examine the idea of trust and civil society as one of the few strategies available in a new world.

The concept of trust, so conveniently wrapped up in the idea of civil society, plays a double role within this notion. Many projects for a new basis of democratic civil society employ the concept of trust in rather circular ways. Firstly, trust – as one of the important sources of cooperation – is seen as a socially desirable aim. Secondly, it is argued that, in order to achieve it, we must proceed in a trustworthy way. It is this double and ambiguous meaning that makes the concept of trust difficult to examine yet simultaneously attractive to use. Thus, while it is not surprising that the concept of trust is so frequently employed, answers provided with the help of this notion are not always sufficient solutions, but rather merely reformulations of problems in 'moral' language. Moreover, this re-emergence of Tocqueville's argument that civic participation, which depends upon trust between members of society, is the only effective means of training responsible and trustworthy citizens suited for liberty (Hall 1992), comes when it is rather difficult to identify clearly the concept of society. While it is not an 'easy task bringing together fellow citizens who had lived for many centuries aloof from, or even hostile, to each other and teaching them to co-operate in their own affairs' (Tocqueville 1955: 107), to create trust in an increasingly underdefined space for 'society' seems almost impossible. The concept of the trustworthy society cannot be defined if we do not have a clear answer to the question of whether 'society' should be vested in nations, smaller groups or wider associations. It should now be clear that the problems of trust are directly connected with the most urgent and important questions of the modern world. In order to be able to address these problems we need to know more about trust and its properties.

## Aims and the structure of the book

As we have seen, many scholars argue that the role of trust in modern society is significant and increasing. The increased importance of this notion is the result of the main structural changes specific to the present transitional stage of Western societies. At the same time there are remarkable commonalities characterizing the various attempts at social reform. Such programmes reject traditional Marxist-inspired concepts of revolutionary change but, at the same time, they are also aware of unmet

potentials in liberal democratic regimes. The proposed remedy, the re-
birth of civil society and active citizenry, is seen as a means of ensuring
cooperation, self-realization, solidarity and freedom. It puts trust at the
centre of an understanding of modern societies and their politics. The
aim of this book is to provide support for the view that trust becomes a
more urgent and central concern in today's contingent, uncertain and
global conditions. It does not propose a vision of politics and of human
life as resting upon trust, but instead attempts to look at modern societies
and their problems from the perspective of the quality of social relationships rather than in terms of goal achievement or performance of the
system. In Western democracies political order is not ensured by a shared
value system or trust in authority. However, to create a new quality of
social relationships, social cooperation, solidarity and tolerance we need
to devote more attention to the relationships among people and to the
relationship between people and decision makers. Because experience of
how societies cooperate and cohere points to the conclusion that it is the
relationships that hold us together, trust and the conditions facilitating
trustworthy relationships should be at the centre of public attention.

The aim of this book is not just to collect evidence in support of the
thesis concerned with the growing significance of trust relationships. I
shall try to demonstrate not only how changes in contemporary societies
are making the construction of trust more urgent but also how they
require a new, more active type of trust and how they make trust more
difficult to attain. The pressures exerted by global changes on the cohesion of national electorates, on the autonomy of national economies and
on the extent of economic inequalities between social groups and between regions make the production of trust increasingly problematic in
ways that I shall outline in detail. In order to be able to address these
problems we need to know more about trust, its properties and its
changing nature. It is also my aim to present various ways of conceptualizing the notion of trust and the ways in which sociological theories
deal with it. Since trust is a very imprecise and confusing notion and our
intellectual understanding of trust is seriously underdeveloped, this over-
view of the field is necessary in order to facilitate an advance in the
debate about this phenomenon. Fourthly, I hope that an incorporation of
the experience of communist and post-communist societies of Europe,
which can be seen as a testing ground for the role of trust, will offer a
particularly instructive insight to both the necessity and the difficulty of
generating social cooperation based on trust.

The first chapter examines various definitions of trust. Aiming at
bridging the interpersonal and systematic levels of analysis, I conceptualize trust as a social mechanism which can be explained by people's beliefs
and motivations. To trust is to believe that results of somebody's in-

tended action will be appropriate from our point of view. Social relations and obligations inherent in them are presented as being mainly responsible for the production of trust. To hold that trust cannot be fully understood without an examination of institutions leads to the argument that the problem of constituting trust in society is an issue concerning the conditions necessary for social order.

The aim of the second chapter is to show the shortcomings of the classical sociologists' conceptualization of trust as a self-evident social good emerging in a spontaneous way. The relationship between trust and collective order in Spencer's utilitarian model, Durkheim's normative approach and in writings of Toennies, Simmel and Weber are examined. It is proposed that, for the purpose of analysing trust, three types of order should be distinguished: stable order, which accounts for the predictability, reliability and legibility of the social reality; cohesive order, which can be seen as based on normative integration; and the third type of order, collaborative order, refering to social cooperation. The main difference between these three types of order is connected not with the types of motivation behind trusting behaviour but with the particular function of trust within each of these models.

Chapter 3 specifies the uniqueness of the role played by trust in these three types of order by analysing contemporary sociological theories which debate the function of trust in modern societies. By examining Parsons' and Luhmann's rational choice theory and Giddens' conceptualization of trust, I shall demonstrate that trust can perform a multitude of functions. It can be a silent background, sustaining the unproblematic, smooth running of cooperative relations. It can be a solution to the free-rider problem. It can help people to reconcile their own interests with those of others. But above all, trust, by keeping our mind open to all evidence, secures communication and dialogue. Combining the theories of social order with some theoretical assumptions about the various functions of trust, I shall argue that the relations between order and trust can only be understood by examining the role of trust relations in stable, cohesive and collaborative orders by asking the following questions: How is the stability of social order protected? Whom do we trust? What are the conditions for collaboration?

Trust understood in the context of three different types of order is a multi-dimensional phenomenon. The three forms of trust, whether understood as habitus, passion or policy, are seen not as alternatives but rather as mutually reinforcing types of social capital. The following part of the book is more narrative in nature and applies these common foundational features of trust to an examination of modern societies.

In chapter 4, which deals with the tendency of the social order to be seen as stable, I shall draw an analogy between Bourdieu's (1977) concept of habitus and trust as a strategy for securing the stability of social order. Trust, understood as a specific type of habitus, allows us to account for the fact that social agents perceive the social world as stable. In order to 'make coherence and necessity out of accident and contingency' (Bourdieu 1977: 87), trust as habitus operates through rules of interaction, rules of distanciation and rules of remembering. I shall illustrate operation of these rules by examining habit, reputation and memory as three practices, which are deployed to sustain the stability of collective order.

Chapter 5 deals with the second type of order – that is, cohesive order – which can be understood in terms of the Parsonian societal community in which trust is based on familiarity, bonds of friendship and common faith and values. In this instance, trust takes on the connotations of passion, out of which motive and belief arise. I shall examine the role of trust as a passion by looking at the three bases of trust – namely, family, friendship and society.

In the third, collaborative, type of order, which is the topic of chapter 6, trust is defined as a device for coping with the freedom of others. Since trust can be seen as a mechanism for solving the problem of cooperation only when people cooperate irrespective of sanctions and rewards, we need to consider trust as a policy aiming at the creation of conditions which foster bonds of solidarity, tolerance and the legitimization of power.

The proposed synthetic approach, which attempts to combine contingency with the importance of sustaining collective order, permits the conclusion that to construct conditions in which people can learn to deal with one another in a trustworthy way without making everyone feel the same involves the generation of a sense of belonging and participation through the politics of democratization.

# 1

# Defining Trust

## What is trust?

> Trustworthiness, the capacity to commit oneself to fulfilling
> the legitimate expectations of others, is both the constitutive
> virtue of, and the key causal precondition for the existence of,
> any society.
>
> Dunn 1984a: 287

Trust is a highly problematic but recurrent feature of social relationships.
Social theories tend to conceive of trust by pointing to the range of
benefits that trust provides. For instance, it is seen as essential for stable
relationships, vital for the maintenance of cooperation, fundamental for
any exchange and necessary for even the most routine of everyday
interactions. 'Without trust only very simple forms of human cooperation which can be transacted on the spot are possible, and even individual action is much too sensitive to disruption to be capable of being
planned, without trust, beyond the immediately assured moment'
(Luhmann 1979: 88).

It is argued that trust, understood often in a very vague and
unsystematic way, shapes all aspects of human life. Whatever matters to
human beings, says Bok, 'trust is the atmosphere in which it thrives. . . .
When it is damaged the community as a whole suffers; and when it is
destroyed, societies falter and collapse' (1979: 31 and 26–7). Also Hirsch
(1977) sees trust as a public good which is necessary for the successful
running of the economy. Trust is also essential for facilitating effective
problem solving, because 'it encourages the exchange of relevant information and determines whether team members are willing to allow
others to influence their decisions and actions' (Carnevale and Wechsler

1992: 471). The role of trust in the constitution and maintenance of systems of empirical knowledge is connected with its property as 'the great civility', which is 'granting the conditions in which others can colonize our minds and expecting the conditions which allow us to colonize theirs' (Shapin 1994: 36).

Furthermore, since autonomy requires trustworthiness in social communication, trust is also a prerequisite for the realization of our essential nature and the formulation of self-identity. Habermas (1984), for example, views the ability of communicative action to negotiate shared understanding, which in turn coordinates interaction, as based on the three validity claims – truth, rightness and sincerity. His communicative ethics presupposes that 'communicating actors always infer that their exchange speech acts satisfy a condition of mutual trust. Communication can continue undisturbed if speakers suppose that they already act in accordance with a sincerity rule' (Keane 1984: 159). Thus, communication, based on mutual trust, coordinates social and political interaction. A similar perspective is adopted by Bok when she notes that '[a] society whose members are unable to distinguish truthful messages from deceptive ones, would collapse' (1979: 18). Following the Tocquevillian tradition, interpersonal trust is also seen as fostering democratic values and as the basis for sustaining republican society or civic community (Putnam 1993). An emphasis on trust as an essential element of our mutual welfare and more broadly as an aspect of a worthwhile life is indeed very common in political science and sociological literature. So, if without trust life would not be possible, what is trust?

The omnipresence of trust and its problematic and multiple meanings have resulted in a unimpressive record on the part of the social sciences in grasping its essence (Dunn 1993). Different disciplines in social science have attempted to study it, or at least register its presence, but without a great deal of effort being devoted to its conceptualization. A survey of the literature on trust in 1985 concludes that 'the social science research on trust has produced a good deal of conceptual confusion regarding the meaning of trust and its place in social life' (Lewis and Weigert 1985: 975). Even though trust has received considerable attention in recent years, the confusion continues with an increased mixture of approaches and perspectives.

In unravelling this conceptual complexity our concern will be limited to the social scientist's perspective. Social science enquiries are designed with an explanatory purpose in mind, and their aim is to test a specific empirical context and the consequences of a given phenomenon. This means that we will not be interested in moral dilemmas since these are topics specific to normative philosophy. Similarly, trust as a psychological trait of personality, as studied by experimental psychologists in laboratory settings, is not part of our immediate interest. Akin to our approach are the volumes of research on trust conducted by political scientists, interested in factors influencing social confidence in political systems and their leaders. Sociologists themselves have seldom studied or measured trust, although there have been some studies which have measured 'confidence' in public opinion surveys.

The sociological literature conceptualizes trust as either the property of individuals, the property of social relationships or the property of the social system explained with attention to behaviour based on actions and orientations at the individual level. The first approach puts emphasis on feelings, emotions and individual values. Trust is seen as a function of individual personality variables (Deutsch 1958; Cole 1973; Wolfe 1976). In this socio-psychological work trust is confused with or closely related to cooperative mentality, honesty, loyalty, sincerity, hope or altruism. These attempts to develop a personality theory of trust are far too simplistic in their lack of attention to the social context (one may trust in some circumstances, not in others, and so on). Methodologically they are also unacceptable because in these studies trust is treated 'in ways which have reductionistic consequences' (Lewis and Weigert 1985: 975).

In the second approach, trust is seen more as a collective attribute, and is thus applicable to the institutional fabric of society. In this way, for example, Fordism as a mode of production is described as a 'low trust system' (Fox 1974), while 'flexible specialisation' or a post-Fordist organization of manufacturing is labelled as a 'trust dependent system' (Sabel 1989; Hirst and Zetlin 1991). Trust is seen as a social resource that can be drawn upon in order to achieved certain organizational goals (Nachmias 1985).

The third approach sees trust as a valued public good, sustained by actions of members of a given society. It can be found, for instance, in Tocqueville's classic description of the civic community as marked by a social fabric of trust and cooperation and reliant upon the activities of a public-spirited citizenry. Also Putnam's (1993) search for an explanation of what 'makes democracy work' in northern Italy points to trust within community. He views trust as social capital, which is the essential condition for effective, responsive and representative institutions. A view of trust as an emergent property of the social system as much as a personal attribute allows this popular approach to apply trust as a valuable concept for overcoming the macro/micro distinction. In the same vein, Luhmann (1979) and Barber (1983), while starting with people's expectations, view trust as a dimension of the social structure which 'cannot be fully understood and studied exclusively on either the psychological level or on the institutional level, because it thoroughly permeates both' (Lewis and Weigert 1985: 974). Seeing trust from this perspective makes it possible to show how building trust on the micro-level contributes to the more abstract trust on the macro-level (Luhmann 1988). Each positive contact with our local doctor, for example, may gradually increase our confidence in the medical system.

Following this perspective, it can be said that an adequate conceptualization of trust as a sociological notion, aimed at bridging the interpersonal and the systematic levels of analysis, should see trust as a social mechanism, that is, 'a specific causal pattern that can be recognised after the event but rarely foreseen' (Elster 1993: 13). Studying trust as a social mechanism involves explaining people's actions by their motivations and beliefs. It raises three questions: firstly, what kind of motivations? secondly, beliefs about what? and lastly, what are the sources of these motivations and beliefs? Before addressing these questions, it will be helpful to examine the most common definitions of trust. The efficient way to grasp the most common connotations of the notion of trust is to analyse some basic definitions, rather than debating various attempts in sociological theory to identify its role and nature. Definitions of trust in sociological literature generally reflect the theoretical stands of the various authors, and as such they need to be discussed in the context of their respective theories (which will be our task in the following two chapters), while dictionary-type definitions show the most common properties of trust and illustrate an evolution of its meaning.

Trust has had many connotations. The oldest one relates this notion to faith or 'the confidence in a supranatural Power on which man feels himself dependent' (*Encyclopedia of Religion and Ethics*, Morgan 1912: 464). Trust of this kind is present in all religious beliefs since to trust God as the source of salvation is an essence of every religion. 'Blessed is the man who trusts in Jaweh and whose confidence Jaweh is', says the Old Testament. 'In God We Trust' is on the coins and notes of the United States. 'Trust in God' is the Islamic suicide bombers' final message. Trust is seen here as in part an article of 'faith' to which is attributed a broader meaning, including trust and some cognitive elements of assessment of a given doctrine. In the idea of faith the emphasis falls on its cognitive aspects, yet faith is always an antithesis to understanding since it relies upon a vague and partial understanding of its object. Faith is not, however, a passive acceptance of the unknown; rather it is, as in Pascal's view, a strategic decision to take a risk in the condition of uncertainty. In Roman languages, the term used for trust, *fede* (translated into English as faith) also implies non-rational and incalculable elements (Pagden 1988: 129). It carries with it an element of duty to keep faith as the foundation of social life. For Giddens (1990: 27), trust is a form of faith, in which 'confidence vested in probable outcomes expresses a commitment to something rather than just a cognitive understanding'. This brings us to another concept closely connected with trust – namely, the notion of confidence.

The main definition of trust in the *Oxford English Dictionary* identifies trust as 'confidence in or reliance on some quality or attributes of a person or thing, or the truth of a statement'. In this definition, trust to a large extent merges with the idea of confidence, which expresses a firm trust. Without going into the debate about the criteria for the distinction between trust and confidence (see the discussion of Luhmann's concept of trust and Giddens' understanding of the notion of trust in chapter 3), it can be accepted that trust is a matter of individual determination and involves choosing between alternatives (I decide to take a risk and trust my new colleague), while confidence is more habitual expectation (I am habitually confident that my milkman will deliver milk to the doorstep tomorrow). The main difference between trust and confidence is connected with the degree of certainty that we attach to our expectations. It is, of course, much easier to decide whether to have confidence or not in one's milkman than to decide which people can be trusted to reciprocate friendly actions, since trust involves a difficult task of assessment of other people's capacities for the action. Thus, anything that facilitates accurate judgement about whom to trust has an important social value. Indeed, it is precisely the existence of many forms of complex interdependence and the freedom of others that creates such an enormous demand for trust and makes it an interesting social phenomenon.

Further pursuing the *Oxford English Dictionary*'s definition of trust, we discover that from an economic perspective trust is identified as 'confidence in the ability and intention of a buyer to pay at a future time for goods supplied without present payment'. This definition points out that trust is an underlying feature of a specific exchange relationship. It is not a barter exchange, where face-to-face transaction takes place without any time delays. It is not a monetary market exchange, where buying and selling is based on common trust in money as the medium of transaction. This type of relationship can be described as a 'credit' type of exchange in which 'trades trust each other' (Anderlini and Sabourian 1992: 100). In this light, trust can be defined as 'a set of expectations shared by those in an exchange' (Zucker 1986: 54), and different types of exchange can be defined according to the level of trust present within the relationship.

Anthropological analyses, which tend to emphasize the normative standards that sustain exchange, show the importance of reciprocity as compelling obligations and prolonging partnerships (Shalins 1972). In his classic work *The Gift*, Mauss argues that the obligations to give, to receive and to return are not to be understood simply with respect to rational calculation. Gift giving is a form of non-immediate reciprocity where reward is neither discussed nor consciously calculated at the moment the offering is made. In the long run, however, one expects gifts to be reciprocated. Thus, in primitive and archaic societies, those societies based on gift-relationships, 'there is no middle path; there is either trust or mistrust' (Mauss 1970: 79). Modern, stratified and divided societies, Mauss argues, by definition are no longer reciprocal. This pessimistic perspective is, however, contradicted by some writers, who point to the importance of gift exchange in our complex, large-scale society (Timuss 1969; Zucker 1986; Davis 1992) or to the significant function of other forms of exchange not based on the expectation of profit, as, for example, exchange between parents and children or charity donations (Davis 1992).

Accepting a broad and non-rigid classification of various types of exchange fosters the image of people as having a complex repertoire of behaviour, allowing them to be market-wise in commerce, reciprocal with friends, generous with their children, and in some situations even altruistic. However, in which types of exchange does trust play an important role? It is certainly not in hostile takeovers, nor in burglary nor in extortion, to mention only some of Davis' repertoires of exchange. Trust seems to play a significant role in any exchange where each partner has clear expectations of the other, and where there is a time lapse between the exchange of goods or services. As Mauss (1970: 34) notes: 'Time has to pass before a counter-presentation can be made and this requires trust.' Thus, only the type of exchange based on mutual expectations (obligations) and involving a time lapse is underpinned by trust as an instrument of social organization. Both credit and gift giving can be included in this category. There is, however, a third case of this type of exchange, which is more interesting to sociologists than to anthropologists – namely, cooperation.

Trust as cooperative exchange is a more complex phenomenon than gift giving because the relationships between cooperation and trust are less straightforward than those between trust and gift giving. Gift exchanges, although also based on trust (when you give gifts you trust to receive one in return and, moreover, you are trusted to consider the welfare and interests of the persons you are giving to – for example, a record of classical music would not be the best present for someone solely devoted to jazz), implicitly produce trust because 'histories of such exchange are usually readily available to the partners and because expectations are often culturally given' (Zucker 1986: 61). Cooperation is seen as a by-product of trust rather than a source of trust and, moreover, a lack of cooperation can be a result of other factors (such as lack of sufficient information) rather than an absence of trust. 'Consequently, while cooperation and trust are intimately related in that the former is a central manifestation of the latter, the former cannot provide, for either the actor or the analyst, a simple redefinition of trust' (Good 1988: 33). Despite this call for caution in identifying cooperation with trust, the definition of trust in the *Blackwell Dictionary of Twentieth-Century Social Thought* (W. Outhwaite and T. Bottomore, eds, 1993) implicitly connects these two concepts.

Trust is defined here as 'the willingness of other agents to fulfil their contractual obligation that is crucial for cooperation'. Identifying trust on the basis of its complex relationships with cooperation stresses only one particular aspect of trust, which is attributed to the problem posed by cooperation and arising 'whenever agents cannot monitor each other's action'. However, to some degree all social situations are arenas of mutual monitoring (Goffman 1963a), and, moreover, the 'reflexive monitoring' of social action (Giddens 1984) is an essential factor in the subjective assessment of the probability of whether others will cooperate. Lewis and Weigert note the other reason for not restricting discussion of the concept of trust to the issue of cooperation. According to them, equating the concept of trust with cooperation is a 'strictly behavioural interpretation of the concept of trust', whose value lies in 'operationalising trust as trusting (i.e., cooperative) choice of behaviour [rather] than in developing an adequate conceptualisation of trust' (1985: 975). Also Dunn's (1993) observation that trust as a passion can be enabling and also disruptive (trust, as love, is blind) challenges the view that identifies the importance of trust solely in terms of cooperative relationships. Generally, it can be said that cooperation is only one type of exchange based on mutual obligations, and that there are other types of exchange as well as other types of relationships in which trust plays an important role. For instance, trust as an expectation of stability of social context (one trusts that the train timetables will be the same tomorrow) refers to the predictable rather than to the cooperative character of social order.

What integrates all the above definitions of trust is their common emphasis on the importance of several properties of trust relationships. The main common characteristic of trust, using *Webster's Third New International Dictionary*'s formulation, is its 'dependence on something future or contingent; confident anticipation'. The trust features are thus derived from the contingency of social reality and they require a time lapse between one's expectations and the other's action. What makes trust so puzzling is that to trust involves more than believing; in fact, to trust is to believe despite uncertainty. Trust always involves an element of risk resulting from our inability to monitor others' behaviour, from our inability to have a complete knowledge about other people's motivations and, generally, from the contingency of social reality. Consequently, one's behaviour is influenced by one's beliefs about the likelihood of others behaving or not behaving in a certain way rather than solely by a cognitive understanding or by firm and certain calculation.

What kind of expectations and beliefs can we have about 'something future'? This question brings us back to our conceptualization of trust as a social mechanism, which can be explained by people's beliefs and motivations. We have posed three questions, asking about types, content and sources of motivation and beliefs. In what follows my objective will be to address these three questions. I will start with an analysis of the sources of motivation and beliefs. A sociological approach, which focuses on the way in which individuals and society interact, generally argues that social relations and interactions are the points of origin of motivations and beliefs. It has already been demonstrated by Garfinkel that trust and shared understanding are inherent in all social interactions. The production of trust motivations is similarly presented by Granovetter (1985) and Wolfe (1989). According to Granovetter (1985: 491), the main factors responsible for the production of trust in economic life are social relations and the obligations inherent in them. Wolfe argues that individuals create their moral rules – that is, mutual obligations – through the social interactions they experience with others. 'We are not social because we are moral; we are moral because we live together with others and therefore need periodically to account for who we are. Morality matters because we have reputations to protect, cooperative tasks to carry out, legacies to leave, others to love and careers to follow' (Wolfe 1989: 215). In this context, people's mutual obligations towards one another are the fruit of the collective rewards of interaction.

By reconciling our needs with the needs of others in daily negotiations, organizing and reflecting on our relationships with others, we construct our expectations and our beliefs about others. Basing our assessment of what to do next on expectations that the actions of others will be constrained by their obligations towards us, helps us to account for the contingency and uncertainty of the situation. However, a cognitive basis of trusting attitudes is limited since the main source of information used by individuals to construct their views of other people is their interactive behaviour.

Clearly, since trust is an aspect of all social relationships, one needs to differentiate between various types of relationships and the various types of obligations connected with them. What one expects from children as a parent is different from what shopkeepers expect from shoppers. Furthermore, parents are expected to behave differently towards their children than shopkeepers towards their shoppers (parents are expected to make losses on the exchange with children, while shopkeepers are expected to make profit in exchange with shoppers (Davis 1992: 42)). This suggests that trust does not need to be based only on familiarity or passion. It can rely on rational expectations, as our trust in money illustrates. However, as Dodd (1994: 137) notes, 'the relationship between trust and rationality is complicated and uneven'. The complexity of this relationship is nowhere more visible than in difficulties faced by all rational attempts to build trust.

Expectations in relationships between patients and doctors, lawyers and clients, employers and employees, husbands and wives, citizens and politicians, students and teachers are all constructed in the process of gradual learning by establishing levels of shared understanding and mutual obligations. For instance, the issue of involuntary unemployment is better explained by levels of mutual obligations and understanding between employers and employees than by the neo-classical model of economics. Akerlof (1984: 145–71), after proving that all other possible factors (such as legislation, distribution of skills and so on) do not fully account for the levels of involuntary unemployment, argues that the shared concept of 'a fair wage for a fair day's work', which creates mutual obligations and expectations between these two sets of actors, is the missing factor. The 'gift of fairness' in the employment relationship, which is learned and developed in the creative process of complex adjustment and negotiation, means that both parties trust each other to meet their respective obligations; workers try to work in excess of the minimum work standard; and the firm provides wages in excess of the market rate.

The duration and the stability of social relationships influence the clarity and visibility of mutual obligations. While we are not sure what is expected of us and what to expect of others in an unknown situation, our familiar and stable relationships with our friends and colleagues are not causes of such anxiety and uncertainty. Modern societies are full of ambiguities, creating opportunities to 'take moral shortcuts' and 'not everyone resists them' (Wolfe 1989: 219). However, the same ambiguity which increases 'free-rider opportunities' also permits the securing of general satisfaction, peace or order by facilitating the avoidance of direct or immediate confrontations or conflicts – for instance, peace-creating misunderstanding (Davis 1992: 54–7). The different ways people exploit this ambiguity must be analysed in order to ascertain whether and which modern conditions provide individuals with the opportunity to learn to trust others and to develop self-confidence and self-mastery. Furthermore, since modern life depends on contingent structures and changeable conditions and familiarity is not its dominant feature, there is also the need to examine the role of depersonalized trust – that is, trust in the ability of the system to maintain conditions and to perform its functions.

To sum up, social relations and the obligations inherent in them are mainly responsible for the production of trust. Central to the concept of trust, seen as embodied in structures of social relations, is uncertainty about other people's motivations. People's commonsense knowledge about what to expect from various types of social relations and their understanding of the motives of others is also central to our second question, which asks about the types of motivations underlying trust relationships. Two assumptions need to be noted here. The first argument, by now a commonplace observation, is that mixed motivations are central ingredients in most interactions (Schelling 1960; Elster 1989; Wolfe 1989). Schelling, for instance, argues that distinctively modern mixed-motive games – that is, games where players must reconcile zero-sum ambitions with the possibility of cooperative gains – are based on the paradoxical combination of trust and manipulation (Schelling 1960: 89–115). Margolis (1990) also shows that most real choices are governed by the mixed character of motivation; people are moved all the time by social as well as egoistic motivation in allocation of their spending.

Secondly, people's actions should be seen as responses governed by various motivations to a plurality of varying circumstances (Elster 1989). Accounting for people's motivation means not only analysing the whole range of motivations (values, reasons and self-interests), but also relating them to different contexts. Motivation to trust seems to be a result of either strong positive personal bonds or affects for the object of trust, or a result of our belief that we have 'good rational reasons' (irrespective of their nature) to trust, or a result of our belief that trust enhances our interests or, more often, a result of a combination of all (Williams 1988; Lewis and Weigert 1985). Trust as an attitude is motivated in everyday situations by a rich mixture of factors, from which we can exclude coercion, since trust 'can be promised and trust can be earned, but it cannot be ordered' (Liberman 1981: 134). Neither can it be purchased or bribed, since, as an age-old truth – immortalized in *King Lear* – illustrates, any attempt to 'buy' trust can only destroy it.

The variety of motivations that lead people to fulfil their obligations in a plurality of contexts make it impossible to classify trust relationships. However, there is a common structure which has its origin in the fact that not meeting somebody's expectations offends our sense of what is appropriate in a given circumstance. For instance, in relationships based on personal trust (that is, based on bonds between people – for example, between lovers, members of the family or friends), it is assumed that each partner could rely on the other partner's consideration of his or her needs, interests and preferences. At the same time we do not expect our banker to consider our emotional needs or preferences in deciding on our credit line. Furthermore, although we do not expect members of any family to be motivated solely by a desire to increase one another's well-being, a family where, for instance, self-interest is the main motivation governing its members' relations will be recognized as not functioning properly. In the same way, customers that expect special, personalized, warm and favoured treatment from their bank may be perceived as rather presumptuous in their aspirations.

One may formulate some general assumptions about the strength of trust expectations in various types of trust relationships. One such example is a hypothesis arguing that 'the stronger the emotional content relative to the cognitive content, the less likely contrary behavioural evidence will weaken the relationship' (Lewis and Weigert 1985: 972) or in Luhmann's (1979: 81) words: 'Love and hate make one blind.' Not surprisingly, people think that those acting out of one single, overriding motivation cannot be trusted. They are not examples, to use Davis' concept, of a 'rounded person'. Those suspected of being cold and calculating all the time or being blinded by emotions cannot be trusted. 'In Britain we certainly think that a purely altruistic person is as unbalanced as someone who is only interested in commerce. A blood donor who donates all his blood is clearly mad' (Davis 1992: 45).

Despite the variety of motivations underlying trust relationships, they show, as we argued above, some common characteristics. These common features of trust relationships result from human beings, as emotional, rational and instrumentally orientated agents, seeking to ensure that their social relations and arrangements meet their emotional, cognitive and instrumental needs and conform to their sense of what is appropriate in each context. Our concept of what is appropriate originates in our vision of a full life and in our concept of ourselves as 'rounded persons'. 'We expect our acquaintances to try to be rounded people with reasonable personal repertoires: then we may call them good of their kind – good men, good women, good shopkeepers, good Registrars' (Davis 1992: 46).

While these common features provide the underlying structure to trust relationships, the issue of the content of beliefs or expectations still remains to be considered. Expectations or actors' beliefs are basic ingredients of social interaction and their fulfilment (or otherwise) has various consequences for the relationship in which actors are engaged. Actors' mutual expectations (seen as a common platform of shared understandings and the meanings attributed to each other) are central factors influencing their choice of which actions are rationally, emotionally or

instrumentally appropriate in a given context. According to Barber, there are three types of expectations that involve some of the fundamental meaning of trust:

> The most general is expectation of the persistence and fulfilment of the natural and the moral social order. Second is expectation of technically competent role performance from those involved with us in social relationship and systems. And third is expectation that partners in interaction will carry out their fiduciary obligations and responsibilities, that is, their duties in certain situations to place others' interests before their own (Barber 1983: 9).

In this perspective the essential meaning of trust is connected with the general and comprehensive definition of trust as an expectation of the persistence of a moral social order, which Barber uses as the context for two further and more specific definitions (trust as technically competent performance and trust as fiduciary obligation). Barber's classification of the content of expectations indirectly points also to causes of distrust. Whereas the absence of trust in the moral social order is very difficult to accept, disappointment in our expectations of others' competence or responsibility is more easily dealt with. Barber's distinction leaves unspecified, however, the social mechanisms which generate trust, and in a more general sense is too normative and optimistic in its assumption that people internalize a 'collectivity-orientation', which leads them to be more concerned with others' interests than with their own.

A similar classification of the content of expectations was used by Lewis and Weigert (1985) in their attempt to conceptualize trust as a multi-faceted phenomenon. They distinguish three dimensions of trust: cognitive, emotional and behavioural. Trust is not seen, however, as an individual attitude (although these three distinct dimensions are normally used to describe attitudes) but as a collective attribute. According to Lewis and Weigert (1985: 969–72) trust is based, firstly, on a cognitive process which discriminates among persons and institutions by classifying them into trustworthy, distrusted and unknown categories. Secondly, it is based on an affective component which consists of an emotional bond among all those who participate in the relationship and which is underwritten by social actions. By including the behavioural content of trust – that is, the undertaking of a risky course of action – this sociological conceptualization of trust does not allow one to see trust as a continuous state and it excludes inaction (which may also be motivated by trust or be risky) from the trust repertoire. Furthermore, Lewis and Weigert do not offer a theory of social mechanisms which generate trust.

In short, the content of expectations is a combination of different kinds of meaning and a variety of shared understanding, which actors develop within their specific relationships. All these expectations have, however, something in common; namely, they are all orientated towards future action. When one says; 'I trust that my fellow students will accept new rules' or 'I trust that our team will win', one anticipates or estimates the probability of some future action. Thus, it can be said that to trust means to hold some expectations about something future or contingent or to have some belief as to how another person will perform on some future occasion. To trust is to believe that the results of somebody's intended action will be appropriate from our point of view.

This definition identifies the content of expectations by pointing out that they are related to future action and that they consist of the evaluation of this action's intended results. Trust can be said to be based on the belief that the person, who has a degree of freedom to disappoint our expectations, will meet an obligation under all circumstances over which they have control. If unforeseen circumstances arise which could prevent the fulfilment of those obligations, through no fault of the parties concerned, it will not be perceived as a case of betrayal. Thus, although we are willing to forgive mistakes or unintended consequences, the intended betrayal of our trust is a cause for enormous pain and distrust.

By 'intended actions' I do not mean only actions which are conscious, planned or calculated but also the possession of expertise to carry out such action. In other words, intended actions consist of a person's intentions and his or her emotional, technical or material ability to perform the intended actions. Because of the variety of such 'expertise', they need to be viewed from within in the context of the specific relationship. For instance, when one trusts a doctor to perform an operation well, one trusts that this doctor intends to perform it well, and this means that one trusts that this particular doctor has the proper qualifications to do it (one trusts that a doctor would not intend to carry out an operation without the proper skills and knowledge) as well as a motivation to succeed (one trusts that a doctor intends to do her or his best). The absence of one or both of these ingredients, on the basis of which one evaluates the probability of the success of the operation, may be a cause for distrust. In another context, for example, between friends, the notion of intended actions means that friends are expected not to intend to harm their partners and to take into consideration their partners' 'utilities' (emotions, values and so on, depending on the context). Here the 'expertise of the friend' is an ability to think about the other's interests, values and so forth. A person who gives her friend, who is allergic to the sun and hates beaches, beach equipment as a birthday present does not show this ability. Her present will be a disappointment to the friend, because one trusts friends to intend to take into consideration one's perspective and

values. The issue of this 'expertise' is even more complex in more intimate relationships, where, to paraphrase Giddens (1992), the 'expertise'
means opening to others, which in turn requires self-identity and integrity. Thus, one trusts one's lover to intend to carry out, and be capable
of, 'emotional communication with other and self in the context of
interpersonal equality' (Giddens 1992: 130). In contrast, inattention
towards strangers can be explained by a shared understanding that
intended actions of parties are without any concern to each other. It also
requires 'expertise' of polite estrangement (Goffman 1963a; Giddens
1990).

As all these examples illustrate, thanks to trust one avoids having to
take account of some possibilities and is able to embrace some action,
which without trust would be impossible. Seen in this light, trust not only
secures the stability of social relationships but is also 'indispensable in
order to increase a social system's potential for action beyond these
elementary forms' (Luhmann 1979: 88). In order to influence the functioning of the system, trust needs to be embodied in social institutions.
However, not all social systems generate the same amount of trust; for
instance, the level of trust in southern Italy is considerably lower than in
northern Italy (Gambetta 1993; Putnam 1993). Some systems, moreover,
can survive without trust; as an historical examination of eighteenth-
century Neapolitan society and politics illustrates, the necessary conditions of micro- and macro-trust within society can be destroyed 'while
still preserving its conditions as a society' (Pagden 1988: 131). Furthermore, in some systems distrust can play an integrative function (Goldfarb
1991). Not one of these options is, however, a context-free choice since
the level of trust depends upon the continuity of certain fundamental
institutional characteristics of a given society.

Thus, trust cannot be fully understood and studied without the examination of institutions as repositories of a legacy of values and without
addressing a practical issue of how far human beings' concepts of duties
and obligations are influenced by the societal institutions which organize
ways in which people are bound together. In essence, the problem of
constituting trust in society is the issue of the conditions necessary for
social order and human action to continue. The question of what holds
societies together and whether they can fall apart had been asked long
before the birth of modern sociology in the nineteenth century. Ever since
then, trust has been an important, although not always an explicit,
element in those sociological theories which have addressed the question
of how to preserve diversity and still maintain social order.

Only a more complete analysis of how these theories understand trust
and conceptualize its role for the preservation of social order can help us
further with our own comprehension of this notion. Moreover, in order

to be able to appreciate the novelty of modern analyses of trust, we must be clear about the contribution that classical social theory has made to the topic.

## Trust – a prerequisite of order?

For anyone attempting . . . to develop an alternative to both the market and the state, trust can be expected to play a crucial role.

Wolfe 1989: 204

Two key issues, bequeathed to the social sciences by philosophy, have ensured the more or less explicit presence of the notion of trust in sociology from its early days until the present time. The first has been concerned with identifying what holds societies together, while the second has focused on the nature of the relationship between the individual and society. The works of the earlier social thinkers, stimulated by the changes occurring around them, have established a long tradition in social theory that analyses tensions between the nature of the individual and the requirements of social order.

Trust as coextensive with the very existence of social order is present in Hobbes' answer to the problem of order. Hobbes' approach to the problem of order explains the social contract and social stability as the outcome of actions of self-interested, rational individuals who intentionally create institutions securing and promoting social order. Since order and peace among egoistic, opportunistic actors is very difficult to sustain, people's only hope for safety is to establish a mighty power over a community. This pessimistic evaluation of the chance to obtain social order without political authority focuses the contractarians' attention on two problems. Firstly, how can such self-interested individuals intentionally establish institutions that promote social order? Secondly, why would they ever allow themselves to be constrained by these institutions (Hechter 1989: 60–5)? The contractarians' answer to these questions relies on the notion of trust. Once Hobbes proposed grounding of political order in the fear of others and in mutual distrust, 'he was bound to accept a new and "artificial" structure of trust to ensure the legitimacy of the new regime and to limit or resolve forms of conflict that could not simply be suppressed by force. This "artificial" structure of trust was necessary to close the gap in the social order left unfilled by force or reason alone' (Weil 1987: 776).

The very foundation of Hobbes' theory lies in the assumption that power was to be trusted and that it was not to be exercised against the people's interest. Thus, there was no need for control over the political authority. However, such confidence in governments and in one's opponents depends either on the trustworthiness of human nature, which is in contradiction with Hobbes' vision of human beings' nature, or on the structural conditions that permit trust. Hobbes argues for the building of 'artificial' structures of authority and trust by a prudential policy, designed to moderate extreme conflicts and relying on a sound balance between the public and private realms.

> In this sense, the growth of trust – which now appears as the reduction or redirection of fear under the social contract – results from the success of the sovereign in (1) assuring security and (2) reducing extreme conflict by a prudential policy of establishing certain controversial practices in the public realm and of banishing the most controversial points from the arena of public to the private realm (Weil 1987: 779).

In contrast to Hobbes' 'artificial' harmony of interests, secured through centralization of sovereignty, followed by the growth of moderation, tolerance and freedom and accompanied by growing trust, other approaches to the question of order, if not pointing to the direct intervention of Providence (which directs individuals' actions towards the common good, which none of them intentionally seek) assumed a 'natural harmony of interests.' Self-regulation, coordination and adjustment of various interests, as in Mandeville's *Fable of the Bees* (1723) and later in Adam Smith's *The Wealth of the Nations* (1776), is seen as a result of 'the invisible hand of nature', perceived still as 'providential in tone and overtone' (Lubasz 1992: 44). Adam Smith not only stressed that 'sympathy' contributes to the stability of the moral order by forming trusting relationships, but he conceived the invisible hand of nature as providentially designed and argued that it 'guides man via their several natural interests and passions so to invest whatever capital they can command as in fact, though without their intending it, to promote the interest of society' (Lubasz 1992: 53). According to this interpretation of Adam Smith's theory, economic actions are not quests for the greatest possible profit but actions orientated to the common good, thus attributed with some moral character. This perspective, unlike the theory of the invisible hand of the market as presented by modern economists, stresses the supra-economic context of the theory and emphasizes that nature has its own law, which rewards virtue independently of human will and mental processes.

Similar assumptions about the supranatural context for trust relationships and a similar broad concept of duties and responsibilities can be found in Locke's writing, which for centuries influenced the perception of trust in liberal political theory. In contrast to Hobbes, Locke's doctrine was based on a belief in the natural sociability of human beings and it

placed emphasis upon social and personal trust as a fundamental principle of order (Silver 1985: 55). Locke understood by the notion of trust
'the duty to observe mutual undertakings and the virtue of consistently
discharging this duty' (Dunn 1988: 81), which also involves the belief
that the object of trust would perform such a duty. Locke, like most
seventeenth-century natural law thinkers, placed particular emphasis
upon the 'promise' as a type of social performance on which human
cooperation depends and upon which the promise creates self-imposed
obligations, 'hence permitting trust to pervade in civil society' (Silver
1985: 56). Trust, seen as the formative force or the foundation of social
life, was both a rational practice and a moral duty. 'It was above all the
rationality of this duty which enabled human beings to live dependably
with one another' (Dunn 1993: 640). And although 'the hand of the
Almighty' visibly backs the sanctions, central to the problem of trust is
the 'cooperative and strategic interaction of individuals and groups'
(Dunn 1988: 81–2). Locke's vision of the nature of legitimate political
authority as a structure of well-founded trust remains at the centre of
modern understanding of the issue of legitimacy of political power.

Hobbes' solution to the problem of order is inconsistent not only with
the vision of the foundation of stability of political order as proposed by
theorists of natural rights but also with theories of republican virtue, as
represented, for example, by Alexis de Tocqueville. For Tocqueville,
social life was not based upon contract, with the idea that one could
withdraw from one's obligations if the terms were not being fulfilled, but
rather on a theory of community, assuming that the pursuit of their own
interest by free individuals brings them into contact with others, which
stimulates concern for those others (Pope 1986: 135–45). He also rejected the fearful psychology of Hobbes and viewed liberty as inherent in
community.

Tocqueville, for his contribution to our understanding of affinities
between trust and liberty, is described as 'the greatest theorist of trust'
(Hall 1992: 16). Tocqueville's belief in the supreme value of political
liberty is based on the assumption that freedom presupposes order and
that freedom is itself the source of order. Only in a free society can people
participate and control their institutions, and identify with them as their
own creation, and only in a free society can people develop cooperative
relationships. According to Tocqueville, trust and freedom, as the main
characteristics of a democratic society, are connected: 'Interpersonal
trust is probably the moral orientation that most needs to be diffused
among the people if republican society is to be maintained' (Poggi 1972:
59). To sustain political liberty both interpersonal trust and trust in one's
capacity are necessary because anxiety-ridden individuals will not be able
actively to exercise their capacity for 'self-government' and, conse-

quently, they will lose confidence in that capacity and will cease to insist on their rights (Tocqueville 1968: 72–97). Living in freedom is a condition of trust, which in turn teaches people to be responsible in their practice of citizenship (Hall 1992: 20–1). Since both political liberty and the practice of citizenship reflect 'a balance between the rights and duties of the individual' (Oldfield 1990: 139), Tocqueville viewed them as synonymous, as seen in his description of a vision of the ideal society:

> Each man having some rights and being a sure of the enjoyment of those rights, there would be established between all classes a manly confidence and a sort of reciprocal courtesy, as far removed from pride as from servility. Understanding its own interests, the people would appreciate that in order to enjoy the benefits of society one must shoulder its obligations. Free associations of the citizens could then take the place of the individual authority of the nobles, and the state would be protected from tyranny (1968: 12).

What allows a nation to be free and democratic is an 'enlightened self-interest' based on an understanding that people are neither self-sufficient nor isolated. Thus, political liberty is founded on a rational calculation of self-interest which proves the effectiveness and importance of cooperation, solidarity and public-spiritedness. The existence of secondary associations, in turn, whilst creating trust, empowers people since, as Tocqueville observed, participation in secondary groups can teach self-discipline, moderation and an appreciation of successful collaboration. Freedom exists where civil associations balance the power of the state. They, in turn, contribute to the effectiveness and stability of democratic government by instilling habits of cooperation and mutual trust in their members. Finally, Tocqueville argued, no democratic society can survive without a religion. His belief in the role of religion in maintaining social order and continuity rested upon the assumption that religion is necessary for liberty because it places some limits on human behaviour (Tocqueville 1968: 355–9).

All the authors discussed above conceived of trust as a crucial basis for social order. Although the problem of order in the nineteenth century was not debated with the same urgency as it was in the seventeenth century, the transition from the 'traditional' to the 'modern' society made the question of social order very topical. The mutual necessity of progress and order became the overriding theme of the origins of positive philosophy. Its main dilemma was the question of how to secure social order in the new type of society, in which many checks on people's conduct had disappeared. Each answer to this question relied on some assumptions about human nature and about the structural conditions sustaining social order.

In its thinking about the character of the individual, classical sociology followed the project of modern philosophy – that is, it aimed at converting egoistic men into altruists (MacIntyre 1981: 212–13). The founding fathers of sociology, driven by intense moral and political commitments, introduced to the new discipline the contradictions between the familiarity, closeness and trust of the old order and the individualism, rationality and distrust of the new society. Thus, analysis of tensions between the demands of new order and the concept of human nature were at the core of their theories.

Saint-Simon and Comte developed theories which emphasized particular elements of the emerging 'industrial society'; a society with a growing division of labour and no longer held together by the spiritual power of the Catholic Church. According to Saint-Simon, society could only progress and achieve the necessary stability if science and industry were put at the service of mankind and scientists became the religious leaders, while for Comte the necessary prerequisite of social order was the consensus of moral beliefs. This moral consensus could be provided by 'a new religion of mankind', based on the dogma of science and which would secure the dominance of altruistic over egoistic feelings. For Comte, therefore, a progressive and well-ordered society is one of moral consensus, in which a religion of humanity binds society together as a moral community. This stand contributed to the later development of an idealistic approach stressing non-rational and non-utilitarian elements of human existence (Martindale 1960: 76).

In the mid- and late nineteenth century, new answers to the question about the connection between order and human nature began to emerge. These theories of social order, as Poggi (1972) notes, can be divided into two strands. The first type assumes that social order is imposed from above (as in Marx's perspective); the second argues that social order is negotiated from below (as in the broad normative approach and utilitarian theories). Marx who, like Hobbes, believed that conflict is endemic in social life, saw society as a power struggle in which groups, differing in their relations to the means of production, attempt to suppress one another. Thus, according to Marx, social order results from power imbalances – that is, from the ability of some classes to have their own way against the resistance and at the expense of other classes (Poggi 1972: 130–40).

'In Marx's view the only possible contacts between individuals behaving according to the *homo economicus* model are antagonistic. No human action aimed at solidarity can ultimately be derived from it. Even if relations deriving from this model will not be explicitly antagonistic, men will still regard other men as means' (Avineri 1968: 17–18, quoted in Poggi 1972: 149). For Marx, to address the problem of order meant an attempt to solve the issue of order between collective units with different economic power rather than between free and equal individuals (Poggi 1972: 149). For him, writing from a macro-structural perspective, because the issues of social cohesiveness and integration were not important, the concepts of relational dimension of internal class solidarity have been left undeveloped. In short, in Marx's political theory there is no place for trust since according to him the dominant mood of interaction is antagonistic and based on conflict of economic interests between collective units. 'The core Marxist view is that rational trust is precluded in principle by exploitation' (Dunn 1988: 77). This perspective assumes not only that trust is precluded by a structurally unjust order but also that the liquidation of private ownership of the means of production is the sole way to secure non-exploitative, thus trustworthy, relationships. Only in communist society can the individual meaningfully enter into social relationships; only there is the individual able to perceive that his or her needs cannot be reduced to the means of physical existence (Avineri 1970: 65–96). 'Marxism was a dream offering the prospect of a society of perfect unity, in which all human aspirations would be fulfilled, and all values reconciled' (Kolakowski 1978: 508), but it was unable to acknowledge the inevitability of conflicts between a plurality of values. Therefore, in our discussion of social order as a condition for trust we will focus on classical non-Marxist perspectives since only this type of theory conceives of social order as the result of social interactions.

Classical non-Marxist social theorists divide order into two broader perspectives. The first, a utilitarian approach, sees spontaneous activities of self-interested individuals as establishing the institutions that promote order, harmony and general well-being. The second perspective tends to emphasize normative factors as the key forces of social control. These two approaches are the most persistent cleavages in the social sciences, and their contrasting views of human nature (*Homo economicus* and *Homo sociologicus*) are the results of their different answers to the question of how social norms and the rational pursuit of interests combine into social action.

Although both approaches place solidarity at the core of social order, they vary in their account of it. The normativist view equates solidarity with social obligations, while a broad utilitarian perspective considers solidarity to be 'the product of rational individual action' (Hechter 1987: 27). It seems that in order to grasp the nature of trust, which is consistently seen as a crucial aspect of solidarity, we need to discuss these two distinct approaches.

In the next chapter I shall examine the theoretical assumptions made about the basis of social order and human nature within Spencer's utilitarian model, in Durkheim's normative approach and in the more

eclectic writings of Toennies, Simmel and Weber. All these writers contributed to the theory of social order and their concepts are cornerstones
for the development of the notion of trust. I shall show that these
classical sociologists not only expanded our understanding of the relationship between trust and collective order, but that they also, in an
illuminating way, elucidated the unique nature of trust.

# 2
# Classical Sociology and the Search for Order

## Utilitarian theory and Spencer's competitive solidarity

Utilitarianism, with its concept of rational and self-interested man, has survived in sociology a long time and still constitutes the basis of many theories such as exchange theory and rational choice theory. Utilitarian theory essentially combines both Hobbes' and Locke's theory of possessive individualism (Macpherson 1962: 270) with the requirement for harmonious social order. Utilitarianism, which has been called 'liberalism in which individualism is putting on a calculating mask' (Merquior 1991: 34), argues that social order is created by rational egoists who are also 'reasonable' enough to recognize that their self-interests are best realized by adhering to common rules. This individualistic standpoint of the utilitarian theory does not mean, however, that utilitarians share the central idea of Hobbes' *Leviathan*. In contrast to Hobbes' solution, which points to the role of a political state in imposing stability, they assume that social order can 'emerge spontaneously from conflicting and divergent human strings' and that 'human interests are in mutual agreement' (Szacki 1979: 109). Social equilibrium is achieved by the concurrent choices of self-seeking, calculating individuals and can be secured without relying on trust. There is no need for mutual trust because people's actions are induced solely by their own interests and in turn these actions automatically produce happiness for everybody. Therefore, it can be said that '[w]ithin this perspective, which we can label utilitarian, the problem of order was not so much solved as discounted' (Poggi 1972: 166).

In the utilitarian view, all moral principles take their character and meaning from the end perceived as the pursuit of happiness. The utilitarian account of private morality as advancing individual pleasure, happiness or welfare also demands some degree of sacrifice of individual rights. However, while the recognition of the equal claims of all others to lead a happy life means that in some cases general welfare overrides individual rights, utilitarian theory does not introduce normative concepts which could explain why people accept the violation of their individual rights. Values, norms, dignity or autonomy of human beings are dismissed since utilitarianism 'speaks with the voice of utility, not with the voice of rights or civic virtue' (Merquior 1991: 34) and 'the citizens' only duty is not to interfere with one another's rights' (Poggi 1972: 170). This illustrates two notorious difficulties in utilitarian philosophy: firstly, the combination of altruistic ethics with hedonistic psychology (Peel 1971: 93); and secondly, utilitarian theory's difficulty in accommodating the concept of right (Sen and Williams 1982; Gray 1991).

The acknowledgement of the fact that individual self-interest is not always sufficient to bring about total harmony since people are not always able to recognize the identity of their own well-being with that of others, resulted in a visible confusion in classical utilitarian theory. Some utilitarians, such as Bentham, argued that society had to rely on the law to bring harmony about and that the function of the liberal state should be to increase compliance with rational law. Others, like Herbert Spencer, regarded the function of the state differently.

This difference of their position was the result of contrasting views concerning the quality of human nature. On the one hand, Bentham, like Hobbes, believed that 'human beings are . . . deficient in altruism and therefore require the threat of coercion to encourage them to seek majority interest rather than their own' (Dowrie and Talfer 1962: 42). Spencer, in contrast, assumed that cooperative or altruistic behaviour is the result of social evolution rather than social engineering.

Spencer, an extreme individualist, argued that 'a society is but a collective name for a number of individuals' and that 'society exists for the benefit of its members; not its members for the benefit of society' (Spencer, quoted in Wiltshire 1978: 236). Accepting the concept of 'natural rights' (which Bentham had dismissed), Spencer advocates the principle of liberty as 'a means to an end', enabling men to pursue selfish objectives on the assumption that these actions would be conducive to social betterment.

Spencer's moral theory or 'rational utilitarianism' holds that the principles of morality, justice and liberty are of secondary importance because they are rooted in the principle of utility (Gray 1991: 109). His ethics also contain evolutionary overtones because, despite his assumption concerning the natural harmony of interest, which allowed him to see social order as being based on contractual relations, he seems unconvinced that self-interest alone would be enough to ensure social cooperation. Thus, Spencer's optimistic vision of the future depended upon the increasing fitness of humanity for the perfect 'social state'. In other words, he believed that the human character will progressively adapt to a less authoritative and less coercive but more complex, cooperative and sophisticated system. Ethical evolution, in Spencer's view, tends towards a perfection of human conduct and an increased moral sense and altruism. In his writing on ethics Spencer not only borrows Comte's notion concerning the growing dominance of altruistic over egoistic feelings, but he also attempts, like Bentham, to reconcile an altruistic ethics with individual hedonistic psychology. Spencer's proposed solution to this problem relies on Adam Smith's concept of the social sentiment of sympathy as reflex of self-love (Peel 1971: 93). Social evolution – that is, a gradual and progressive transition from a military to an industrial type of society – is demonstrative of a mutuality of influence between character, institutions and environmental adaptation. The first type of society, the military one, although based on a system of compulsory cooperation, is not, however, perceived as illegitimate. Members of military societies are motivated by patriotism, which legitimizes official control. They must have reverence for, and faith in authority and their behaviour is characterized by obedience, conformism, loyalty, acceptance of routine, lack of initiative, dependence on authority and inflexibility (Szacki 1979: 226; Coser 1977: 93). Confidence, loyalty and faith in rulers, who are seen by the ruled as 'divinely ordered', are the necessary requirements enabling a military society to wield all its forces in cases of attack or defence. In this particular instance there is no need to base cooperation on other resources such as trust or interest, because the nature of 'the little civilized man' driven by primitive forces does not require it (Spencer 1969: 185).

By way of contrast, cooperation in the forthcoming industrial type of society, according to Spencer, would be voluntary and is based upon individual self-restraint rather than on utilizing coercive discipline (1896: 569). Cooperation in this instance would depend on the fulfilment of contracts and when these contracts were unhindered and their performance certain, 'the growth is great and the social life active' (Spencer 1969: 174). The industrial type of society is a decentralized, *laissez-faire*, socially mobile, self-regulating, liberal society, where the state exists for the benefit of individuals. Members of this type of society would be characterized by their independence, respect for others, resistance to coercion, initiative, truthfulness and kindness. Consistent with his evolutionary scheme, Spencer argues that industrialism generates altruism by allowing the sympathies free play and it favours the growth of altruistic sentiments and norms. In peaceful industrial societies social structure becomes flexible, just and open, and individuals enjoy freedom of movement and a high level of social mobility, which does not destroy social cohesion (Rumney 1966: 290).

Spencer sees societies in his time as being in a transitional stage. Contemporary societies, he argues, whilst still preserving many characteristics of the military type, have additionally acquired some features of industrial society. Moreover, this transitional stage in modern society itself is one of the main causes of social disintegration and a general lack of trust. 'Men may work together in a society under either of . . . two forms of control: forms which, though in many cases mingled, are essentially contrasted. Using the word cooperation in its wide sense . . . we may say that social life must be carried on by either voluntary cooperation or compulsory cooperation' (Spencer 1969: 317). As he viewed the system 'under which we at present live' as fostering 'dishonesty and lying', Spencer focused his attention on a search for rules of cooperation and trustworthiness (1969: 315). Since social order can only be changed gradually through the evolutionary process of the modification which makes the individual fit for the 'the social state', Spencer's theory in fact provides justification for the continuation of the *status quo*. Although Spencer, like Marx, presupposes a 'withering away of the state', he admits that in existing modern societies the worship of authority is still an indispensable aid to social cohesion and the maintenance of order. According to Spencer, social life is dominated by the universality of competition, yet with the advancement of the process of social evolution the coexistence of competition and cooperation becomes unproblematic. Thus, progress towards the ideal 'social state' of the future, while approaching the achievement of social harmony, order, altruistic feelings, voluntary cooperation and self-control, does not eliminate competition.

Essentially, Spencer's anticipated industrial society can be described as a type of cooperative community consisting of a series of market relations and free from state compulsion. In such a society of 'self-respecting and worthy individuals' self-government would be based on democratic principles, and it would be possible to reconcile the maximum individual freedom with social stability and coherence by balancing 'self-love and social sentiments' and, consequently, securing equal freedom for everyone. For Spencer, in accordance with his organicist analogy, social order is the result of a mutual dependence of different parts whose particular contributions and rewards are settled by bargaining. This act of balancing individuals' interests and social ends is contained and expressed itself through fulfilment of contract. A breach of contract is considered to be a type of indirect aggression since it undermines the conditions of normal social life and order (Spencer 1969: 177). To preserve social stability and harmony the conditions for the fulfilment of contracts need to be established.

Thus contract, as a form of imposing restrictions on the parties, 'shifts the focus of trust on the efficacy of sanctions, and either our or a third party's ability to enforce them if a contract is broken' (Gambetta 1988b: 221). However, Spencer prefers not to rely on the state or on negative sanctions. Instead, he proposes a normative basis for securing contractual obligation and positive sanctions. According to him, contract as an act of autonomous will between trustworthy people and as an instrument of mutual benefit is a device for producing the general well-being of society which, in turn, increases societal trust in contract. Spencer appears to have realized that cooperation is conditional on the belief that the other party is trustworthy and will not take advantage of us and that, while interest may generate pressure to behave honestly, for a 'concert of interest to be played', egoistic motives are not sufficient for contractual success. He saw the modification of human nature as the necessary condition for social cooperation since cooperation requires 'trust in the sense that dependent parties need some degree of assurance that non-dependent parties will not defect' (Williams 1988: 8). However, this modification, based on Spencer's belief in the evolutionary increase of moral sense and sentiments, offers a completely anachronistic solution to the problem of cooperation.

Spencer's conservative utilitarianism advocates *laissez-faire*, a distrust of modern political structures and the right to ignore the state. His belief in the changeability of human nature along with his view that moral institutions are themselves the product of social evolution contributed to his posthumous defeat. Spencer's theory, like most evolutionary concepts, is intensely optimistic in its assumption that things get better as they evolve. Our twentieth-century experience does not allow us to share this illusion. Furthermore, the increasing role of the state and the common recognition of the role of political authority in all dimensions of social life have cast Spencer's vision of the natural harmony of interests in a market society into the shade. However, despite the fact that his evolutionist sociology and organicist analogies currently do not attract much attention, one of his principal questions – namely, 'how much regulation, even in the case of virtue, can man and society bear and still retain individual liberty and independence' (Macrae 1969: 53) – seems to be particularly pertinent now. Equally challenging is his belief that a flexible, mobile and open society can only be based on trust and cooperation.

Sociological criticism of utilitarian theory also attacks Spencer's perspective for his narrow view of individual action as being intrinsically self-seeking and calculating. According to Durkheim, for example, free exchange cannot be a model for all social relationships. Parsons (1949) also criticizes the utilitarian assumption concerning random wants or desires and the fact that utilitarian theory fails to explain where the ends come from and how the ends of one individual come to be integrated with the ends of others. This criticism relies on the assumption that social order and harmony can only be secured if people are united towards some collective ends. Social cohesion, seen as the consequence of shared common goals and the result of an acceptance of common aims as a duty, is best described by Toennies.

## Toennies' communal ethic

Where utilitarian theory maintains that man is generally rational, Toennies argues that human beings are neither exclusively rational nor irrational. Instead of debating human nature Toennies focuses on social relationships. His influential typology of types of social relationships captures the great transition from the 'pre-modern' to the 'modern'. Toennies addresses the onset of modernity in terms of change in the nature of human associations from *Gemeinschaft* to *Gesellschaft*. His account of the change emphasizes the stability, harmony, sentiment, warmth and wholeness of social relationships in community and stresses the unnatural hypocrisy and the coolness of modern urban society. It creates the image of modern society as destructive of the human spirit and man's potential for happiness and binds social order, moral conduct and stability with community life.

Toennies assumes that different societies produced different social 'wills' and that social will was experienced by the individual as a moral commandment. He sought to show that all social relationships are created by human will and that, consequently, social relationships are associations among and between the wills of human beings. In community, where people form associations because they value the relations as an end in themselves, natural will predominates, which is expressed in 'the mental world of individual as causal force, but is carried in the individual in the form of habit, habit produced by repetitive action in accordance with this *Wille*' (Turner 1994: 52). With the emergence of *Gesellschaft* the unity of collective will or collective intention is lost. In society, where rational will prevails, social relationships are valued only as means to a particular end.

> There is a contrast between a social order which – being based upon consensus of wills – rests on harmony and is developed and ennobled by folkways, mores and religion and an order being based on a union of rational wills – rests on convention and agreement, is safeguarded by

political legislation, and finds its ideological justification in public opinion (Toennies 1988: 223).

According to Toennies, a *Gemeinschaft* community is in many ways like an extended family group. 'The closeness and mutual dependence of family life involve strongly shared sentiments based on natural instincts and emotions reinforced through shared activities and experience' (Francis 1987: 7). Although these natural relationships are not without conflicts, tensions and crises are peacefully solved thanks to the shared and accepted ways of dealing with and balancing authority with consensus.

In *Gesellschaft* people enter into relationships with others only for purely instrumental reasons because the quest for profit and power is inherent in modern man. This leads to the manipulative treatment of others, who are viewed as means to the subjects' goals. 'In the end, rational will shunned attainable purposes: wealth and authority both looked beyond themselves to a happiness that could not exist. Striving rather than attainment, thus became the goal of modern people. Hence, the ruthlessly instrumental character of modern reason drained all meaning from human action' (Samples 1988: xviii). Thus, modern human beings are not only faced with a crisis of meaning but are simultaneously losing their freedom since '[m]eans develop their own logic and their own laws, which men must obey, although they may continue to live under the impression that they are masters of their instruments. The power of the isolated means over human thought and action is highly characteristic for the spirit of modernity' (Toennies, quoted in Samples 1988: xix). In all spheres of *Gesellschaft*, individual choice and decision are perceived to be more important than shared sentiments and obligations.

In light of the above it is clear that, according to Toennies, relationships based on trust can only exist in *Gemeinschaft*. Trust is a virtue which occurs within the *Gemeinschaft* social and economic context. Relationships based on trust and trustworthy people are only natural in community. They are the result of natural will, based on natural instincts and emotions. One trusts members of one's family and friends because feelings towards them are based on mutual affirmation, understanding and similarities, and this process is continuously reinforced through common experience and activities. Thus, trust cannot be artificially created; it is an automatic by-product of community social and economic conditions. More specifically, it is community integration, reinforced by moral and religious values, which facilitates trust relationships and which in turn stimulates further community cohesion. By way of contrast, the anxious, calculating and self-interested modern person cannot be trusted, and does not trust others, since to fulfil their needs each person requires the possessions of others, and this leads to manipulation and instrumentality.

Toennies directly addresses the issue of trust in one of his last articles, in which he sums up the *Gemeinschaft/Gesellschaft* debate. While discussing the distinction between these two types, he presents the difference between *confidence* (with which we treat people we know and like) and *mistrust* (with which we treat strangers, people with whom we are not familiar). In community, trust is based on a person's personality and his or her behaviour as a member of the community. 'Personal confidence is essentially conditioned by the personalities of those who confide; that is, by their intelligence, their knowledge of human nature, and their experience, on which the latter is based' (Toennies 1988: 241). Trust in this situation is seen as a by-product of familiarity and friendship, both of which imply that those involved have some knowledge of each other and a degree of respect for the other's welfare.

In *Gesellschaft*, confidence becomes highly impersonalized and is based on reputation. This type of impersonal trust is the result of increased economic cooperation and growing professionalization. Consequently, '[p]ersonality has come to be of little or no importance. Only the "wealth" of the person counts, for it is assumed, and usually on valid grounds, that self-interest will induce even the personally less reliable businessman to pay his debts as long as he is able to do so' (ibid.). A second type of impersonal trust occurs when we are not familiar with the other party but reliant upon them for their skill, knowledge or volition, such as doctors or lawyers. We trust experts because of their professional accomplishment:

> as far as volition is concerned, we put our trust in (a) certain moral qualities and the assumption that the individual in whose care we entrust ourselves could not possibly follow this profession if he did not possess at least a modicum of such qualities. Closely connected with it is (b) his own self-interest, either material or non-material, both of which usually merge into each other (Toennies 1988: 241).

In *Gesellschaft*, cooperation is motivated by self-interest, thereby making small demands on personal trust, but increasingly relying on impersonal trust. Thus, while interest enables cooperation to occur, an accumulation of knowledge about others' behaviour, their interests, resources and skills, results in the stabilization of cooperation through the development of impersonal trust. However, Toennies, unlike the utilitarians, did not believe that the type of society in which interest governs people's action can be harmonious, free and autonomous. He believed that when personal morality is not connected with professional or business morality, professional standards can easily be eroded. In this context he makes two salient assumptions. Firstly, he assumes that because our personality is a complete entity, it is impossible to separate standards of behaviour in occupational roles from private morality. It is not sufficient to be an honest lawyer; one must also be an honest person in order to preserve a high standard as a lawyer. The second assumption says that societal cooperation based solely on interest will eventually erode the social cohesion of that society. According to Toennies, the contractual and calculating relationship necessitates, encourages and extends 'immoral qualities' (Fletcher 1971: 55). Although on the surface the relationships could be characterized by politeness, a removal of this veil of 'civilised manners' would reveal that:

> they were all consciously, and even ruthlessly, pursuing their own interests; trying to manipulate each other, to outwit each other, in such contractual ways as to maximize their own profit.... The attitudes of mind in such 'society' were therefore those of deception, of scheming, of calculatedly measuring and using others in order to further and secure ends of your own (Fletcher 1971: 55).

In *Gemeinschaft* relationships rest on mutual dependence resulting from 'mutual promise' and they are fulfilled in 'mutual performance' (Toennies 1988: 252). On the other hand, in *Gesellschaft* relationships resemble exchange relationships with the contracting parties being both independent and strangers to each other. 'Do, ut des (I give, so that you will give) is the only principle of such relationships' (ibid.).

Toennies' exchange theory of society, which sees social relations as a special instance of general exchange between means and ends characteristic of modern rationality and his concept of 'happiness' as a final and complete pleasure after which each modern individual strives, realigns him with utilitarian theory. Nevertheless, Toennies was aware of the fundamental flaw in the concept of happiness as utility. He demonstrated that the expectation of happiness is only an illusion and that striving after it results only in a general state of anxiety since 'humans always feared that happiness might escape or be taken by another' (Samples 1988: xviii). More importantly, he recognized the need for something more than sole interest as a means to ensure cooperation.

In numerous criticisms of Toennies' typology it has been pointed out that his picture of *Gemeinschaft* is too glorified and that he overemphasizes the destructive and dehumanizing aspects of *Gesellschaft*, which is too explicitly modelled upon the unhealthy conditions of Hobbes' civil society (Fletcher 1971; Wolin 1960). Toennies' relevance for us today is connected with the growing romantic appeal of community as an answer to the uncertainty and impersonality of our modern societies. His contribution to our understanding of the concept of trust is associated with his emphasis on the plurality of 'communities' penetrating the modern self and limiting the individual's capacity for forming personal attachments. Equally important seems to be his argument that, in order to stabilize social order based on convention and agreement and motived by self-interest, there is a need for impersonal trust, understood as moral standards and reputations. Although his project of explaining how individual habits become collective moral obligation was a failure, he showed the importance of the force of habit in the individual. Toennies' vision of social order as based on balancing authority and consensus awaits translation into more practical language. His emphasis on community as a source of moral norms was questioned by Durkheim, who not only criticized Toennies' assumption that the moral bases of unity have disappeared in modern society, but also provided a new explanation for social cohesion in this type of society. It was Durkheim's task to demonstrate that modern industrial society creates conditions for the establishment of solidarity and moral order.

## Durkheim's organic solidarity

According to Emile Durkheim, the consolidation of industrial capitalism and its impact on contemporary institutions and relations demanded a reformulation of the Comtean notion of social order based on the consensus of moral beliefs. Although Durkheim was convinced that the disappearance of traditional religion does not necessarily entail a dissolution of society, he thought it imperative for contemporary society to develop a new moral code to coincide with changed social conditions.

By admitting that morality 'is going through a real crisis', that faith 'has been troubled; tradition has lost its way; individual judgment has been freed from collective judgment' (Durkheim 1964: 408), he defines his task as a search for the means of achieving a new order. His concern for societal order and the mechanisms of social integration led him to believe that the aim of social science should be to establish a morality which could overcome the social condition of anomie. Durkheim's interest in the origin of shared perception of the world and his belief that the development of humanity requires an optimal level of solidarity has placed him at the centre of discussion about the trust relationship.

Durkheim, like Toennies, acknowledges the contrast between traditional and modern societies. However, in contrast to Toennies, he insists that modern society has preserved a character of 'moral unity'. Durkheim's theory of a social evolution from a 'mechanical solidarity', where social cohesion was based on identity between individuals, to an 'organic solidarity' of modern industrial societies, assumes that the division of labour produces solidarity because it 'creates among men an entire system of rights and duties which link them together in a durable way' (Durkheim 1964: 406). This new type of social cooperation results in a new moral order, which – in turn – integrates society. For Durkheim social integration is primarily a matter of morality or, in other words, a problem of the coordination of individual activity within a social system on the basis of personal commitment to collective standards and rules.

Durkheim's vision of a modern, integrated and moral society assumes that a correspondence between one's needs and somebody else's needs can only be established when people are bound together in common faith. Social order is seen as based on submission to the supreme moral authority of society. Durkheim stresses the dualistic nature of the attachment of the individual to society, as involving both obligation and a positive commitment to ideals. In opposition to utilitarian theory, Durkheim argues that the main demand society makes on the individual is *selflessness*. 'If man is to be a moral being, he must be devoted to something other than than himself; he must feel at one with a society' (Durkheim 1973: 79). Feelings of obligation and altruism as well as moral pressure, which restrains egoistic behaviour, are the bases of solidarity. 'Men cannot live together without acknowledging, and consequently, making mutual sacrifices, without tying themselves to one another with strong, durable bonds' (Durkheim 1964: 228). In his polemic against Herbert Spencer .and the utilitarian individualists, Durkheim strongly asserts the existence of a moral element in social life. Every society, as Durkheim expresses it, is 'a moral society, and a state of order . . . among men cannot follow from any entirely material causes, from any blind mechanism. . . . It is a moral task' (1957: 12).

According to Durkheim, a society composed of egoistic, self-interested and calculating individuals would not be a society at all since acquisitiveness and rational self-interest destroy social solidarity. A need for a morality of cooperation means that individuals must consider not only their interests but also their duties to the community, because without this social integration order would be impossible. Human society should submit to moral restraints because what is fundamental 'is not the state of our economy, but rather the state of our morality' (Durkheim 1957: 16).

The growing division of labour not only leads to solidarity but also enhances individuality. Durkheim's concept of the duality of human existence – that is, the existence of both interest-motivated action and altruistic-idealistic sources for social action – led him to reject Spencer's definition of individualism as 'utilitarian egoism'. In contrast to the utilitarian doctrine of rational ethics, the individual and the collectivity are seen here as dependent on each other. Individualism itself, says Durkheim, is a moral phenomenon since it supports a morality of cooperation. And '[t]he only power which can serve to moderate individual egotism is the power which embraces ... the group' (Durkheim 1964: 405).

In the modern context, moral conduct must be intentional and intelligible rather than unreflective and mysterious. It is the morality of individualism, 'the religion of the individual', centred on liberty and equality, which is 'the sole link which binds us one to another' and 'has penetrated our institutions and custom' (Durkheim 1969: 22). The cult of the individual, which attributes a sacred status to human beings, is inseparable from both a responsibility to the community and an attachment to it. In the same way the modern rational community necessarily attaches the value to the individual, and this commitment is, argues Durkheim, the secular equivalent of the religious collective conscience.

Durkheim reduces the probability of any conflict or tension between the individual and society by glorifying society, which he sees as an all-embracing unity that 'implants in each individual an aspect of itself so that in effect it creates him' (Zeitlin 1968: 257). He takes the image of a small, well-integrated group and extends it into society. 'So long as similarity and/or dependence are recognized affective links may extend and proliferate, an emotionally underpinned altruism may sustain a social organisation of any size' (Barnes 1988: 157). However, it can be said that the sentiment binding the individual to the society is crucial in Durkheim not 'because it is *necessary* to society, but because it is *desirable* in society' (Barnes 1988: 158). Furthermore, Durkheim does not allow for different perceptions of society by its individual members because in his approach patterns of solidarity are seen as irrespective of particular persons, while the division of labour is presented as involving relationships between social roles rather than between particular persons. Consequently, what people think is merely a manifestation of deeper causal structures and moral rules, as shared mental objects are effective guides and controls of conduct.

It is the task of society to ensure consensus on ultimate values ('a single Faith'), which is a necessary condition for social order and integration. In modern societies, where moral conduct must be connected with an enlightened understanding of self-interest rather than a passive performance of rituals, this function of binding together is performed by the state. The state, as the collective agency responsible for planning and organizing social sentiments and representations, provides a moral dimension to altruistic feelings and actions towards others (Durkheim 1972: 192). The state, as an 'organ of reflection', embodies the rationality of its citizens and plays an important role in the process of achieving consensus on the principal values and beliefs. For Durkheim, the political society is a moral one and represents 'the end, *par excellence*, of moral conduct' (1973: 80). Moreover, only 'the State is capable of translating the emancipatory ideals of modern individualism into social practice' (Bach 1990: 193) and of protecting and enlarging individual rights.

Accordingly, all social institutions are organized and receive their directions from the state. Secondary groups, while being the counter-balance to state power, become also the basis of an occupational ethic and serve as a framework for the regulation of relations among various occupational groups. 'A nation can be maintained only if, between the State and the individual, there is intercalated a whole series of secondary groups near enough of the individuals to attract them strongly in their sphere of action and drag them, in this way, into the general torrent of social life' (Durkheim 1964: 28).

If consensus on ultimate values ('a single Faith') is a necessary condition for social order and integration, the absence of such a consensus entails disorder, anomie and, closely related, egoism. Durkheim's concept of disorder, as the result of random forces disrupting the common value system is, however, unable to explain what is really the antithesis of solidarity. According to Lockwood (1992), Durkheim's rejection of the utilitarian action schema and his optimistic vision of society as normatively integrated resulted in his inability to theorize disorder. Focusing on the normative integration of ends allowed Durkheim to identify only one way of explaining disorder, that is, by the restoration of 'precisely the concept of action the rejected theory takes as axiomatic: a purely rational "egoism" oriented to material ends such as power and wealth' (Lockwood 1992: 156). Lockwood argues that, in consequence, Durkheim draws upon instrumental action and the non-normatively regulated social structures (power, wealth, class) in an under-theorized manner when explaining disorder.

Other criticisms of Durkheim's normative position highlight his absolute identification of social with moral (Poggi 1972), as well as his neglect of the issue of variability of values and beliefs. Durkheim also failed to recognize the difference between the state and the nation or between a form of authority and culture. In modern society people live in a complex environment and participate in many groups, whose values are often obscure to them. Moreover, in contemporary societies 'there is abundant evidence to show that, as far as one crucial area of central values and institutions is concerned, most citizens do not have either a clear understanding of or intense or consistent attachment to, the values and principles of democratic procedures' (Lockwood 1992: 23). The stability of contemporary societies does not exclusively depend upon a consensus of norms and values but is rather the result of relative silence regarding the value system and depends on a continuation of the debate about how much diversity a society can accommodate without losing its cohesion. Furthermore, by being concerned with a 'moral' and integrated society, Durkheim failed to acknowledge that some individuals and groups in society might be more subordinate to, and benefit less by, some moral codes, than others. Current debates about the nature of the relationship between immigrants and the host society clearly demonstrate a need for greater attention to this problem. Also, Durkheim's naïve optimism about the role of the state, which he saw only as saviour, not as oppressor, weakens his theory.

What then is Durkheim's contribution to our understanding of the concept of trust? In sociological literature trust is often associated with the Durkheimian vision of society as a 'moral community', and is frequently presented as belonging to 'Durkheimian vocabulary'. This approach, by accepting Durkheim dualism, faces the problem of the simultaneously collective and private character of practices. It argues that, in a well-integrated order, one can trust others to be honest and truth-telling, and to respect their promises, because of the shared morality and common conformity to norms. However, what is the role of trust if we all behave in a morally correct manner and can thus predict other people's actions with a high degree of certainty? Clearly, there is no need for trust in such situations because it is already there. This reasoning shows the attractiveness of dualism, which 'avoids the problem of the achievement of mutuality or "sharing" by definition – the collective part of the mind . . . is mutual by definition' (Turner 1994: 52). Furthermore, by assuming that individual and collective practices are both located in the individual mind as well as in a collective consciousness, the Durkheimian perspective is forced to identify causal mechanisms as located in the collective consciousness and to see collective order as exercising constraints on individual actions. The failure of Durkheim's projects is thus the result of a total lack of awareness of social psychology as well as the circularity of his solution to the dualism of individual and society.

Durkheim's effort to construct the laws of *conscience collective* (shared categories of judgement), which arises from social interaction and which makes possible 'precontractual solidarity', also faced him with the dilemma of control versus freedom. On the one hand, modern moral individuals are viewed by Durkheim as rational and reflective, who in a morally integrated community would be able to recognize the benefit and necessity of subordinating themselves to society. On the other hand, unreflective conformity and the habitual acceptance of social rules and norms cannot be taken as the equivalent of an integrated moral order. Consequently, Durkheim locates 'freedom in subordination to social forces' (Pope 1986: 116) and presents control not as imposed from outside but rather as a moral obligation to obey a rule. Thus, Durkheim's solution to the problem of control versus freedom is unable to provide any convincing evidence as to how social necessities could be reconciled with individual freedom in our modern societies. The Durkheimian claim that the moral system of a society is a function of its social organization does not account for the fact that modern societies consist of many moral systems, quite often with overlapping and conflictual norms and, moreover, systems in the process of continuous change.

Durkheim's approach is also pertinent to discussions of the character of social relations. His vision of the dualistic nature of the attachment of the individual to society, combined with his emphasis on a collective order as dependent upon the stabilizing influence of common norms and values, brings into focus the issue of the regularity and repeatability of social behaviour. According to Durkheim, every moral society has a certain need for regularity and shows some ability to develop habits. This makes the social environment more predictable and orderly and, thus, more trustworthy. Furthermore, moral rules not only secure regularity but also reduce confusion, uncertainty and complexity by providing guidelines and lowering individual investment in new situations. Continuing in this functionalist vein, Durhkeim argues that moral rules disperse conflicts and increase the possibility of cooperation by informing individuals about their duties and teaching them discipline and the moderation of aspirations. One could argue that in this type of society there is no need for rationality since people do not need to consider or reflect on their aims. Social norms provide them with clear guidance as to what to desire and how to achieve their goals as well with a full knowledge of what to expect from others. The security and predictability of the environment creates conditions for trust seen as a consequence of the compliance with moral norms for reasons of discipline or pleasure.

Conformity to order is periodically reinforced by societal rituals, which re-affirm the faith. In the process of universalization the *conscience collective*, which consists of collective representations (that is, ideas and beliefs held in common by the members of a society and which define what their mutual relations ought to be), becomes abstract and general. In modern, secularized societies, as in archaic ones, the laws of collective idealization 'sacralise a culture's core, which in turn defines the social identity of society and specifies the regulating norms for the social integration of its members' (Muller 1988: 144). Modern societies have to devise new rituals at the level of the nation-state in order to try to cement divergent groups together. Abstract symbols of unity and rituals, according to Durkheim, perform an important function of integration. They make individuals 'more confident' and 'stronger', 'because forces which were languishing are now re-awakened in the consciousness' (Durkheim

1965: 387). Highly participatory rituals are a 'kind of machinery for charging such objects with sacredness . . . they are "batteries" for carrying over the moral energy into subsequent situations, when individuals are away from the intense source of moral power' (Collins 1988: 111). National flags, symbols and sentiments become collective representations of society's values and norms. 'They represent what the group shares in common and they help to mark off one group from another; whom to trust? who is us?' (Bocock 1992: 242).

Durkheim's perspective and subsequent attempts to extend his theory in a functionalist way have been criticized for their too consensual and conservative overtones (Zeitlin 1968; Abercrombie et al. 1990; Birnbaum 1955). Durkheim, however, seems to have been aware of the integration problem of modern societies (as illustrated by the issue of suicide), and although he insists that some symbols and some national rituals are important because they may generate a sense of common identity, he never specifies the degree of their actual contribution to integration in modern societies. 'Durkheim seems to have been proved right in coming to the conclusion that there would continue some solidarity ties that resulted from the awe and reverence inspired by symbols and ceremonies expressive of the experience of the transcendence and power of the collectivity itself' (Thompson 1992: 346).

Today, when we experience the loss of solidarity within nation-states, Durkheim's vision of that nation-state as the stage of successful efforts at human solidarity becomes even more appealing. Durkheim's idea of an integrated society in which professional organizations overcome economic anomies and restore dialogues between citizens and the state, and welfare institutions secure economic efficiency and social justice and democracy, is not far away from many recently proposed strategies of national renewal. These projects, while seeing disintegration and demoralization as caused by the abandonment of full employment, a slashing of welfare and a mediocrity of the elites, propose a solution in terms of a recreation of conditions for national solidarity since there 'is no other available framework for most power and policy, or for our sense of community and place' (Woollacott 1993: 4). Durkheim's conception of democratic government, his concern with the weakening of social bonds and his view of culture and religion have also been elaborated upon in twentieth-century sociology. Robert Bellah, for example, argues, like Durkheim, that modernity has generated its own configuration of religious beliefs and practices centred on our national experience.

It is often argued that for Durkheim social order was more important than social justice. In this light Durkheim is seen as a conservative thinker interested in the preservation of social order at any cost, and one for whom the issue of social justice is of a relatively unimportant or secondary nature (Zeitlin 1968: 251). This criticism follows the classical Marxist canon in assuming that both solidarity and justice cannot co-exist, and that in egalitarian society there would be no disruptive conflicts resulting from a plurality of aspirations. However, the growing number of attempts to understand sociologically the issue of the reconcilability of solidarity and justice means restoring Durkheimian abstract reconciliation of these two values (Lukes 1991a). In debates about civil society, the concept of solidarity, understood as a willingness to share the faith of others, is seen as complementary to discourse and as an integral part of a universal theory of justice (Cohen and Arato 1992). Similarly, Durkheim's contribution to the debate about individualism has again become the centre of attention. His attempt to enrich the classical liberalism concept of right by stressing the importance of duties is at the heart of new liberal-communitarianism discussions, aiming to avoid both a solidarity which engulfs community and an autonomy which estranges individuals (Watts Miller 1993). These debates, by following the Durkheimian thesis that only a highly complex and specialized society makes rationalism and individualism possible, have brought to our attention the fact that we not only have rights and duties within a system of organic solidarity but we also have a general duty to uphold this form of society (Torrance 1993).

Durkheim's ambitious dream to 'discover through science, the moral restraint' which could regulate economic life, and through this regulation 'control selfishness and thus gratify needs' (quoted in Stasser 1976: 119) will probably never be realized. Nevertheless, his attempt to integrate the interplay between culture, institutions and the individual still provides one of the most interesting answers to the issue of social solidarity.

## Simmel's constitutive forms of relationship – exchange and reciprocity

Simmel, like his contemporaries Toennies, Durkheim and Weber, sought to grasp the nature of the 'modern' in contemporary societies. His critique of modernity emphasizes the impersonal and fragmented character of modern society and draws attention to the various forms through which social interactions are expressed. Because Simmel was 'one of the least methodical authors who ever wrote on sociology' (Szacki 1979: 346), it is rather difficult to reconstruct his total perspective on trust. However, his contribution to the sociological conceptualization of this notion is significant. Many of his brilliant analyses of the nature of trust relationships were later adopted and developed by scholars such as Luhmann and Giddens. Simmel's theory of trust provides a theoretical framework for analysing personal as well as generalized (or impersonal) trust. His description of the conditions, role and function of trust in modern societies has also proved valuable for sociological theory. Society, says Simmel, 'is merely the name for a number of individuals, connected by interaction' (1950: 10).

Sociologists should therefore study society as a composite of forms of relationship (or forms of sociation). For Simmel the dominant social relation in modern societies is exchange. Not only is exchange 'the purest and most concentrated form of all human interactions in which serious interests are at stake' (Simmel 1971: 43), but social interaction itself is an exchange as 'every interaction has to be regarded as an exchange' (Simmel 1978: 89). Exchange, as 'a sacrifice in return for a gain' (Simmel 1971: 51), teaches us not only the relative value of things, since we value what we sacrificed for, but it also teaches reciprocity, which is regarded by Simmel as a constitutive factor in all social relationships. Exchange is 'one of the functions that creates an inner bond between people – a society, in place of a mere collection of individuals' (Simmel 1978: 175). Consequently, the preconditions for the functioning of exchange also constitute the preconditions for the continuation of society (Frisby 1992: 117). One of the most important conditions of exchange (and, by the same token, societal survival) is trust. 'Without the general trust that people have in each other, society itself would disintegrate, for very few relationships are based entirely upon what is known with certainty about another person, and very few relationships would endure if trust were not as strong as, or stronger than, rational proof or personal observation' (Simmel 1978: 178–9).

Thus, trust is 'one of the most important synthetic forces within society' (Simmel 1950: 326) and, while it may be based on some knowledge, it cannot be explained by it. Trust is a form of faith defined as assured reliance on a person or principle. Trust 'expresses the feeling that there exists between our idea of being and the being itself a definite connection and unity, a certain consistency in our conception of it, an assurance and lack of resistance in the surrender of the Ego to this conception, which may rest upon particular reasons, but is not explained by them' (Simmel 1978: 179). Trust or mistrust exists when one cannot make an assessment of probabilities, when – in a situation of uncertainty – one decides to believe or not to believe in someone or something. People who know everything do not need trust. On the other hand, people who know nothing cannot be rationally confident. Trust is, Simmel notes, unprovable, based on knowledge and non-knowledge since it involves a degree of cognitive familiarity with the object of trust which lies somewhere between total knowledge and total ignorance (Simmel 1950: 318).

Modern life, despite competition, distance, repulsion and lies, 'is based to a much larger extent than is usually realised upon faith in the honesty of the other' (1950: 313). The functioning of complex societies depends on a multitude of promises, contracts and arrangements. Since 'the single individual cannot trace and verify their roots at all', we must 'take them on faith' (Simmel 1950: 313). Simmel devotes much of his attention to an investigation of these subtle social relations, such as courtesy, gratitude or faithfulness, without which 'society could simply not exist, as it does, for any length of time. The elements which keep it alive, self-interests of its members, suggestion, coercion, idealism, mechanical habit, sense of duty, love, inertia – could not save it from breaking apart if they were not supplemented by [faithfulness]' (1950: 379). Faithfulness, or loyalty, refers to the feeling of 'preservation of the relationship to the *other*' (1950: 387). Thanks to its unifying function, 'the personal, fluctuating inner life actually adopts the character of the fixed, stable form of relation' (1950: 386).

On the other hand, Simmel considers gratitude and honour to be supplements of the legal forms. While economic cooperation is reinforced by legal rules, social cohesion needs to be secured by such feelings as gratitude and honour (1950: 386–7). These feelings create an atmosphere of obligation which ties 'one element of society to another, and thus eventually all of them together in a stable collective life' (1950: 387). Thus, while exchange is the most common social interaction, the motives behind it are defined by their social context. In reality, exchange can be motivated by many different forces, trust being one of them.

Much of Simmel's attention is devoted to discussion of how money, as an instrument and measure of exchange, has transformed human relations. In his famous study of money (*The Philosophy of Money*, originally published in 1900), Simmel provides a historical account of how money achieves an abstract and timeless status. He shows how money has replaced personal ties of traditional societies by establishing impersonal relations limited to a specific purpose. The superiority of money as a tool of economic exchange contributes to the establishment of its symbolic function of expressing varied and sometimes contradictory aspects of modern culture.

Viewed from a sociological perspective, money is 'a promise' that exchange will be honoured. Money functions best when people trust in it strongly, and cannot function at all without people trusting in the economic system. Thus, cash transactions cannot occur without a twofold trust: public confidence in the issuing government as well as confidence in the ability of the economic community to ensure the value of accepted money (Simmel 1978: 178–9). However, trust in money is closer to faith than to confidence because it is based on the prediction or calculation of the reliability of likely future events, which Simmel describes as 'a weak form of inductive knowledge'. Economic credit involves some element of quasi-religious faith or supra-theoretical belief that 'the community will assure the validity of the tokens for which we have exchanged the products of our labour in exchange against material goods . . . the feeling of personal security that the possession of money gives is perhaps the most concentrated and pointed form and manifestation of confidence in the socio-political organisation and order' (1978: 179). However, in the last instance it is not the monetary system that has to be trusted but the individuals who operate it.

Simmel's main contribution in the study of money is his essentialist characterization of money. According to him, the symbolic power of money generates a 'pattern of practices and dispositions within economic life which are real because they are consequential. In other words, our ideas about money are intrinsically connected to how we use it, to our propensity to spend, invest, save or hoard the money we have' (Dodd 1994: 57). Our beliefs or trust in the state as the agency responsible for the administration of money sustains the stability of the monetary system. The functioning of the monetary system illustrates how under the condition of modernity personal trust is converted into a generalized trust in the ability of systems to perform, and it shows our 'willingness to accept fictions' (Frankel 1977: 38).

The fragmentation of subjective culture, the increasing detachment of objective culture, alienation and impersonality are all dimensions of modern life that Simmel considers to have either originated or been accentuated by the universalization of money relationships (Frisby 1992: 123–8). Simmel's analysis of the alienating consequences of the money economy shows that exchange relationships within the mature money economy are not 'directly reciprocal'. This is due to the fact that money's empowering characteristics 'have compromised that very freedom which money itself promises to embrace' (Dodd 1994: 49), consequently, fragmenting and distorting the 'inner life' of individuals. Thus, while money empowers its holder, the freedom it provides is a source of alienation. In the transformation of money from the ultimate economic instrument to the ultimate economic goal Simmel identifies the main feature of modernity as ambivalence, 'which explains our age, which, on the whole, certainly possesses more freedom than any previous one, is unable to enjoy it properly . . . why the freedom of liberalism has brought about so much instability, disorder and dissatisfaction' (Simmel 1978: 403–4).

Simmel's analysis of the alienating consequences of the money economy to exchange relationships shows, on the one hand, the growing impersonal dependence between individuals and, on the other, the intensification of opportunities for inner independence, which brings in

people 'the feeling of individual self-sufficiency' (1978: 298). The impersonality of modern society, as Simmel argues, frees us from 'personal
dependence' on particular others for a range of practical needs, thereby
enhancing the possibility of personal relationships valued as expressions
of an inner personality. In modern societies individuals belong to many
groups, none of which make a claim upon the whole of their personalities. The increasing objectification of modern culture has fragmented
and localized the whole social and moral area of *confidence*, and hence
there is no need in modern relationships for personal knowledge. It seems
that one of the paradoxes of modern times is that 'general affairs become
ever more public, and individual affairs ever more secret' (Simmel 1950:
336). Consequently, even in intimate relationships such as those based on
friendship and love, complete intimacy and knowledge is difficult to
achieve. For this reason, as well as a result of growing individualization,
modern individuals show tendencies to differentiate friendships, 'which
cover only one side of the personality, without playing into other aspects
of it' (1950: 326).

The dialectic of human relations means that social relations are always
characterized by ambivalence; they always involve both secrecy and
trust, harmony and conflict, truth and lies. Since trust is connected with
our faith in others' moral or intellectual qualities, which can so easily be
undermined by a moment of excitement, unconscious behaviour and so
on, then trust is necessarily risky and is constantly threatened by betrayal. According to Simmel, the most impressive examples of moral
solidarity are found in secret societies, in which mutual trust sustains
silence and whose members are often subject to painful betrayal (1950:
331–2). Simmel's emphasis on the role of conflict in maintaining unity or
the role of betrayal in enhancing solidarity prevents any simplistic reconstruction of his theory. For example, although, according to Simmel, all
social relationships are based upon trust, it would be unreasonable to
assume that the wage labour–capital relationship is based solely on
'trust' (Frisby 1992: 119). In fact, Simmel considers the relationship
between the superior and the subordinate to be the most important form
of social interaction and sees the nature of this relationship to be based
not merely on imposition but also on reciprocity (Stasser 1976: 160).
This way of thinking opens the possibility to conceptualize work relationships in more complex terms than those offered by a solely antagonistic or cooperative perspective.

The preceding discussion has highlighted a number of characteristics
for trust in a modern context. Uncertainty and the experience of social
differentiation, along with increasing individualization, accentuate the
need for trust, which in turn reduces social complexity by increasing the
'tolerance of uncertainty'. Thus, trust sustains social relationships and is

'one of the most important synthetic forces within society' (Simmel 1950: 318).

The originality of Simmel's work comes from his complex conceptualization of the nature of modernity, which allows him to express varied and ambivalent aspects of modern culture. Simmel moves between a description stressing the freedom brought to individuals by the dissolution of traditional bonds and an emphasis on the sense of belonging and reliance on the social system. Thus, according to Simmel's less restrictive concept of modernity, a human agent, although socially embedded, is still able to enjoy individual liberty and autonomy, mainly thanks to shifting involvements among various fragmented spheres of life and among various groups. Consequently, a study of societal trust will require a combination of a culturalist approach with a micro-orientated perspective.

## Weber's conflation of communal and associative relationships

Simmel's interest in the prospect of freedom and individuality in a rationalized and disenchanted world was shared by Max Weber. Weber, like Simmel, believes that modern society is constituted of and by individuals; that society is a product of their interactions rather than traditional forms of social organization, and that only an individual can be a social actor. However, Weber rejects Simmel's concept of interaction as not being specific enough and instead focuses on social action, its intentionality and the meanings individuals attach to such action.

Weber's aim was to explain how values would affect individuals and social structures. He assumes that all actions have meaning only within a context of value. Weber proposes that motives should be understood as publicly constituted phenomena by establishing a relation between action and goal. The recognition that all meanings are social in character implies that particular actions can be seen as rational in one society but not in another. Weber was primarily concerned with modern Western society, and his studies of non-Western societies served mostly to underline the uniqueness of Western nations, which were seen as dominated by goal-orientated rationality. Weber's systematic and historical sociology is based on his classification of social action into four types: goal-orientated, value-orientated, affectual and traditional action.

Weber concentrates his attention mainly on instrumentally rational (or rational goal-orientated) actions, which are based on the calculation of alternative means to the end. A second type of social action, value-rational actions, is 'determined by a conscious belief in the value for its own sake of some ethical, aesthetical, religious, or other form of behaviour, independently of its prospect' (Weber 1968: 25). Both types of action are based on consciously regulated comparison and choice – that is, on rationality. The self-reinforcement and stability of the first type of action is ensured by its reliance on people's self-interest as a motivational force. Mutual self-interest contributes to the predictability of the behaviour of economic actors, who are all bound by the rule of efficiency. And although this process involves comparison and choice, this type of action does not involve an evaluation of others' motivation and behaviour because self-interest or calculation is assumed to be an inherent or natural capacity, which does not need to be supplied by society with interpretative standards (Alexander and Giesen 1989: 11). The process of individualization and rationalization, as shown by Weber in *The Protestant Ethics*, contributed towards the creation of new collective identities and new solidarities. These new bonds are often muted and invisible, resulting, however, in solidarities of enterpreneurs based on a common interest which is largely mediated through the market. 'The commitment to profit and accumulation, the necessity of dealing with competitive threats, the demands of building up and managing the firm – all these requirements impose upon the entrepreneur's existence constraints more objective and abstract, and publicly less validated, than those associated with estate membership, but no less cogent and less capable of sustaining a collective identity' (Poggi 1983: 108). This market community is characterized by impersonality, an orientation to commodity, and 'there is no brotherliness or reverence, and none of those spontaneous human relations that are sustained by personal unions' (Weber 1968: 636). This new type of trust relationship, founded on the mutual interest and functional interdependence of modern societies, is different from the trust of the pre-modern era, which was based on commonly held beliefs.

For Weber, one of the preconditions for the success of modern capitalism was the transition from personal trust to impersonal trust. It is exemplified in the abstract and universal trust of the Puritan enterpreneurs, who were loyal to their *calling*, without considering what benefits it would secure for them. 'This made them *individually* and *unconditionally* trustworthy and thus, according to the theory, they made the modern world possible' (Gellner 1988: 152). Their mutual trustworthiness was their social capital, which benefited the group, and in the longer run established the framework underlying capitalist relationships.

The ends of value-rational actions are socially learned and individually constructed. This type of orientation includes actions motivated by personal loyalty, honour or duty, which are undertaken regardless of cost involved. From the viewpoint of instrumental rationality, value-rational action is 'always irrational' because it is based on the principle of effectiveness, not efficiency, and because it does not take into consideration consequences of action (Weber 1968: 26). The rationality of ultimate values, which the individual learns from his or her culture, manifests itself in 'its clearly self-conscious formulation of the ultimate values governing the action and the consistently planned orientation of its detailed courses to these values' (1968: 25). Because this type of action involves duty or obligation towards the chosen values, it creates bonds based on codes of honour, and therefore the quality of persons is measured by the extent to which they observe those values. We can trust 'the person of quality' because we recognize 'the virtue in virtue' (Hawthorn 1988: 115). However, this type of trust is not self-reinforcing, and there is no good reason, as Hawthorn convincingly argues, to set store by this type of interpersonal trust since '[i]t may indeed be the case that betrayal is something that we have always to expect and accept where there is any honour and virtue at all' (1988: 115).

Two other types of social action, the traditional and the affectual, do not involve comparison and choice, so they can be classified in terms of confidence rather than trust. Traditional actions are 'automatic' reactions to 'habitual' stimuli and hence do not involve any choice of means. Affectual actions, on the other hand, are 'determined by the actors' specific affects and feeling states . . . [and] . . . may, for instance, consist of uncontrolled reaction to some exceptional stimulus' (Weber 1968: 25). Thus, traditional action is descriptive of the situation of confidence and conformity found in traditional communities in which customs, values and beliefs are shared. Affectual action is carried out as the result of certain emotional states, for instance, such as a need for revenge or gratification. Due to the irrationality of this orientation, our confidence in another's behaviour is not the result of our ability to evaluate the probability of the occurrence of this type of behaviour; instead, it is connected with our ability to identify ourselves with this type of conduct. Affectual reactions, as Weber sees them, are not learned but 'innate to the individual and latent there until called out by some stimulus innately recognised as appropriate' (Wallace 1990: 217). The best-known example of this type of action is charisma; that is, an 'emotional' orientation to holders of power.

The preceding discussion has pinpointed Weber's analysis of four types of action and the mechanisms by which mutual bonds within these types of action are achieved. First, there is the rational type of action based on mutual self-interest; second, the value-rational type of action based on trust in virtue; third, the traditional action based on custom and conformity; and finally, affectual action, which is based on faith. Only in the first and third cases – namely, in rational-goal action and in the traditional type of action – are trust and confidence self-reinforcing. The stability of these two types of action is secured by their uniformity, which is determined by conformity/custom and self-interest respectively. Accordingly, since there are only two types of action capable of self-reinforcement, there can only be two types of social relationships – the communal and the associative.

Acknowledging the similarity of his classification to Toennies' *Gemeinschaft* and *Gesellschaft* typology, Weber stresses that it is not the absence of coercion and conflict which constitutes communal relationships but the probability that the actors will direct their actions to the community's end and interest. In contrast to communal relationship, which rests on various types of affectual, emotional or traditional bases, the associative relationship is based on a rationally motivated adjustment of interests (Weber 1968: 40–1). Even though 'communal relationships' are typical features of pre-modern societies, Weber does not mechanically assume, as Toennies does, that the transformation to modern societies eliminates irrational behaviour. Weber notes that the majority of social interactions show characteristics of both types of relationship.

Weber's concept of social relationships as 'the reciprocal adjustment' of people's behaviour to one another 'with respect to the meaning which they give to it' (1968: 30) assumes that the subjective 'meaning' imputed by the parties does need to be the same (1968: 27). In addition, the subjective meaning of social relationships may change; for example, a political relationship can shift from one of solidarity to one involving a conflict of interest. The highest probability of achieving a rational formulation of the intended meaning can be found in the contractual relationship in commerce. There is also the possibility of determining the meaning of social relationships by means of mutual agreement. Entering into a relationship based on mutual obligation means that the parties' rational behaviour is now motivated by a dual rationality. Firstly, the actor is motivated by the value rationality; that is, by a sense of duty. Secondly, he is motivated by the 'means-ends' rationality, and 'the meaning of this action is more or less based on fidelity to his expectations' (Weber 1978: 32). In addition, Weber goes beyond the simple distinction between communal and associative relationships by insisting that both may be seen in the same social unit.

Weber's conception of the nature of social action and of the forms which communal actions taken together with his three dimensions of stratification (class, status and power) can provide interesting hints for the development of the social theory of boundary maintenance and, consequently, trust. In contrast to classes, which may or may not be communal groupings, status groups are normally communities which are held together by notions of 'a specifically regulated life style' and 'a restriction on "social" intercourse' and by social esteem and honour accorded to them by others (Weber 1968: 932). Weber strongly emphasizes the economic role of status groups; that is, their monopolization of goods and opportunities. In order for status groups to exist and to carry out their exclusionary and monopolistic strategies – that is, reserving specific goods opportunities to members and denying them to outsiders, the most typical problem of collective action – the free rider dilemma – needs to be solved (Barnes 1992). Since it is individually irrational for members of the group to support its exclusionary and monopolistic strategies, the group needs to facilitate the collective action of members. 'If a status group is to persist, and hence to exist, its members must generate a stream of collective action directly oriented to that objective. Such a stream cannot be sustained by "economic" arrangements, and must rather be secured by processes of honouring and dishonouring embedded in ongoing communicative interaction' (1992: 264). In Weber's account the 'special honour' functions as a symbolic reward, which is allocated by members themselves and 'distributed among the membership and inalienable from them: action related to such honour is autonomous group-oriented action, decoupled from the influence of outsiders' (1992: 265). Individuals of the same status may cooperate to promote shared ends because of the ability of the membership to withdraw recognition and to deny 'the special honour' to disobedient members. Status groups as groups with the specific characteristics may generate a stream of collective actions because of their ability to communicate their approval and disapproval to its members. This task of boundary-maintenance, while – at the same time – conveying to members whom to trust and whom not to trust, makes the continued existence of the group possible.

According to Weber, therefore, the maintenance of social order requires collective actions. In addition, Weber argues that the optimal case from the point of view of social order occurs when action motivated by self-interest – that is, rational-goal action – overlaps with value-rational action. This is a situation in which individuals follow freely chosen values and retain a clear understanding of the consequences of a given choice while respecting other individuals' interests and values. This combination of reason, responsibility and freedom is seen by Weber as the most desirable option in the modern world, where a conflict of values is inevitable.

The fact that individuals bring various types of motives to social relationships contributes to the significance of rules as the common point of orientation for the involved parties. When 'the rules were invested additionally with the quality of legitimacy, and that quality itself was justified by individuals, regarded as "right" on some grounds, then the motives for accepting the order were correspondingly strengthened and its endurance more securely guaranteed' (Albrow 1990: 163). In brief, Weber conceptualizes social order as uniformity and stability governed by rules and, at the same time, as being contingent upon a variety of individual orientations and backed by custom and pure self-interest. It seems that a legitimate order is a situation where the meaning of social relationships is agreed upon by mutual consent, and where parties are motivated by both mutual duties and obligations as well as by self-interest. A legitimate order 'enjoys the prestige of being considered binding' (Weber 1968: 31), and is founded upon an agreement which brings trust in virtue and self-interest together. This mutual agreement gradually establishes itself as an order based on a belief in its legitimacy. Consequently, this belief in the binding power of the rule or trust in the validity of the rule becomes routinized as a universal trust in the principles of the legal-rational bases of associative relationship.

The general issues that preoccupied Weber were the prevailing cultural crisis and the effects of modernity on the individual. Unlike Durkheim, he does not believe in value consensus and in the inevitability of periodic revivals of sacred social ties. Weber is more pessimistic, as he views a modern, secular and materialistic society as being overwhelmingly dominated by the process of rationalization, which leads to the domination of instrumental reason and specialists 'without spirit', and, subsequently, to disenchantment (Weber 1948: 155).

The processes of bureaucratization and rationalization may also result in 'legitimacy without trust' (Pakulski 1992: 24). Weber's warning of the emerging danger in modern rational societies, where moral commitments are no longer ascertained by institutional arrangments, leaving, for example, the market or the state without their previous moral support, is still very relevant. How to repair or avoid the danger of 'order without trust'? How to stop the process of erosion of informal reciprocity among people? How to prevent the decline of credibility of many institutions on which a mature and free society depends? These are today's most urgent social questions.

In terms of a general theory of trust, Weber's contribution is essential because he puts forward the question of complexity, discontinuity and transformation of trust relationships. He also demonstrates, from the viewpoint of social order, the desirability of the situation where reason, responsibility and values combined together create the conditions for a legitimate order, and, thus, for trust relations.

In Weber's model, interests are the motor of action but ideas, which define ends, can – by constructing and regulating patterns of conduct – serve interests. In this perspective, trust, as the value behind action, can be seen as constructed and sustained by pragmatic interests; however, at the same time, it creates new possibilities for action and for regulating the action of others. Weber's attention to the possibility of evolution of any type of relationship makes it possible to assume different levels of importance of trust in various periods of societal life. Moreover, Weber's successful weakening of the distinction between communal and associative relationships permits a disavowal that there is a simplistic differentiation between interpersonal trust and abstract trust and enables them to show their interdependence. Thus, to follow Weber does not necessarily entail privileging instrumental rationality but, rather, to pay attention to the tensions between normative and instrumental aspects of human behaviour and the search for links between a confidence and conformity of communal relationship and the universal trust of associative relationship.

## Types of order and trust

The concept of social order depends upon which element of compliance is brought to the fore: interest, norms or coercion. The general perception of classical sociology points to its assumption regarding the normative vision of social order as maintained only in the presence of common culture rooted in a well-integrated society. However, despite the common belief of the fathers of sociology that self-interest could not be the sole condition of social order, their theory of order is far from conclusive, and it was unable to come to terms with the issue of the relative significance of social norms versus interest. Their attempts to solve the dilemma of how mutual concerted action was possible focused their attention on the question of how we understand the meaning of actions. It can be said that the classical theorists built their conceptualization of social order on theories of meaning and attempts to explain it. 'They were concerned with the origin of shared perceptions of the world (Durkheim). If understanding actions required understanding intentions, intentions themselves must be socially defined (Weber). . . . The epistemological basis of meaning was a focus for all of them' (Rawls 1992: 234).

All classical sociologists stressed that the very construction of the social division of labour generated uncertainties, and they saw the implementation of various institutional arrangements as necessary for the continuity of social order. They attempted to solve the problem of order by addressing the issue of people's mutual interaction and connected with it executions of the conduct of others and by searching for the means of finding moral individualism in egoistic individualism. The earlier writers, whilst emphasizing normative forces, recognized that social pressure towards integration could be based on routine and custom, or it could also be the spontaneous outcome of activities of rational individuals. All of them noted negative aspects of modern civilization, and they searched for a remedy by focusing on factors which could balance the processes of secularization, rationalization and the weakening of social bonds. The results of their search for the bases of social order in modern societies illustrate the main differences between their theories, and, ever since, sociology has attempted to accommodate these differences. Utilitarian theory believes that social order results from the unplanned convergence of independently pursued interests and is not imposed by any transcendental entity. Spencer claims that modern industrial society is held together by an organic web of individualistic contracts, and thus order for him means voluntary cooperation based on contractual relations, where competition and cooperation balance each other. For Toennies, social order means social cohesion based upon consensus of wills, where familiarity, tradition and sentiments, reinforced by shared experience, safeguard integration. For Durkheim, morality is the essential source of social integration, and social order is based on the submission of the individual to the supreme authority of society; moral consensus is viewed as the source of social integration. The Durkheimian perspective points to the crucial role of the consciousness of obligations, which is imposed by society as a whole. It views people as obeying because they share certain common values and beliefs that are reaffirmed by means of reunion and rituals. Trust here seems to be a normative obligation inherent in social relations. For Simmel, social life is in a state of constant flux. Nevertheless, he shows how social stability is sustained by underlying interpersonal practices and rituals of everyday life which are reliable and based on trust. For Weber, one of the preconditions of the success of modern capitalism was the transition from the order and trust of communal relations to the universalistic trust of the Puritan entrepreneurs. In his vision of a new legitimate order emphases are put on an individual's perception of the order as binding and on a variety of motivations which lead to mutual consent. Although Toennies, Weber and Simmel were more pessimistic than Durkheim and Spencer in their critiques of the reality of modern bureaucratic societies, all of them recognized the importance of social integration and address the problem of trust directly or indirectly. Apart from Toennies, who considered modern societies to be moving dangerously in the direction of a Hobbesian state of war, classical sociologists, even though noting the loss of objective meaning and the emergence of mutually incompatible values, still did not recommend a return to traditional existence. However, their perceived solutions to the problem of modern culture differed markedly. While Toennies recommended breaking out of humanity's self-confinement with rational culture, and while Simmel perceived 'the subjectivity of pre-objective inner experience as the locus of the true unity of life' (Burger 1993: 816), Weber rejected all these solutions and proposed instead 'the ethics of responsibility'. Both Weber and Simmel demonstrated that the experience of modernity is more diverse in terms of involvement and motivation than it was previously assumed.

Weber's exposé of the tensions between the normative and the instrumental aspects of social reality illustrated, for example, that norms do not necessary contrast with self-interest. As seen in his description of the economic relationship, the norms of trust, honesty and fairness are supplementary to a contract-based market exchange. Weber, moreover, professes value-pluralism and does not share Durkheim's belief in the normative consensus based on the morality of individualism. How, then, is the existence of a collective order, and consequently, trust relationship, possible in the world of pluralistic or even conflictual values? How can Durkheimian normative consensus, which proved to be the most influential for subsequent sociological formulations of the theory of social integration, be combined with Weberian value-pluralism?

This question can be answered 'when we see that Weberian value-pluralism can manifest itself through divergent interpretations of abstract Durkheimian values' (Lukes 1991b: 62). Durkheim's moral individualism is centred on the two abstract values of liberty and equality, and the generality of these values permits us to combine Weberian and Durkheimian perspectives at a high level of abstraction, leaving unresolved only the problem of 'the interpretation of what they mean' (ibid.). In this light, social consensus can be maintained at a general, abstract level, while, through negotiation on a lower level, we can arrive at a compromise interpretation of the main values. Furthermore, this type of order can be seen as relatively stable since in daily life conflicts over particular values do not often occur because of the routine ('business as usual') character of daily life. Moreover, debates aiming at achieving common understanding and common interpretation of these highly abstract values mainly occur in transitional periods – that is, when people are forced to learn new ways of organizing individual and collective actions. In these 'unsettled periods', to borrow Swidler's phrase, the importance of normative consensus increases significantly because of the need for 'the collective sentiment' to provide a unified answer to the question of how people should live. In 'settled periods' a consensus at a high and abstract level is not questioned, although silence on this issue often only cancels real disagreements (Lukes 1991b; Swidler 1986).

Consequently, it can be said that in 'settled' or 'normal' periods the issue of trust, even in the context of a culture with a low level of coherence and unity of values, is not perceived as a social problem. In transitional periods, in contrast, the role of trust as the basis for negoti-ations and dialogues becomes more important and more visible. How-ever, in reality the picture is more complicated because distrust can also be the base of social order. For example, Goldfarb (1991) shows that cynicism, as a 'form of legitimation through disbelief', can become a means of social integration since it produces passivity and compliance by dissolving people's capacity to be critical and to initiate their own pro-gramme of change. Moreover, the absence of trust does not necessarily entail a lack of social order since order can be sustained by effective government based on fear. For example, in traditional Islamic societies the central authorities based their effective rules on the destruction of subunits in urban societies, consequently destroying trust (Gellner 1988). The same can be said about state socialism in Eastern Europe, where social order was maintained and controlled by the central authority whose strength was based on spreading distrust and the atomization of society. Thus, to identify trust with social order is not sufficient. We need to problematize the issue further by asking what kinds of order are supported by trust and in what kinds of order does trust really play an important role.

According to Elster (1989), two types of social order can be distin-guished. The first type of order is characterized by the predictability of social life and is maintained by the existence of habitual rules and social norms. A normal and routine life would not be possible without an implicit and unconsidered trust that everyday life does not carry major threats. Consequently, the absence of predictable order entails chaos rather than mistrust. Thus, the predictability of social order should be seen as a collective achievement to which we all contribute by following rules of daily life. More importantly, as Goffman (1970) notes, these rules do not produce social order; they are, rather, a way of exhibiting social order. Trust in such a case can be seen, according to Simmel, as a mechanism which allows us to accept the fiction of order because it functions.

The second type of order refers to the cooperative type, within which, according to Elster, the main problem is the free-rider dilemma. While social norms are extremely important for solving the problem of the first type of order, their contribution to the second type of order is more 'ambiguous' since 'social norms do not coordinate expectations', thus they 'may or may not help people to cooperate' (Elster 1989: 97). A situation in which people exhibit uncooperative behaviour does not need to lead to chaos; instead; it would result in the loss of possible cooper-ative gains and in the distrust of uncooperative partners. Moreover, as cooperation can be achieved not only by means of fear or coercion, but also on the bases of common values or self-interest, the key issue concerns the possibility for creating and maintaining trust and the role of trust when motives are mixed. Furthermore, predictability and cooperation do not necessarily include aspects of social order described as social cohesion or social integration, where individuals are connected by some bonds of allegiance, and consequently their actions are influenced by their identification with their group and its norms. It is in this mood that British officials, for example, reject the idea of the European integration, whilst accepting the plan for European cooperation.

Therefore, for the purpose of analysing trust, three types of order should be distinguished: stable order, which accounts for the predictability, reliability and legibility of the social reality; cohesive order, which can be seen as based on normative integration; and collaborative order, which refers to social cooperation. This approach excludes from further discussion a zero-sum game or model of order as ruled by 'pure conflict' and is thus irrelevant to the trust debate (Schelling 1960: 67). The main difference between the three types of order is connected not with types of motivation behind trusting behaviour (since, as we have already established, it always consists of a mixture of interest, reason and values) but with the function of trust. While all three types of order benefit from trust, since trust facilitates stability, cooperation and cohesion, the key question concerns its particular function within each of these models. In the next chapter I shall specify the uniqueness of the role played by trust in these three types of order by analysing contemporary sociological theories which debate the function of trust in modern societies.

# 3
# Functions of Trust

## The integrative function of trust – Talcott Parsons

Talcott Parsons was probably the last of the great sociologists who placed the problem of order at the centre of his concern. His analysis of the place of trust and meaning in the construction of social order and his analysis of the manner in which both of them were institutionalized can be seen as the expansion of the main concern of classical sociology. Parsons' attempt to find a solution to the problem of order which would be able to overcome the atomist and rationalistic tendency of the utilitarian view and which would also avoid the misgivings of solidaristic theories, 'which swallow up the individual in a larger whole' (Parsons 1949: 52), concentrated his attention on the commonalities of a plurality of actors mutually orientated to one another's action. Consequently, he stresses the integrative role played by shared values, and a normative, consensual-orientated explanation of social cohesion. His more practical aspiration, to address the problems of the social transition which America experienced after the Great Depression, led to the definition that these problems were caused by a gap in integration resulting from the lagging of the process of the institutionalization of norms, capable of providing a sufficient level of motivation, legitimacy and solidarity, behind the process of social differentiation.

Assuming, like Durkheim, that social order resting on self-interest cannot be stable, Parsons rejects individualistic accounts of society and argues that normative structures are the only route to a collective order. As he saw societies constituted of stable cooperative interactions, Parsons viewed social order not as based on rational self-interest or on externally imposed sanctions alone, but as resting on a common value system which 'is one of the required conditions for a society to be a stable system in equilibrium' (Parsons 1949: 389). The mutuality of interaction in a stable system is mediated and stabilized by moral standards seen as 'the core of the stabilizing mechanisms of the system of social interaction' (Parsons 1964: 22). This assumption leads to the analytical preponderance of society over the individual and, by seeing values as the stabilizing factor, makes them 'unmoved movers in the theory of action' (Swidler 1986: 274), lowering – by the same token – the explanatory thrust of his theory. The idea of normative regulations as fulfilling an integrative function forced Parsons to give priority to the common value system over the social actor. This resulted in a blending together of action and order in his theory. In subsequent years Parsons began to focus his attention on action, not so much from the perspective of the actor as from the view of the social system, in which the actor happens to be acting. Consequently, the stability of the social system is seen as resulting from conceptualizing role sets in terms of their inherent reciprocity and tendencies towards equilibrium.

As social order was based on a core of institutionalized values and social systems were viewed as a constellation of roles, the task of sociology as an analysis of the social system 'centred on the phenomena of the institutionalisation of patterns of value orientation in roles' (Parsons 1951: vii). The patterns' variables, describing alternatives possible from the point of view of the social system and the choices that are faced by individuals in their orientation towards roles, mould the processes of integration between individual actors and the social system. When there is a consistency between institutionalized roles and orientations of individual actors, societal integration is optimized (1951: 52–4). The perfectly integrated system would be one in which there is a greater convergence between the social system and the individual actor – that is, the system in which 'the "deeper" layers of motivation become harnessed to the fulfilment of role expectation' (1951: 42). Thus, the problem is how to make sure that appropriate values and norms will motivate actors and guide their role performance. If moral codes are incorporated into the roles, it can be argued, as Wolfe (1989: 204) does, that Parsons locates the basis of trust in the roles that actors perform. For example, we trust professionals because the moral code inscribed in their roles ensures that they act according to our expectations of how people in these roles should act.

Wolfe argues that 'Parsons' scheme represents a plurality of moral roles, each one taking moral obligation away from both individual choice and social constraint and giving it instead to the role' (1989: 203). He criticizes this 'role-based' vision of morality by pointing out that in such cases any change in roles will necessarily entail a change in morality.

Therefore, Wolfe concludes, there is no independent basis for trust in Parsons' analysis. 'Without a compelling reason to explain why voluntaristic action should lead to binding moral obligation, Parsons opts for sentiments not unlike the social conformity' (1989: 205). Although there are many difficulties with Parsons' concept of morality, Wolfe's argument that for Parsons the notion of plurality of roles constitutes a theory of morality seems to be too simplistic. It overlooks the importance of cultural patterns of constraints in Parsons' theory and it runs against the most common criticism of Parsons' normative functionalism which labels him 'moralist' for believing in the existence of some kind of supra-individual context for human behaviour which secures societal order (Andersen 1990).

Parsons' real ambition was to develop an explanation for the binding nature of moral obligations without attempting to advance an accompanying conception of the place of morality in human life. He recognized that the categorization of various roles according to pattern variables was not a substitute for a theory of morality and that there was a need for a theory of group solidarity. None the less, apart from a tentative explanation of solidarity as being linked to the development of affective ties generated during socialization, this theory was not satisfactorily elaborated. In what follows I shall interpret Parsons' understanding of the concept of solidarity since in this context the notion of trust is debated.

The concept of solidarity is used by Parsons to cope with the difficult task of the conceptualization of the interrelation of social and cultural systems. Solidarity is seen as the main characteristic of a legitimate order of societal community, whose primary function is to define the obligations of loyalty to the societal collectivity (Parsons 1971: 12). The integration is secured thanks to the capacity of a societal community to produce solidarity, understood as a generalized capacity 'to control and to "bring into line" the behaviour of the system's units in accordance with the integrative needs of the site, to check or reverse disruptive tendencies to deviant behaviour, and to promote the conditions of harmonious cooperation' (Parsons 1971: 49). Solidarity, identified by the institutionalization of shared values (Parsons 1951: 193), is a dimension of social order produced by mutual constraints and reinforced by a common fate and mutual feeling of responsibility. Patterns of solidarity are generated by a collective orientation (the second pattern variables) by enhancing responsibility through common identity. While self-orientation implies an indifference to 'the integrity of a valued social system of action' (1951: 97), a collective orientation enables generalization of loyalty. Hence, according to Parsons (1969a: 142), trust is 'the attitudinal ground – in affectively motivated loyalty – for the acceptance of solidarity relationships'. Trust resides in the individual's belief that others will put self-interest aside in favour of a collectivity orientation. When trust acquires sufficient autonomy to become an examined assumption, it can – through the governing expectations of participants – control the behaviour of people.

From this perspective trust is viewed as synonymous with conformity and familiarity, while motivation to cooperate is seen as a result of collectivity norms being reinforced by the mechanism of social control. The granting of trust entails the expectations that others will meet their obligations and responsibilities, that they will show 'other-orientation'. And this is by itself a mechanism of social control which enables the monitoring of others, especially of those in positions of power. As an aspect of actors' value-orientations which commits them to norms of reciprocity and complementarity, trust also plays an integrative role. An integrated system is thus a system in which actors are trustworthy in the performance of their roles, which in turn contributes to the stability and orderliness of the system. They are trustworthy because of the solidarity of their collectivity, which imposes discipline upon them but also helps them to 'live up to these kind of expectations' and cope with the uncertainty of less clear situations (Parsons 1951: 193). What are the sources of solidarity?

There are two models of solidarity present in Parsons' writing. The first type of solidarity, bearing a clear resemblance to the Durkheimian concept of solidaristic organizations, is based on consensus on norms and values as described in the ideal type of voluntary associations (Parsons 1969b: 503). A fascination with the issue of societal community and a search for the possibility of enlarging the moral capacity of polity resulted in Parsons' view of associational groups as the basis of social and political trust. The solidarity of these groups is a result of 'discussion and deliberation among individuals who freely choose to participate in an association' (Cohen and Arato 1992: 131). The existence of solidarity within professional communities is also a source of the layman's trust towards representatives of a given profession. To sustain this social trust, associations or solidarity groups exert pressure on their members – through leadership, ideology or norms – to play the expected roles in the process of interaction. While the generation of trust depends in this type of solidarity relationships upon such factors as common values and interests (Parsons 1969a: 127), it can be said that trust is viewed here as synonymous with conformity.

Parsons insisted on the centrality of the category of integration through associations without being able to see other alternatives to social organization. This failure was a result of the fact that he never took into account the selectivity and asymmetry built into the contemporary institutions (Cohen and Arato 1992: 131–7). Parsons was also unable to notice the negative potential of modern associations. His 'morality of association' failed to account for the fact that in modern democracies the politicization of many groups creates collective anomie instead of absorbing individuals into the collectivity (Wolfe 1989: 115–16).

The second model of solidarity, as an indicator of Parsons' search for a functional equivalent to *Gemeinschaft*, has its roots in 'common belongings' (Parsons 1969b: 416–18). In this model, solidarity is seen as dependent on and, at the same time, reinforcing, the constitution of collective identity. Cohen and Arato (1992: 131) sum up this type of solidarity as being grounded on 'the generation of consensus among individuals on the basis of preexisting, diffuse solidarity that is not open to questioning or thematization'. The role of these collectivities is essential in the maintenance of adequate levels of motivation. This task is carried out mainly by the social structures concerned with socialization, particularly kinship. Although Parsons incorporated Durkheim's understanding of the continuity of sacred values in a secular society, he saw that in modern complex societies it is often therapy rather than religion which 'supplements kinship' in securing an adequate level of motivation (Parsons 1966: 13). Parsons also insisted on the continuing importance of friendship in shaping our moral standards (1969b: 251). Anchoring morality in cultural patterns of constraints – that is, basing it on familiarity – opens Parsons' theory up to the problems inherent in pure collectivism. Parsons partly managed to escape these problems by arguing that both models of solidarity, based on the familiarity type of solidarity and the associational activities and relationships, can coexist. Although Parsons' concept of solidaristic communities allows mainly for a normative coordination of action and conventional relations to standards, and although the institutionalized roles include a pattern conformity with collective orientation, yet moral codes are not inscribed, as Wolfe argues, on to roles but are grounded in the solidaristic collectivities. Seen in this way, morality is not founded on religion nor does it depend on something outside of society nor is it a matter of individual choice, but it is viewed as something internalized by members of solidaristic communities.

In the Parsonsian approach, personal trust relationships are secured by a reciprocity of perspective acting as a reward. It is assumed that all members of the same collectivity use the same interpretative framework since they share a common culture based either on kinship, shared intimacies, familiarity or common interest and background. However, it still raises a question of how trust is produced in other than relatively informal and homogeneous communities. Explaining solidarity by norms alone, without making clear how the norms are enforced, 'amounts to a tautology' (Hechter 1987: 23). Thus, the main problem with Parsons' concept of trust is that it does not explain how compliance with norms is generated and how institutions promote solidarity. It seems that the assumption that solidarity is a result of the development of affective ties generated during socialization allowed Parsons to not problematize the issue of trust, and, consequently, the concept was left underdeveloped.

The concept of trust, viewed as the equivalent of solidarity, is conceived by Parsons not only in terms of relations among individuals in a society but also as concerning integration between subsystems of the social system. To look at the social system as the interaction of a plurality of actors focuses attention on a personal trust, while switching over to system-integration stresses the significance of symbolic trust in four subsystems (the economy, the polity, the legal and integration subsystem and the family and tradition) of the social system. What holds for individual actors with regard to the social system also holds for the subsystems: 'it makes sense to talk of the various kinds of expectations and trust that supraindividual systems have of one another' (Barber 1983: 18). Within each subsystem, a steering medium functions both to bind together the operations of the subsystem itself and to control its relationship with other subsystems. Parsons, who assumes that symbolic processes have primacy over social structural factors, explains the operation of the steering media in terms of a cybernetic hierarchy (Dodd 1994: 60–5). Operations within the social system and between its subsystems are carried out by way of four media of interchange, which are characterized as symbolic media, thus having connotions of value consensus (Alexander 1989). Trust on this level exists to the degree that interchange between generalized media – namely, commitment, influence, power and money (each originated in different subsystems) – is effective. Trust is associated with symbolic legitimation and seen as a consequence of commitment, which involves appeals to obligation in terms of basic norms and values. For example, power, a medium generated within the political subsystem, is provided with the symbolic legitimation produced by effective integration with norms and values. If trust is maintained, legitimate power based on individuals' trust in those who rule them will be used to achieve collective goals (Parsons 1963). However, if the political power is symbolically delegitimated, if symbolic trust is eroded, then exchange moves to 'the kind of purely individualistic exchange that disrupts, randomizes social life' (Alexander 1989: 256). Eventually trust will be withdrawn and actions correspondingly instrumentalized; thus, without trust, only an individualistic order becomes possible. Staying with the example of the political subsystem, political institutions without trust would be forced to rely solely on force and coercion for obedience. This would be not only more costly, more time-consuming and a less flexible solution, but, as Parsons argues, it would carry the threat of instability. 'Only if the media of exchange can generate trust, if they can mobilise or plug into some functionally specific consensus, can societal production occur without the continual, crippling withdrawal of resources by participating groups or individuals' (Alexander 1989: 142). In short, a medium from which trust has been withdrawn may only recover its value from above 'by calling on ... various cybernetically higher forces' (Parsons 1975: 101). Parsons here, however, 'ignores the possibility that one medium might be used to bolster another, in which case redemption need not be from above at all. This, for instance, would make the interrelation of economic and political power – buying political influence – difficult to explain' (Dodd 1994: 64). This shortcoming in Parsons' theory is not only the result of the way in which he addresses the relationship between money and power but also of the more general problem stemming from incorporation of trust to normative integration. According to Williams (1988), unless cooperation also serves an egoistic motivation, the practices of cooperation will be unstable. This means that a social order based on trust not grounded in self-interest will be unpredictable and unstable, and, for this reason, trust is not always functional.

In Parsons' theory, trust not only performs an important function in increasing the effectiveness of the system, but it also secures conditions for the flourishing of 'institutionalized individualism'. The presence of trust means that 'creative individuals are allowed greater freedom and autonomy. Further, simply by facilitating cooperation among diverse individuals and groups, trust contributes to a more inclusive, cosmopolitan community' (Alexander 1989: 142). Unfortunately, Parsons' solution for achieving this better world – a world free from excessive individualism, instability, fragmentation of communities, abuses of power – is totally unrealistic. How can people get along peacefully with little besides mutual trust to help them? And if they are so cooperative and trustworthy, how can they be sure that their trust will be not abused?

According to Parsons, symbolic legitimation, which is produced by effective integration norms and values and equated with media generalization (and, consequently, with symbolic trust) is the sole route to social order. Many critical points have been raised against this vision (Black 1961; Craib 1984; Dawe 1978; Giddens 1977; Gouldner 1970; Hamilton 1983). It is often pointed out that Parsons' assumptions are idealistic and lack empirical support, that his zero-sum concept of power is too simplistic and too naïve, that trust can be generated not only through symbolic means but also can be achieved by, for example, an increasing effectiveness in production or a higher level of services or provision to a community.

Parsons stresses the institutionalization of norms which are capable of generating sufficiently high levels of motivation, legitimacy and solidarity. However, an increasing concern with the production of personalities through socialization is not enough to make coordination possible, neither does it provide a guarantee that institutionalized values will secure use of knowledge and power solely for positive purposes. It is clear that it is not enough to look at trust as a simple dependant of symbolic legitimation and normative structures. Since social life is also structured by people's access to goods and property, the concept of trust needs to be considered not only in relation to social integration and system integration, but also in the relations between various groups within society. By excluding the possibility that the normative order may arise from calculative conformity and the calculative sanctioning of others into conformity, Parsons is also unable to see how actors' self-consciously calculative orientation to a situation can result in routinized practices, which could sustain societal trust (Barnes 1988: 21–54). In Parsons' vision of value-integrated society, with its emphasis on normative uniformity rather than diversity, consensus rather than conflict, there is no space for distrust based on conflictual interests or mistrust of a political authority as a result of economic exclusion and political alienation. Consequently, it leaves unspecified social mechanisms which generate trust in spite of unmet expectations and does not recognize the potentially positive function of distrust in some situations.

The picture of society as a solidarity of interaction in which continued stability depends solely upon actors' cognitive performance, cultural standards and motivational commitment excludes more structural concerns. It brings into attention the notion of trust as the condition which regulates and controls roles as well as the condition of the system integration. In Parsons' theory the significance of trust as a single explanatory device is clearly overstated. The notion of trust, used as a substitute for familiarity, conformity and symbolic legitimation, does not provide us with an effective instrument with which to analyse social reality. However, Parsons' contribution does indicate a fruitful way of showing the consequences of trust for the functioning of different social systems. Parsons not only noticed two types of solidarity, but he also pointed to the fact of their simultaneous occurrence in the modern world. For example, the obligations between professionals and their clients combined some elements of a *Gesellschaft* relationship with some main *Gemeinschaft* dimensions. This opens up an interesting perspective of seeing trust as a continuum or a spectrum, ranging from personal trust to abstract trust.

## Reduction of complexity – trust in Niklas Luhmann's writing

Niklas Luhmann was the first to provide a theoretical clarification of the concept of trust and to elaborate the theoretical framework within which the role of this notion could be adequately evaluated. His perspective is the continuation of the functional approach found in Parsons' discussion of system integration and symbolic trust. However, for Luhmann, unlike Parsons, the relevance of trust is not so much a result of his interest in the general and fundamental theoretical problems of order and constancy in society, but rather a consequence of the importance which he attaches to two interdependent structural changes taking place in the modern world. Firstly, the modern world is and presents itself as an 'unmanageable complexity' because of 'the increasing diversification and particular-isation of familiarities and unfamiliarities' (Luhmann 1988: 105). The second process is 'the increasing replacement of danger by risk' – that is, by the possibility of future damaging consequences of our actions (1988: 105). Therefore, in a more contingent and complex world, risk-taking rationality is required; 'and risk-taking will as far as others are involved, require trust' (1988: 105).

Luhmann solves the problem of the contingency of modern life by creatively incorporating and developing Parsons' media theory and his concept of symbolic generalization. The characterization of modern life as increasingly complex and contingent led to the observation that there is a need for generalized media that generate trust without eliminating the reality of choice. Consequently, trust is seen as one of the generalized media of communication (others being love, money and power), and as such reduces the complexity of the world faced by the individual actor by providing the capacity for 'intersubjective transmission of acts of selec-tion over shorter or longer chains' (Luhmann 1979: 49). One of the most important points made by Luhmann is that trust can be understood and compared with other functionally equivalent mechanisms only from the point of view of its function. Historically, trust can have different shapes, can occur on different levels and can be more or less spontaneous but it always performs the same function; it 'reduces social complexity by going beyond available information and generalising expectations of behaviour in that it replaces missing information with an internally guaranteed security' (1979: 93). Trust serves to increase the potential of a system for complexity, and its function is the reduction of social complexity by increasing the 'tolerance of uncertainty' (1979: 150). Despite this functionalist assumption that trust is integral to the capacity of a system to reduce complexity, it is, however, 'not clear whether trust actually is functional in the way intended within systems-theory' (Dodd 1994: 139). Furthermore, Luhmann is less forthcoming on the issue of how this function of trust helps to explain the actual formation of trust. Trust, while it is not the only mechanism for the reduction of complexity and cannot be reduced or replaced totally by the other phenomena, is presented by Luhmann as a rational answer to the complexity or uncertainty of social life.

Luhmann argues that social order in modern society is no longer based on the personal trust that characterized small, traditional societies. In civilized social systems personal trust is built up in a tactical-perceptive manner rather than spontaneously, and it 'becomes a type of system trust in the ability of the systems to maintain conditions or performances which are, within certain limits, identical' (Luhmann 1979: 68). Under the conditions set by civilized society, readiness to trust is achieved more through flexibility of self-presentation and less through emotion. It incorporates an element of reflexivity, and in this form personal trust 'becomes trust in perceptive tact and expressive discipline' (1979: 68). Trust, as the result of one's ability to control self-presentation and ability to maintain boundaries, is also very much the subject of interest of Garfinkel, who defines a trustworthy person as one who can master the discrepancy of prescribed attitudes with respect to reality 'in such fashion as to maintain a public show of respect of them' (1963: 238). However, while according to Garfinkel, the orderliness of social life is founded on the mutual trust members have displayed towards one another, Luhmann does not take trust for granted because actors are always conscious of the possibilities of distrust.

In the modern world we are no longer placed in a fixed social setting and these new conditions of expanded choices, opportunities and dependences require commitment and a sustained belief in the ability of systems to perform and maintain conditions, rather than personal trust. For Luhmann, as for Parsons and later Giddens, modern society is not necessarily less integrated than the traditional one. However, unlike Durkheim, Luhmann thinks that the symbols that represent the unity of the system – that is, the highly general and non-controversial ideologies and symbols – do not perform an integrative function but only symbolize the meaning of integration. Hence, trust resides in the actors' ability to read meaning and their rational perception that human beings' ability to function rests on 'trust in trust'.

Thus, modern societies are characterized by the increasing importance of 'system trust', which is built upon the belief that others also trust. It does not rest on bonds between people but includes reflexivity and a conscious approach (Luhmann 1979: 66–9). Both the system and the actors benefit from trust's ability to reduce the uncertainty caused by social complexity. This notion of trust, roughly analogous to the idea of public good, rests on a 'presentational' base. It ensures that everything seems in proper order, which, in turn, increases our 'trust in trust'. Thus, the cognitive basis of trust lies in that 'each trusts on the assumption that others trust', or trust in trust (1979: 69). The mechanism of the formation of trust in abstract systems takes the form of a perception of the social world as a 'fabricated appearance' which provides 'a durable basis for the continuation of contacts as long as everyone observes the rules of the game and works together, in trust, to maintain the representation' (1979: 67).

This kind of confidence that our expectations will not be disappointed, being part of our daily routine and normal behaviour, is not concerned with knowing the essential truth about a matter. For example we have confidence in the purchasing power of money, which is based more on our familiarity with it rather than on our precise knowledge of the working of the currency. Moreover, we are not involved in the process of deciding whether or not to accept money each time we encounter it. We assign our expectations to it, knowing – on the basis of our previous experience – that the danger of disappointment is minimal. This form of trust, which neglects the possibility of disappointment, is learned as behaviour and involves a feeling of familiarity. It covers the risk involved and the reflexivity, initially necessary for these relationships (1979: 66–9). In his recent writing Luhmann proposes calling this type of trust in abstract systems 'confidence'.

The distinction between confidence and trust in many ways resembles Simmel's discussion of confidence and ignorance. It is based on the perception and evaluation of a given situation – that is, on our ability to distinguish between danger and risk. 'If you do not consider alternatives, you are in a situation of confidence. If you choose one action in preference to others in spite of the possibility of being disappointed by the action of others, you define the situation as one of trust' (Luhmann 1988: 97). Thus, trust is not a continous state but is connected to the specific circumstance in which individuals consciously contemplate alternative courses of action.

However, while confidence in the system is essential for its functioning, to overcome any crisis the system needs more than passive, pragmatic acceptance. In order to maximize utilization of resources in situations of uncertainty or risk the system requires additional trust input. This type of trust can only be developed on the ground of the first form of trust – that is, confidence in the system. However, a lack of confidence, causing disappointment with the system's performance, may or may not have an impact on the level of trust in the political system or the economy. The withdrawal of attitudes allowing for active support 'is not an immediate and necessary' result of lack of pragmatic commitment' (Luhmann 1988: 104).

This picture of the circular relationships, between confidence and trust on the level of the supra-individual systems parallels Luhmann's earlier remarks about the interdependence between trust and self-confidence on the level of the individual. Generally, it seems, writes Luhmann, that people are more willing to trust if they possess inner security. This readiness to trust, based on self-confidence, enables people to cope with disappointments in a more composed and positive manner. Thus, the importance of self-confidence is connected with the fact that it makes insecurity 'bearable' and increases our ability to deal with unexpected problems (Luhmann 1979: 79–81).

Luhmann, unlike Parsons, makes it clear that he does not assume that trust is the sole foundation of the world. Moreover, he introduces distrust as a functional alternative to trust, arguing that system rationality cannot be attributed to trust alone and that in some situations distrust is only a healthy sign and therefore must be institutionalized. However, distrust should never be allowed to gain the upper hand because it may turn into a destructive force (Luhmann 1979: 75). At the same time, trust is not a ready-made solution to the world's problems. Trust in the systems as a whole depends 'decisively on trust being curtailed at critical points and distrust being switched in. Conversely, only in systems which are trusted can distrust be so institutionalized and restricted that it is not regarded as personal, and so reciprocated, and remain in this way protected from extensions into conflicts' (1979: 92).

Trust itself presents a problem because it is not a means that can be chosen for a particular end and its achievement cannot be designed and optimized. And, at the same time, a highly differentiated society needs more trust for the reduction of its complexity. With the disappearance of the old bases of forming social trust and the emergence of more contingent structures and changeable conditions, the reconstruction of trust presents many problems. Moreover, due to its fragility, trust can be learned only very gradually on the basis of previous experience. However, the fact that trust is the easier option allows Luhmann to be an optimist and to believe that there is 'a strong incentive to begin a relationship with trust' (1979: 72).

Luhmann's notion of trust rests as on a 'presentational' base ensuring that everything seems in proper order. It transforms the problem of trust from a question about the actual characteristics of trust relationships into one concerning the beliefs people hold about other people's beliefs about it. In so doing, it empties the concept of trust of any objective reference or moral content. Although the removal of normative overtones is a positive step, the separation of people's trust attitudes from objective grounds and the reason for having confidence in someone or something is less justified. People not only trust 'on the assumption that others trust' (Luhmann 1979: 69), but they also evaluate their conditions as less or more encouraging trusting attitudes (you trust more political leaders when your salary increases, but – at the same time – your neighbour, whose salary declines, may distrust them), they calculate the probability of some events and they hold some specific beliefs and feelings justifying or not justifying the specific relations. Thus, Luhmann's presentational approach could be enriched by a framework providing the basis for assessing the degree of discrepancy between people's values and beliefs (for example, their concepts of a good political system) and the conditions in which they live (for example, the type of prevailing political regime).

In Luhmann's perspective, trust as a property of the system is rational because it is indispensable in order to increase a system's potential for complexity. In this context, 'rational' refers to systems, not to individuals, and to mechanisms for maintaining systems, rather than to decision-making processes. Consequently, Luhmann's concept of trust is much broader than the understanding of this term in the rational choice perspective, which, according to him, missed the point of the question of trust by equating it with a model for calculating correct decisions.

## Trust as a lubricant of cooperation – the rational choice approach

In the last decade the popularity of rational choice theory has extended from economics and political science to sociology. This expansion can be attributed to specific features of this approach, such as its methodological individualism, its potential for the micro–macro linkage, and the elegance and simplicity of its model of motivation. Its popularity can be viewed as a theoretical reaction to a priori macro-structural and functionalist arguments. It has resulted in claims that the elementary postulate of rational choice theory about human behaviour can provide a micro-foundation for 'the most general and elaborated individualistic theory in social science' (Hechter 1987: 30).

In a general way, rational choice theory assumes that any participation in collective action can be explained by models of rational individual action, where rationality is understood in utilitarian terms as a matter of satisfying the individual's preference, and consists in choosing that action that is most likely to produce the highest 'utility' for the actor. Focusing on the motivations and beliefs of actors, such explanations begin with 'the logically most simple type of motivation: rational, selfish, outcome-oriented behaviour' (Elster 1989: 37). Since the aim of this type of explanation is to link micro- and macro-levels of analysis, they involve, apart from individuals, two other elements – namely, institutions and social outcomes. Rational choice argues that social life constitutes the aggregated outcomes of all individual's rational choices. The maximized individual outcome is contingent upon the effects of others' actions. Consequently, the decision process is best analysed by utilizing the methodology of game theory, in which 'each actor considers what others are likely to do and then makes the best choice to attain her end, given the probable behaviour of others' (Turner 1991: 84). The incorporation of game theory enhances the theoretical credibility of rational choice models. Rational choice theory also attracts attention because it addresses the central issue for any social system – that is, the question of how public goods are produced. The question of collective action, or the free-rider problem, is crucial to any understanding of what makes people choose cooperation when there are no external mechanisms enforcing their commitments. Since nobody can be excluded from consumption of public goods once the good is produced, there is a question of what does motivate rational actors, who are always choosing that course of action which satisfies their most preferred goals with the greatest efficiency, to contribute voluntarily to the provision of collective goods. As individual rationality does not imply the rationality of collective behaviour, this approach also tries to understand how rationality on the part of individuals leads to coherence at the level of society.

Since there is nothing in the theory that excludes the view of human beings as being able to act in pro-social manners, rational choice theories represent a spectrum of perspectives. Some stress egoistic self-interest, while others underline the role of self-interest by admitting that pro-social behaviour can spontaneously emerge and be sustained by repeated exchange. More eclectic approaches emphasize both norms and interest as determinants of human behaviour. In this way various explanations of cooperation can be divided according to their assumption about the relative importance of self-interest *vis-à-vis* norms. Accordingly, the place of trust and its role in the process of cooperation is conceptualized differently, with some writers stressing that trust can be generated by the rational pursuit of self-interest alone and others noticing the role of familiarity or normative contexts in the construction of the trust relationship. Nevertheless, rational choice theory commonly highlights the relationship between trust and rationality, and points out risks and benefits which accompany trust.

The expansion of rational choice theory from economics to sociology has resulted in attempts to incorporate economists' definition of trust in social science literature. Trust from the economists' perspective is a remarkably efficient lubricant to economic exchange or the most efficient mechanism for governing transactions (Arrow 1974). Trust is viewed as 'implicit contracting' or as a unique commodity, which cannot be 'bought very easily' and which is fragile with respect to substitutes, such as insurance, monitoring, rewards or sanctions (Arrow 1974: 23). Economic situations can be seen as a continuum of options: from cases based on partners' mutual trust, through ones based on conventions or limited mutual trust, to situations based on a lack of trust. Literature on game theory assumes that conventions (for example, in employment relations) are solutions to the prisoner's dilemma, since they 'operate as a coordination mechanism so that one of the many possible solutions will be the one chosen' (Leibenstein 1987: 609). The central issue raised by this type of economic study – that is, the question of the relationship between self-interest and trust – is still the underlying problem of mainstream rational theory in contemporary sociology.

The latest major work written in this perspective, James Coleman's *Foundations of Social Theory*, tries to combine political and moral questions and the use of rational choice models. Coleman equates interests with goals and sees them as the driving force of action, motivated by the rationality of maximizing utility (1990: 509–11). In a vein very similar to neo-classical accounts of economic behaviour, Coleman assumes actors to be not only rational but also unconstrained by norms and purely self-interested. Consequently, interests are viewed as the ultimate source of all social explanation, and an analysis of trust is constructed on the basis of simple relationships between a person's expected gains and the expected losses from another person.

Coleman notes that all trust situations involve a time lag, and it is this time asymmetry in delivery which introduces risk into unilateral action. Consequently, for him, as for Luhmann, the trust situation consists of a sub-class of those involving risk. 'They are situations in which the risk one takes depends on the performance of another actor' (1990: 91). Trust is a purposive behaviour aiming at the maximization of utility under risk. Mutual trust is seen as a form of social capital since it reduces the cost of monitoring and sanctioning activities (1990: 306–10). While assuming rationality on behalf of both trustors and trustees, Coleman shows that the trustor's decision to place trust is based 'not simply on his estimate of the probability of the trustee's keeping the trust, but also in part on the use of negative sanction' (1990: 115). Rational individuals place trust only when both potential gains are bigger than potential losses and trust relations are supported by negative sanctions.

Coleman in his discussion of personal trust assumes a more rational account of human behaviour than Parsons, and in his version trust is a less emotional, more calculating, colder device for policing free riders. It echoes Blau's statement that we trust one another only to the degree that our own interest is served. In both approaches trust is based on self-interest, and a good reputation is compared to 'a high credit rating' (Blau 1964: 259). Coleman, however, is more realistic than Parsons in arguing that demand for a normative system is not a sufficient condition for bringing it into existence. He argues that solidarity is produced consciously, by explicit communication about joint interests and joint sanctioning, which contrasts with the Durkheimian perspective, according to which solidarity is produced unconsciously by the process of shared emotions and interactions. Because sanctions – as, for example, mistrust – reduce the volume of exchange in a system, they can be seen as 'a public good' (Coleman 1990: 116). Since this public good needs to be supported by a normative system, Coleman admits that trust can only be produced in informal, small, closed and homogeneous communities which are able to reinforce normative sanctions. Hence, in Coleman's theory, norms are not really contrasted with self-interest since in his theory the pursuit of self-interest exploits social norms to punish untrustworthiness (Lukes 1991a: 148). Furthermore, by limiting his argument to social structures that are not normatively based and adopting the power theory of norms, Coleman is unable to explain the strength of norms and consequently the importance of trust in social relations (Stinchcombe 1992). He also fails to provide an account of shared meaning as the condition of trust relations since he does not address questions of 'how would isolated individuals achieve meaning in common with one another' and 'whether meaning requires some social orienting on its own behalf?' (Rawls 1992: 229).

The awareness of the limitation of rational choice theory has led Jon Elster (1989) to acknowledge that it needs to be complemented with an analysis of social norms; and that norms provide sources of motivation that are 'irreducible to rationality'. Elster admits that much of what we call moral behaviour involves more than satisfying self-interest and that norms which help society stay cemented together cannot be explained as outcome-orientated rationality. He concludes by arguing that the mixture of self-interest and normative commitment (for example, trust and credibility) that guides human action contributes to social stability and cooperation; however, to know how they interact we must analyse particular cases.

According to his eclectic view, both rationality and social norms are among the determinants of most action. Envy, self-interest and codes of honour, or the ability to make credible threats and promises, are seen as motivations which provide the 'cement of society' without 'which chaos and anarchy would prevail' (Elster 1989: 250). The concept of trust, seen as a social 'lubricant', which facilitates cooperation, is closely related to the notion of credibility, which – by enhancing the probability of carrying out promises and threats – promotes cooperation but may also promote violence. Hence, credibility is a more ambiguous concept than trust, which is more desirable on all levels since it does not promote violence but solely fosters cooperation.

Elster discusses two types of trust. The first amounts 'to the ability to make credible promises', while the second type introduces a concept of trust in a wider sense by viewing trust as a 'part of a code of honour' (1989: 274). From the second perspective, trust is seen as a broader concept than credibility because it includes 'a belief that the other party will act honourably even under unforeseen circumstances not covered by contract or promises' (1989: 274). However, under some conditions – namely, when long-term self-interest is involved – credibility and trust might bring about the same outcome. Hence, although trust as a code of honour cannot easily occur among strangers as credibility does, in iterated games or prolonged contacts their consequences are similar.

In the modern world economic, social and technological changes are undermining our ability to make credible threats, thereby making our societies 'safer and bleaker' than the societies of the past. 'They are safer because fewer threats are made and carried out, and bleaker because fewer promises are made and kept. People are less violent but also less helpful and cooperative' (Elster 1989: 284). The social and geographical mobility of modern societies tends to erode trust and credibility by undermining bonds of solidarity and reducing the importance of long-term self-interest since dominant interactions are becoming increasingly ephemeral and in a state of flux. Hence, Elster proposes a strategy of economizing on trust, arguing that it is less risky and costly to concentrate on cooperation than on trust. According to him, without assuming that the prior level of trust will eventually be high enough to bring about cooperation on its own account, we should promote the right conditions for cooperation, relying above all on constraint and interest.

A more optimistic stand on this issue is presented in a volume edited by Gambetta (1988a) and entitled *Trust: Making and Breaking Cooperative Relations*. Although the contributors to the book address various problems of trust, talk about trust in different contexts and place emphasis differently, there is, however, some degree of convergence on the conceptual issues, which allows for the common presentation of the book. The authors of this illuminating volume would agree with Elster that the contrast between norms and self-interests does not need to generate a distinction among different kinds of actions. Yet they would stress a belief in the rationality of placing faith in trust and point to the danger of both; banking on trust as well as failing to understand how it works. While Elster's strategy of economizing on trust sees trust as a by-product of a good economic system but too risky to rely on, Gambetta and his colleagues argue that, although promoting trust is costly, a lack of trust is more costly still. They also note that even though trust is often a by-product of objective conditions, yet it is not always the case (Gambetta 1988b: 225). By assuming that the predisposition to trust 'can be perceived and adopted as a rational pursuit even by moderately forward-looking egoists' (1988b: 228), Gambetta and his contributors see trust as a precondition of cooperation. It is assumed that cooperation 'requires trust in the sense that dependent parties need some degree of assurance that non-dependent parties will not defect' (Williams 1988: 8). The similarity of perspectives presented in the volume is captured in Gambetta's summarizing definition of trust as 'a particular level of subjective probability with which an agent assesses that another agent or group of agents will perform a particular action, both before he can monitor such action (or independently of his capacity ever to be able to monitor it) and in a context in which it affects his own action' (1988b: 217). In this perspective, trust is seen as a form of reliance on other people, which involves beliefs about the likelihood of their behaving in a certain way. A person is trustworthy when we have evaluated that the probability of her or his behaving in a way that is damaging to us is low; then we can consider cooperation. While this definition of trust is relevant for the description of formal relationships in the economy and polity, it does not capture the nature of trust in intimate relationships, where friends or partners trust each other's good will towards them.

By viewing trust as a social lubricant which makes possible production and exchange, the contributors to the volume assigned to trust a status of public good. In this context the role of trust is to narrow down the set of viable outcomes by limiting numbers of strategies at the player's disposal by subordinating self-interest to social norms. As Dasgupta concludes, 'repeated games need some form of friction to generate predictable outcome. Moral codes are a form of friction. There are certain things, while feasible, that are "not done"' (1988: 71). For example, our feeling of a sense of obligation not to betray someone's trust will exclude dishonest actions from our choice of behaviour. Trust facilitates cooperation because it is a kind of pre-commitment, a device 'whereby we can impose some restraint on ourselves and thus restrict the extent to which others have to worry about our trustworthiness' (Gambetta 1988b: 221).

In order to explain the conditions for cooperation, the contributors to the volume turn for inspiration to some of the recent work in the theory of repeated games under uncertainty. Game theorists' account of the role of communication in undetermined conditions points out that strategic rationality alone cannot adequately coordinate interaction. Confronted with the limits of rationality, game theorists restricted themselves to listing other options available to players for fostering cooperation. For example, looking at the performance of agents in the prisoner's dilemma game, Good (1988: 34–7) argues that the players' behaviour becomes more cooperative, and consequently trust develops, when the their long-term interest is emphasized, when there is a need for collaboration or when there are conditions present for successful communication. However, at this level of generality it is rather difficult to solve the problem of cooperation (Williams 1988: 12). All contributors to the volume are aware that the demand for trust can be varied, depending on the specific circumstances and conditions of cooperation. And, moreover, with a high degree of convergence, they all point to the significance of self-interest in stabilizing cooperation. Although analytically four motives for cooperation are distinguished (coercion, interest, values and personal bonds), it is assumed that they operate together and that the promotion of cooperation ought to rely on interests. For example, Williams (1988: 11) notes that unless cooperation also serves an egoistic motivation, the practices of cooperation will be unstable. The importance of interests is not only connected with its ability to generate the pressure to behave honestly, but also with its potential to make cooperative behaviour more predictable. A more general conclusion, which can be derived from chapters on the political and economic spheres, maintains that any attempt to 'produce trust which was not in fact an attempt to produce something else, something self-reinforcing, must fail' (Lorenz 1988: 208).

The contributors to the volume dispute the assumption of economists that the narrow pursuit of interest results in efficient economic exchange by pointing out that human rationality is limited and the environment is uncertain and ambiguous. The importance of trust is a result not only of our inability to monitor of others' behaviour due to a time lag (as in Coleman's approach) but also because of the unobservability of some of these actions (Dasgupta 1988: 53). Trust is also important because of our freedom and that of our partners to disappoint each other's expectations (Gambetta 1988b: 218). Hence, solving the trust problem means overcoming our ignorance and, consequently, stabilizing cooperation. However, trust is not easily achieved. Good (1988: 38–46) stresses that the assumption about unbounded, cost-free rationality is rarely met and that the uncertainty and ambiguity of many social situations result in interpretations of information by individuals in line with their preconceptions. This means that neither habits nor reputation are readily changeable in the face of new information. Hence, says Good, we need to abandon 'the cleaner and simpler assumption of perfect rationality' (1988: 46). What is required is a more complex view of a political and economic agent.

Lessons from the well-known case of the prisoner's dilemma game suggest that beneficial cooperation may not occur even when players possess motives for cooperation. As many writers in the volumes already discussed point out, the issue is one of communication. 'It is necessary not only to trust others before acting cooperatively, but also to believe that one is trusted by others' (Gambetta 1988b: 216). Pagden, Lorenz and Gambetta, among others, illustrate how a lack of information can result in distrust. They show how distrust filters through society, and how the unpredictability of sanctions generates uncertainty in agreements, stagnation in commerce and industry, and a general reluctance towards impersonal and extensive forms of cooperation.

Although it is assumed that trust is rather difficult to produce at will, many of the contributors searched for conditions which facilitate trust. Among many of these conditions, time and experience are mentioned as critical for deciding whether to trust or not to trust. We are learning to trust in successive stages, tentatively and conditionally. In economic relationships, as in a finitely repeated prisoner's dilemma game (where it will pay one player to signal to other players an intention to cooperate in the hope that they will reciprocate in a series of mutually productive games), a favourable reputation is something which economic agents will be concerned to establish. As Dasgupta (1988: 63–70) points out, decisions about whether or not one should trust another person depend on that person's reputation. Since building up such a reputation requires not only an investment of resources but also takes time, people with a good reputation can be trusted because they would not like to lose this valuable asset.

This incremental notion of trust is further enriched by the incorporation of the role of personal relations in establishing trust between parties. Personal contacts, while allowing for easier exchange of information, facilitate an easier, quicker adaptation to contingencies of the environment, and thus contribute positively to cooperation. Although trust as a feeling or passion can be seen as a by-product of personal bonds, it cannot be intentionally induced (Gambetta 1988b: 230–2). However, since trust is, as Hirschman (1984) argues, a commodity which may increase through use, it is always better to start with trust than defection. Despite its optimistic conclusion, *Trust: Making and Breaking Cooperative Relations*, however, does not present any realistic strategy to counter social distrust.

To sum up, Gambetta and his contributors argue that the best way to explain human behaviour is by assuming that the individuals are likely to behave rationally and that the best strategy for cooperation is to put faith in trust. The strong emphasis on the incremental properties of trust provides an interesting foundation for trust analysis. However, the usefulness of this approach seems to be reduced by not enough attention being given to the diversity and contingency of social situations as determining factors of the needed level of monitoring at a given level of the shared norms. The argument of Gambetta and his colleagues that the role of trust is connected with our inability to monitor others' actions (we trust before we know how the other will behave) presumes the superiority of the moral mechanism over the monitoring system. However, many scholars do not believe that moral obligation, trust or commitment by itself can solve the problem of asymmetry of information, and thus the problem of cooperation. These critics maintain that the weight of the explanation should not fall on a single variable.

This criticism can be found in Ostrom's (1990) approach, which overcomes the too simplistic assumption of rational choice theory that trust is a synonym with rational expectations. In her analysis of the conditions under which common-pool resource problems have been solved, Ostrom demonstrates that in this type of situation people are tied together and are dependent on one another. Unlike the prisoner's dilemma game, they are not coerced into acting independently. Their problem is how to develop a strategy of cooperation which obtains joint benefits. The development of self-organizing and self-governing forms of collective actions needs to overcome problems such as 'lack of predictability, information, and trust as well as high levels of complexity and transactional difficulties' (Ostrom 1990: 25–6).

Ostrom views people as fallible and norm-adopting, and pursuing contingent strategies in complex and uncertain environments. Such individuals can be expected to make a commitment to rules, which described their mutual rights and obligations. These rules are developed internally in the process of interactions and trust relationships help to monitor and sanction them (1990: 185–6). She shows how individuals imperfectly but persistently try to follow the norms and engage in mutual monitoring whilst building institutional arrangements in many different empirical situations. While it can generally be said that shared norms can reduce the cost of monitoring and sanctioning (1990: 36), Ostrom notes that in some settings, long-term commitment can be undertaken with 'only modest investment in monitoring and sanctioning', while in others just the opposite is needed. In reality, people, knowing the uncertainty and ambiguity of social scenarios, tend to utilize contingent strategies in relating to one another. This contingent rule-following commitment requires that individuals obtain information about rates of rule conformance adopted by others, hence adopting contingent strategies, which facilitate monitoring. At the same time, monitoring enhances the probability of adopting actions contingent on conditions in a given case or situation. 'Adding the capacity to use graduated sanctions initially for their information value and eventually for their deterrence value, one can begin to understand how a complex configuration of rules used by strategic individuals helps to solve both the problems of commitment and the problems of mutual monitoring' (1990: 187). Ostrom's perspective states that a sociological explanation of cooperation cannot be formulated wholly in 'economic' terms since, in order to understand collective action, we also need to account for other factors which encourage collective action. In the same vein, Barnes argues that 'the key to understanding collective action lies in the existence of mutual *symbolic* sanctioning considered as an aspect of communicative interaction, that is normal and natural to us as social beings' (1992: 263).

Since the rational choice perspective does not explain differences in the extent of group obligations and does not have a lot to say about when members will honour these obligations, recent efforts to modify the theory have focused on variables internal to the situation (size, leadership and so on). For example, Hechter (1987: 10–15), who like Ostrom notes the importance of the need to include information and transaction costs to the general model of collective action, stresses the importance of the size of the group for the understanding of the problem of solidarity. While trust can be a spin-off of participation in small and informal groups, which do not need formal control to secure communication, exchange or common understanding (such as family or friends), trust needs to be secured in larger groups because common knowledge, required to sustain cooperation, is unlikely to be available in such groups. According to Hechter, what is necessary for cooperation in large groups is formal control. Hence, the solidarity of a group is assumed to increase with the extent of normative obligations to the group, on the one hand, and the effectiveness of social control on the other. Both variables, in turn, are assumed to increase with the increasing dependence of group members on jointly produced goods and increasing mutual visibility and, hence, controllability of the members (Hechter 1987: 181–3).

Although Hechter is right in taking account of the importance of the size of the group for understanding the problem of solidarity, he fails to notice the incremental, self-transforming nature of organizational change. Trust relationships established in a small-scale organization can be used as an initial social capital allowing the organization to expand and consequently solve new problems, which means that the size of the group does not necessarily limit solidarity. According to Hechter, the coordination or cooperation problem is not the same one as that of trust, because formal control based on sanctioning and monitoring excludes or tends to lessen the significance of trust in facilitating cooperation in larger groups. In a situation where there is a lack of communication between the members of a group, distrust could emerge even if all members of a large group were moral, trustworthy and altruistic. This argument that distrust is not the only factor behind a lack of cooperation is the main difference between Hechter's approach and Gambetta's perspective (1988c: 162–8), which equates distrust with a lack of co-operation. Hechter's conceptualization of solidarity means that trust among members of larger groups may be possible only in those groups which are able to offer access to joint goods (dependence) and which have a relatively high control capacity. Yet, at the same time, mutual trust or group solidarity is viewed as 'the degree . . . [to which] its members comply with corporate rules in the absence of compensation' (Hechter 1987: 39). This circular definition of solidarity 'leads to a peculiar tension, if not contradiction, in the very concept of solidarity, since both joining and membership, according to Hechter, depend on dependence' (Lechner 1990: 103). Consequently, the inability of his theory to solve the 'normative' side of solidarity and its exclusion of other than opportunistic behaviour diminishes the appeal of this theory's explanation of the process of accretion of trust.

The most general and the oldest criticism of rational choice theory points to its lack of assumptions about the genesis, nature and strength of the individual preferences. Hechter argues that in much of rational choice theory 'preferences are denied an independent role in the determination of behaviour' (1987: 184). Wildavsky (1994) criticizes rational choice theory for being rooted in a single form of cultural rationality – competitive individualism – and postulates that rational choice theory be improved by incorporating a culturally pluralistic theory of preference formation. Others point out that rational choice theory employs too narrow an understanding of trust since trust is not a mean that can be chosen for a particular end (Luhmann 1979: 89) and that it fails to provide an account of shared meaning as the condition of trust relations (Rawls 1992).

In the 1990s attempts to introduce moral criteria directly to theoretical models in social science and economics has resulted in a revision of the rational choice approach. The essence of the new developments in rational choice theory is to re-train the concept of human rationality while simultaneously introducing norms and beliefs. This revision rejects self-interest as the sole factor in human behaviour, while, at the same time, postulating that individuals maximize cooperation subject to some constraint – that is, trust. The example of the new, far-reaching criticism of rational choice approach is the volume titled *Beyond Self-interest*, edited by Mansbridge (1990), which proposes solutions to the prisoner's dilemma game not based on self-interest but on empathy and love. She and her contributors criticize rational choice theory for its emphasis on the individual as always choosing that course of action which satisfies their preferred goals with the greatest efficiency. According to *Beyond Self-interest*, human beings are not merely rational individuals behaving in a coherent, purposeful, maximizing and occasionally far-sighted fashion. However, when self-interest is replaced with unegoistic and pro-social behaviour, the problem of trust is absent because the difference between honesty and altruism is overlooked and because selfishness is perceived as the sole source of conflict. Despite the possibly similar outcome of altruism and honesty (or trust), they are distinctively different. While altruism 'may yield socially desirable outcomes even in the absence of honesty', the honesty of selfish agents may also result in a positive outcome – that is, in a healthy market competition (Elster 1990: 50). Secondly, as Lukes (1991b: 270) notes, in some circumstances self-interest or egoism can result in social harmony even in conditions of scarcity. Following Rawls' statement that 'the plurality of distinct persons with distinct systems of ends is an essential feature of human societies' (Rawls 1972: 28–9), Lukes sees the roots of conflict in social diversity rather than in self-interest. Hence, it can be said that the source of distrust is not, or not only, a conflict of self-interests but it may also be the results of the diversity of human ends. In this framework, the roots of distrust between groups are deeper than their interests, since those interests are defined by the groups' different conceptions of what is good.

To sum up, rational choice theory holds some promise as being effective in analysing situations involving some specific type of action – that is, instrumentally rational action. However, it is less successful in dealing with a variety of actions motivated by passions, emotions or pro-social orientations. It also does not explain traditional actions arising out of the habits and routine of everyday life. None the less, even accepting that the 'advancement of self interest is not the dominant natural human goal in all situations' (Turner 1991: 91), the concept still permits the notion of rationality or the image of rational human beings to have some plausibility in predicting some types of behaviour. This more sectoral view of rational choice theory does not alleviate many of the criticisms of it, but, by assigning 'a dominant role to norms in some areas of behavior and interests in others' or by opting for a more historical approach, which 'predicts shifts in the motivational mix' (Offe 1991a: 83), it espouses positive aspects of the rational choice perspective.

## Trust and modernity: Giddens' approach

Giddens' diagnosis of modernity and his analysis of the notion of society starts with the reformulation of the question of order. Instead of the traditional problem of order which, as stated by Parsons, searched for sources of social integration, Giddens poses the question of order as a 'problem of how it comes about that social systems "bind" time and space' (1990: 14). The issue of order, formulated as the problem of time–space distanciation, is one of three forces behind the essential characteristics of modernity. These forces are: the separation of time and space, the development of disembedding mechanisms, which 'lift out of social relations from local contexts of interaction and their restructuring across undefined spans of time–space; and the reflexive appropriation of knowledge (1990: 21). Modernity, which presents a threat to our confidence in the continuity of our personal identity and in the social and material environment, cannot be completely controlled. Yet trust relations, as a basis of time–space distanciation, may provide a solution to the modern condition of risk and danger.

Giddens' description of the transition from traditional to modern societies shows how the three above-mentioned dynamic forces of modernity disengaged some basic forms of trust relations from the attributes of local contexts. Modern institutions are grounded in 'reflexivity' and modern individuals, without the guidance of traditional authority, must self-reflexively construct their identities. Consequently, the conditions of trust in pre-modern and modern societies are totally different, with the former based on personal trust secured by kinship, community, religion and tradition, and the latter resting on trust in abstract systems. However, although Giddens contrasts the sources of trust in modern and pre-modern times, he does not assume a deficiency of trust in modern society. Rather, he stresses the search for the balance between trust and risk in the modern world as the equivalent of the pre-modern balance between security and danger. Modernity involves not only the destruction of traditional orders but it also reconstitutes them at a new global level. Modernity is a 'risk culture', since its globalizing tendencies, together with the circularity of knowledge in conditions of modernity, has extended and intensified risk environments, seen not as a result of natural hazard but as socially constructed (for example, the risk of nuclear war). Consequently, it requires and provides us with different means of achieving trust.

This quest for trust is now a reflexive project based on the knowledge that the world is not simply given but is a product of a human transforming activity (Giddens 1991: 3–34). Since trust is bound up with modes of organizing interactions across time–space, it is vested in abstract capacities characteristic of the institutions of modernity, itself brought about by disembedding mechanisms depending on trust. According to Giddens, there are two types of such mechanisms which provide 'guarantees' of expectations across distanciated time–space and which require a more abstract form of trust than in pre-modern conditions. These are symbolic tokens (media of interchange, such as media of political legitimacy and money) and expert systems – that is, systems of technical and professional knowledge, where trust is placed in a body of reflexive knowledge. Giddens also suggests that in a period of high modernity there is renewed re-embedding and growing importance of personalized trust, based on deliberately cultivated, face-to-face relationships. His approach no longer dismisses interpersonal trust as a declining or vanished traditional form, but rather investigates its changing features and its continuing or renewed role in modern society, as a supplement to trust in abstract systems. Because trust in abstract systems is not so psychologically rewarding, confidence in such conditions ought to be 'actively regrounding' in personal ties with others. The fragility of the modern trust relationship, left without the external support of kinship ties, local community, tradition or the authority of religion, and the less satisfying nature of abstract trust have increased the importance of trust in our societies and have changed its relation to day-to-day routine. Now, more than ever, trust needs to be actively built by 'opening ourselves out' to others, and it also has to be negotiated and bargained for (Giddens 1992).

The globalizing tendencies of modernity lead to the transformation of intimacy (Giddens 1990: 112–14) and to the extension and intensification of risk environments. These two issues are the most interesting of Giddens' contributions to trust debate. The first is connected with the building up of trust mechanisms in an intimate situation in which the construction of the self becomes a reflexive project. The second relates to the consequences of global risk as 'key elements of the runaway, juggernaut character of modernity' (1990: 131). Before beginning a more detailed discussion of these two environments – trust and risk – it is worth analysing Giddens' concept of trust.

Although trust has already become the core concept in all three of Giddens' latest books, it is a relatively new notion in his writing. Yet it is firmly grounded within his previously developed concept of ontological security and it relates to the main characteristic of modernity as developed in many of his earlier works. Giddens' classification of trust into two categories – trust in persons (or facework commitments) and trust in abstract systems (faceless commitments) – can be seen as an attempt to overcome distinctions between macro- and micro-sociological theorizing. Consequently, he defines trust as 'confidence in the reality of a person or system, regarding a given set of outcomes or events, when that confidence expresses a faith in the probity or love of another, or in the correctness of abstract principles' (Giddens 1990: 34). Apart from these two categories of trust – personal and in abstract systems – Giddens also speaks of 'basic' trust or 'elementary' trust. This differentiation is possible because Giddens assumes that trust is 'a continuous state' (1990: 32), or a particular type of confidence which is presumed as a foundation in our social relations. Although Giddens uses the concepts of basic and elementary trust interchangeably, the context of his discussion seems to suggest that basic trust is connected with the genesis of our ontological security – that is, our confidence in the continuity of personal identity – while elementary trust is connected with the predictability of daily encounters.

Elementary trust, which any initiation of an encounter presumes, tends to be sanctioned by a perception of 'established trustworthiness' and/or by the maintenance of informal rituals – again, often of a complex kind (Giddens 1990: 82). An absence of the elementary trust in the possible intentions of others assumes a total hostility and unpredictability of the social environment. Giddens' explanation of the routine of everyday life as one of the means of maintaining trust and predictability in social order is enriched by Goffman's analyses of the background assumptions that greatly sustain and reproduce trust among strangers on an occasion of face-to-face interaction. Giddens' concept of elementary trust resembles Goffman's concept of 'civil inattention', which is a general method of sustaining trust as the essential background for social conventions. This conceptualization of the notion of trust is also very much in the mood of Garfinkel's definition of trust, which underlines its unreflective qualities. Giddens, like Garfinkel, sees the process of the formation of elementary trust as leading to the development of 'practical consciousness, which is a continuing protective device against the anxieties which even the most casual encounter with others can provoke' (Giddens 1990: 99).

In his discussion of basic trust, Giddens follows the work of Erik Erikson, which illustrates how the development of trust in infancy determines the core of our ego identity. Basic trust, as the basis of 'a stable self-identity' presupposes the development of trust in oneself together with the building of trust in others (Giddens 1990: 94–9). Ontological security, as the most important psychological need, is founded upon the formation of trust relationships, and centres initially on parents, members of the family and friends. Without the development of this basic trust, people may experience persistent existential anxiety, and a lack of confidence in the continuity of their self-identity and the constancy of their environment. A stable informal environment protects us from deep-seated anxiety by developing our trust in others and in taken-for-granted ways of living or elementary trust. Here connections between basic and elementary trust become visible. Elementary trust contributes indirectly to our sense of psychological security – that is, our basic trust – because it makes our world look predictable by preserving the routine of daily life. In this way attachment to routine plays a role not only as the mean of the sustaining of elementary trust but also as the condition of basic trust. In this context, basic trust, seen as synonymous with ontological security, and elementary trust, seen as synonymous with practical consciousness, are connected by the third common factor, routine or tact, seen as a cluster of rules which regulate activities in ways that make them predictable and orderly.

In an extreme situation when the individual lacks both ontological security and practical consciousness, she or he would be unable to maintain tact and routine. Generally, however, encounters with strangers or acquaintances are based on the balancing of 'trust, tact and power' (Giddens 1990: 82). Moreover, since in a normal situation attitudes of trust towards those unknown or towards abstract systems are routinely incorporated into the continuity of day-to-day activities, elementary and basic trust can both be seen as 'a tacit acceptance of circumstances in which other alternatives are largely foreclosed' (1990: 90). This trust, which in Giddens' perspective is always 'in a certain sense blind trust' (1990: 33), and the integration of routines into abstract systems are central foundations of ontological security in the conditions of modernity.

Routines, however, which are structured by abstract systems, are not psychologically rewarding. Because they reduce the size of personal life and increase impersonalized organized structures, they have more to do with effectiveness than with emotional satisfaction (Giddens 1990: 120). Moreover, the new nature of personal relations, which makes them subject to greater negations than before, facilitates the centrality of trust (Giddens 1992: 138). Given the importance of personal trust, mistrust, as its opposite, would be too weak a concept. In our modern societies, 'the antithesis of trust is thus a state of mind which could best be summed up as existential *angst and dread*' (Giddens 1990: 100). In order to avoid anxiety we need to construct the self as a reflective project. We can no longer rely on kinships, religion or tradition, because with modernity the nature of interpersonal intimacy has changed.

> Trust in persons is not focused by personalised connections within the local community and kinship networks. Trust on a personal level becomes a project, to be 'worked at' by the parties involved, and demands *the opening out of the individual to the other*. Where it cannot be controlled by fixed normative codes, trust has to be won, and the means of doing this is demonstrable warmth and openness (Giddens 1990: 121).

Opening to others requires self-identity, discovery of which is a project shaped by the reflexivity and globalizing tendencies of modernity. In the context of interpersonal equality, integrity of persons is a core source of intimacy understood as 'a matter of emotional communication, with other and with self' (Giddens 1992: 130). The same properties of trust and understanding that trust 'begins with keeping oneself open to evidence' were acknowledged in Gambetta (1988b: 235), although acting as if one trusted others is not seen there as caused by the need for self-actualization but by the rational calculation of benefits expected out of the placing of confidence in trust.

Giddens' emphasis on the need for self-management and on the need for working on establishing relations of trust resemble Ervin Goffman's writing on roles and role management, The essence of professionalism is identified by Giddens, with the help of Goffman's concepts, as the division between 'front-stage' and 'back-stage' performance. It sustains a faith in the working of expert knowledge of which the lay person is ignorant. However, even though in the modern global situation trust in abstract systems is a matter of 'the calculation of benefits and risk', we still cannot ignore expert knowledge because 'one cannot completely opt out of the abstract systems involved in modern institutions' (Giddens 1990: 84). Consequently, the mechanisms of trust in abstract systems are essential in shaping modern societies.

Although modern societies are increasingly becoming 'risk societies', our main problem is not the sheer number of serious risks but rather their inevitability, the fact that 'these are not risks anyone chooses to run' (Giddens 1990: 131) and that they are intertwined with our personal life. Following Urlich Beck's (1992) ideas, Giddens argues that we are living under the threat of low-probability, high-consequence risks. Globalizing risk means that risk and danger are a part of our daily lives. At the same time they are out of our control and there is nobody who could be held accountable. Moreover, risk and danger do not respect social boundaries; we are all equal in the face of nuclear disaster. This characteristic of modernity with its array of risks reduces lay trust in expert systems and has a negative impact on individual ontological security (Giddens 1990: 131–47). A retreat to privacy and passivism would seem to be a natural reaction in such a situation. Giddens is more optimistic, however. He thinks that collective political actions and social movements are not only possible but also necessary, globally and locally. How and where, then, can modern people find the sense of security to allow them to search and construct strategies for the preservation of the world as a liveable habitat?

According to Giddens, modern conditions of life offer us a new chance for the increase of social activism. For Giddens modernity does not mean only subjective difficulties with identity or a fragmented, unstable and ambiguous social reality. In the mood of his dialectically constructed experiences of modernity, Giddens argues that the paradoxical features of modernity not only deskilled and made people powerless but they also empowered and skilled them. The conditions of modernity and the democratic structures of modern nation-states furnish opportunities for activism. Of course, adaptive reactions to the risk profile of modernity can vary from pragmatic acceptance to cynical pessimism, yet the important role played by social movements demonstrates that activism and radical engagement, not only privatism, are part of our modern experience (Giddens 1990: 134–48). Social movements are seen as the prime vehicle of the radical response to the risky profile of modernity, and women 'became charged with managing the transformation of intimacy which modernity set in train' (Giddens 1992: 178).

The widening scope and increased importance of intimacy could, as argued by some (such as Marcuse 1964; Lasch 1985), make public life less intelligible. This delimination of individual autonomy into realms of subjective experience does not seem to worry Giddens. He assumes that the concern with intimacy is connected to the very reflexive nature of modernity and represents new forms of social activity. Nevertheless, he does not provide a full answer to the question of how people who are shaped by the experience of comfort and personal trust can 'be strong enough to move in a world founded on injustice' (Sennett 1974: 260). Maybe people – in order to be able to undertake actions orientated towards change – should be faced with fear and anxiety, and learn how to live with it? If it is true that the structure of an intimate society develops a personality which is open, warm and trustworthy, yet full of 'fear of public life' and unable to distance itself from intimate desires (Sennett 1974), should we not be more cautious in assuming that intimate experience would permit people to create a new kind of sociability and activism?

Giddens' approach establishes mutual links between societal changes and individual attitudes, thereby successfully combining micro- and macro-levels of analysis. The uniqueness of his theory of trust is a result of the dialectical concept of the conditions of modernity seen as determining the trust environment. Giddens revitalized the notion of trust by convincingly establishing a connection between the increased importance of trust and change in social, political and economic realities. He shows how active processes of reflective self-identity are made possible by modernity and how it, in turn, increases the role of trust in the public and private spheres of life. Giddens' contribution to the theory of trust redirects interest in the notion of trust from more deterministic and single-order explanations to an approach which combines the psychology of trust with a multi-dimensional sociological understanding of the conditions of trust.

## How to study trust

Trust should not be the sole concept used to characterize modern society. However, as we have seen, many scholars argue that its role in modern society is significant and apparently increasing. The increased popularity of this notion is the result of the main structural changes, such as the increasing diversification and particularization of familiarities and unfamiliarities (Luhmann 1988; Elster 1989), or the separation of time and space, the development of disembedding mechanisms, the reflexive appropriation of the results of knowledge (Giddens 1990) and the increasing replacement of danger by risk (Beck 1992; Giddens 1990; Luhmann 1988).

Trust can perform a multitude of functions. It can be a silent background, sustaining unproblematic and smooth-running cooperative relations. It can be a solution to the free-rider problem. It can help people to reconcile their own interests with those of others. It can provide political leaders with the necessary time to carry out reforms. It can offer friends or lovers a platform from which to negotiate their relations. But above all, trust, by keeping our mind open to all evidence, secures communication and dialogue. An analysis of trust may be concerned with either personal trust or trust in abstract systems. We may examine the role of trust in fostering collaborative relationships or analyse the psychological impact of trust on the individual. This diversity of assumed functions and various classifications, together with an ambiguous and diversified context of trust relations as well as an overload emotional and overstated explanatory value of the concept, makes trust one of the most difficult concepts to handle in empirical research.

The review of the main theoretical perspectives on trust has offered us an opportunity to compare and supplement the arguments. My proposed synthetic approach will combine theories of social order with some theoretical assumptions about the various functions of trust. It can be argued that the relations between order and trust can only be understood by investigations of individuals' conformist, binding and collaborative behaviours.

As the starting position I accept one of Luhmann's most important assumption about trust; namely, that trust should be understood only from the point of view of its function and that this function cannot be reduced or replaced totally by the phenomena. In contrast to Luhmann's statement that trust always performs one function (it reduces social complexity), I would propose that trust may perform at least two more functions. This assumption is connected with viewing social order not only as a stable system but also as a cohesive and collaborative one. The identification of social order as stable, cohesive or collaborative necessitates a different function of trust within each type of system. Thus, we examine trust relations in modern societies by asking what kind of functions trust plays in each of these orders.

I would also argue, following Giddens, that there is a connection between our inner traits and our ability to trust (basic trust) and more general trust attitudes. As Giddens says: 'Trust, ontological security and feeling of the continuity of things and persons remain closely bound up with one another in the adult personality' (1990: 97). While certain commitments are constitutive of our personality, integrity can be seen as an essential factor enabling us to carry out these commitments and obligations.

However, individuals can only acquire and maintain goals through continuous familiarity with social forms because the meaning of our duties and activities come from society. Our conceptions of self and our duties towards others depend upon social and political institutions which both produce and constrain the realization of social values. Thus, trust requires the existence of not only ontological security but also a variety of social forms; namely, the provision of conditions in which bonds of solidarity can flourish. 'It is now reasonable to believe that establishing a social frame that facilitates human flourishing does depend on establishing and sustaining structure of government and responsibility which merit and earn trust' (Dunn 1990: 32).

My third assumption is connected with a specific characteristic of trust, which is often described as its ability to play the role of a social lubricant, collective good or social capital (Coleman 1990; Gambetta 1988a; Putnam 1993; Luhmann 1979). Trust, as social capital which facilitates cooperation, is an attribute of the social structure and can benefit the wider community. At the same time, social capital is not produced automatically; it must 'often be produced as a by-product of other social activities' (Putnam 1993: 170). This property of trust, indicating that it is in some way external to the individual and able to promote other social goods such as the good of an open society, allows us to assume that it is possible and worthwhile to think about designing rational strategies for the 'supply' of trust to the system. To answer our initial question about what kind of functions trust plays in three types of collective orders, we should examine the role of trust relations in stable, cohesive and collaborative orders by asking respectively: how is the stability of social order protected? Whom do we trust? What are the conditions for collaboration?

Starting with the stability of collective order, we can say that here trust is a device for coping with the contingency and arbitrariness of social

reality. Our perception of social order as stable is not a natural phenomenon but is a result of a generally held set of rules to which each of us
contributes daily. Our perception of collective order as stable is sustained
by rule-following behaviour, which makes our world predictable, reliable
and legible. All these rules rest in actors' trust or expectations of 'things
as usual' with the agent being 'able to take for granted, to take under
trust, a vast array of features of the social order' (Garfinkel 1967: 173).
Social regularities are obtained in an unreflective manner because we act
in habitual ways for day-to-day purposes. Hence, trust plays the role of
a protective mechanism, which prevents chaos and disorder by helping us
to cope with the volume and complexity of information. It reduces the
anxiety caused by ambiguity and the uncertainty of many social situations. It also tends to endow social order with meaning and neutralizes
its arbitrariness. The predictability, reliability and legibility of social life,
following Goffman (1970), can be seen as an issue of rule-following, and
trust is therefore a necessary condition for routine social life to be
possible.

To account for the tendency of the social order to be seen as stable we
need to conceptualize trust as a routine background to everyday interaction through which the predictability, legibility and reliability of collective order is sustained, while the perception of its complexity and
uncertainty is restricted. Social life, however, is predictable, reliable and
legible not only because of cognition, but also because of the constraining
functions of external structures. According to Bourdieu, at the heart of
this dialectic between objective structures and subjective perception is
habitus – that is, 'systems of durable, transposable dispositions', that are
produced by objective structures and conditions, but are capable of
producing and reproducing those structures (Bourdieu 1977: 72).
Habitus as the system of dispositions, 'a past which survives in the
present and tends to perpetuate itself into the future by making itself
present in practices structured according to its principles', is 'the principle of the continuity and regularity' (1977: 82). It is the structuring
mechanism or 'socialized subjectivity' which enables agents to cope with
unforeseen and ever-changing situations (1977: 72). The notion of
habitus avoids the deterministic or free-will extremes by stressing an
openness of the system of dispositions, which are constantly subjected to
experiences, and by emphasizing the role of habitus as 'the product of the
embodiment of the immanent regularities and tendencies of the world'
(Bourdieu and Wacquant 1992: 138). Although people internalized 'the
immanent law of the structure in the form of habitus' (1992: 140), they
are still capable of creativity within the limits of the structure. Since
habitus is the system of strategies and practices through which social
order 'accomplishes itself' and makes itself 'self-evident' and 'meaning-

ful' (1992: 127–8), we can draw an analogy between habitus and trust as a strategy for securing the stability of social order. Consequently, trust can be viewed as 'a system of lasting and transposable dispositions which, integrating past experience, functions at every moment as a matrix of perceptions, appreciation and actions, and makes possible the achievement of [an] infinitely diversified task' (Bourdieu 1977: 83), endowing the social order with predictability, reliability and legibility, Trust understood as a specific type of habitus accounts for the fact that social agents perceive the social world as stable. Trust as habitus is a mechanism deployed to sustain the predictability, regularity and legibility of the collective order. To 'make coherence and necessity out of accident and contingency' (1977: 87), trust as habitus operates through rules of interaction, rules of distanciation and rules of remembering. I shall illustrate the operation of these rules by examining habit, reputation and memory as three practices, which are deployed to sustain the stability of collective order.

These practices, by replacing missing information with an internally guaranteed security, simplify the process of formulation of generalized expectations about others' behaviour. The first one consists of practices which sustain a common definition or perception of situations. In such a case trust can be seen as 'background noise', which includes routinized behaviour, background assumptions and rituals. The second type of practice, reputation, is a device for restricting the behaviour not only of the people who have invested in it, but also of others, who have to decide how far they can trust the former. In the third category of habitus practices we include collective memory as a strategy deployed by people to interpret the present according to strategic preconceptions, which allows for the preservation of identity, legibility and continuity of their experience. All three – habit, reputation and memory – are customary practices of calculative and knowlegeable agents, who accept and trust a given system of routines. Reconstitution of routines in the course of calculative action, which are conceptualized in socially defined ways, contributes to people's knowledge of rules, norms and regularities. 'And this knowledge, along with everything else they know, leads them to act so that the normative order continues' (Barnes 1988: 45).

In the case of the second type of order (the cohesive one), which can be understood in terms of the Parsonian societal community, trust is based on familiarity, bonds of friendship and common faith and values. Trust here takes on the connotation of passion, out of which motive and belief arise. Trust is seen here as operating through internalization and moral commitment. This original form of trust, since it brings together feelings, motives and beliefs, is an important part of a person's identity: it is the core of her or his integrity and a source of ontological security. As the basis of a stable self-identity, trust is also the foundation of our relationships with a wider world.

As a device for coping with other people's authenticity, trust can here be defined as an 'affective condition, linked to expectations of others' future action' (Dunn 1993: 641). The essence of trust as a passion (affiliation) is 'the confident expectation of benign intentions in another free agent' (Dunn 1988: 74). This type of trust is based on our reliance on others' good will, or, as Parsons says, on their 'collectivity-orientation'. Trust as a passion is not strategic and rational, and although in the majority of cases it rests on conformity and familiarity, it may be based on massive social distance. I shall examine the role of trust as a passion by asking a question: whom do we trust? Sociological research has shown that we tend to trust members of our families, friends and fellow countrymen rather than non-members of these groups. There is a clear continuum of a feeling of confidence and obligation, which starts with the absolute trust in the dearest person and ends with the less intimate feeling of reliance on others who share some of our characteristics (religion, ethnicity, nationhood and so on). Hence, in order to answer the question of whom we trust, I shall examine the three bases of trust – namely, family, friendship relationships and society.

Moving now to the third type of order – that is, collaborative – we can define trust as a device for coping with the freedom of others. Its function here is to foster cooperation. As Williams (1988) argues, the mechanisms which motivate cooperation consist of four basic elements: coercion, interests, values and personal bonds. However, a system in which people decide to cooperate only for fear of sanctions cannot be described as a cooperative one. Trust can be seen as a mechanism for solving the problem of cooperation only when people cooperate irrespective of sanctions and rewards. Thus, as Turner (1989) argues, the existence of collaborative order is associated with the perception of the mechanisms of social control not as constraints on individual freedom, but rather as aids in collaboration, and this happens only in solidaristic, fair and just systems. Turner characterizes a number of conditions which foster this type of perception of control, and consequently the order based on it, as cooperative. Firstly, it depends on a culturally embedded view of the relationship between self and society (the issue of solidarity). Secondly, it is influenced by the degree of inclusion of individuals and groups to the system (the issue of toleration). Thirdly, the perception of control as non-constraining is shaped by the level of social support for the system and is measured by the degree to which the system is viewed as fair (the issue of legitimacy).

In order to account for the tendency of the social order to be seen primarily as collaborative we need to consider trust as a policy aiming at the creation of conditions which foster bonds of solidarity, mutual respect and discourage uncooperative attitudes. Of course, the promotion of trust as a mechanism for facilitating the perception of control as non-coercive is also dependent on the satisfaction of economic interests. Our concentration on the examination of three issues – namely, those of solidarity, toleration and legitimacy – does not mean that the issue of social justice is seen as unimportant. As Habermas (1990) notes, justice and solidarity do not represent two distinct moral principles; they are two aspects of the same value. Seeing these concepts as complementary allows us to stress the role of trust as policy concerned with the equal freedom and welfare of unique and self-determining individuals. Sustaining a cooperative order requires the existence of a variety of social forms and the provision of many collective goods, such as freedom of association and expression, freedom of the press and religion. Moreover, to base collaboration on trust requires political support for the construction of the conditions of equality, which give people a genuine sense of an equal consideration and stake in society. This strategy, by providing people with a reason why they should obey and cooperate, lessens the likelihood of social controls being perceived as constraints.

The concept of trust as a policy was introduced by Dunn (1988) as a contrast to the view of trust as a passion. Dunn stresses that trust is 'a more or less consciously chosen policy for handling the freedom of others human agents or agencies' (1988: 73). Trust as a policy is 'a method of dealing with the fact that most important human interests depend profoundly on the future free action of other human beings' (Dunn 1993: 641). Consequently, this strategic shaping of collective life depends on the role of human intelligence and practical skill as well as on the use people choose to make of their freedom of action. Thus, political elites can achieve the confidence of society by well-designed, strategic and rational policy, seen as 'the properly sceptical choice of human political expedients' (Dunn 1988: 90). As mentioned above, in order to examine trust as a policy we need to consider the issues of solidarity, toleration and legitimacy and to analyse the methods by which the problems inherent in each are solved. All these problems can also be related to the dilemma of normative order. However, while the conditions of collaborative order are designed to protect equal treatment and respect for all, normative order refers more directly to the concept of self and identity. Thus, when we talk about trust as a policy we stress the issue of solidarity as not requiring empathy and sameness with others but as a solidarity 'with others with whom we share a collective identity without sharing or even necessarily liking their personal needs and values' (Cohen and Arato 1992: 385).

**Table 3.1**  Trust: forms and practices

| Order | Trust | Practice |
|---|---|---|
| Stable | Habitus | Habit |
|  |  | Reputation |
|  |  | Memory |
| Cohesive | Passion | Family |
|  |  | Friends |
|  |  | Society |
| Collaborative | Policy | Solidarity |
|  |  | Toleration |
|  |  | Legitimacy |

The proposed synthetic approach, while trying to combine contingency with sustaining collective order, allows us to specify the conditions of collaborative order, which is seen as the terrain for impersonal trust relationships, to identify the supportive bases of trust, which are found within the normative system, and to describe habitus practices through which we communicate to others our trust in the stability of social order. An adoption of this broader approach allows the choice between methodological individualism or the more collectivistic perspective to be evaded.

Trust understood in the context of three different types of order is a multi-dimensional phenomenon. The three types of order are not alternatives since they all contribute to trust relationships. They all provide us with grounds for stability, cooperation and identity. All forms of trust, whether understood as habitus, passion or policy, can be modified by reflection and interests. However, each is different, and has its characteristic symmetrical equivalent of trust. These are, respectively, confusion or chaos (disruption of trust) when background expectations are not met; distrust when intentionality is attributed to untrustworthy strategies (deficit of trust); and betrayal when emotional outrage is caused by the untrustworthiness of important others. These main elements, constituting the basic criteria for trust relations, are presented as general concepts which can be applied to any historical context of a specific society. They are portrayed as underlying the common logic of trust relationships in any type of society. Our task in the next part of the book will be to apply these common foundational features of trust to an examination of modern societies.

# 4

# Trust as Habitus

## Habits and rules of social interactions: predictability

> to assure regularity, it is only necessary that habits be strongly founded.
>
> Durkheim 1973: 32

Trust as habitus is a protective mechanism relying on everyday routines, stable reputations and tacit memories, which together push out of modern life fear and uncertainty as well as moral problems. For most people the existence of social order, which dwells in day-to-day predictability, is convenient and comforting. Daily routines, in particular, create a feeling of security. Since the world of everyday life is the most important reality with which human beings are in contact, the habits of everyday life can be seen as devices to sustain the predictability and stability of social life. Although unreflective or 'taken-for-granted' attitudes with which we engage in habitual practices conceal these functions from us, a closer look at habits shows their role in the presentation of social order as predictable, since habit 'makes us expect, for the future, a similar train of events which have appeared in the past' (Hume 1985: 43). The aim of this chapter is to analyse the significance of habit in sustaining the perception of social order as a predictable one, and, by the same token, in maintaining our trust in our social environment. Seeing the usefulness of this concept does not mean, however, that it is assumed that modern individuals' behaviour is equally restricted by habit or ruled by custom as in the past or that contemporary habits are not subject to questioning and reflexive adjustment. In order to understand the nature and role of habit in modern, rational and reflective societies and its relation with trust it will be helpful to clarify the meaning of the concept itself.

Although habit forms a key part of any established relationship and is often at the core of activities marking social division, it is not often studied by contemporary sociologists because of its presumed 'automatic' and 'unreflective' nature. Yet habit and its social forms – that is, custom and tradition – were seen by earlier researchers as 'the real forces which govern us' (Durkheim 1956: 152), which are 'often a matter of almost automatic reaction to habitual stimuli which guide behaviour in a course which has been repeatedly followed' (Weber 1964: 116). Habit was 'intentionally expunged from the vocabulary of sociology' not only, however, because the discipline subject (namely, modern people) had become less habit-bound, but also because this step was seen as necessary for the establishment of the autonomy of the discipline (Camic 1986: 1077). Furthermore, this exclusion of the notion of routinized behaviour was part of the broader disrespect with which the 1960s' generation treated the artifice of convention, ceremony or etiquette. Some sociologists have recently tried to bring habit back by pointing out that habit captures 'the tendency we all have, in greater or lesser measure, to do again what we done before' (Young 1988: 75).

The word 'habit' colloquially refers to routine actions of a personal nature (such as hygienic practices, eating habits and so on) as well as to regular practices connected with daily rhythms (like the habit of reading a newspaper after dinner). Consequently, habits are our 'second nature' because, as Hobbes said, 'manners maketh man' (quoted in Turner 1994: 6). The common-sense classification of habits into good habits (which we are proud of) and bad habits (which we try to quit, such as the habit of smoking) refers mainly to these types of behaviour. Even so, in a more general way, being 'a creature of habit' does not imply a positive connotation, regardless of the type of activity involved. It is a consequence of the dominant perception of habit as a relatively elementary routine which automatically prompts the old ways of thinking, feeling and acting.

This ambiguity of habit, captured in common language, is also present in social science literature. For example, while some writers see habit as 'virtually automatic behaviour', playing the role of a 'conservative agent' (James 1950: 121) and 'a trained inability' (Veblen, quoted in Turner 1994: 107), others, in contrast, tend to stress habit's virtues (Young 1988: 78). From one point of view, habits can be seen as 'human comfort' (as illustrated by Marcel Proust's writing), while from another, habits are, to use Sartre's words, 'bad faith'. Both these positions describe people as binding themselves in daily life to a set of voluntarily accepted rules – that is, their habits. However, the first position sees habits as enabling people to achieve some security and warmth in daily life, while the second one points out the damage to the individual's authenticity, creativity and openness caused by the numbing daily grind of habits.

Yet this is not the only ambiguity connected with the concept of habit. Since habits are more than repetitive behaviour, which could also be a result of instincts, reason or impulse, to have habits 'is to have a particular kind of mental cause operating' (Turner 1994: 16). Consequently, it can be said that there is an invisible 'mental' element by 'virtue of which the visible pattern of behaviour persists' (1994: 16). Furthermore, habit is a hybrid term not only because it is 'at once mentalistic and observational' (1994: 16) but also because it is individual and social at the same time. This two-level structure of the concept of habit, that is its individual substance and some sort of social and historical substance, contributes to the ambiguity of the concept and raises many unanswered questions. 'If one starts with habits and they are understood solely as individual psychological facts, it is difficult to see how these become something else, such as a moral obligation shared by others' (1994: 27). Habits seem, moreover, to be both causal (individual, thus not transmitted) and persistent (thus collective objects). On the one hand, it can be said that habits die with individuals; on the other hand, the continuation of traditions persist. 'So traditions cannot consist of habits alone. This is a simple formulation of a problem with no simple solution' (1994: 78).

All of these ambiguities of the concept of habit explain its unpopularity in sociology, which has become more conscious that attempts to bring together some sort of hidden collective objects (habit as tradition or mores) with its individual bases are rather fruitless. These problems are especially urgent in the discussion of the issue of the transmission of habits, which requires an account of their origin and persistence. Since my task here is solely a descriptive one, I shall assume, consistently with the previous acceptance of Bourdieu's notion of habitus, that habits, as characteristics of individuals, lead to the persistence of similar forms of behaviour and that 'by performing in certain ways, people acquire habits which lead them to continue to perform, more or less in the same way' (Turner 1994: 100). Not wanting to restrict the usages of the word 'habit' to too narrow a meaning, I follow Dewey's definition of habit as a 'kind of activity which is influenced by prior activity and in that sense acquired; which contains within itself a certain ordering or systematisation of minor elements or action; which is projective, dynamic in quality, ready for over manifestation; and which is operative in some subdued subordinate form even when not obviously dominating activity' (quoted in Young 1988: 76–7). This definition allows us to view habit as a continuum of practices and dispositions to perform 'a previously adopted or acquired form of action' (Camic 1986: 1046). It is close to Bourdieu's theory of practical sense since this approach, like Bourdieu's concept, rejects dualism of objectivity and subjectivity or individual and social and also stresses the central and active role of the habit. 'Through habits formed in intercourse with the world, we also in-habit the world. It becomes a home, and the home is part of our every experience' (Dewey 1958: 104). Our attention will focus not on the lower spectrum of the habit continuum (habits as elementary, specific activities) but, rather, on the middle range of the scale. Thus, our interest is in habits as patterns of disposition and activity in the social world. Since the ability of a person to interact more or less successfully with other members of the community is a matter of habit, a matter of having properly responded to feedback and having developed habits of response that enable them to sustain interactions, I shall concentrate on the habits of ordinary social interactions.

I propose to divide this broad form of interpersonal habit into three types of habits: social habits of conduct or routinized practices; mental habits or background/taken-for-granted assumptions; and ceremonial habits or rituals. The first type of routinized interpersonal interaction – that is, the habit of conduct – refers to our repetitive behaviour towards others or in connection with others and thus plays an important social function. The most interesting feature of the second type – that is, mental habits or taken-for-granted (background) assumptions – is that breaching them, although they are not social norms, can result in social sanctions. The third type – namely, ceremonial habits or rituals, which can be viewed as rules of etiquette and rites of passage in the life cycle – are important since they enhance feelings of group solidarity and identity. All three types of habit have at least two features in common. All of them replicate the past in the present and, in doing so, all of them increase the predictability of social order. In what follows I shall discuss the contribution that each of these three types of habit makes to our sustained perception of the social environment as predictable.

Starting with habit as routinized practice, it can be said that among many functions attributed to it, such as its ability to make life simpler as well as its potential for economizing on the effort needed in any activity (Young 1988), the most important is probably its capacity for 'ordering' or for 'patterning' our daily life. Understood in this way, because habit is a means of reducing social complexity, it therefore can be seen as playing the same role as trust. Both trust and habit achieve this by reducing the length and the significance of the process of deliberation. Habit of conduct secures it by cutting short the selection process and, by the same token, helping us not to become victims of 'an overload of information'. 'Habit, by allowing predictable events or features of event to be managed with hardly any effort, enables people to concentrate most of their attention on the unpredictable' (Young 1988: 83).

By switching us on 'automatic pilot', the habit of conduct allows us to perform daily activities without spending unnecessary time considering them. This is possible because a habit 'is a memory unconsciously edited for action' (Young 1988: 85). Trust also shortens the length of deliberation. However, it allows us to make a decision without the possession of all the necessary knowledge, not by providing us, like habit, with well-known patterns of practices, but by facilitating the taking of a risk. Simplifying social complexity by taking a risk (the function of trust) and simplifying social complexity by dependence on familiar practices (habit) can be seen as part of the same process. 'One trusts if one assumes that this behaviour will fit in meaningfully with one's own pattern of life; one distrusts if one reckons that this will not be the case' (Luhmann 1979: 72). Seeing trust as an expectation that familiar things will remain stable (which is Luhmann's concept of confidence) brings to our attention the importance of the routine of daily life in ensuring that our expectations will not be disappointed. On the other hand, we continue our routinized practices because we are confident that 'life goes on as usual'. Thus, our daily habitual practices can be seen as supported by the shared trust in the stability of our daily lives, without which we would be living in 'a state of permanent uncertainty' (Luhmann 1988: 97). The interdependence of trust and familiarity founded on habitual practices can be best illustrated by any example of our frequent reliance on other people's habits. For instance, knowing the daily routine of my postman, I expect that my mail will be delivered before lunchtime. My confidence, in this instance, can be explained by my general trust in the institution (the Australian post) and in my postman's habits. Furthermore, on the basis of this event, I develop my daily routine of reading my newspaper and letters while having lunch. Similarly, many of our habits are developed on the basis of our confidence in the habitual behaviour of people with whom we work, sometimes to the point of the total predictability of (and boredom in) some meetings. And in turn our habits form a key part of others' trust in the predictability of social relationships and public order.

Another similarity in the way in which trust and the habit of conduct function is connected with their potential for drawing boundaries between familiar and unfamiliar, known and unknown, or them and us. Habits and routines influence the way in which we divide and classify our surroundings because they influence what we notice and what we ignore (for example, habits determine what we eat and what we avoid, what programmes we watch on TV and which newspaper we buy, and so on). The way in which people become habits for one another defines boundaries of individuals' social world since by the established routine of social contact (such as whose birthday we celebrate and whose not) people sustain and confirm their relationships with families, friends and members of the professions – that is, the main groups among whom the individual moves every day and with whom she or he establishes various types of relationships and shares various types of activities. While routinized practices are not the sole way of preserving social closure (it can be preserved by various formal restrictions on access, such as the requirement of a title or an immigration quota), the differentiation of the group from its environment is often achieved by the implementation of various exclusionary habitual practices. For instance, white neighbourhoods can set up various means of preserving their distinction by reinforcing their shared habits and rules of avoidance of non-whites.

By not walking their dogs across Bellewether or Warrington, the Villagers [residence of a white area] themselves help create and enforce lines of division between their own neighbourhood and Northton [a black neighbourhood]. Although one usually thinks first of stone throwing or other forms of harassment as determining where boundaries are drawn, it is also through daily activities like dog walking that borders are made and remade by people on both side of the dividing line (Anderson 1990: 225).

Some groups still manage to preserve a distinction between themselves and others by simply maintaining their old habitual practices; for instance, the so-called 'old-boy network' groups are practically inaccessible to women since their home duties too often do not allow them to share the group's habitual (after-work) activities. Because conventional and habitual behaviour, which is socially recognized and easily understood, neutralize or increase acts of distrust, these types of behaviour are a critical part of the self-presentation and the process of drawing boundaries between them and us. The fact that these habitual boundaries are normally taken for granted and that we experience social reality as made up of insular entities without really questioning it (Zerubavel 1991) helps to give meaning to our environment and to preserve the stability of the context of daily life. Consequently, this stability or predictability in daily life, protected by habits of conduct and routines, can be seen as the permanent system of reference for the individual. Seen from this perspective, habits contribute to the establishment and stability of trust relationships by drawing boundaries between familiar and non-familiar and intercepting distrust.

Probably the most important contribution of routine behaviour to the reinforcement of trust in social order is connected with the potential of habitual practices to render distrust as 'aberration' or an insignificant 'accident'. By preserving the routine of daily life people reinforce, in themselves and one another, the feeling of normality, which conceals the unpredictability of the reality, thus increasing the perception of general trustworthiness and ontological security. This feeling of normality is the most common way in which we relate to the world surrounding us, and at the same time the most obvious frame of reference for attitudes of general trust. 'The world of everyday reality presents itself as self-evident facticity. In order to live a "normal" life in society, it must be taken for granted as such' (Berger 1978: 347). Everyday reality preserves its taken-for-granted character and takes on the appearance of 'normality' thanks to a balancing act between the reconciling predictability of social order and a variety of the reality-shattering experiences. This act of compromise is secured – at least to some degree – with the help of routinized practices whose comforting presence suspends the arbitrary character of the reality.

Normality is based either on our perception of regularity, universality and the frequency of events and people's behaviour (its practical dimension) or on our classification of action as rule/norm-following (its normative dimension) (Lukasiewicz 1987). Consequently, the predictability and normality of social order can be seen as synthetic criteria of the normality of social order. However, the implications of their absence differ. Without seeing the system as predictable, we will be in a state of 'permanent uncertainty' (Lukhmann 1979), puzzling all the time what to do. The unpredictable refers to changes in our environment that cannot be reduced to rules and require adaptability (an absence of the practical dimension of normality). In a situation which is felt by individuals as 'not normal' (which is due to changes in circumstances uncontrolled by and independent of people's will as well as to a loss of the controlling power of social norms), people try to preserve the 'practical normality' (that is, the predictability) by repeating daily routines as though nothing had happened. Many stories from concentration camps illustrate people's attempts to preserve predictability by maintaining small habits. 'What is important is feeling a certain continuity of life, even in small matters, defence against accepting an exceptional state which would overturn previous hierarchies of importance of human affairs in the face of a total threat to one's existence' (Werner, quoted in Lukasiewicz 1987: 57).

Since the predictability and habit of conduct are 'our chief tools for survival' (Young 1988: 83), habit (like trust) plays an important part in sustaining our ontological security. While routinized practice achieves this by allowing everyday reality to preserve its taken-for-granted character and to take on the appearance of 'normality', trust, by being a basis of 'stable self-identity' permits us to form meaningful relationships which contribute to the continuity of self-confidence and the constancy of our environment. 'Ontological security and routine are intimately connected, via the pervasive influence of habit' (Giddens 1990: 98).

But what is 'normal' or 'conventional life' in our modern or post-modern world? Can habit or routine continue to play an important role in our less stable, less predictable and more fluid social reality? Contemporary societies are often considered to be going through a crisis of normality in which norms are questioned and behavioural guidelines are eroded. In their search for personal identity and self-confidence, people find themselves in the context of a plurality of values, a variety of forms of family life and a diversity of life styles. These tensions inherent in modern life require that the individual becomes self-reflexive, considerate and responsible. Modern conditions tend also to undermine the traditional or 'customary' nature of habitual behaviour, and as a consequence self-reflection and individualism become part of our feeling of normality. Habits become more than ever a matter of our own choosing.

In the modern world habits of conduct are not only 'always being created anew' (Young 1988: 79) but they are more than ever the results of reflexive choices based on informed decisions. For example, my routine way to get to university is a result of my experience and knowledge about the daily distribution of traffic on the surrounding roads. Thus, during the early morning rush hour I will avoid some roads, while in the quiet time of late morning I will take them. But all the time I will habitually drive on the correct side of the road and do not spare much attention to decide which road to take at a specific time of day. Hence, even if one recognizes the importance of reflexivity in modern conditions, one must also acknowledge the existence of the human tendency to simplification of the available information and to rely on 'simple and usually habit-oriented heuristic procedures for reducing complexity' (Collins 1992: 89).

Furthermore, while in the past routine was connected to tradition and rituals (Giddens 1990: 104), in modern societies routinized social practices are integrated into the system of institutions. In modern societies, trust in abstract systems, rather than in tradition, offers security in day-to-day life, and routine practices preserve the correspondence between the order of institutionalized conventions and the subjective principles of organizations. With the development of abstract systems, trust 'in impersonal principles, as well as in anonymous others, becomes indispensable to social existence' (1990: 120) and as such it is routinely incorporated into the continuity of day-to-day activities. The integration of routine into abstract systems encourages the acceptance of existing conditions since we cannot avoid the 'bargain with modernity' or the participation in socio-economic life because 'such is life'. Consequently, '[b]usiness as usual is a prime element in the stabilising trust and ontological security' (1990: 147).

While Giddens is right that the taken-for-granted way in which every-day actions are structured by abstract systems has 'an empty, unmoralised character' (1990), it is also worth remembering a deeply comforting dimension of routinized practices. On the one hand, it is a result of our trust in abstract systems, even though trust is the only available option. For instance, we feel safe and out of the 'danger zone' of illness because we have undergone regular and routine medical check-ups, even though we have virtually no chance of checking the validity of the evaluation of our results since we are dependent on the information provided by experts. On the other hand, it is a result of the attempts by modern institutions to settle us into the consolation of comfort; for example, as consumers we are encouraged to feel more confident and better about ourselves with every dollar we spend. Regardless how illusionary is the security offered by the institutionalized world, its effect can be felt as real, as many examples illustrate. Some extreme examples point to our dependence on the mass media; for instance, the increase in the rates of illness and death among the elderly population of Australia during the summer months has been claimed to be caused by the absence of soap operas on TV viewing which consti-tuted the daily routine for these people (ABC, 7.30, Report, 26 April 1994).

It seems that if there is a need for trust as well as for distrust (Luhmann 1979: 71–5), there is also a need for habit and spontaneity. Routinized practices and outlooks on life are an important part of the individual's defence against anxiety and are a means of simplification. When this type of behaviour gains the upper hand, however, routine activities can reduce complexity and re-affirm preconceptions about social reality, thus en-abling the individual to act not only creatively but even rationally. This can happen in two ways: through the processes of routinization and ritualization.

The processes of routinization is 'one of the principal continually operating forces in everyday life' (Weber 1964: 372). Generalizing from Weber's remarks about the routinization of charisma, it could be said that this tendency to replace spontaneity and originality with routine is the result of 'striving for security' and can be seen as 'the objective necessity of adaptation' to normal, everyday needs and conditions (1964: 370). It happens when an individual's or organization's routine takes on a life of its own and poses obstacles to innovation or improvement. Although, from a long-term perspective routinization can be seen as playing an important role in creating a predictable environment (because it makes even failures recur in predictable ways), its more immediate impact cuts off any spontaneous type of behaviour and lowers the capacity of individuals to choose actions appropriate for the situation.

The incapacity of individuals to change and respond to change can also contribute to the process of ritualization, which, according to Merton (1957), occurs sooner or later when people abandon or lose sight of their original goals and values and compulsively continue to perform routinalized practices; for instance, the ritualist will continue to perform boring tasks even though this behaviour no longer offers any prospect of success. This way of reducing the discrepancy between socially endorsed values and the limited means of achieving them is illustrated by ritualist behaviour in the context of American culture, which, as Merton describes it, stresses monetary success but fails to provide everybody with an equal means of becoming wealthy.

In short, routinization and ritualization can tame the individual and, by the same token, re-make his or her social world. The extreme example of the outcome of both processes is presented by Patterson in the following way: 'the ordinary workman by the water's edge slips into his groove and will be likely to stay there till the end of his day. . . . At thirty a man has given up playing games, making love to his wife, reading books, or building castles in the air. He is dangerously contented with his daily work' (quoted in Abrams 1982: 264). In this way, habits and routine activities are seen as preserving the predictability of social order, thus being one of the available means of coping with tension within socio-cultural systems, while also being barriers to innovation, change and creativity. Sadly, the force of creativity is mainly released, as many examples – not only from literature – illustrate, by some traumatic event such as illness, invalidism or the loss of a spouse, which, by breaking and closing the path of the normal routine, demand new attitudes and new behaviour.

Paradoxically, we are trapped into the web of habit even when we try to develop means of protection against routinized practices or when we try to liberate ourselves from the power of unreflective forces. Since to master one's fate by correcting routine practices requires an enormous discipline and by viewing life as a business that has to be handled with efficiency, routinization is a natural consequence of it. The Weberian ethics of responsibility, while recommending a self-depreciating dedication to larger causes as the way to overcome the contradictions and banalities of everyday life, creates, at the same time, a person of poise, self-control and moderation, who through self-discipline and routinized practices preserves order (Collins 1993: 861–9).

The importance of self-discipline and self-control in the making of the modern individual is also emphasized by Elias. According to him, the civilizing process, understood as leading to a new self-image and stronger self-control, to new rules of social distanciation and to a new etiquette, involves a redefinition of 'normal' behaviour. The making of the civilized

individual meant a 'particularly strong shift in the individual self-control
– above all, in self-activating automatism' (Elias 1978: 257). New 'normal' behaviour is uniformly restrained and internal compulsions 'prevent
all spontaneous impulses from manifesting themselves directly' (1978:
258). Other writers – for example, Luhmann – also stress self-presentation and perceptive tact as a basis of trust independent of emotion. This
type of trust demands more discretion and reflexivity from partners than
spontaneous trust, however, under a 'particularly secure and continually
sustained circumstance – for example, as the mode of behaviour proper
to a uniformly educated higher class of society, or the upper level of
bureaucracy' (Luhmann 1979: 68). While for Luhmann a characteristic
feature of trust is that in almost all conditions (except in stable and
transparent systems where an extension of more routinized relationships
would be possible) it incorporates an element of reflexivity, for Garfinkel
trust is a taken-for-granted 'confidence of one's expectation'. Garfinkel's
attempt to show what it is that secures the individual's compliance
with the prescriptions and conventions of the common-sense world,
which resulted in the demonstration of the constraining power of taken-
for-granted frameworks of common constructions, moves our discussion
to the second type of habit – that is, *mental habits* or *background
assumptions*, which explain the emergence and the role of routine
structures.

Routine structures are, according to Garfinkel, 'emergence products of
the perceivedly normal values of interpersonal events that members of a
group seek through their adjustive activities to maintain' (1963: 188).
'Normal' social reality is a 'contingent ongoing accomplishment' of
competent social actors who continually construct their social world via
'the organized artful practices of everyday life' (Garfinkel 1967: 11). In
contrast with structuralist objectivism, social order is seen here as the
emergent product of decisions and actions of individuals to whom
the social reality is given as immediately familiar and meaningful.
'Ethnomethodology shows that actors have a preference for normalcy,
and resist having to rearrange their practical actions in a way that
disturbs the working consensus of everyday life. . . . Any social order
becomes accepted as long as it has been in existence long enough to seem
routine or normal' (Collins 1992: 85).

By developing Schultz's 'thesis of reciprocity of perspectives', Garfinkel
shows how rules, as taken-for-granted assumptions that make up attitudes of daily life, produce actions that confirm the individuals' expectations and how individual actors, in order to cover new events, elaborate
and extend the existing rules through various techniques of normalization. In short, '[w]ith respect to the production of normatively appropriate conduct, all that is required is that the actors have, and attribute to
one another, a reflexive awareness of the normative accountability of

their actions' (Heritage 1984: 117). However, this reflexive characteristic of actions is rarely consulted in a normal daily life. Garfinkel strongly emphasizes the role of habit in generating social order. He also stresses the routine nature of the implementation of the common procedures for maintaining normal courses of action. Normally people are interested in following ordinary routine since they routinely find that it is the best way to secure the realization of their tasks. According to ethnomethodology, the human reliance on a taken-for-granted sense of order shows a preference for normalcy. People 'strongly resist efforts to make them see that it is in any sense constructed; the main procedures of common-sense reasoning are to be unquestioning, to trust in normal appearances, and repair breaches as soon as possible' (Collins 1992: 81). Only when the breach of common-sense assumptions occurs – that is, when the 'accommodative work' (attempts to normalize situations in accordance with the procedures) is unable to make sense of the new development (because it actually violated the shared expectations), the reflexive aspect of conduct is activated. 'Garfinkel's actor is virtually the opposite of the wilful rebel and creator; s/he certainly has no taste for living in conscious awareness of reflexivity' (ibid.). Garfinkel's 'breaching experiments' show how upsetting the order by disturbing the routine of ordinary conversation destroys mutual trust – that is, the basis of social order. Thus, the maintenance of a reciprocity of perspectives is the result of trust which each actor has that others will share her or his assumption as a matter of moral necessity. The trusted use of shared expectations in the constitution of the orderliness of social life, along with rituals, rules and conventions, can be seen as the significant interactional resources contributing to the routinization of daily encounters.

Rituals, our third type of habit, are routine social activities, which are important rules and resources for mastering social encounters. According to Goffman, we always tend to 'reinstate the ritual order' by employing our repertoire of 'face-work' or face-saving practices, by this kind of capacity that is 'sometimes called tact, savoir-faire, diplomacy, or social skill' (1972: 13). We also tend to cooperate in face-saving by helping others to perform their face-work.

> Since each participant in an undertaking is concerned, albeit for different reasons, with saving his own face and the face of others, then tacit cooperation will naturally arise so that the participants together can attain their shared but differently motivated objectives. . . . The person not only defends his own face and protects the face of the others, but also acts so as to make it possible and even easy for the others to employ face-work for themselves and him (Goffman 1972: 29).

Goffman views the construction of self as a ritual process of exchange, which constrains the individual from the outside in. In performing these practices we show a 'willingness to abide by the ground rules of social interaction' (1972: 31); hence, interaction rituals pull the individual into locally compelling membership ties. Goffman's interaction ritual model entails individuals orientated to the formal structure of their encounters, including, especially, its rules. Nevertheless, rules can only be partial guides to conduct because of their indexicality and indeterminacy, and this means that they always depend upon a sense of the local context and they leave room for interpretation. Since there are two types of inter-action – unfocused (those 'interpersonal communications that result solely by virtue of persons being in one another's presents') and focused interaction (which 'occurs when people effectively agree to sustain for a time a single focus of cognitive and visual attention') – there are two kinds of 'face-work' or social rituals. Civil inattention – that is, the courtesy performed between two persons passing on the street – is 'the slightest of interpersonal rituals, yet one that constantly regulates the social intercourse of persons in our society' (Goffman 1963a: 84). This routine of non-personal treatment employed by people on the street ensures others that there is nothing to be afraid of and that she or he is going to behave tactfully by keeping an orderly appearance. Society also needs to mobilize their members to maintain their obligations and rules of conduct in more focused interactions, such as, for example, in conver-sation. Normally we take for granted our obligations and expectations underlying these rules of conduct. Our unreflexive attachment to rules leads to 'constancy and patterning of behaviour; while this is not the only source of regularity in human affairs is it certainly an important one' (Goffman 1972: 49).

Goffman divides rules of conduct into two types; first, substantive rules, which guide conduct in significant matters; and second, ceremonial rules, which are conventionalized means of communication. This divi-sion of rules of conduct, together with the assumption that in all societies these rules are organized into codes, leads him to conclude that '[i]n our society the code which governs substantive rules and substantive ex-pressions compromises our law, morality, and ethics, while the code which governs ceremonial rules and ceremonial expressions is incorpo-rated in what we call etiquette' (1972: 55). Social courtesy, rituals of etiquette or, even more generally, civility, can be seen as important tools for achieving orderly social interactions due to their several crucial functions. Firstly, civility allows us to deal with others without special attention, simplifying and smoothing social interaction. Secondly, since people 'can be sociable only when they have some protection from each other; without barriers, boundaries, without the mutual distance which is the essence of impersonality, people are destructive' (Sennett 1974: 311), manners and conventions are significant factors facilitating sociability.

Thirdly, rituals of etiquette are essential for promoting greater social trust and integration since it 'is unusual for a society to distrust ritual or ritualised gesture, unusual for a society to see formal behaviour as inauthentic' (1974: 315). Thus, ceremonial rules of conduct are perceived as rules which not only constrain and guide actions but also as resources used in interaction for ensuring integration and lowering confusion and increasing trust. Yet, these rules of social interaction do not compel us to act, they exhibit rather than produce social order (Manning 1992: 10).

In Goffman's cooperative vision rules of conduct are seen mainly through their neutralizing function. Hence people's behaviour is presented as being motivated by the desire to establish a situation of equilibrium, which would allow for stability and reciprocity of mutual expectations. However, in modern life, wherein intimate relations are given more significance than ever before, civility, manners or etiquette are often seen more as obstructions to intimate expression and authenticity than as tools for sustaining social life. At the same time, with the decline in the importance of various social distinctions, many conventions have been losing their relevance and clarity; for example, many men feel confused as to what now constitutes 'proper manners' towards women: should men open doors for women or not? Furthermore, in today's so-called 'impolite' society, rules and rituals of social behaviour seem to be more orientated towards securing physical safety than social harmony. We are less concerned with conforming to traditional rules of etiquette but more concerned with conveying a 'stay away from me' message. 'Street wisdom', a term coined by Anderson, 'is really street etiquette wisely enacted' (1990: 231).

Writing about race and class in a changing American urban community, Anderson notes that the mutual 'trust and moral cohesion that once prevailed are undermined, and an atmosphere of distrust, alienation, and crime pervades the area, further disrupting its social organisation' (1990: 3). He discovers the problems which accompany racial and class transition by studying relationships between two neighbourhoods: a run-down and deteriorating black ghetto (Northton) and a middle- to upper-income, predominantly white community (the Village). The underlying social perception in both these areas is that local streets and public places are uncertain at best and hostile at worst. In such a situation, where the streets are more and more seen as a jungle and when interpersonal trust is gone, negotiating public space requires a sophisticated etiquette.

To lower the chance of trouble and conflict, residents of the community develop informal rules which allow them to use the public space with some safety. Concern for personal safety activates new street etiquette and 'inspires the social process of mental note taking, which lays a foundation for trust among strangers, dictated by the situation and proceeding by repeated face-to face encounters' (Anderson 1990: 210). Residents can no longer rely on unreflective routine or simplistic etiquette. In order to 'keep up a guard' they need to be continuously engaged in 'field research' (learning the safety signals which various people display – items such as conservative clothing, a tie or a book) and be aware that each situation is unique.

Fortunately, not all streets in the contemporary world resemble a jungle. Nevertheless, the general feeling of safety and simplicity of relationships in the public spaces, particularly in big cities, has been eroded. Regardless of one's city, be it Moscow, Oxford, Chicago, Bangkok or Sydney, the fact remains that in order to have the upper hand, to ensure safe passage and to prove one's knowledge of the rules, one needs to develop increasingly sophisticated skills of reading and interpreting symbols and signs that others exhibit in everyday life. Moreover, apart from the safety issue, our difficulties in public places result from the ambiguity of many signals as well as the frequency with which they change. It raises several questions. How should we behave in a post-modern, uncommunicative, ambiguous, fast and fluid world?

Are manners still a lubricant of the social machine? It seems that we can no longer assume that we all believe in relying on good manners alone to get us through life. An instruction I overheard, which a middle-class Englishwoman was giving to her eight-year-old daughter who was complaining of having been kicked by her girlfriend, helped me to realize this. The mother, who was angry with the daughter for being passive, strongly insisted that the only possible response to such an offence was to take an aggressive stand, and she demanded that her daughter respond physically to any bullying. We can all identify multiple examples highlighting breaches of civility in our daily lives. However, my example points to something more: it illustrates a virtual fetishizing of the necessity of brusque and blunt manners in today's world. Are we witnessing the emergence of a new type of manners, better suited for individualist culture and the world of the competitive global economy?

I think that the situation can best be described as one of confusion rather than novelty. A journalistic description of a grotesque lapse of urban manners which took place on the London Underground illustrates the point.

> A young businessman, dressed in regulation grey and carrying a smart briefcase, was attempting to make his way down the carriage. His path was blocked by another young businessman, clearly not of management material, whose back was turned.
> 'Excuse me', said businessman Number One. 'May I get by?'
> 'Excuse me', replied businessman Number Two, not missing a beat. 'But would you like a punch in the mouth?'

Needless to say, the carriage stiffened with gleeful anticipation of a
general slanging match and possibly a clumsy fight. But none was forthcoming. 'You're very rude,' said businessman Number One, glancing about his
fellow passengers for support (Bracewell 1993: 24).

This example points to the failure of background assumptions in
unfocused interaction (civil inattention), to the dissociation of the
relationship between manners and class and to the fact that the threat
of impoliteness is a part of our urban life. But more importantly it
also points to some confusion, ambiguity and a fear of being misunder-
stood in the world in which we live. On the other hand, the disappearance of good manners has been answered by a counter-movement aiming
at the re-birth of civility. Many national newspapers and new clubs
committed to good manners (for instance, *Polite Society* in the United
Kingdom) become involved in campaigns to improve manners, to
propagate the formality of daily encounters, to increase social awareness
of the need for social courtesy and in covering the return of such
events as débutantes' balls and a 'National Day of Courtesy'. All these
actions aim at solving or disguising the ambiguity of social relationships
through the introduction of new symbolism and new content to rites of
transition.

Rites of transition and other group rituals can be seen as contributing
to members' self-confidence and mutual trust within the group as well
as to mapping out whom to trust to outside the group (Gluckman
1962: 24). Ritual action influences the actor's understanding of the
situation by modelling her or his perception through the capacity of
rituals for objectification, 'that is the endowment with authority of
shared meaning, through presentation in forms external to the subjective experience of the individual' (Lane 1981: 17). One normally
thinks about rites of transition as an expression of shared values, beliefs
or religious identity; however, as Harrison shows, rituals are also a
display of the power relations within the group itself; they are part
of people's identities in their relations to others. 'From this perspective,
a ritual is an objectified schema of action, with a complex of privileges
and obligations defining the categories of persons that may perform
the acts or roles that constitute it' (Harrison 1992: 241). Hence
rituals can be seen as one of the schemas of enforcing social order
or making social order appear normal and stable. Their social relevance
'lies in their use to justify or oppose the arrangement of power and
the positions within this arrangement of the powerful' (Mills 1970:
77).

In very a similar way Bourdieu says that symbolic systems are not
simply instruments of knowledge; they are also instruments of domination, since they promote the social integration of an arbitrary order: 'The
conservation of social order is decisively reinforced by . . . the orchestra-

tion of categories of perception of the social world which, being adjusted
to the divisions of the established order (and therefore, to the interests
of those who dominate it) and common to all minds structured in
accordance with those structures, impose themselves with all appearances of objective necessity' (Bourdieu and Wacquant 1992: 13). The
socially constituted classificatory schemes through which we actively
construct society tend to represent the structures out of which they are
issued as natural and necessary, rather than as historically contingent
fall-outs of a given balance of power between classes, ethnic groups or
genders.

A good illustration of the manipulability of the meanings of rituals
has recently been presented by Gajek (1990) in her study 'Christmas
under the Third Reich'. In the late 1930s the National party began a
systematic attempt to transform Christmas for propaganda purposes into
a Germanic, specifically National Socialist festival, and to dissociate it
from Christianity and the Church. The changes in the celebration of
Christmas, while preserving many basic elements such as the family
gathering, the decorated tree, the exchange of presents and so forth, were
designed to explain the link 'between the home and the Front' and to
conform 'the family's identification with the National Socialist State
and its Führer' (Gajek 1990: 8). The appropriation of this ritual by the
Third Reich was based on the change of the Christmas message from a
message of peace to one of militaristic nationalism and the duty of self-
sacrifice in war, and as Harrison notes, it can be seen as an attempt to
'redefine the structure of property rights in which the ritual was located'
(1992: 232).

Similar examples of rituals as embodiments of ideology and as a means
of preserving the fundamentals of the political system can be found in
countries of the former Soviet bloc. As Lane (1981) shows, the utilization
of rituals, possible because the unified political elite manipulated the
masses in order to ensure the viability of the social and political order,
was the essential mechanism of maintaining social order. Ritual, as a
form of political socialization, was also, by implication, regarded as a
means of increasing group solidarity. 'The common performance of
ritual, as it is assumed, can transform a collective of associational kind
into a political community which is able to mobilize individuals on its
behalf' (Lane 1981: 19). The aspiration of the Soviet elites to secure
integration, combined with their structurally conditioned inability to
face up to conflicts, led them to overestimate the role of ritual. Ritual
became an important means of 'glossing over conflictual social relationships' (1981: 33). Today, we see the disappearance of practically
all Soviet rituals (from the May Day parade to wedding rites) and a
return to religious rituals. It becomes clear that the impact of socialist

rituals on attitudes and behaviour was not a lasting one and the task of changing the world cannot be achieved by solely transforming its representation.

While the role of rituals in Soviet bloc countries was unique because they were institutionally supported by the regimes' united elites, in modern industrial societies rituals, although still in existence, are more marginal and less important for the stability of political and social order (Lane 1981: 251–9). The majority of writers tend to agree that rituals, which relate the individual to the whole society, have become difficult to sustain in modern Western societies not only because of the plurality of values but also because of the absence of structural support for rituals from authoritative institutions. Bocock (1974) is the only researcher who argues that rituals in advanced industrial and secular societies are substancially undervalued. 'Ritual is a crucial part of the process whereby any society maintains itself, and contains dissident elements within it' (1974: 175). Bocock believes that they still play an integrative, affirmative and strengthening role in relation to key areas of our lives: 'to our sense of community or lack of it; to social cohesion or social conflict; to the human body, death, illness, health, sexuality; and symbols of beauty and holiness' (1974: 24).

It seems that although many of the rites of passage in the life cycle have become secularized and individualized, some are still occasions for collective commemoration. Weddings, for example, are still great celebrations, often well-staged performances of an individual rite of transition. In the annual cycle of the Christian world Christmas, and Thanksgiving in the United States, are the most important rituals. And although these rituals have become thoroughly secularized and commercialized, they still seem to play an important role in sustaining the cohesion of families.

On the one hand, in contemporary societies, rather than being a source of comfort and a reinforcement of order, the ritual is often a source of confusion or distrust. On the other hand, public opinion, while rejecting existing rituals as irrelevant, often supports the creation of new ones as being expressions of new values. In addition, because rituals can also take on the role of expressing protest and releasing aggression (Lukes 1975), they do not simply mirror social relations but help constitute them.

To sum up, it can be said that all three types of habitual action discussed here constitute effective mechanisms for re-affirming the predictability of social order as well as re-ordering the ambiguous aspects of a given situation. Habit, to paraphrase Geertz (1968: 7), provides 'a model of' and 'a model for' social relationships, permitting the removal of ambiguity in social conditions and an adjustment of our perception of changing conditions. The maintenance of habits and routine is also extremely important for a feeling of ontological security, and consequently for the individual's capacity to act and think innovatively. While too compulsive a commitment to routines endangers creativity, routine as 'a central element of autonomy . . . is not inimical to creativity, but presumes and is presumed by it' (Giddens 1991: 40–1). All three types of habit also help to economize on the effort, attention and memory needed in any activity; and by making 'coherence and necessity out of accident and contigency' (Bourdieu 1977: 83 and 87) they are principles of continuity and regularity. By emphasizing the communicatory function of routinized actions, background assumptions and rituals, I have demonstrated that all these habitual actions – by transmitting knowledge about the stability of social order – sustain the individual's sense of living in an ordered social context, which manifests reliability, legibility and predictability at the level of action.

## Reputation and rules of social distanciation: reliability

> A problem of the acquisition of meaning by things or forming habits of simple apprehension, is thus the problem of introducing (a) definiteness and distinction and (b) consistency or stability of meaning into what is otherwise vague and wavering.
>
> Dewey 1910: 122

The notion of definiteness and consistency to which Dewey is referring above depends upon what our culture and our past experience have already defined for us. From within a confusing and ambiguous social reality we tend to select and identify people, things and events according to preconceived concepts, established reputations or stereotypes. 'Society establishes the means of categorizing persons and the complement of attributes felt to be ordinary and natural for members of each of these categories' (Goffman 1963b: 2). The existence of society and its continuity, in turn, is made possible because of people's ability to communicate their approval or disapproval to other members of their groups. Opinions, evaluations and views about others shape our social relations, the nature of social institutions and, consequently, play a significant role in the maintenance of social order. This task of categorization and boundary maintenance, and the conveying to members of whom to trust and whom not to trust 'without special attention and thought' (Goffman 1963b: 2) is performed through a common recognition of one's standing in terms of trustworthiness – that is, reputation. Reputation permits us to trust another person by providing us with some information about the sort of person we are dealing with, before we have had a chance to have contact with that person.

A person's reputation, by shaping our anticipation of what a given type of individual should be, serves as a warrant for trust and as a measure of distanciation. Thus, reputation helps us to manage the complexity of social life by singling out trustworthy people – in whose interest it is to meet promises. It also facilitates reliability of social surroundings by helping us to decide whom we can empower to act in our interest.

The notion of reputation, like trust, promotes cooperation by enhancing the probability of carrying out promises. Reputation, however, is a more ambiguous concept than trust since, as publicly held opinion, it is open to manipulation and stereotyping. While to enjoy a favourable reputation entails the public recognition of one's ability to make credible promises, to be trusted also involves broader and less specific expectations of behaving properly or adequately in all circumstances. Nevertheless, both reputation and trust can be seen as important means for reducing the complexity and ambiguity of social reality.

A reputation is founded and sustained by the anticipation of particularistic rewards and sanctions linked to group membership. The expectation of utilities associated with good standing in a given group, organization or community motivates members committed to long-term relationships to live up to performance criteria. We can trust their interest in protecting their reputation – reputation for making credible promises – since they have invested resources for the purpose of building a reputation for credibility. What are the rewards that people, who follow the old truth that 'a good name is rather to be chosen than great riches' (Proverbs 22: 1) can expect?

A good reputation allows economic agents locked into the relation to cut the transaction costs and overcome limited information, and thus to facilitate efficient contractual relations (Lorenz 1988: 198–202; Dasgupta 1988). A good reputation in all types of businesses attracts customers and clients and increases a company's competitive advantages. A group's reputation contributes to the group's continuing existence by ensuring its cohesion and increasing its members' loyalty. At the same time, the existence of the group's reputation allows outsiders, such as clients, customers and traders, to go beyond available inadequate information and to operate within a set of generalized expectations of 'proper' behaviour on the part of the reputation holder. Groups or individuals able to acquire a reputation, which is defined in game theory as 'the perception others have of the players' value which determines its choice of strategies' (Greif 1989: 867), can overcome contractual problems and the inherent problems in the business world connected with difficulties of distinguishing good quality products or services from bad. Symbols of reputational status, such as brand-name goods or chains, counteract the effect of quality uncertainty (Akerlof 1984: 21).

An individual's reputation, in conditions where there is uncertainty about other people's motives, is an essential device permitting others' to evaluate that individual's capability to meet their specific expectations. 'A man's reputation is what is said about him. It is the overall response of people to both actor and role performance; an assessment not only of the results achieved but also of the manner in which they were achieved' (Layton 1971: 79).

A person's reputation is created out of a multitude of events and actions past and present, which build up an image of a member of a community. This shared image of a member of a community which is stable over time – that is, her or his reputation – affects how people behave and what they expect from a given person. The construction of a reputation within the community depends on the group members having complete information about one another's past behaviour. Whereas in smaller and more homogeneous communities people's judgements about the reputation of others were in accordance and they were the result of face-to-face contacts, in modern societies we tend to rely on more formal evidence of reputation. The practice of asking for referees' reports when applying for jobs, checking credit lines when applying for bank credit or making sure that a contractor one wants to employ is a member of the appropriate professional body – are all examples of these formal indicators of reputation. Investments in reputation or attempts to excel above others and thereby attain a higher evaluation are now less than ever based on 'the canon of reputability', which, according to Veblen, originated among the leisure class but permeated the whole social structure. Unproductive consumption of goods is no longer seen as 'honorable in itself' or as 'a prerequisite of human dignity' (Veblen 1959: 61). Conspicuous consumption and conspicuous life style are no longer 'means of reputability to the gentlemen of leisure' (1959: 64). In the modern world, instead of one common 'canon of reputability', there is a variety of standards, relevant in different contexts and frameworks. Although there is no one clear pattern of consumption and pattern of behaviour which could be taken for the manifestation of a person's or group's reputation, it seems that reputation still plays an important role in enhancing status. In the contemporary situation, where not many status symbols are available, the enhancement of our status in the eyes of other people by investing in one's reputation is challenging but nevertheless rewarding.

Not only are we constantly thrown into contact with new groups of people; new students, new colleagues, new clients, new salespersons, new neighbours and so on, but we also participate in various discrete arenas such as our work environment, leisure activities, voluntary work, activities with our children and so on. None the less we value – to a different degree – a high opinion of all these people, since a 'good reputation in the community is like a high credit rating . . . which enables a person to obtain benefits that are not available to others' (Blau 1989: 259). Moreover, we can trade off 'credit' from one phase or area of our life for positions in another sphere. This is practised by some High Court judges in Australia, for example, who, after retiring from the bench sell their high reputation to private companies, which are willing to pay a lot to boost their own reputation by having ex-High Court judges as their consultants.

Reputation, as part of a simplifying process in which the unknown and fearful becomes familiar, singles out individuals or groups noted for distinction, respectability or good name. While reputation, like trust, can be a spin-off from participation in small and informal groups, which do not need formal control to secure communication, it needs to be secured in more uncertain and complex environments. In small and informal groups, such as within the circle of family or friends, reputation, based on complete information and enriched by the incorporation of personal relations, is easily established and does not differ from trust. Reputations within kin groups, for example, are symbols of personal identities since they are both a product of past behaviour with kin and a component of future acceptance of actions of kin. 'The kin group as a whole, through the shared images which its members hold and transmit, has the power to confer or withhold a "good" reputation' (Finch and Mason 1992: 161). In informal groups reputations are confirmed, sustained and modified by face-to-face interactions, conversations and contacts. Yet, in a larger and more complex context, acquiring and sustaining a reputation for being trustworthy depends on more formal characteristics of a given group or organization. To establish a reputation in such circumstances depends upon the availability, circulation of information and the functioning of formal control (monitoring and sanctioning) and the structure of the system. A person's reputation, understood as a means of spreading information about what sort of person a given individual is, can therefore be seen as social capital – that is, 'those expectations for action, within a collectivity that affect the economic goals and goals-seeking behavior of its members, even if these expectations are not oriented toward the economic sphere' (Portes and Sensenbrenner 1993: 1323). Accordingly, it can be said that a group's reputation, as social capital, is generated by the disciplined compliance with group expectations of its individual members. There are several motivating forces behind this: value convictions, the pursuit of self-interest backed by the norm of reciprocity (conformity ) and the anticipation of utilities associated with good standing in a particular collectivity. In order to establish a favourable reputation, a group must be able to impose strong constraints forcing individuals to set aside their personal interest for the sake of those of the collectivity. This function can be performed by mechanisms of formal control, moral commitment or by societal pressure.

To start with the latter, societal pressure to conform, according to Blau, is one of the most important factors influencing people's behaviour; 'men are anxious to receive social approval for their decisions and actions, for their opinion and suggestions' (1989: 62). Consequently, a favourable reputation rests on calculative conformity, which 'entails sacrificing rewards that could be attained through direct exchange, but it brings other rewards indirectly' (1989: 259). If one does not pay back favours to a neighbour, the neighbour will become less friendly, more distrustful and less cooperative. 'Chances are, moreover, that the neighbor will tell other neighbors about the ingratitude of this individual, with the result that this person's general reputation in the community suffers' (1989: 97). According to this social exchange perspective, people motivated by self-interest reciprocate exchange because they fear that others, who are seen as concerned with protecting their own self-interest, would distrust them, and, consequently, it could mean their exclusion from any further beneficial exchange. The social disapproval that would follow nonconformist behaviour costs more than giving in to social pressure. This approach thus assumes that reputation arises from individual calculative reciprocity of exchanges – that is, from the 'reciprocity of transactions' – and that reputation is based on 'previous good deeds to others, backed by the norm of reciprocity' (Portes and Sensenbrenner 1993: 1324). Thus, when trust is seen as a function of self-interest, the establishment of a superior reputation in the community involves conformity to its obligations. However, with modern culture so diffused and fragmented and with the decreasing role of social disapproval, the growing number of exchanges with strangers and lack of a total monitoring system, the mechanism of conformity to social pressure does not seem so easy to construct and sustain. While in traditional societies, conformity and group pressure were mechanisms able to force obligation, today, with the increase in 'free-rider' opportunity, individual reputation is less arbitrated by public opinion. In such a situation, where the opportunities to take short-cuts are enormous, a reputation cannot be sustained only by conformity to social pressure. At the same time, with the declining cost of exit, giving in to groups' demands is no longer necessarily backed by self-interest. This raises the question of what alternative mechanisms of reputation we have.

According to the main sociological tradition, individuals do not show naked greed because of their value imperatives learned during the process of socialization. This is central to the Parsonian-Durkheiman-Weberian perspective, and a moral commitment or 'an obligation which an individual is supposed to feel and does feel towards the content of his professional activity' (Weber 1958: 54) is the source of 'noncontractual elements of contract' (Durkheim 1964: 162). Accounts of reputation as social capital which arises out of the interjection of established values seems to be regaining popularity in the social sciences (Bellah et al. 1985; Wolfe 1989; Casson 1991). By assuming that moral commitment rather than self-interest is the basis for reputation, these scholars reject the concept of economic man and instead maintain that people are able both to be morally committed and to recognize the same potential in others. 'Trust in other people need not, therefore, be based on a complicated calculation of how economic man would respond to a particular incentive structure, but rather on a simple judgment as to whether one is dealing with an "ethical man" rather than an "economic" man' (Casson 1991: 16). The moral mechanism also solves the main problem in constructing trust relations – that is, the need for a large amount of information – by assuming that people are self-monitoring agents, and thus there is no need for external monitoring.

Accordingly, people are seen to strive to achieve a good reputation because it engenders their pride and self-satisfaction, whereas being unable to perform well induces feelings of inadequacy and embarrassment. However, while it is probably true of those people who committed themselves to a moral imperative, several question remain: how do we know who is honest and who is not, and whose reputation do we trust?

The third type of mechanism which forces individuals to look beyond their personal interest for the sake of those of the collectivity, and by the same token permits trust in their reputation, is the mechanism of formal control. Most organizations can provide evidence of this mechanism since formal control is a necessary condition for cooperation in large groups. Formal control, which is based on the sanctioning and monitoring of members' behaviour, increases the volume of cooperation. At the same time, since formal control ensures compliance with corporate obligations, it contributes to a group's reputation (Hechter 1987: 52). The predictability of members' behaviour within a given group is linked to its particularistic rewards, sanctions and monitoring. 'The greater the ability of community to confer unique rewards on its members and the more developed its internal means of communication' (Portes and Sensenbrenner 1993: 1327), the higher the level of social capital, or the more favourable and stable the group's reputation.

Among the many conditions which contribute to the formation of a reputation, time and experience are critical for deciding whether to trust or not to trust. One important source of reputational information is the past – that is, an individual's previous behaviour. For reputation to be really effective, individuals must recognize that their own behaviour has consequences for their reputation. As many studies show, we are learning to trust and we are building reputation in successive stages, tentatively and conditionally (Good 1988). In economic relationships, as in a finitely repeated prisoner's dilemma game, a favourable reputation is something which economic agents will be concerned to establish. Since building up such a reputation requires not only an investment of resources but also takes time, people with good reputations can be trusted because they would not like to lose this valuable asset (Dasgupta 1988; Casson 1991). 'Loss of reputation is particularly serious for people who are locked into a group where barriers to exit are high. In fact it can be shown that reputation effects succeed quite well in sustaining trust in small, compact, and isolated social groups' (Casson 1991: 16).

When there is a scarcity of information, particularly when we have more information about the group than an individual member, there is a tendency to simplify the perception of the social environment by identifying all individuals with the group to which they belong. An important way of achieving this is by mechanisms of labelling or stereotyping. Publicly held opinion about any person is often formed on the basis of the theory we hold about the effect of culture, class membership, family life and the like, on a person's motivation and thus his or her behaviour (Dasgupta 1988). However, while, in the past, people's social standing and, consequently, reputation were easily known and recognized, in the present urban environment it is much more difficult to single people out according to their occupation, education and so on. 'The material conditions of life in the city weakened any trust people could place in the "natural", routine labelling of others by origin, family background or occupation' (Sennett 1974: 60).

Furthermore, it is often not a lack of information or of communication which prevents trust between individuals or groups but rather people's bias or preconceptions. Decisions about whether to trust or not to trust another person depend not only on information about that person but also on the way in which this reputational information is interpreted and which particular aspect of it is seen as significant. As Good (1988: 38–42) notes, the interpretation of reputation is always open to many readings and is a function of the interpreter's perception of the nature of the social world. When individuals are confronted by uncertainty and ambiguity, they tend to interpret incomplete information 'in line with the individual's preconception. Such interpretations will, of course, serve to reinforce those preconceptions' (1988: 41).

This tendency for sustaining the previously formulated perception of other people is rooted in the specific nature of trust as 'a peculiar belief predicated not on evidence but on the lack of *contrary* evidence' (Gambetta 1988b: 234). This bias, consequently, plays an important role in the preservation of the existing order. Due to the way in which people process or interpret unclear information, neither reputations nor preconceptions are readily changed, even in the face of challenging evidence. This strategy of coping with the limits of our rationality and knowledge is underlined by our cognitive capacities. The fact that cognitive inertia may prevent people from changing their beliefs is clearly visible in any intergroup exchange, be it conflict or cooperation, where groups' respective opinions about each other determine the level of their mutual trust. The role of reputation as a guarantee of trust is connected with setting rules of social distanciation – who should be trusted or who should not. If we generalize Casson's (1991: 100) observation that poor economic performance is associated not so much with actual cheating as with fear of being cheated, it can be said that the absence of cooperation is a result not so much of bad reputation as of the lack of reputation. In other words, the existence of reputation is an important social capital which facilitates people's willingness to cooperate by helping to overcome a scarcity of information. Furthermore, a given group's reputation not only facilitates the group's contact with others, but also increases the group's integrity and its ethics since members' self-interest encourages them to defer exit or cheating.

The three mechanisms of reputation – a code of ethics (values), conformity to social pressure (reciprocity of exchanges) and formal control (sanctioning, monitoring and discipline) – are not mutually exclusive. Furthermore, because even an individual's ends and interests are conceptualized in a socially defined way, the mechanism of reputation is complex and rests – to a different degree – on all three components. 'An individual may be knowledgeable and calculative, yet the knowledge he possesses and the scheme of calculation he employs will be those of his society, and the calculations he makes will be social actions, the actions of someone who accepts and trusts a given system of routines' (Barnes 1988: 35). If we assume that calculative reciprocity, as the base of reputation arising out of conformity, is shaped not only by self-interest but also by knowledge of socially available actions and socially formed judgement, it can be seen as a general mechanism present in all type of groups and organiz-ations. For the purpose of simplicity of argument, however, in what follows I shall concentrate on only two types of mechanism of reputation construction: firstly, arising out of self-interest (that is, out of the anticipation of utilities associated with good standing in a given group, organization or community); and secondly, out of values (that is, out of moral obligation). Moreover, since it is difficult to differentiate between reputation stemming out of familiarity and trust resulting from the participation in small and informal groups (which is the topic of the next chapter), I shall focus here rather on the denial of a favourable reputation as a result of unfamiliarity. For the purpose of clarity of argument, I shall use three analytical categories: reputation for virtue (honour), reputation for making credible promises (credibility) and denial of reputation (stereotypes).

Honour, according to the *Oxford English Dictionary*, is now commonly defined as a reputation for high virtue, honesty or integrity. The ethic of honour was an aristocratic concept 'strongly influenced by the medieval codes of chivalry', which were 'rooted in the social structures of feudalism' (Berger et al. 1974: 80). In hierarchical societies, where titles were instantly recognized, honour was a source of solidarity among equals. It was also a mark of distanciation; for example, duels were fought only between equals. The attribution of truth and honesty as inner qualities to honourable men supported the existing social order. The central motive of the honour ethic was 'the strong sense of one's worth and honour which pushed men to conquer their fears and baser desires and do great things' (Taylor 1992: 153). In this scheme, two senses of honour coexisted: 'one external, public and reputational (having to do with one's standing *vis-à-vis* others), and the other internal, personal, and private (referring to indwelling virtues and one's awareness of having those virtues)' (Shapin 1994: 68). However, since the seventeenth century the ethic of honour has been the subject of criticism, which labels the search for honour as being concerned with mere appearance and undisciplined self-indulgence. 'A new model of civility emerges in the eighteenth century, in which the life of commerce and acquisition gains an unprecedentedly positive place' (Taylor 1992: 214). Instead of the aristocratic search for military glory, commerce came to be seen as a constructive and civilizing force (Hirschmann 1976), which gave rise to new views of social order and new moralities and 'most specifically of a historically unprecedented concern for the dignity and the rise of the rights of the individual' (Berger et al. 1974: 79).

In sociology, honour is perceived mainly through a Weberian perspective, which assumes that it is the characteristic of specific groups – that is, status groups. Honour comes with membership in these specific groups, which have potential for social control based on the ability of the membership to withdraw recognition from disobedient individuals and to remove their special honour. Concepts of social recognition and of allocation of resources, so central to this perspective, are also present in the anthropological approach, which sees honour as prescribing 'appropriate behaviour for people at the various points of the hierarchy' (Davis 1977: 98).

For Bourdieu, honour as symbolic capital, 'is always *credit* in the widest sense of the word, i.e. a sort of advance which the group alone can grant those who give it the best material and symbolic *guarantees*, it can be seen that the exhibition of capital is one of the mechanisms which make capital go to capital' (1977: 181). Seen in this way, honour is not only a matter of pride ('the social recognition of self-importance') but also of practical utility, since 'appeals to honour, the justification of behaviour in terms of honour are means of acquiring power and wealth' (Davis 1969: 69). Honour is important in the pre-modern societies because there 'the dominant agents have a vested interest in virtue; they can accumulate political power only by paying a *personal* price, and not simply by redistributing their goods and money; they must have the "virtue" of their power because the only basis of their power is "virtue"' (Bourdieu 1977: 194). Honour is 'the non-transferable ticket of entry into the political arena' and people who have no honour, and seen therefore as not trustworthy and having less to offer by the way of guarantee and reliability, are not included (Davis 1969: 76). Furthermore, honour is translated to power by a way of knowledge. 'If the relations of a man of honor were to be believed, then such a man might unconditionally colonize others' minds, constituting their sense of what was the case' (Shapin 1994: 65).

In order to maintain their honour intact people conform to group expectations and perform their obligations and duties. This, in return, creates expectations about how they should behave in specific circumstances. Honour requires knowledge about 'a man and his family', his economic standing and about the way in which he controls his women, hence only small pre-modern communities are able to carry out this continually task of assessing honour (Davis 1969: 80). People in such communities 'know that their behaviour will be observed and gossiped about; this, they recognise freely, is the chief constraint on their behaviour and it is one which many people resent bitterly. On the other hand, they cannot afford to do without the reputation which gossip gives them' (1969: 74).

The role of honour as a crucial control mechanism on people's behaviour is not significant in the modern urban world. Urbanization, development of the monetary system and institutionalization weakened reciprocal controls, leading to the collapse of the collectively maintained ethic of honour. In today's larger and more fluid societies, where one's reputation is not known, contract law replaces informal social sanctions. Institutionalization of the delegation of authority, which is accompanied by an explicit definition of responsibilities, has been eroding the relationship between power and honour. Honour is no longer a necessary symbolic foundation of power, yet we still find it difficult to accept that power is rooted not in 'virtue' but in 'naked self-interests' (Bourdieu 1977: 196).

Our nostalgic yearning for more 'honourable' social arrangements underpins contemporary concern with the type of morality of the institutionalized world. It leads to the questioning of confidence in institutions and demands competence and integrity from people in power. 'Perhaps honour is too old fashioned a word but what it comes down to. A well run society needs to know that the servants and ministers responsible for bad decisions are prepared to resign' (Porter 1992: 7). This demand for public scrutiny of the morality of politics is based on the assumption that the absence of integrity and responsibility of political leaders can, in the long run, destroy key institutions, thereby leading to the disintegration of society. The public concern with the ethics of those in top jobs is best illustrated by the 1993 failure of President Clinton's nominees for Attorney-General to be accepted by American public opinion. Two successive candidates were forced to withdraw, because they were declared morally unsuitable for the position after the public learned about their hiring of illegal immigrants as housekeepers.

Although high standards are not expected of politicians alone, there is, as Weber notes, a qualitative difference between the honourable behaviour expected of politicians and that of administrative staff because they are subject to 'exactly the opposite principle of responsibility'. According to Weber:' [t]he honour of a civil servant is vested in his ability to execute conscientiously the order of the superior authority, exactly as if the order agreed with his own conviction. . . . The honour of the political leader . . . however, lies precisely in an exclusive personal responsibility for what he does, a responsibility he cannot and must not reject or transfer' (1958: 95). Weber's model can be criticized for being too simplistic, outdated and overlooking many overlaps of these two sets of authorities (Thompson 1987). However, his normative stand claiming that the political leader should act on an 'ethic of responsibility' grasps well the core aspect of politicians' honour. Many examples demonstrate a high public expectation of political leaders and that their honourable behaviour is seen as necessary for societal trust and consensus.

The behaviour of Secretary of State Cyrus Vance in 1980 is one of such cases. His resignation from the office after the abortive raid to rescue the Iranian hostages was commonly perceived as an honourable act. His acceptance of guilt for deceiving the allies – in order to increase the chances of success of the raid he supposedly told the European officials that the United States would not undertake military action (Thompson

1987: 18) – was identified as honest behaviour. Similarly, despite his unpopular decisions (such as the 1981 introduction of martial law), the Polish General Jaruzelski enjoys a high reputation for honesty, integrity and generosity (according to a opinion poll, 52 per cent of Poles surveyed declared that Jaruzelski was a better president than Walesa (*Polityka*, 16 April 1994: 1)). None the less, not many of today's politicians would willingly accept Mark Antony's line: 'If I lose mine honour, I lost myself' (Shakespeare, *Antony and Cleopatra*, III, 4).

Apart from politicians, the interest at stake in the conduct of honour is common to professions such as law or medicine, in which those who practise them must be 'above suspicion'. These people have a vital interest in keeping their profession's capital of honour – that is, its capital of honourability – safe from suspicion. There are several ways of securing professional reputation. Apart from the special rituals and life-style requirements, which sustain the group's control, there is a need for members of a given professional group to become aware of its cultural specificity and to become sensitive to its internal evaluations. Consequently, 'for the need of honor to be satisfied in professional life, every profession must have some association really capable of keeping alive the memory of all the nobility, heroism, probity, generosity and genius spent in the exercise of that profession' (Weil 1952: 20). As Durkheim (1983: 8) notes, the ethics of each profession are localized within a limited region and the nature of professional ethics is influenced by its group structure, size and coherence. Professional associations, by 'bringing men's minds into mutual understanding' (1983: 15), provide an important focus for loyalties, and consequently, for communicative interactions within which honouring and dishonouring occurs. Members of a given profession experience a sense of honour or shame only in communication with other members of the same profession since the features of professional ethics are not common to the public; 'they are rather outside the common consciousness' (1983: 6). Consequently, the fact of 'not honouring one's signature is a disgrace, almost the supremely shameful act, in business. Elsewhere it is looked on with a very different eye' (1983: 6).

The morality of professions, rooted in group solidarity, is not the only way in which people of the same professions may operate cooperatively to further their reputation. Contemporary professions aim to achieve and sustain a high social reputation with the help of a variety of strategies and techniques of control which are based on a monopoly of knowledge and expertise rather than solely on an emphasis on honour, shame and pride. As the moral and emotional aspects of professional collectives become marginalized and less visible, the sensitivity to dishonouring and honouring declines. In the context of the declining importance of internal communicative structures within which disapproval and approval could take place, the process accelerated by the growing size, specialization and bureaucratization of professions, the significance of formal control in ensuring a professional reputation, has been increasing.

One of the most important techniques of control within professions is discipline, which implies specific knowledge, skills, imposed procedures of normalization (such as educational standards), as well as trained control over professional practice. Discipline constitutes the main claim for legitimacy of professional authority and contributes to the reputation of a given profession (Foucault 1984). We trust our doctors, lawyers and teachers because of the reputation for discipline inherent in their professions. The expertise of individuals is itself guaranteed by the institutions from which they speak and which are the ultimate source of that expertise.

However, modernity can be characterized not only by the processes of specialization and bureaucratization of professions, resulting in a wider choice of expert systems and knowledge, but also by its reflexivity, which undermines the belief in a rational system and in the power of science and knowledge. Thus, the dominance of a common scepticism results from the contradictory processes, which, on the one hand, tend to increase the complexity and specialization of knowledge, therefore making us more illiterate about the way the world works, and on the other hand, making us more critical of experts. Consequently, modern Western society has become the litigious society (Lieberman 1981), where courts are expected to remedy the failure of trust and where the emotion of shame is disguised and repressed. 'But litigation is not an ideal means of building community; its procedures and its impact do much to sow mistrust, and its limited successes may blind us to the need for reforms that lie outside the ceaseless cycle of plaintiff and defendant' (1981: 186). Yet even reforms will not so easily restore the mutual trust since professional ethics are undermined by the very high profile of science and technology, the growing level of education and, consequently, the increased demand for autonomy and a higher level of scepticism (Barber 1983). However, although we cannot take everything on trust, we cannot also doubt everything except what we have established single-handedly for ourselves (Coady 1993). Thus, if we have to rely on the testimony of other people, the issue is how to know when such testimony can be trusted.

The new science in the seventeenth century based knowledge on social conventions, ensuring trust and trustfulness by arguing that only the integrity and disinterestedness of the witness could secure the true testimony (Shapin 1994). The testimony was trusted if it came from people with a reputation of being 'men of honour'. Therefore, individuals' reputation, their credibility and trustfulness, as embedded in the gentry class, was a base for the knowledge of things. Although the way in which modern scientific knowledge gains credibility does not have much to do with gentlemanly culture and values of gentlemanly conversation, Shapin suggests that 'that there is a legitimate sense in which modern science is much more trusting' (1994: 417). Even though contemporary scientific knowledge is based on anonymous scientific expertise rather than on the good manners of scientists, personal contact, informal exchanges and reputation of credibility are still important factors. In a similar vein, although a profession's discipline serves as guarantee for trust, people – regardless of their level of trust in an abstract system – still trust one doctor and not another on the basis of familiarity. Because our trust in a local doctor is negotiated at 'access points' (Giddens 1991: 84–7), the question is 'Does this particular doctor meet our expectations?' rather than 'Do we trust bodies of specialized knowledge?' There is, of course, a growing public suspicion of experts' knowledge and scepticism about bodies of specialized knowledge. This scepticism, however, while increasing anxiety, does not allow for total mistrust because it would make our lives difficult or impossible. Therefore, since we are forced to live within 'system trust' (Luhmann 1979) – that is, trust without familiarity and without the effective possibility of mistrust – we should try to sustain as many opportunities as possible where reputation is rooted in personal trust.

Although, in our search for goods and services we rely on the ranking of reputations, which can be supplied by informal or formal networks (now often prepared by various agencies keeping track of quality of products and enterprises, such as various consumers' and professional associations), our final decision (for instance, which builder to trust with our house improvements) is often influenced by our personal impression of a person. We tend to opt for people with whom we can develop 'an understanding', which would encourage better communication and a common interpretation of situations. Basing relationships on personal trust helps to solve one of the pervasive problems in continuing economic relations: 'the need to adapt to contingency' (Lorentz 1988: 208). Unanticipated contingencies are particularly connected with the system of flexible specialization, which is characterized by a high degree of uncertainty associated with competition based on product and process innovation, consequently making reputation based on personal contacts even more important. Japanese and the Third World companies are especially famous for the construction of their reputation, which enforces obligations and trust in the industrial context. In Japan, an employee's life commitment to the company 'makes the firm's reputation of great importance to all employees and so helps to guarantee to a supplier that "the firm" will not renege on its obligations' (Dore 1993: 75). In a more competitive and technologically sophisticated environment a good reputation is important because it facilitates firms' cooperation with suppliers, which is necessary in order to meet changing demands and to share the risks of increasingly complex and uncertain investment projects.

Lorenz's argument that partners in economic cooperation still 'appreciate the reciprocal nature of learning process' (1993: 319) seems to imply the importance of both time and personal experience as additional means of strengthening a fragile reputation. Nevertheless, conditions in the modern world, especially with the development of new technologies, are becoming more conducive to the facilitating and spreading of impersonal trust or institutional-based reputation. Consequently, reputation does not need to be acquired solely through personal experience over time. It is not a new trend. In the United States from the turn of the century reputation construction has been handled by 'rational bureaucratic organisations, professional credentialing, the service economy, including financial intermediaries and government, and regulation and legislation' (Zucker 1986: 101). Moreover, since – in order to cope with the potential risks of the defection of the 'reputation holder' – economic institutions increasingly rely on various types of insurance companies (for example, stock markets insure investors against fraud and misrepresentation), a company's or product's reputation has become protected by insurance-like arrangements. Furthermore, new computer-based technologies could undermine the role of time and personal experience in constructing reputation. 'Once communication moves on-line, having a core group of subcontractors turns from strength to weakness. . . . Having placed an order on line, the purchaser can wait to see which supplier offers to fulfil it most efficiently. By scouring the world for the best deal, technology favours on-line opportunists' (*The Economist*, 9 July 1994: 10). A new communication revolution, by changing the type of cooperative relations between economic agents and by allowing for a new type of shopping (electronic retailing or interactive shopping), could promote a shift towards sources of reputation less embedded in social relations. However, this new development does not necessarily exclude the emergence – out of initially opportunistic contracting – of more stable and obligated exchange networks. Moreover, one may doubt if the use of these new technologies would eliminate disadvantages always faced by outsiders in any exchange.

Since we are 'better at predicting the behaviour of those most like ourselves' (Hardin 1993: 512), strangers are given fewer opportunities to demonstrate their trustworthiness. One of the main problems faced by immigrants, especially by the educated ones, is their lack of reputation in a new country, which – in the absence of some external guarantee – acts as a barrier to their entry into the labour market. A lack of Australian, American or Swedish job experience is one of the most frequent reasons given for turning down immigrants' applications for jobs. This, of course, facilitates community among immigrants and the development of self-employment in ethnic communities.

To overcome the lack of reputation outsiders are forced to turn to their own communities as the only source of their reputation. Tightly knit immigrant networks enable ethnic entrepreneurs to recruit clients and workers and to achieve strong competitive advantages. In such communities access to credit (as, for example, in rotating credit associations), suppliers, subcontractors and customers (for instance, small enterprises) depends on personal reputation, guaranteed by the ethnic enclaves' monitoring and sanctioning capacity (Light 1972; Waldinger 1984; Ward and Jenkins 1984). 'In a personalistic business community . . . a personal reputation is a man's lifeline to credit, suppliers and customers. Merchants are mutually dependent hence susceptible to opinion, because they owe their reputation to their community mates, with whom they share their sociocultural life' (Omohundro 1981: 113). Lever-Tracy's study of small ethnic businesses in Australia emphasizes the role of reputations as it permeates all aspects of business. For example, personal reputation was seen by 75 per cent of business people as the best way to find labour because it ensures reliability of employees (1992: 59). In the same vein, Omohundro notes that a person's 'solid reputation earns him an inexhaustible supply of easy credit, and it is the reputation of individuals that makes or breaks whole businesses' (Omohundro 1981: 63).

Among Dominicans in New York the circulation of money available for business start-ups is based 'first on the reputation of the recipient and second on swift retribution against those who default' (Portes and Sensenbrenner 1993: 1333). The most famous case of a community created by outsiders to increase the opportunity to demonstrate their trustworthiness, thus to make their reputation known, is the Cuban business sector in Miami. Its success is attributed to rotating credit associations, which – in order to lower the risk of default – made loans 'exclusively on the personal reputation of the recipient in Cuba' (1993: 1334). These so-called 'character loans' were backed by the sanctioning capacity of the migrant business community and were not extended to new refugees coming from the mid-1970s, since their reputation for honesty and reliability was unknown to Cubans from the first exodus.

Not all immigrants, however, have the same opportunity to turn to their ethnic enclaves for support. Some groups, which are without their own cultural and material resources, are forced 'to accept definitions of their own identity based on host-society stereotypes' (1993: 1331).

Stereotypes coined by the host community are normally highly simplified representations, based on the acceptance of rigid and unequal divisions. They are, as Lippmann noted, not neutral, and their function is wider than merely to introduce order and simplicity to complex social surroundings. A pattern of stereotypes is

> not merely a short cut. It is all these things and something more. It is a guarantee of our self-respect; it is the projection upon the world of our own sense of our value, our own position and our own rights. The stereotypes are, therefore, highly charged with the feelings that are attached to them. They are the fortress of our tradition, and behind its defenses we can continue to feel ourselves safe in the position we occupy (Lippmann 1949: 63–4).

Many of these old fortresses are already empty; however, new ones are emerging all the time. The most visible change in the last three decades has been occurring in gender stereotyping. What is interesting, however, is the fact that gender stereotyping has not disappeared but simply changed. Even in Norway, which is at the forefront of women's participation in politics – the country has one of the highest proportions of women in parliament (Matland 1994: 274) – societal views on women as political leaders are still coloured by stereotyping. An experimental evaluation of gender stereotyping of political candidates discovered that gender is still a significant consideration in evaluating political leaders (respondents distinguish between male and female candidates in a number of policy areas, rating traditionally male politicians as more effective in defence, foreign and economic policy, while female politicians were seen as strong in environmental, agricultural and women's rights policy). Surprisingly, it also demonstrated that a new gender stereotyping has emerged which picture women as being competent in different policy areas than men. The new stereotyping (also visible, for example, in the now common presentation of women not as being inefficient in business but simply being better in small businesses) is 'not radically different from traditional gender stereotyping, but with an important proviso that women's areas of expertise are of equal importance to men's areas of expertise' (1994: 288).

Other types of relatively stable stereotypes are those connected with race and national identity. As the process of globalization advances, the issue of classification of various national and ethnic groups and attachment to these images of various expectations of behaviour becomes less clear and more complex. 'Modern living means living with strangers, and living with strangers is at all times a precarious, unnerving and testing life' (Bauman 1993: 161). When people are confronted with a confusing variety of patterns of behaviour, cultures and so on, the process of classification can be messy and full of tensions and misunderstandings. Many people could find themselves in between or in a 'zone of choice' because there are not – at least, not yet – ready-made labels for them. And although providing a label is no longer an easy task, the tendency to do so remains. A study of members of an international organization discovered that even these cosmopolitan people believed that nations are characterized by different mentalities and character traits. Moreover, they assume for each nation a cluster of character traits, which describe, for example, the French as nationalistic, arrogant, individualistic and charming, the British as nationalist, isolationist, reserved and friendly and Germans as orderly, hard-working, romantic and complex (Wilterdink 1992: 33–5). The study also demonstrates that people's evaluations of national character are not value-neutral descriptions of social reality. Stereotypes help people to come to grips with social reality and to make it more comprehensible; however, 'their popularity makes it possible for indifference to flourish' (Herzfeld 1992: 96). Stereotyping by denial of identity or selfhood generates and justifies indifference, and therefore lowers the likelihood of mutual trust.

Another collectivity, apart from strangers, which often finds its social standing to be ambiguous is now old-age group. On the one hand, until very recently, old age was seen as a stigma, as something discrediting and exclusionary from normal social life. On the other hand, demographic trends – in 1990 over 17 per cent of people in the OECD countries were aged 60 or above and by 2030 it will be more than 30 per cent (*The Economist*, 13 August 1994: 17–18) – and changes in the quality of life and economic status of older people imply a necessity to see the capacity and needs of the aged in more constructive and positive terms. Older people, like Goffman's stigmatized people, are faced with a choice to control the circulation of discrediting information about themselves with the help of various concealment techniques (such as dyeing their grey hair), or by trying to pass in the community by acting in a 'normal' way (like taking on younger people's life style) or opt for disclosure (perhaps by joining 'grey power' parties). This third solution – that is, the transformation of the stigmatized person from someone with information difficult to manage into someone with an uneasy social situation to get through (the best illustration of this transformation, to use another example, can be provided by gays 'coming out of the closet') – not only constitutes a turning point in the person's moral career (Goffman 1963b: 100–1) but also exposes the wider community to a new moral dilemma. 'For society as a whole moral questions are raised whenever an outcast group seeks entry, no matter what the reason for its liminal status – social class, gender, sexual preference, geography, color' (Wolfe 1989: 216).

Looking at strangers, social outcasts, 'different' or 'socially deviant' –
those who are outside the framework of the 'respectable' – can show not
only how labelling and stereotyping is spread, but it can also contribute
to our understanding of the main societal problems. Since the structure of
power and status in everyday life influences which groups or individuals
are seen as 'different', any discussion of the rule of social distanciation is
– by the same token – a debate of morality as the politics of new relations
among human beings.

If it is nothing more than natural that we are better in predicting the
behaviour of people like ourselves and that for us all strangers of another
race 'proverbially look alike' (Dewey 1910: 121), can we assume that we
are all naturally prejudiced and racist, or, in other words, do not feel an
obligation to strangers? If we tend to give strangers fewer opportunities
to demonstrate their trustworthiness – to establish their reputation – how
can mutual suspicion be overcome?

These questions point to the need for consideration of the issue of
reputation (or its lack) in connection with the problem of people's
mutual obligations. Both factors are shaped by the wider social context
– for example, by the type and function of the state. Not being able to
trust the state, people would not trust one another and would limit their
obligation to their families (Banfield 1958). Also the possibility of exit
(such as a high level of migration) lowers the significance of reputation
(the cost of leaving the group is not high, so the loss of reputation is also
not costly), and lessens the sense of obligation on the part of those who
stay (since they assume that others will also eventually leave). Investment
in obligation to others does not also mean, in all societies at the same
time, investment in reputation. In traditional societies, individuals' fulfilment of their obligation to their families determined their reputation or
honour in the community. However, in the modern world obligation
becomes more complicated, the scope of obligation expands and the
opportunity for investment in reputation becomes less clear and less
profitable. 'To be modern is to face the consequences of decisions made
by complete strangers while making decisions that will affect the lives of
people one will never know' (Wolfe 1989: 3). Thus, in the contemporary
world there is a need for the extension of obligation to strangers; however, at the same time the context of social life is more messy than ever
and is full of ambivalence. In such a context, full of confusing, incoherent
signals of approval and disapproval and in the process of continuous
change, which undermines our ability to establish a social standing, it is
difficult to know what kind of investment, if any investment at all, could
contribute to a favourable reputation.

It seems that the type of relationship between reputation and the
obligation of members of society may indicate the type of social order in

terms of its general trustworthiness or moral standards. However, we now know that 'we will face forever moral dilemmas without unambiguously good (that is, universally agreed upon, uncontested) solutions, and that we will be never sure where such solutions are to be found; not even whether it would be good to find them' (Bauman 1993: 31). Yet, even in this ambivalent modern context there is a space for practices of friendship, love and compassion, which together with policies aiming at the creation of a cooperative, just and tolerant society, could increase societal trust.

## Rules of remembrance: legibility

> Alike with the individual, and with the group, the past is being continually re-made, reconstructed in the interests of the present.
>
> F.C. Bartlett 1932: 309

Memory, seen as a part of the patterned practices, reduces the complexity and restricts the uncertainty of our social environment. Individuals seek to impose legibility on the irregularities in institutions and values and thus provide for comprehension and continuity of their historical experience (Smith 1982). Memory provides the shared sense of ideals about the past that can link people together and it secures a sense of continuity 'with what they think they know in order to be able to deal with what they don't know' (Hamer 1994: 184).

Memory is intimately connected to identity; in John Locke's words: 'I am what I remember myself being'. This perspective raises many questions about the relationship between, for example, lost memories and identity. However, since we are not concerned here with the cognitive problem of remembering, we can exclude from our discussion the issue of to what extent an individual's memory is distorted, fragmented or inadequate. When discussing the issues of memory and trust we will also not be troubling ourselves with the question of whether our memory is objective or subjective. In the same way that we accept information from the person on the street when we ask him or her for directions, we need to accept memory as a source of information about how 'we represent ourselves to ourselves and to those around us' (Fentress and Wickham 1992: 7).

Our main concern will be with one of the most significant characteristics of memory; that is, with the fact that our memories are not solely personal: they are constructed, sustained and transmitted by families and the many other collectivities to which we belong. All memories are, according to Halbwachs (1992), a leading follower of Durkheim, collec-

tive memories. Memory, as Halbwachs argues, is not a mechanical ability
to register passing events and to preserve the vision of the past. Memory
is the process of a continuous reconstruction of the past by the remembering subject. The individual is able to carry out this reconstruction only
as a member of a given social group which provides him or her with a
framework for each process of recalling the past and secures the legibility
of the present. Since 'one cannot in fact think about events of one's past
without discoursing them' (Halbwachs 1992: 53), which connects one's
memory with a specific set of ideas of one's collectivity, it can be said that
memories are structured by group identities. People remember their past
thanks to their belonging to various groups, be it either a family or social,
religious or national group, with which they identify themselves.
Halbwachs also notes that any change in belonging results in the reconstruction of an individual's memory. The specificity and uniqueness of
social groups in various historical epochs leads to the different character
of their respective collective memories. Groups construct their images of
the world by establishing an agreed version of the past, and this is
achieved, according to Halbwachs, by communication and not by private
remembrance. From this Durkheimian perspective, memory is not an
individual property; it comes from outside since it is coded in language,
which is the social fact, not an individual choice. Seen in this way,
collective memories, as social facts, have their own history and are
important mechanisms for securing the legibility and stability of the
world surrounding us.

Collective memories, like customs, traditions and habits, can be seen as
constant efforts to maintain and reconstruct societal stability. However,
unlike habit, memory can often be 'a highly active, effortful process'
(Young 1988: 97). Our recollection of the past needs to be deliberately
and consciously recalled. Whatever memories 'route into consciousness,
they need to be organized into patterns so that they make some kind of
continuing sense in an everchanging present' (1988: 97–8). The selectivity of this recollection, resulting in recovering only the relevant to the
present moments of our past, supports a construction of the social world
as legible and stable.

Memory, for Halbwachs, 'mediates between the social world and the
mind but only so as to reproduce society' (Tonkin 1992: 97). Regarding
social memory as an expression of collective experience, which 'identifies
a group, giving it a sense of its past and defining its aspirations for the
future' (Fentress and Wickham 1992: 25), excludes the question of the
historical truthfulness of a given group memory. Instead, it focuses our
attention on the issue of whether the group regards this memory as true,
and if so, why it does so. The answer to this question is connected with
the role that collective memory plays in drawing boundaries that mark

groups' identities. We know from Durkheim and Simmel that symbolic boundaries presuppose both inclusion and exclusion and in this way they legitimate differences and inequalities. Thus, boundaries and identity can be seen as occupying the centre stage of the memory and trust debate. Symbolic boundaries are conceptual distinctions that we draw between ourselves and others, using available cultural resources in order to define who we are. 'By generating distinctions, we also signal our identity and develop a sense of security, dignity and honour; a significant proportion of our daily activities is oriented toward avoiding shame and maintaining a positive self-identity by patrolling the borders of our groups' (Lamont 1992: 11). The people excluded by our boundaries are those whom we do not trust and those whom we trust are included. Since most of the boundaries 'have to do with a public evaluation of behaviour, with degrees of conformity to social codes, rather than with a hypothetical inner state' (Herzfeld 1980: 341), the main role in the process of justifying and legitimating differences between outsiders and insiders is played by collective memory.

Before we move to a more detailed discussion of the connection between memory and trust, let us briefly identify the analytical distinctions between memory and trust since an awareness of them is essential for any dialogue between groups with different, even conflictual memories. Apart from the similarities between trust as 'weak inductive knowledge' (Simmel 1950) and memory as 'uncertain and unstable knowledge' (Fentress and Wickham 1992: 541–86), both of them perform a similar function: they help us to cope with uncertainty and complexity of social reality and provide our social world with some coherence. 'Whether we are aware of it or not, what is valuable about memory is not its capacity to provide an unshakeable foundation for knowledge but, simply, its capacity to keep us afloat' (Fentress and Wickham 1992: 10). Both, trust and memory, serve as the platform from which we 'leap' to conclusions, which would be impossible on the basis of insufficient information alone.

When we decide to trust someone, as well as when we recall our memory of somebody, we refer to some kind of past experience framed within a social context of our interaction with a given person. However, memory and trust, both being nothing more than beliefs, are equally fragile. Trust can be easily destroyed since it is, as we already noted, a belief predicated on the lack of *contrary* evidence (Gambetta 1988b: 234). In a similar way our confidence in memory is limited by 'the possibility that they [memories] will be contradicted by new experience or better ideas' (Fentress and Wickham 1992: 10). In both cases, the level of uncertainty of the information is relatively high. The way to overcome this uncertainty lies in the continuous connections between the past and the present. In the first case, it is overcome owing to a collective cognitive reality described by Luhmann (1979) as 'trust in trust', which cuts short any further search for information or evidence of trustworthiness and allows one to trust because others trust too. In the second case, we recognize our memory as true only as long as its usefulness is secured by continually positive testing in everyday life. Thus, it than can be said that a *usable* memory is nothing more than a collective belief in some vision of the past as being 'the true' one in a specific moment of the group's life. Furthermore, as an evolution of the content of Israeli high school history, described as 'the shifting moods of remembrance and rejection', shows, even the most traumatic past can also be 'manipulated by politicians and ideologues' (Elon 1993a: 3). The possibility of the use of memory as a political instrument and institutionalization of 'remembrance' within the national ritual and educational system, which can only feed a belief that 'the whole world is against us', raises the question of how to prevent collective memory from becoming the legitimizing myth of a nation's uniqueness? Is it possible to separate collective memory from the passions of identity politics?

Paradoxically, the best means of securing a more 'cooperative' mood of memory would be, as the evaluation of a repeated prisoner's dilemma games suggests, 'to have no memory, to forget that past defections may be repeated in subsequent moves' (Gambetta 1988b: 228). In the real world, however, people's cooperative attitudes are based on their past experiences and trust relations cannot be expected to emerge naturally. Reasonable and intentional trust not only requires the absence of good grounds for expecting others' ill will but also taking the risk of having confidence in others, that is 'a good risk', based on the evaluation 'of what we may generally gain and what we may lose from the willingness to take such risks' (Baier 1986: 236). It demands a critical attitude to a society's own past as an essential factor securing cooperation and trust between societal members (internal solidarity) and trust towards others (tolerance). In a similar vein, ongoing debates on the 'politics of memory' seem to suggest that while collective memory is an inseparable part of any culture, life in any true sense is impossible without some forgetfulness, without assuming that it is 'wisely to remember and wisely to forget' (Elon 1993a: 5) or that political reconciliation should be based on 'forgiving without forgetting' (Sa'adah 1992: 94). Although, as Irwin-Zarecka (1993: 350) notes, there is no guide-line of how 'to come to terms with a morally challenging past, nor how to balance remembering, forgetting and celebrating', it seems that there is no other way than a critical evaluation of the past. In a similar way Cohen and Arato (1992) argue for the importance of critically evaluated tradition and Abrams (1982) points to the role of history seen not only as a background to the present but as a part of a struggle to create a future out of the past, which involves a search for rules of remembering. Furthermore, Keane (1988) suggests that an active democratic memory recognizes that the development of fresh and stimulating perspectives on the present depends upon criticisms that break up habitual ways of thinking in part through types of criticism which remember what is in danger of being forgotten. All these studies seem to imply that collective memory should not be used to construct barriers between groups or to close boundaries of national, ethnic or any other identities. It should not be used to preserve distrust of others and distrust should not be allowed to become the dominant element determining the future of society. We can clearly see here connections between collective memory and trust: collective memory can only resist becoming a national, ethnic or other myth by standing aside from the unreasonable distrust of others and by allowing for a new cooperative future to be established on the basis of 'forgiving without forgetting'. In this way trust is not only a belief based on past experience, that is, a product of memory, but it is also a source of memory, guiding what we should remember or what should we forget from our past. The core of the issue of trust and memory is the question of how to avoid putting blame for our failures and insecurities on to others; how to avoid confusion of nostalgia with memory, and, last but not least, how to construct rules of remembering and forgetting in such a way that trust within society and towards others will be possible.

According to Sabel's (1992: 218) optimistic view, supported by his empirical observations, the line between mistrust and trust is much easier to cross than any theory suggests. He argues further that 'the extension of trust in any particular setting depends in part on the actors' reinterpreting their collective past, and especially their conflicts, in such way that trusting co-operation comes to seem a natural feature, at once accidental and ineluctable, of their common heritage' (1992: 218). Nevertheless, it is a difficult task since it requires societies to search for historical truth and resist the temptation of using it to glorify their nation. It is not, as we have argued above, simply an issue of truth. It is, rather, a case of negotiating a 'usable' past relevant to the present, and it means a past which is 'true for the society' and which can restore and secure internal and external trust relations. Bringing some symbols back in from the past to boost national confidence and political unity can in some situations be helpful, but in other cases it may only contribute, for example, to imperial aspirations of a nation or be irrelevant to present conditions. From what was said before it should be clear that the redefinition or search for rules of remembering or forgetting can only be achieved when groups share a common understanding of mutual dependence. Two groups, two cultures or two nations in conflict can establish the grounds for a common self-definition, and by this enlarge the realm of trusting behaviour, if their revision of their boundaries and conditions in which these boundaries were formed is based on shared reflective awareness of mutual vulnerability and dependence (Sabel 1992: 220–3).

The process of recalling and selecting from past experience is not so essential and not so difficult in stable and integrated societies, which are lucky enough to have established and preserved the cognitive stability and trust relations, that – in turn – contribute to the cultivation of such a vision of the past which reinforces and reproduces a cohesive society. However, for a less fortunate society, one in the process of transition and a search for its identity, the main task is to avoid the various dangers connected with the choice of a particular past in the situation of contradictory pressures for social integration, political gains or moral justice. While a stable and cohesive society can afford the healthy assumption that trust in trust pays off, the second type of society needs, before establishing new general definitions of valued traits, to overcome the fear of losing its old 'tool-kits' or its irrelevant general cultural repertoire from the past. It has to address the questions of its identity and its future. This entails the re-opening of taboos and requires the overcoming of many disappointments with the past and the present as well uncertainty about the future. Confusion, difficulty and anxiety underlying the process of negotiating the past were all visible, for example, in the three year-long process of putting together a treaty between Poland and its new neighbour, Lithuania. Since both countries were unable to agree upon an already classic formula, 'Forgive and ask for forgiveness', they got involved in a lengthy debate, which could not establish a common interpretation of the past – especially sensitive being the issue of the 1920 Polish capture of Vilnius, which provokes a strong resentment among Lithuanians but is glorified as a national victory by Poles (Burant and Zubel 1993). At the end, a common denominator was agreed upon and, consequently, the treaty avoids any reference to history, and no dates and no names of national heroes are mentioned. This inability to overcome unreflective nationalism was due mainly to many misconceptions carried from the past which have never been openly discussed (Milosz 1993).

The importance of the debate about ways of dealing with the past has been growing in recent years, with new generations asking new questions. Maybe, as Pomian notes, now is the time when 'an era of the past may serve as a screen on which new generations can project their contradictions, controversies, and conflicts in objective form' (quoted in Rousso 1991: 51). In addition, the decline of communism and a number of events (such as Kurt Waldheim's case, the fate of Bosnia, the opening of the Stasi files, Russia's identity crisis, the D-Day celebrations, or the Catholic

Church's attempts to confront its past) have triggered more than scholarly interest in the past. While historians have initiated debates over Vichy France, Nazi Germany and the civil war in Italy in the last years of the Second World War, governments have been forced to take a stand on many issues related to the past (as illustrated by a new German law making the denial of the Holocaust a criminal offence (*The European*, 20–26 May 1994: 2)). In this search for the past, we are told that postwar identities were false, that they were based on 'the erection of an unnatural and unsustainable frontier between past and present in European public memory' (Judt 1992: 84). Equally interesting is the process of searching for collective memory which is taking place within communities of black Americans. Many new books bring an Africanist perspective to North American history and culture and move African-American studies from the margins of discourse to its very centre. The moral potential of such a discourse, which brings together people with different, often painful, memories, is best illustrated by the new Australian legislation, named the 'Mabo judgment' after Eddy Mabo, a Murray Islander, the plaintiff in the case. Since this case illuminates new aspects of the relationship between trust and memory, I shall look at it in more detail.

In 1992 the High Court decided that Queensland's annexation of the Torres Strait in 1879 had not lawfully extinguished Eddie Mabo's customary ownership of the portion of Murray Island that had long been passed down through his family. The High Court judgments in the Mabo case rejected the view of Australian common law, that confirmed the doctrine of *terra nullius* on the issue of land tenure, and recognized a form of native title which reflects the entitlement of indigenous inhabitants to their traditional lands in accordance with their customs and laws. The powerful symbolism of this decision, reinforced by the Federal Government's legislation of land rights of indigenous people, comes from the perception of this verdict as being the 'binding basis for reconciliation between white and black in Australia' and as having 'the potential to work the miracle' (Paul Keating, the Prime Minister, quoted in Flood 1994: 15). While the practical outcome of the native title legislation is yet to affect people's lives, it seems that this new law opens up the new possibility of building a national consensus based not on a dominant group's rules and memory but on a common search for a mutually acceptable vision of the future shaped by an agreed vision of the past. Moreover, since the Mabo legislation is the result of skilful negotiations between interested parties, 'it created a precedent for how future decisions are to be negotiated' (Lafitte 1994: 20). Although the process of negotiating was far from the first principle of Habermas' 'discourse ethics', that communication be freed from domination, the Aborigines involved in discussions with the Cabinet managed to 'maintain a level of transparency' and overcome internal divisions (1994: 20). Consequently, new bases of trust emerged. Whereas in the past whites have trusted indigenous people in a similar way to that in which powerful people trust their subordinates to do the menial work, while leaving the position of power to them, this new approach provides opportunities to move away from 'morally indecent trust' to 'morally decent trust', in which we could entrust 'knowledge of each party's reasons for confident reliance on the other to continue the relationship' (Baier 1986: 259). Thus, while in the past whites have traditionally taken inequality to be non-discussable, now the range of people having the right to be 'us', to be partners in discussion of the positional power, is enlarged. The indigenous people are not only interested in receiving compensation, but they also want to be treated as equal moral subjects. This means that they want the authorities not only to act justly, but they also want to be able to trust authorities' motives behind the action. This approach stresses the importance of asking Baier's question of whether 'their trust in us is morally decent' rather than checking if 'we are acting justly'. The significance of this question is that it 'instantly raises the question: can we tell them everything we know and still keep their trust?' (Rorty 1994: 6). Moral progress for Baier is connected with the enlargement of groups' boundaries, with the movement from individual rights to collective rights, with the enlargement of categories of people who matter to us, rather than with the setting of criteria for right action. It means that boundaries between in-groups and out-groups have to be learned and learning them – that is, learning who to trust and who not to trust, rather than of the importance of principles in general – constitutes our education in the group morality. If partners are to entrust their respective reasons for mutual confidence in each other, their past needs to be a part of this relationship and they need to recognize the rights of their respective collectivities. How they are going to negotiate the past is another question; however, knowledge of the conditions of that reliance needs to be mutually accepted. In this way, the Mabo judgment can be seen as creating a common Australian memory since for the first time Australia has the opportunity to be 'a nation with moral foundation' (Rowse 1993: 20). For the first time Australia has the chance to think about setting up common rules of what should be remembered and what should be forgotten in the process of national reconciliation.

Equally pressing is the need for critical reconstructions of the collective memories of Eastern European societies. Leaving this task unattended could result in instability for more than this region alone. Eastern European countries are facing the danger that by 'adjusting it [memory] to suit new national borders' (Zarecka-Irwin 1993: 32), which means the

exclusion of minorities from their vision of the past and basing international relations on a particularistic understanding of their rights, they
are losing the opportunity to build more tolerant and trustworthy societies. Taking into account that this process of searching for a usable past
is extremely dangerous and that these countries have plenty of other
problems to contend with (an economic one being the most prominent),
is it really worth taking it on? Some writers propose leaving taboos in
place since 'ruthless honesty' about the Eastern European past can only
awake traditional motifs of resentment and self-pity, consequently causing more harm than good. This option, which is a specific interpretation
of Santayana's argument, concludes that 'the best way to avoid repeating
the past may be to forget about it' (Judt 1994: 4). We should not,
however, forget that Santayana also warns that not to learn from
the past may result in the repetition of the past mistakes. This leaves us
with a 'middle-way' position, a more common-sense approach which,
while not totally rejecting interest in the past, points out that too obses-
sive use of the past can be an obstacle to the effective functioning of a
country.

I would argue that although the process of 'coming to terms with
the past' is not harmless, nevertheless the specific situation of Eastern
European countries – namely, their need to construct a basis of national
identity – demands a re-opening and discussion of the past. We need only
to remember 'the historical deficit' of the post-war era and disastrous
results of the absence of any open public debate over such issues as
ethnicity, religion or race. The emergence of anti-Semitism in Poland, a
country with no more than 5,000 Jews among its 38 million population,
is the best illustration of what not opening but 'freezing' taboos could
lead to. Furthermore, Eastern European people, unlike the Western
Europeans, have lived for centuries in fear of their own extinction. For
them, as for all colonized societies, memory is especially important. And
while it is true that their own independence was often gained at the
expense of other ethnic groups and that they too often protected their
autonomy with the help of undemocratic means, they cannot now be
denied a chance to formulate the rules of normative order. Eastern
Europeans' search for their memory is the sole path to setting trust
relations within their societies and with their neighbours.

Moreover, it must be acknowledged that the emancipation brought by
the events of 1989 not only did not elevate the importance of memory,
but paradoxically, reinforced the significance of collective memory. For
example, Polish sociological research shows that only recently thousands
of Poles – first- and second-generation migrants to the so-called 'recovered territories' (which Poland acquired from Germany after 1945) –
have started questioning their rights and identities by asking who they

are? What are their connections with these localities? Are they from there or are they still from Vilnius, Lvov and so on? What are their rights to the land (Wejchert 1993)? Many factors contribute to this increasing insecurity and the emergence of feelings of instability, such as the increasing voices of native people (like 'Silesia for Silesians'), more open politics, which allows for the re-emergence of the manipulation of various beliefs, the decline of social provision and growing competition for jobs, services and so on. In other parts of Eastern Europe similar feelings of insecurity are additionally reinforced by worries about the future of existing borders. Kaliningrad and the Baltic republics, for example, are consumed by 'rumours' that 'an East Prussian government in exile has already been formed by right-wing German politicians' (Elon 1993b: 28). Consequently, distrust between various groups is growing. Attacks on Gypsies in Romania, anti-Semitism in Hungary and Poland and the increase in nostalgic nationalism, as illustrated by the bringing back in of old right-wing heroes such as Ion Antononescu in Romania or Miklosa Horthy in Hungary or Josef Pilsudcki in Poland, are all evidence that some segments of Eastern Europe are in danger of giving up any attempts of carrying out a critical revision of their mythological or nationalist histories.

Conversely, as Hobsbawm (1993) notes, the Israeli and Irish examples give us hope. Israel has recently been relatively successful in separating its history from myths, rituals and politics (Elon 1993a). Similarly, changes in Irish history aim at distancing it from national propaganda. Both these moves allow Hobsbawm to conclude that 'a new generation has grown up which can stand back from the passions of the great traumatic and formative movements of their countries' history' (1993: 64). There are already some very interesting indicators pointing out that debates over Eastern Europe's past are bringing positive results in terms of the construction of new trust relationships and building more solidaristic collectivities. Whether East Europeans manage or not to resist the temptation to replace history with myths and inventions and what kind of memory they are going to glorify will depend on many factors – for example, help to some degree from the West to overcome post-communist societies' feelings of low self-confidence and uncertainty. In what follows I will describe the Eastern European search for the rules of remembering and forgetting as an illustration of the connections between trust and memory.

In one of the scenes from the German film *Heimat*, a young hero, who came from a small village to study in Munich, says that he started feeling at home in that city only when, after his friend's death, he acquired 'his own' grave in a Munich cemetery. By perceiving his identification with the city through the memory of his friend's death, he points to the fact that a search for a place is mediated by memory. Since memory is context-dependent information, moving to new surroundings means an absence of clues which can prompt our memory; while staying in the same place means that 'the external environment itself takes over the job of ordering memory into sequence' (Fentress and Wickham 1992: 73). Thus, our cemeteries are evidence that we are part of the past of a certain place, the proof of our existence there or our duration in that place. The significance of 'cemetery' as a token of the past or an indicator of our rights to a place is particularly visible in unsettled cultures or societies under threat. In this type of uprooted society, the importance of private memory can often lead to the fetishization of tokens of the past, to the extent that the tokens replace, or at least displace, real memory. The ambiguity of relationships between real and token memory, official and private memory brings the issue of trust back into focus. The Polish situation is perhaps the best illustration of Eastern Europe's unique relationship between memory and trust.

As a child, I used to spend hours with my grandmother cleaning French pilots' graves in a small Polish city, which until 1945 belonged to Germany. My family, like the majority of people in our town, had settled there just after the Second World War and, like many Poles living in these 'regained Polish historical lands', from which more than 6 million Germans were expelled, we made a conscious effort to construct a home there. Although official propaganda tried to ease their insecurity by providing evidence of the 'Polishness' of the land, 'the Poles managed to make that past into their own' (Elon 1993b: 29), not because of the role of the official propaganda but mainly because of their individual attempts to construct a new memory. My grandmother felt that in this new city she did not have anything that was 'her own', not even 'her graves', and that by caring for the French soldiers' graves from the Second World War she could attach herself to a new locality. I believe that she was simply doing what many others do when not having the actual remains; they invent their own past in the new place. Her choice of the graves, however, was also a statement about the conditions on which she accepted the present. She didn't choose Soviet soldiers' graves, firstly because they were taken care of officially (for example, my primary school was responsible for several rows of them) and, secondly, because these graves, uplifted to the role of official monuments, were an expression of propaganda, which aimed at providing one kind of memory. Her distrust for this 'ready-made memory' also came from her memories of the property confiscated by the Soviet authorities and hard labour in the Soviet Union, where she had spent seven years as a deportee and prisoner. These memories were not only painful but also, more importantly, not officially acknowledged. She did not choose the German soldiers' graves, although they were not officially provided for, probably because she saw Germans, as the majority of Poles did, as aggressors, and, probably because – since their graves were located at an old Evangelical German cemetery – it would require her to overcome her rather narrow understanding of the meaning of being a devoted Catholic and a Pole. Her choice of French pilots' graves was determined mainly by the fact that she believed that somewhere in the West there was somebody taking care of the grave of her only son, who was killed by Germans while on a flying mission. Her positive experience of the British Red Cross while searching for her son and – at the same time – the hostility she encountered from the Polish authorities on account of being in contact with 'the West', only confirmed her anti-Soviet, anti-public attitudes and orientated her towards the Catholic Church.

This example illustrates the main problems of memory and trust encountered – to a greater or lesser extent – by East European countries since 1945. Firstly, it shows the separation between official and private memory and its consequences for trust. The official version claimed that Eastern Europe after the Second World War was not 'cut from its history', but on the contrary that it was 'saved' from its memory. However, the continuity of the richness of unofficial memories points out that for Eastern Europeans their pre-communist past remained important. Their history was not just 'another country' but

> a positive archipelago of vulnerable historical territories, to be preserved from attacks and distortions perpetrated by the occupants of a neighbouring island of memory, a dilemma made the more cruel because the enemy is almost always within: most of these dates refer to a moment at which one part of the community took advantage of the misfortunes of another to help itself to land, property or power (Judt 1992: 100).

Secondly, it points out that while in the West history was what people learned from history books, magazine articles and TV programmes, in Eastern Europe oral narratives were more important. Since 1945 officially written and taught Eastern European history was distorted or set aside according to political needs, people relied on various sources of transmission of unofficial collective memory, such as that of family and other informal circles. In addition there was also the Church's preaching and rituals, information from foreign radios, and later the second circle's publications, which provided additional information.

Thirdly, many Eastern Europeans, because of repatriation, the high level of industrialization and the speed of urbanization in the post-war era, found themselves in a new social, physical and political environment, which only increased their anxiety and limited their trust to close family or friendship groups. As Polish sociologists researching affiliations and emotional attachments have proved, Poles identified themselves only with their family groups and with the abstractly conceived idea of nation, while at the same time showing a total lack of trust in intermediate structures between these two levels (Nowak 1989). In other words, the dismissal of the official memories as mere propaganda, combined with a strong tendency to fetishize tokens of the past, resulted in a vacuum or gap between these two levels, which was filled with mutual distrust.

Fourthly, the stability of collective memory in a closed system, in which access to information and contacts with the outside world are limited, is higher than in a more open system, which allows for more confrontation with new ideas and facts, and thus a higher level of dynamism and education in collective memory. Although it is assumed that written, not oral, memories are frozen, paradoxically, the closeness of the Eastern European situation and later the opposition's attempts to consolidate the nation against the communist state resulted in a compromised and unrevised version of 'the only truth'.

The effects of this situation on the post-war generations is difficult to overestimate, especially if we also take into account the evolution of social, political and economic conditions and changes in official memory. On the one hand, many of the post-war generations of Eastern Europeans, especially East Germans, were confused and unable to choose among many, often incoherent, voices. They 'grew up deprived of any usable' past by which to measure or attach themselves (Judt 1994: 4). On the other hand, the lack of any critical evaluation of tradition by unofficial narratives, aiming rather to defend and to protect the national memory against the communist influence, led many to adopt unreflective nationalism. Thus, while the first group did not know whom to trust, the latter was based on distrust and demands for conformity.

It can be said that the communist regimes failed to create a new national identity, and that the events of 1989 can be seen as 'the rebirth of history' (to use the title of Misha Glenny's book). Whereas the communist past 'left a vacuum into which ethnic particularism, nationalism, nostalgia, xenophobia and ancient quarrels could flow' (Judt 1992: 100), the new conditions since 1989 have shown that nothing as simple as 'true history' can replace it. Although history textbooks began to be revised and the majority of streets were renamed, an indispensable part of creating a common usable memory, based on societal reconciliation and requiring a self-redefinition as a nation, in many cases was missing. Instead, many attempts to control collective memory have taken place. The examples from former Yugoslavia and Russia point out that the memory of the past has been used selectively to suit the construction of new national identities. Russians' search for their national identity, distinct from both the Soviet Union and the pre-revolutionary empire, seems to have resulted in a new consensus, tinged with nationalism and old values. In Poland liberal elites have been accused of restoring a communist-like control over the past in order to expose only the glorious events of the pre-1945 period, while labelling everything not good as 'legacies of communism', in the same way that all pre-1989 failures were presented as 'legacies of capitalism'. In former Yugoslavia, the revival led by Milosevic and re-legitimization of the bad memories of inter-ethnic conflicts and nationalist rhetoric have resulted in mass ethnic intolerance and a prolonged war.

If, as Ignatieff (1993) argues, the search for identity, for roots and for cohesion is our fate as human beings, does it follow that nationalism is only one answer to these aspirations? What are the alternatives to nationalism? It seems that there are at least three possibilities. Each of these three attempts to overcome shortcomings of nationalism proposes different means of constructing trust relations, but they will only be effective if they are put to use together to build new inter-group relations. The first one, relying on overcoming distrust between nations by building trans-regional or even supra-national alliances, points to the symbolic importance of diplomatic contacts. The second solution depends upon intellectual dialogue between nations, which aims at selection and critical evaluation of tradition and creation of trust by boosting tolerance and solidarity. The third solution is based on direct contacts of members of various nations, leading to overcoming distrust and establishing a mutual understanding of a common fate. These three mutually reinforcing solutions can be seen as addressing the issue of trust on international, national and local levels.

To continue with our Polish example, it could be claimed that while good relationships between Poles and Germans cannot develop without achieving some level of trust, this trust needs to be based on the established ground or mutual knowledge of what are the rules of remembering and forgetting, on clear information and mutual recognition of who, representing what, is to be trusted and who is expected to trust. In order to foster better relations between Poland and Germany there is a need to establish 'whose heritage should be celebrated and where may be symbols that carry profound implications for international policy' (Zarecka-Irwin 1993: 33). The role of diplomatic relations and the role of political leaders is extremely important, as Willy Brandt's break-through behaviour showed. On the occasion of the signing of the Polish-German treaty in Warsaw in 1970, federal Chancellor Willy Brandt said:

The flight from reality creates dangerous illusion. . . . A clear sense of history cannot tolerate demands that can never be fulfilled. . . . We must look towards the future and recognise morality as a political force. We must break the chain of wrongs. If we do this we shall be practising not the politics of resignation, but the politics of reason (quoted in Donhoff 1982: 134).

At the same time, during his visit to the former Jewish ghetto in Warsaw, Brandt, 'in the presence of his anti-Semitic hosts, fell upon his knees in front of the monument in remembrance of the murdered Jews' (Donhoff 1982: 15). The importance of both of Brandt's acts for both nations was enormous and for many it was the real beginning of a new relationship between Poland and Federal Germany.

Apart from satisfying a symbolic transformation of the images of the past, there is also a need for a dialogue, which could clarify how the past is used and how it fits the present political arena. Here, for example, the most important act in post-war Polish history was the 1965 letter of the Polish bishops to their German Catholic co-partners which not only offered forgiveness but asked for it as well. 'In spite of everything, in spite of this situation burdened almost hopelessly by the past, or rather just because of this situation , we cry out to you: let us try to forget' (quoted in Ash 1993: 299). The letter had been attacked by the communist regime, which tried to achieve societal legitimacy and support by playing on nationalistic feelings, mostly by manipulating the nation's anti-German sentiments. In such a climate it took courage to admit, as the bishops did, that Poland's western territories were not 'recovered territories' but, for the most part, had never been Polish in recent history. This message, so unpopular with official propaganda, did not have a big impact on public opinion, which had been taught by the authorities to believe that 'patriotism meant hatred of the Germans' (Ash 1993: 307). Nevertheless, the impact of German *Ostpolitik*, consciously aiming at the removal of the sense of a German threat, and the challenge of the bishops' message, both slowly facilitated a new way of thinking among independent Catholic and opposition circles, and this created the basis for a new type of discourse, which recognizes morality as a political force. In an 'open letter to all Germans who wish to work for German-Polish reconciliation', written in 1981, the Polish intellectual Jan Jozef Lipski, a man widely recognized as the spokesman of the Poles' moral conscience, observed that it would be 'favourable for a future reconciliation and friendship' if 'each should make the reckoning with their own guilt and rather with their own than with the other's (Ash 1993: 302). The symbolism of both the bishops' and Lipski's letters did not achieve very much because in pre-1989 Poland there were not the conditions for an open discussion of Polish-German relations. Only after 1989, when the real possibility for contacts and exchange on the local level emerged, local education of memory and, when required, local negotiations of the content of collective memory could take place. The best example of this third type of effort to create a new trust between people carrying different memories is the East Prussian local organization named *Borussia*.

*Borussia* is an association established in 1990 by young humanists from Olsztyn, a city in north-east Poland (former Allenstein). Its name comes from the old Latin, pre-national and trans-national description of the region located between the lower Vistula and the Nemunas rivers. This name expresses, the founders of the association claim, the renunciation of any exclusive rights to this region. It recalls East Prussia before the spirit of nationalism began to poison all international relations. In this period

> what comes first is not loyalty to one's liege-lord, as it does in the West, but one's ties to the land. The rules kept changing; first there were the Teutonic Knights; then the Poles, Swedes, Danes, Russians and Prussians; they were of secondary importance; what mattered was to cling to the land, to belong to that landscape (Donhoff 1982: 137).

*Borussia* describes the region as a part of Europe, and pronounces the recognition of humanistic, universal values and memories of all groups as its main goal. Their platform is based on their vision of East Prussia's future as a part of 'an harmonious and free Europe of nations' (Rexheuser 1993: 161). The association brings together people from Lithuania, Ukraine, Germany, Poland and Belarus. They cooperate in an attempt to create a new identity for the region; an identity which would overcome both the German vision of East Prussia as the 'cultural or spiritual community' and the Polish one as 'the victim of Germanization'. *Borussia*'s open debates (such as at the 1991 conference in Olsztyn, where more than one-third of the participants came from Germany), are designed more to enlarge the scope of collective memory (for example, by giving a voice to all groups – those as new in the region as Russians from Kaliningrad or those as old as Jews). In addition, these debates increase the understanding of how the emergence of nationalism has influenced the past of all the regional groups rather than searching for a common interpretation or a common denominator.

It is interesting to note that all the most important fathers of Western European unification – Schumann, Mannet and de Gasperi – were also people from borderlands. The importance for the wider community of dialogues which emanate from culturally and ethnically mixed regions is endorsed by the first issue of a journal published by the association, which opens with a joint article by a Pole and a German (R. Polsakiewicz and Christian Moser), entitled 'Idea as a political factor: Kant's project "Towards eternal peace" – between utopia and reality'. Other actions initiated by *Borussia* – for example, bringing together youth peace groups from Germany and Poland to clean the graves of German soldiers from the First World War in a small village in East Prussia (which was an occasion for Germans to overcome their feelings of guilt and fear that this type of task could only be seen as glorification of German militarism and for all of them to talk about their past and reflect on their common history) – teach how 'to avoid conflicts without avoiding the past' or how to trust one another without demanding a total censorship of history. Although the region's history cannot be changed, and the cemetery remains a part of its landscape, it is now a monument against war; reproach coming from the '183 soldiers killed and from the Polish and German youth who have worked on the restoration of the cemetery'. Although what is an important event of the past is to some degree designated by forces and factors external to local societies – that is, by national or even international communities – a local community still has some degree of freedom of decision making or choice of what is worth remembering. The concept of collective memory as a reflective exchange between external and local visions of events closely relates to Stanislaw Ossowski's (1962) concept of a private homeland, which is based on the assumption that we are able to reflect on our memory. A community of reflexive selves is, by definition, both prudent and other-regarding, since 'I can imagine a trusting world and imagine others imagining the same' (Sabel 1992: 223). If it is true that the more isolated and independent the group, the higher will be the likelihood that its memory will be constructed in opposition to the outside world (Fentress and Wickham 1992), then it follows that growing interdependence and increased understanding of mutual dependency on a global scale reinforces Sabel's optimistic conclusion that we now have more reason to trust one another.

To conclude, an analytical distinction between trust and memory proves not only to have theoretical implications but also to be of practical importance since it paves the way for increased inter-group understanding and opens up new ways in which various groups can deliberately deal with their past. The most important factors allowing the group to interpret its past in a more 'trustworthy' manner towards others is an openness to an external world, which provides the group with the material for conscious reflection, and conditions for discourse as well as enabling the exchange of the group's experience of its surroundings. Memory as a practice of overcoming uncertainty by the continuous connections between the past and the present enables us to perceive our social world as coherent and legible. Habit, reputation and memory are all means of preserving the past exprience in order to construct a more predictable, reliable and legible present. They are all different but complementary strategies designed to help us to acquire a general sense of trust towards the social world.

# 5
# Trust as Passion

## Trust and family

It is an everyday and valued conception in our society that the
family is the primordial source and location of trust. The
expression, 'if you cannot trust your family, then whom can
you trust?' has a large value and ideological appeal for us.

Barber 1983: 26

Barber's remark points out something essential about the nature of
family relations. It also reflects an assumption about an automatic relationship between the family and trust. However, this and many other
sociological truisms about family life are now under close scrutiny. Many
changes, both external and internal to the family, are forcing all of us to
inspect the 'roots of trust' within the family. The process of achieving
mutual awareness of new bases of trust in family relations is a painful
one and some forms of trust relations are unable to survive it.

Attempts to reflect on trust relations in the family are not evidence of
a denial of the importance of trust. They should be seen, rather, as a
necessary revision of the family's emotional base so it can meet the new
needs and aspirations of its members. The modern family, which is faced
with growing expectations as to the quality of mutual relations, to
the nature of trust relations and with the growing demand for equal
opportunities and options for men and women in all aspects of everyday
life, is open to new requests and to many anxieties. How can the modern
family meet these demands and overcome anxieties? What kind of processes or trends can be seen as helpful in creating a new trust relationship
in the family; which ones can be described as only constructing obstacles
to it?

There are many processes affecting family life which from the point of view of trust relationships could be influential. Such processes include the growing reliance of the family on external institutions, changes in the roles of women and men in the family, changes in forms of family life, and the increased quantity of disclosed information about hidden or dark aspects of family life. It seems, however, that all the main aspects of change are well represented by referring to the broader process of *decentring* forms of family life. Intended and unintended consequences of this process of decentring on trust relations within the family will be the main topic in this chapter.

The process of decentring in patterns of family life describes a shift from known traditional forms of family life (Wolfe 1991). When traditional models of family life no longer seem adequate and valid and when there is an absence of well-defined new patterns of behaviour, which can determine what to expect from partners, people have to define for themselves the rules by which they structure their lives. Consequently, modern society is involved in a search for a new basis upon which a more just and perhaps more emotionally satisfying family can be created (Wolfe 1991: 462–5). The main consequence of this is a kind of institutional and emotional ambivalence. If today's society is characterized by the centrality of ambivalence, ambivalence about contemporary family conditions is probably the most distressing one. This feature of modern society is grounded in the tensions resulting from the growing process of individualization and commitment to conventional institutions. The family is seen both as an obsolete institution and as the main orientation and identification model for the individual. The ambivalence about today's family situation is best illustrated by the difficulty we face whenever we try to arrive at a common definition of family (a lack of consensus on the definition of the family during the UN conference on population in Cairo in 1994 best illustrates this problem). The broadest definition proposed by Giddens seems to be the most suitable for our purpose: a family is 'a group of individuals related to one another by blood ties, marriage or adoption, who form an economic unit, the adult members of which are responsible for the upbringing of children' (Giddens 1989: 740). In modern societies the main form of family is the nuclear family; however, there is no longer only one type of family. A study by the American Census Bureau has found that in 1991 50.8 per cent of children live in families consisting of themselves and married biological parents, in comparison to 57 per cent in 1980 and 66 per cent in 1970 (*The Economist*, 3 September 1994: 32).

Dual thinking about today's family conditions can also be attributed to our contradictory emotions and expectations towards family life. On the one hand, the majority of people in Europe as well in America declare that the family is the central focus of their life. In 1990 Western European studies showed that for more than eight out of ten respondents family is very important, while 78 per cent declare that marriage is not an outdated institution (Ashford and Timms 1992: 49–51). In a similar vein, the family is seen by three out of four Americans as 'a group of people who love and care for each other' (Stacey 1993: 270). On the other hand, 60 per cent of the US national sample answered negatively the proposition that 'most couples getting married today expect to remain married for the rest of their lives' (Bellah et al. 1985: 90). In Western Europe only 16 per cent of those asked disapproved of divorce (Ashford and Timms 1992: 62). Maintaining traditional attitudes and opinions also goes hand in hand with a growing acceptance of different modes of cohabitation and various family patterns (Ester et al. 1993: 98–105). Thus family life has not lost its importance but the conventional nature of family and commitment to this conventional form have been declining.

Another ambivalence is grounded in the contradictory perceptions of family life. On the one hand, the majority of those surveyed in a Yale University study gave negative ratings to the quality of American family life, while, on the other hand, 71 per cent of them declared themselves 'at least very satisfied' with their own family lives (Stacey 1993: 270). The same results can be seen in West European research, where the highest degree of satisfaction is to be found in relations to family life and where on average almost 80 per cent of respondents have complete trust in their families, while at the same time they worry about the shape of the family. In 1990 87 per cent (in comparison with 83 per cent in 1981) would like to see more emphasis placed on family life (Ashford and Timms 1992: 13, 67).

What we are witnessing here are growing tensions between individuals' preoccupation and satisfaction with their families and their fear of more general family crisis. While this fear is to some degree stimulated by frequent manipulation for political reasons of public nostalgia for 'traditional family values', it also has some ground in people's perception of the reality of family life and their difficulties in coping with contradictory emotions. Since ambivalence can be a difficult experience (it can lead to uncertainty and indecision regarding appropriate action) and since culture and society, while being the main source of ambivalence, provide fewer and less effective means of dealing with it, people are under pressure to search for their own personal solution. This leads to the growing importance of individually negotiated arrangements between partners and between members of the family – in other words, to the increased reliance on less institutionalized forms or codes of behaviour. To be sure, these new solutions based on negotiation and consensus are even more fragile and difficult to maintain than old ones. In the modern family and modern marriage, or more generally intimate companionship, there is more awareness of risk along with the confidence that it is a good risk. Because there is knowledge of the risk involved and some realization of why we take the risk of committing ourselves, the modern family requires more and depends more on mutual trust. If so, how does the modern family ensure trust relations? The significance of trust in family life is normally considered in connection with parent–children relations and in connection with the relationship between partners. The first type of relations are seen as the source of basic trust and, consequently, ontological security, while the second is seen as the most important basis of intimacy, which ensures emotional and moral development.

It seems that there is no doubt among social scientists that the family is one of the main groups securing the individual's self-identity. At the heart of lasting ego-identity is basic trust, which creates a sense of ontological security that will carry the individual through periods of change and crisis. The role of the family in the development of trusting and trustworthy personalities has recently been reconstructed by Giddens (1990 and 1991), Hardin (1993) and Baier (1986). This argument connects the assumption of D.W. Winnicott and Erik Erikson about the importance of the early childhood experience of basic trust with that about the formation of an inner sense of trustworthiness, which subseqently provides the basis of a stable self-identity. Infant trust, which 'normally does not need to be won but is there unless and until it is destroyed' (Baier 1986: 242) is blind and uncritical, and points to the relative power of parents on whom a young child is totally dependent. The infant learns to rely upon the consistency and attention of its providers and this constitutes the basis of its capacity to be trusting and the elaboration of self-identity. Infants' translation into competent adults proceeds via learning, and learning presupposes trust in the reliability of knowledge sources – that is, parents. 'Trust and co-operation are manifest of the quest for standing as a competent member in the relevant context. In the acquisition of language and in the acquisition of knowledge, the child reveals an inherent sociability. That sociability is essential; verbally mediated learning would be impossible in its absence' (Barnes 1988: 88–9). Early trust, as a by-product of the family's activities and attitudes, is a 'protective cocoon' that screens out many potential dangers individuals could face in adult life. Infant trust, rewarded and stimulated by the experience of trustworthiness in the family, encourages the development of a more optimistic trusting approach to the world and others. It can be seen, argues Giddens, 'as a sort of *emotional inculcation* against existential anxieties – a protection against future threats and dangers which allows the individual to sustain hope and courage in the face of whatever debilitating circumstance she or he might later confront' (1991:

39). The formation of the basic structures of trust in the personality allows us to take full advantage of emerging opportunities, which brings – on all accounts – much more beneficial outcomes than results of avoiding risk actions, which are characteristic of people who learned distrust (Hardin 1993). Believing that others are trustworthy, particularly when further reinforced by new experience, ensures a feeling of security and stability of self-identity. All of these together create cruel divisions; between those lucky enough to be optimistically trusting, whose families enable them to learn to trust, and two disadvantaged groups consisting of 'those whose early years are spent in fractured conditions of caprice and neglect ... and those, perhaps especially women, who have suffered substantial abuse in their early years from the very persons who might have provided the first experience of trustworthiness' (Hardin 1993: 514).

Although the number of disclosed incidences of child abuse has never been so high, it is mainly due to the growing public awareness of the seriousness of this type of crime. Today parents realize more than ever their responsibilities to children. Modern parenthood is a matter of free choice and parental roles in general have changed since child-rearing has become less a process of disciplinary supervision and more a question of personal attention to the emotional and relational aspects of a child's development. A recent Australian study discovered that 87 per cent of respondents agree that a 'child's sense of self-esteem and self-worth needed to be protected at all costs'; 9 per cent disagree (*The Australian*, 7 September 1994: 3). In this new and more democratic family parents need to earn children's respect and children are treated as individuals with their own rights; in 1990 only 42 per cent surveyed people from the Netherlands, 45 per cent from Norway and 47 per cent from Denmark declared that a child should love and respect their parents irrespective of their behaviour (Ester et al. 1993: 111). At the same time, however, the majority of the people interviewed expressed a more traditional view of parenthood by endorsing the statement that parents must always do their best for their children; 75 per cent of Americans, 79 per cent of Italians, 78 per cent of Spaniards agree with this statement (1993: 111). Despite the individualizing trends of today's culture, which makes all of us more aware of our own needs, modern parents still accept limits to their pursuit of happiness brought by the presence and needs of the children. None the less, the quantity of anxiety and stress, especially felt by women in relation to their children, is continuously growing. Many factors can be seen to be contributing to this.

Firstly, more than ever before parents are now surrounded by advisers, experts, new demands and new professional knowledge about what to do in order to facilitate the personal development of their children. These constant constraints on parents' confidence (as well as on their time and resources) make them insecure and stressed, but more ambitious parents. 'In competing with the professionals on different aspects of children's affairs, parents are realizing that they lose control over their children and confidence in their capacity to take care of them' (Bjornberg 1992: 9). Secondly, with the growing divorce rate, with the separation of parenthood from marriage, with the fragmentation and disintegration of the traditional family and with a decline in the number of births, the importance of the child is rising, which subsequently puts some constraints on the individualization process. 'The child is the source of the last *remaining, irrevocable, unexchangeable primary relationship*. . . . Everything that is desired, but not realizable in the relationship, is directed to the child. With the increasing fragility of the relationships between sexes the child acquires a monopoly on practical companionship' (Beck 1992: 118). The process of individualization, which removes the traditional dictates of gender roles and the family, conversely brings a longing for the child seen as *the final alternative to loneliness* (1992: 118). However, the same trends can also undermine the centrality of the child in the family. Remarriages in general and the increasingly complex stepfamilies (whose problems will be discussed further) often put children in ambiguous positions and force partners to negotiate the priority of the needs of various members of the new unit (Beer 1992). This paradoxical situation of an excessive affection for children along with the realization of the enormous growth in the needs and the demands related to the development of a child (Beck-Gernsheim 1992) and the need to balance the expectations of adults and children, result in confusion, a lack of self-confidence and anxiety on the part of many parents. Does it consequently mean that today's parents are not always capable of providing a child with the basis for a stable self-identity because their own inner sense of security is not well formed? I do not think so.

Firstly, the family is only one of many contemporary institutions to pass confusing and mixed messages to children. Although the modern family sends many confusing messages (about competing and not competing, about making money and not making money, about assertiveness and subordination), children are getting equally confusing information from schools and the mass media as well. Secondly, the modern family teaches children how to live with ambivalence, which is one of the main characteristics not only of today's family but also of today's world. Thirdly, basic trust, developed through the loving attentions of parents to their infants, does not presume an absence of parental anxiety. Modern parents, regardless of the complexity and ambivalence of their situations, are able to provide the basis of trust and love because they care about their children's happiness, and this is the foundation of the child's trust in the parents. When children grow and become conscious of trusting parents, they have good reason to believe that their parents will continue to care for them because they know that parents care about the same good as they do; that is, their happiness. 'They will be common goods, so that for the trusted to harm them would be self-harm as well as harm to the child. . . . She can have plenty of evidence that, for reasons such as pride, desire to perpetuate their name, or whatever, they do care as she herself does about her health, her success, and her ties with them' (Baier 1986: 243).

Trust is the necessary condition for the elaboration of self-identity not only because it provides security, stability and safety, but also because it provides freedom for the child's self-exploration, which often expresses itself in anger, demands or conflicts. A prominent part in the search for the self undertaken by children and teenagers is confrontation with their caretakers. The family is a supportive and empathic environment where even conflict can be a catalyst for growing. Parents are solely people, whom children trust enough to be able – without losing their love and their trust – to oppose them in order to check their own limits, abilities and boundaries of the self. Tensions in mother–daughter relationships as well as conflicts between fathers and sons are well described in literature. An interesting account of mother–daughter relationships can be found in Erica Jong's personal story *Fear of Fifty* (1994). She admits that while she emancipated herself to 'cut free' from her mother with her first published book, it was her mother's trust in her that allowed her to achieve this. 'I wrote a manifesto against my mother. And it was she herself who had given me the courage to do this' (Jong 1994: 377). Subsequently, she realizes that

> there is something in the beating of daughters against maternal limitations that pushes us to find out who we are. I see my own daughter demolishing me, deconstructing me. She has to do this to get free of me. . . . She has to do these things to establish her identity in opposition to mine. This is the way she grows (Jong 1994: 366).

For the development of an individual's creative personality there is a need not only for the security of basic trust but also for the freedom provided by unconditional parental trust. Jong is aware that parental trust, seen as 'a building site' or 'a ground' from which children 'push off' to establish themselves, is the precondition for their freedom. Seen from this perspective, the development of an individual personality is a heroic achievement, which is possible because of the formation of the basic structure of trust built upon the mutuality of responses between members of the family. Trust, ontological security and attempts at separation and achievement of individual self-identity are important elements of the adult personality. The modern family plays a significant role as a source of trust not only in early childhood.

In the pre-modern world, where personal relationships were based on externally reinforced obligations, kinship played an important role in ensuring trust between people. The reliance on external support to keep close relations together meant that trust was taken for granted, that there was no need for trust to be won since it was tied to the position. This type of trust between a married couple was based on the marriage contract, which used to be 'a bill of rights, which essentially formalised the "separate but unequal" nature of the tie' (Giddens 1992: 192). Thus, trust was not only geared to established positions but was also morally indecent because the inequality of power relations between partners was often behind men's confident reliance on women. According to Baier (1986: 248–50), morally indecent trust occurs when either party relies on qualities in the other which would be weakened by the knowledge that the other relies on them. It is the kind of trust which 'men typically have in women; trust that they will uncomplainingly do the dirty work, raise the children to be trustworthy citizens while changing their nappies, and leave "any position of superiority in any realm" to men' (Rorty 1994: 6). When the inequality of power between men and women was a non-discussable topic, the quality of trust in the family was also not a suitable subject for scrutiny since it meant 'to take a very risky bet on the justice, if not the "civilization", of the system of trust one inhabits' (Baier 1986: 260).

Whereas in the past kinship obligation provided stable conditions of trust within which daily life was organized, today's family relationships demand a new form of trust and, moreover, trust in the family or in kinship can no longer be taken for granted. Yet both the family and kinship are still a framework for negotiation and bargaining for trust. The family still remains a well-suited institution for the building of trust relationships because it can offer the nurturing atmosphere of caring which allows for the partners' mutual disclosure, which is a necessary condition of trust. The family is a place where our full personalities are known, where our real identities are not only established but, if accepted, translated into reputational terms (Finch and Mason 1992). Because of the distinctive characteristic of family, especially family of origin (social relationships that are not chosen and of a lifelong permanency), for most people their image within their kin groups matters. If we want to be trusted, to be a holder of a 'good reputation' within our family, we need to behave properly to other members of the family not only according to our criteria but according to the family's values and opinions. Reputations within families are results of past experience and actions. They also are components of what we can expect in the future from our kin.

The usefulness of being seen as trustworthy within kin groups is not limited, however, to providing the basis on which exchanges of assistance can be negotiated; they are also 'treated as valuable in their own right – symbols of personal identity which are worth fostering (Finch and Mason 1992: 160). We can, of course, withdraw totally from contacts with family and develop other elements of our identities, which are not tied to the family. Nevertheless, for many, especially women or the elderly – the family is the most important source of identity and of material support and assistance (Moore 1990; Duck 1990). Results of cross-national comparision have proved that cooperative family and kinship relationships are still prevalent in all social groups in modern societies and that close kin and friends are still seen as the main source of instrumental and emotional support (Hollinger and Haller 1990). Even after divorce many couples and their parents sustain kinships ties with their former spouses and their relatives, and for working women kinship resources are still of enormous value (Stacey 1993: 255).

None the less, the growing individualism within the family and the rejection of socially grounded obligations make family life increasingly subject to complex and difficult negotiations, through which it tries to meet new expectations and build a new type of trust. Personal ties in this new type of intimate relationship are based on voluntary commitments and intensified intimacy. This new partnership involves neither submission nor domination: 'the partners try to listen to each other, while each remains a separate person, conscious that intimacy can be a cause of conflicts, or become too close and stifling, or too defensive' (Zeldin 1994: 326). It evolves in the direction of pure relationships or friendship, as illustrated by the findings of a 1980 American enquiry, which discovered that 60 per cent of married men and 50 per cent of married women described their spouses as a very close friend, or of a pure relationship (1994). The pure relationship is described as a situation where 'a social relation is entered into for its own sake, for what can be derived by each person from a sustained association with another; and which is continued only in so far as it is thought by both parties to deliver enough satisfactions for each individual to stay within it' (Giddens 1992: 58). This type of relation rests on commitment, which is based on the acceptance of the risk and the range of rewards available within the relationship, and is open to negotiations through honest discussions about the nature of the relationship. Pure relationships depend on mutual trust between partners, which needs to be constructed through mutual disclosure, closely connected to the achievement of intimacy. 'What matters in the building of trust in the pure relationship is that each person should know the other's personality, and be able to rely on regularly eliciting certain sorts of desired responses from the other' (Giddens 1991: 96). In pure relationships based on voluntary commitment and intimacy, trust plays an important function of ensuring feelings of stability and security. However, pure relationships can be psychologically very damaging and, moreover, they are more vulnerable than any other types of relationships. This vulnerability is expanded by tensions between the family's need to meet expectations as to the quality of mutual relations, especially as to their being emotionally gratifying, and the demands imposed on the family to be rational agents in an over-rationalized world.

The increased importance attached to expectations of decent trust, which is 'the confident expectation of benign intentions in another free agent' (Dunn 1988: 74), has been proved in many studies of the simul-taneously occurring consequences of the process of individualization. In one such study, respondents from nine West European countries rated the following factors in contributing to a successful marriage as being 'very important': faithfulness (82 per cent), interpersonal trust (81 per cent) and understanding (77 per cent) (Ashford and Timms 1993: 52–3). Characteristically, compared with trust and intimacy factors, material conditions (such as housing that is good and independent from that of in-laws) were less often mentioned as bases for a successful marriage. The rise of a general outlook on love which advocates full, open and honest communication among self-actualized, independent individuals and the mutual sharing of feelings is indicative of the 'therapeutic' mode of thinking about love (Bellah et al. 1985).

To some degree the spread of therapeutic attitudes and language is connected with the emergence of the pure relationship, which – in turn – is closely related to the rise of therapy since 'the more the pure relation-ships become dominant, the more crucial becomes an in-depth under-standing, which allows one to feel "all right" with oneself' (Giddens 1991: 186). The growing importance of intimacy and, connected with it, therapeutic work, however, is double-edged. Firstly, the intensification of intimacy, which is accompanied by the 'therapeutic' mode of thinking about love, by postulating the mutual sharing of feelings rather than enduring commitment resting on binding obligation, replaces the ideal of love with the concept of communication and introduces confusion and ambivalence about obligations (Bellah et al. 1985: 101–3). The continu-ous verbalization of emotions, which is seen as the path to reaching intimacy in the face of the erosion of traditions and binding norms, does not restore bonds other than those based on free choice. 'No binding obligations nor wider social understanding justify a relationship. And should it no longer meet their needs, it must end' (Bellah et al. 1985: 107).

Secondly, the much desired intimacy, seen as the basis of a new quality of trust in the pure relationship, contributes to a new confusion of intimacy and privacy. On the one hand, modern couples experience freedom from the institutionalized aspects of marriage, while, on the other hand, new constraints appear in their place – for example, the idea of complete frankness in expressing one's feelings, as well as the overstressed importance of continuous verbal communications. The tyranny of intimacy (Sennett 1974) characterizes the way in which many couples attempt to live together, especially those in upwardly mobile milieus. The acceptance of the family as the main identity and solidarity group as well as the intensified private life may lead to a limitation in the quality of family life. The basis of this self-limiting characteristic of families, which perceive themselves as a whole world, is 'the existence, or the belief in the existence of long-term trust. For families to believe they are all-important there has to be the conviction that no betrayal and breakup will occur over the long term' (Sennett 1973: 54). In the bounded, small, nuclear family with its enforced intimacy, the intensity of relations feeds a demand for order, coherence, harmony and trust. Because this enforced trust presupposes both equality of power and aspirations, which is alien to most families' experience, it can lead to the suppression of diversity, the avoidance of conflicts and tensions, which together freeze the development and maturing of personalities. Yet, only well-differentiated adults may experience passionate intimacy (Rubin 1983). Looking at American couples, who through their quest for openness, honesty and total intimacy, lose their passions, Rubin argues that these 'intimate strangers' substituted maturity and autonomy for childhood experiences. The tyranny of intimacy, with its implicit prohibition on maintaining privacy and personal secrets, is closely related to a lack of differentiation of the spouses from each other, reducing, by the same token, opportunity for autonomy, which is an essential condition of building trust relations based on self-actualization.

Thirdly, the intensification of intimacy can also result in ambivalence about the private realm and public arena. Today, on the one hand, it becomes more difficult to discern just what to assign to the private domain and what to the public; for example, reproductive rights are fought for in the public realm. On the other hand, there is growing evidence of public withdrawal from the public realm. Consequently, the family is 'the core of the private sphere, whose aim is not to link individuals to the public world but to avoid it as far as possible' (Bellah et al. 1985: 112). The intensification of private life leads to a diminution of the quality of public life (Sennett 1973) since it assumes total openness and warmth in private life as a counterpoint to the continuous process of control and coldness in public life (Welter-Enderlin 1993).

All these contradictory trends and the unsettling conditions of the modern world make families' attempts to balance the desires and aspirations of their members a uniquely difficult task. The removal of many salient assumptions about relationships between family members, the erosion of traditions and externally supported roles and obligations and the acceptance of new members to the family have created a new situation, which demands more clearly defined obligations and responsibilities as well as a clearly defined basis of trust. This is a paradoxical request since, as I have just argued, the transformation of intimacy has resulted in confusions about obligation. In some way, the new awareness of the importance of sharing and communication, as the main characteristic of the pure relationship, has become as much a burden as a means of self-actualization. Where once it helped the family to escape from its unsatisfactory form, now it introduces ambivalence, insecurity and distress, which often fuels nostalgia for the 'traditional' family. This new trend, for instance, may account for the appeal of fundamentalist religions and the return of some elements of patriarchal ideology.

Stacey's (1993) ethnographic survey of American families experiencing unsettling economic and social conditions during the 1980s shows how working women found ways to re-organize and diversify their families. It demonstrates the demise of the dominant type of family, and documents how post-modern conditions, which fuelled 'cravings for security and spirituality' and the retreat from rationalism and secularism (which resulted in a 'resurgence of fundamentalist religious revivalism'), contributed to the emergence of varieties of new forms of family (1993: 260).

Stacey's case-studies illustrate how women are grappling with the contradictory character of their post-modern family options. Although freed from the restrictions and protections of the modern family, they often experience difficult choices. One such woman, Pamela, sympathetic to feminist and union movements, after an emotional family and economic crisis, decided to resume her unsatisfactory marriage by having a fundamentalist wedding. Pamela's conversion to patriarchal Christianity, seen by her friends as a violation of her emotional and political integrity, was her attempt to find a shelter, which would help her to stay in the marriage and which could protect her from her too high expectations for total honesty and openness that she realized could not be met. The main attraction of the Christian marriage rested on the fact that, although it did not change her husband's inability to be open and to communicate (which was Pamela's main disappointment), it did, however, provide her with the security of the 'absolute commitment' which was comparable with the value of emotional intimacy. 'I think that absolute commitment, that rock-bottom commitment, that's so important; otherwise everything is so contingent. . . . He is more committed, and he's more trusting,' says Pamela (1993: 82).

This example illustrates that the transformation of women's consciousness, which once helped women to flee from their marriages now often demands from them a disciplining of those impulses in order to overcome marriage breakdown and family crisis. 'Whereas once it helped them to reform or leave unsatisfactory relationships, now it can intensify the pain and difficulty of the compromises many feel they must make to sustain intimacy and to cope with family crisis under postindustrial circumstances' (Stacey 1993: 263).

Pamela's creative use of patriarchal ideology to serve her family's purposes is also indicative of another characteristic mark of today's intimate relationship; that is, its self-reflexivity. The growing awareness of the need to construct and negotiate decent trust, which could provide a good ground for emotionally gratifying relations, necessarily incorporates an element of reflexivity. Trust as a passion is not strategic and rational but, because it is tangled and often threatened by ordinary life, we sometimes suddenly become aware of its existence or its absence. The painful process by which such awareness actually comes about can be illustrated by two extreme examples of family situations in which the process of negotiating and defining obligations exposes the 'roots of trust'. In what follows I shall look at step-families, which are the best example of a new demand for trust, and at the extreme problem connected with the issue of custody, which sheds light on the dual function of trust.

The step-family is a type of family with unique relationships worked out by its members with little cultural guidance. It is becoming increasingly common due to higher divorce rates and higher re-marriage rates among divorcees. Up to 10 per cent of all Australian families are step-families with dependent children (*The Australian*, 9 March 1994: 31). Step-families, as a recent study shows, break down a lot faster in the first two years than other types of families. But if they last the six years, they tend to be more stable than first-time families. It means that initially there is a very high level of conflict between partners in step-families, resulting from their unrealized, often unrealistic expectations and difficulties involved in negotiating new obligations and duties. 'New couples often argue over the management of their children and this is the one area they cannot talk rationally about' (ibid.). It usually takes about five years for the step-family to settle down, stabilize and established patterns of functioning. The lives of step-families are far more complicated than those of nuclear families in many ways. From the point of view of trust relations, ambiguity in norms about relationship is the most important differentiating factor. Not only are the legal, normative and emotional responsibilities of the step-parents to the step-children not well defined, but the relationships between siblings and step-siblings also lack clear definition.

The children's position within a newly created step-family is often very ambiguous and complicated especially by the arrival of children born to the new couple. Children need to negotiate not only their own ranking within their new family group but they often face the same problem while visiting new families of their non-custodial parents. Many elements of this complex process are simply impossible to predict and control. It often leaves children on their own. Even in situations where they do not question parental love and parental trustworthiness, they realize that, although not excluded, they are not necessarily at the core of their parents' happiness. So, although some form of trust may survive, this newly achieved awareness may shape more reflective and cautious attitudes in general.

Children are often caught between two families and are expected to be able to preserve and respect the rules of both; in addition, they may carry a burden of distrust between their biological parents. It is estimated that about half of remarried spouses have 'strained, openly hostile, or nearly impossible' relations with former spouses (Beer 1992: 34). When an emotional divorce is incomplete, a child's loyalty is sought by both parents, resulting in stress in the children, since they lose no matter which side they choose, and if they decide not to choose they risk alienating both parents. Since children in step-families have a relatively greater power (and desire) to disintegrate marriages than in conventional families, they are often thus elevated to quasi-adult status. It produces frustration and fear because they feel that they fail parental trust since they cannot make everybody happy. However, it is not only the role of the child in step-families which is limited and full of tensions. The roles of adults are also not so broad as in nuclear families, where parents have more control over the family.

The most important issue in the step-family requiring negotiation is the problem of the relative priority of the relationship of the step-parents as a couple and the step-family as a whole compared with the priority of needs of its individual members. Step-families are in most cases a result of the remarriage of people who have experienced distrust and disillusionment in their previous marriage. They start with a new couple's task of re-establishing trust and becoming friends (Keshet 1988). In order to function successfully, couples in step-families, like partners in nuclear families, have to put their relationship above that of the previously established biological relationship between parents and children. The painful difficulties that are characteristic of step-families are illustrated by William Beer (1992) by means of many interesting case-studies. Problems experienced by Randy and Linda, for instance, whose family consists of them and their children from both their previous marriages, are typical. They are a relatively happily organized family;

however, they do not know what to do about Randy's son Alex, who is emotionally disturbed and neglected by his mother, his custodial parent. Although Randy initiated the court procedure to protect Alex, he decided not to accept custody of Alex because of the potential disturbance for his new family, which could cause more difficulties and problems and affect many people. Randy explains his motives in the following way:

> Well, this was one of the toughest decisions in my life. I still have a lot of guilt. I thought that whatever the good it might do for Alex, it would ruin a lot of other lives. So we went back to court. His mother said, 'I don't want him', and I said, as nicely as I could, 'I don't want him' (Beer 1992: 4).

Alex subsequently spent several months in foster care until his mother remarried and took him back. The problems faced by this family shed light on the kinds of difficulties and the kinds of bases of new trust which are characteristic of step-families. Were Alex's parents betraying his trust? Why is nobody able to figure out to which family Alex belongs? Was Randy's new role as a step-father more important than his parental obligations to Alex? Whose expectations and affections should be met? How can trust in parents and partners be preserved when their actions are seen and presented as justified by calculations of costs and benefits? How can trust in the family be sustained when the negotiation process makes visible whose needs are gratified and whose not? How should trust be sustained when there is confusing ambiguity in norms about relationships?

Trust in members of the traditional family rests on conformity and familiarity. This type of trust is based on the individual's reliance on other's good will and the sharing of devotion to common goods – that is, the well-being of the family. However, step-families are more complex in comparison to conventional families, their boundaries are less clear, their composition changes over time and they do not have 'a fixed cast of characters' (Beer 1992: 8). This complexity is the result of the fact that most persons, in addition to having the standard roles appropriate for conventional families such as father, husband, brother and so on, also have additional roles, whose multiple demands pull people in different directions. The rules in step-families are also contradictory, ambiguous, unclear, complicated and in a continuous process of negotiation. Moreover, while in a conventional family people adjust and learn to trust each other in stages, as it is formed, in step-families the adjustment comes after the family is formed. Taking into account tensions within this type of family and its lack of control over many potentially disruptive developments, one can understand why it becomes necessary for the step-family to be constantly able to renegotiate rules and membership.

Numerous studies comparing the performance of children from various types of families do not provide any evidence suggesting that there are striking differences between children from step-families and those from nuclear families. There is, however, much inconsistency in results; for example, some British studies show that boys from step-families are more likely to be delinquent, whereas American studies do not confirm this result (Beer 1992: 119–205). None the less, some studies provide an opportunity to look at the long-term effect of step-family living. In the yearly General Social Survey Americans were asked: 'Generally speaking, would you say that most people can be trusted or that you can't be too careful in dealing with people?' Cumulative results from 1972–84 show that adults from nuclear families were more likely to say that people can be trusted, while people who grew up in step-families were less trusting (1992: 211). In many other questions seeking to measure a general adjustment, people from nuclear families score better than adults brought up in step-families. However, although the relative psychological benefits of growing up in families that are intact are very clear, there is no proof of any clear disadvantages experienced by adults from step-families. 'Depending on how one looks at it, then, the step family's glass is half-empty or half-full' (1992: 224). In short, the step-family is a substitute for the nuclear family and as such is here to stay. Step-families are going to search for an answer as to how to combine the parental need for emotional gratification in pure relationships with the children's need for trust and security.

All these problems of trust and security become even more urgent when we look at the issue of custody, particularly at its extreme case – parental kidnapping. While custody arrangements are a direct consequence of a high divorce rate, incidents of child abduction by an non-custodial parent are implicitly connected with the growing process of internationalization of modern societies, an increasing geographical mobility, as well as with a growing intrusion of the law into family life. Nobody really knows how many cases of abduction of children by parents occur yearly. Only the most complex cases to come before the courts are known. The only figures available on international custody battles come from those that involve the thirty-seven nations that are signatories of the Hague Convention, which obligates members to return children wrongfully removed to their country of residence. In Australia, the United States and Britain alone more than 20,000 children had been kidnapped by a parent in the 1980s (*The Australian*, 8 November 1994: 20). In 1988, in Britain there were 105 unresolved cases involving children abducted to countries that are not signatories and 19 still outstanding cases where children were abducted to the signatory countries (Toynbee 1988: 24). In other countries the situation looks similar. These statistics refer only to international parental kidnapping, which represents only the tip of the child-abduction iceberg. In the United States, particularly, the main issue is removal of children from one state to another. The problem has been gaining momentum since the 1970s, when the Library of Congress estimated that some 25,000 incidents of child-snatching occurred annually, while a parents' group seeking to stop it, Children's Rights Inc., believed that figure may be closer to 100,000 (Wallop 1979: 249).

Overall, the examination of parental kidnapping from the point of view of trust relationships points to contradictory functions played by trust. Firstly, reading parents' account of incidents, it becomes clear that not all of them know to what degree their legal system can be trusted. They feel not only misguided by the criminal laws, which in many countries are still ineffective in deterring child-snatching, but also almost entrapped by the custody laws, which are frequently seen as contributing to the problem. However, what is important here is not that parents question policies implemented by the courts, but that they are faced with a question of whom to trust, which presents them with a dilemma as to what kind of criteria should be used to make this decision. They need to decide whether to trust the police and legal systems or whether to act outside the law, yet they do not know what measures will serve their children's interests best and nor even if their children's best interests should be the main factor behind their decision. 'I began to realize [notes one frustrated parent] that unless I broke the law I would never see my children again' (Parental Kidnapping 1979: 74).

Secondly, those parents who understand that their children are the true victims of the situation, face the dilemma of how to combine a healthy distrust of their previous partners (who kidnapped their children) with the ability to preserve the healthy, trusting attitudes of children towards their parents. As one mother, who has recently been through a long court battle to get her son Ryan back and who still feared another abduction attempt, says: 'It doesn't do Ryan any good if I don't trust him [ex-husband]. But do I trust him not to do it again? I don't think so. That will take years to get that kind of trust back' (*The Australian*, 9 June 1994: 4). The family who after divorce goes through this type of experience can be described as a group where trust and distrust are both functional at the same time. The result for the individual is an increased emotional and cognitive work-load and considerable anxiety. Their position at the intersection of public and private law and morality, trust and distrust exposes these families to anguish, frustration and feelings of powerlessness and assigns to them an enormous task to overcome it all.

It can be said that the modern family demands from its members the need to be more active agents, able to adjust to new circumstances and reflect on trust and its consequences. Is the family able to carry out this task, which is its own transformation? In a world where decentred families cannot provide a stable emotional anchor, where social structures become increasingly decentred and where there are many relational possibilities and alternative identities, variations in response to these transformative processes can be enormous. These differences are not only visible in the variety of ways in which people have been coping with the new realities, but they are also expressed in the language of social theory and political debates. On the one hand, there are writers such as Giddens, who optimistically perceive the self as active and substantial, therefore able to adapt and respond to change. Furthermore, modern social life is seen here as furthering 'the appropriation of new possibilities' (Giddens 1991: 175). On the other hand, a more pessimistic perspective places doubts on the very assumption of a bounded identity and the authenticity of the self. The failure of the modern family to provide a trusting, warm, attentive environment, which is required for the development of the functional self for the modern world (that is, an independent and autonomous self), creates *the empty self* (Cushman 1990). Emptiness, a lack of internal sense of self, makes individuals particularly vulnerable to influence from various cultural forms, and consequently the self is becoming increasingly saturated because of the perpetual flow of images.

> Social saturation furnishes us with a multiplicity of incoherent and unrelated languages of the self. . . . This fragmentation of self conceptions corresponds to a multiplicity of incoherent and disconnected relationships. These relationships pull us in myriads of directions, inviting us to play such a variety of roles that the very concept of an 'authentic self' with knowable characteristics recedes from view. The fully saturated self becomes no self at all (Gergen 1991: 7).

This way of arguing sees a modern self as a construct of modern conditions and as a 'disappointment to itself' (Cushman 1990: 608). As the category of 'real self' continues to recede from view, emotion and passion cease to be a significant essence of individuals and the concepts of trust and sincerity also slip from view. The fractionalization of relationships, which, consequently, do not require full expression of the self, reduces family functions by lowering dependence on family members and replacing the family with professional services. In the modern family '[c]ontinuity is replaced by contingency, unity by fragmentation, and authenticity by artfulness' (Gergen 1991: 181).

Repercussions from the transitions and new forms of family life are also discussed in the political realm. These debates about the modern family fluctuate between nostalgia for the past and the acceptance of change. On the one hand, a pessimistic picture is painted in which

'poverty of values', devaluation of fatherhood, 'ethical cancer' and decline in family's values are the main themes. All these factors are seen as
leading to rising crime, children's educational disadvantage and emotional difficulties, disintegration, fragmentation of families and separation of parenthood from marriage. On the other hand, optimists point
out that although once powerful, intimate ties are weakened, others may
be formed or strengthened, and that the issue of how to support these
new forms of families and how to connect them with a wider community
should be explored. Instead of stressing, as conservatives do, a process of
disintegration, they underline people's active engagement in creating new
forms of family organizations, growing opportunities for the self-
actualization of women, the increased importance of children in the
family, the growing amount of time devoted to children by parents, the
changing balance of duties and rights between partners. Both positions,
somehow in a Tocquevillian mood, accept that the family is an institution able to tie individuals securely into a sustaining social order and
that today's individualism is 'inside the family as well as outside it'
(Bellah et al. 1985: 90). However, because they accept different assumptions about the ability of the self to be an active agent in the process of
change, they differ in their evaluation of today's families' lives and in
their remedies for how to improve it. Somewhere in between there are
voices of writers such as Lasch, Etzioni and Wolfe, who aspire to see the
family as an integral part of a larger moral ecology, tying the individual
to the community and the nation. These authors, although not calling for
a revival of the patriarchial family, show some nostalgia for the stronger
distinction between public and private and the stronger authority of the
family. Lasch (1977), who sees the family as a mediator between the
individual and society, criticizes the invasion of the family by the spirit of
economic rationality, consumerism, public policy and state intervention.
Etzioni (1993), like Lasch and Wolfe, criticizes modern societies for
overstressing rights and de-emphasizes the significance of responsibilities,
the fostering of selfishness and self-absorption rather than awareness of
the needs of others. He recommends that parents spend more time with
children, even at the expense of their careers. To cut the divorce rate,
Etzioni suggests pre-nuptial counselling sessions on joint decision-making and mutual respect as well as tax incentives to keep families together.
Although Wolfe (1989) does not suggest that women return to traditional roles, his analysis shows how the women's move to paid jobs led
to many family functions being taken over by other institutions, resulting
in the calculation of family obligations in terms of self-interest and the
erosion of established social obligations.

All these voices of concern for the family's well-being perpetuate
confusion. None the less, they also remove the many illusions about

families. Today we cannot automatically assume that the family is always a realm of solidarity as opposed to the anxiety that is in the professional realm. But it also must be acknowledged that, despite all the difficulties faced by today's family, people still value their families and see them as a place of love, trust and happiness. None the less, people's ability to operate within less traditional forms of family relationships varies. In order to support people's effort to construct and sustain rewarding family relations there is a need for policy which would facilitate and sustain trust in the family.

## Trust and friendship

What loneliness is more lonely than distrust?

G. Eliot

Loneliness is often connected with an absence of friends; it is assumed that those who have few friends or none are more apt to experience loneliness. Although solitude can be accepted, when not enforced by distrust of others and when people feel that they have chosen it themselves, most of us want to belong and be accepted. It is one of the main paradoxes of our time that, while the contemporary society is increasingly perceived as a society of the lonely crowd, where even the family is no longer unquestionably the source of belonging, at the same time the need and search for support, company and security is a dominant feature of modern culture. The fulfilment of this need for belonging and 'reliable alliance' – that is, for a bond that can be trusted to be there for you when you need it (Weiss 1974) – can be provided by friendship. As illustrated by various opinion polls, the importance attached by people to friendship in comparison with other values – such as family, freedom, independence, justice, work and so on – is always very high, and in one French poll it scored 96 per cent (Zeldin 1994: 33).

Trust between friends, as trust between parents and children or intimate partners, involves reliance on others' good will towards one. Epicurus said that what 'helps us in friendship is not so much the help our friends actually give as the assurance we feel concerning that help' (quoted in Enright and Rawlinson 1991: 10). It is trust based not on the understanding of each other's interest or evaluation of the likelihood of others behaving in a certain way, but trust based on the belief in another's inner attributes. 'The act of trust extends commitment beyond extrapolated experience, by resolving uncertainties about others in the direction of unconditional confidence in their essential qualities and enduring dispositions' (Silver 1989: 227). Thus trust, as a basis for friendship, involves a distinctive solution to problems of interpersonal uncertainty (1989: 275). Since we are always faced with 'the unknowability of others' (Simmel 1950) and since they are free to act against our interest, believing in others' good will involves the element of risk. Trusting despite the uncertainty 'affirms the impossibility of betrayal despite its existential possibility' (Silver 1989: 276).

A friend is prepared to accept a risk because she or he values the relationship for its own sake. Thus, a friend is 'someone with whom one has a relationship unprompted by anything other than the rewards that the relationship provides' and 'one stays a friend of another only in so far as sentiments of closeness are reciprocated for their own sake' (Giddens 1991: 90).

In friendship the consciousness of the degree of uncertainty is high, yet it is accompanied by a total commitment or feeling of an absolute belief in the friend's good will (White 1993: 72). Studies of friendship show that people see the violation of confidentiality as the main risk, while they appreciate the cognitive and affective support provided by friendship (Morgan 1990; Duck 1991). This dilemma, between risk and commitment, is well illustrated by a 19-year-old girl's remark: 'I seldom talk to anyone about my romantic problems. . . . I only discuss problems such as lack of understanding between the two of us with my closest friend whom I can trust' (quoted in Goldsmith and Parks 1990: 110). Only relationships with close friends, apart from the family, involve intimate self-disclosure, which assumes a shared feeling of solidarity (Berg 1984). Friendship, according to Simmel, even more than marriage, is able to 'connect a whole person with another person in its entirety' (1950: 325). None the less, any communication, even with the closest friends, involves selection as well as the hiding of some ideas. Modern people, particularly, because of their individualistic personalities, fragmented social life and differentiated interests, have 'too much to hide to sustain a friendship in the ancient sense' (1950: 326). Yet, the closer the relationship, the more painful a lie is to bear. 'The farther removed individuals are from our most intimate personality, the more easily can we come to terms with their untruthfulness . . . while if the few persons closest to us lie, life becomes unbearable' (1950: 313).

Life becomes unbearable because a lie is a violation of friendship, which is seen as a voluntary bond in which people are expected to be honest, open, affectionate, trusting and trustworthy, sharing and helpful. One of the strongest rules of friendship, according to Argyle and Henderson (1985), is not to disclose this confidence to other people. A study of 306 English middle-aged, married couples, discovered that the most common definitions of 'friend' were: 'A friend is someone I can talk to and trust' and 'A friend is someone I can call on for help' (Crawford 1977: 116–17). Furthermore, a betrayal by a friend is painful because

friendship bonds reflect on us and our self-esteem. Friendships not only
provide us with a sense of being part of a social group or community but
they enhance our self-esteem by reassuring us of our own personal worth
and value and, consequently, they are an important source of our
emotional and psychological stability. Friends contribute to our self-
evaluation by accepting us and acting in ways that indicate that they
value our company and our opinion and thus bolster our attitudes,
opinion and beliefs. In addition, in our culture there is a popular belief
that a number of friends is a good measure of social and personal success.
Someone who can claim a wide network of friends is usually regarded as
happy and successful. Thus, losing friends could be perceived as a negative or even threatening experience because it can be seen by others as
indicative of one's more general failure in life. A high-quality friendship
is characterized by emotional support, an ability to reciprocate, trust and
confide, yet the reality is less reassuring and we keep on learning to be
tolerant of our friends' failings. Since friendship rarely lives up to the
ideal picture, maybe real friendship is, to use Shakespeare's words,
'mostly feigning'. Behind this type of question there is the myth of
friendship, which was passed to us from antiquity and which later was
reinforced by a spirit of romanticism. Yet, the aim of friendship as being
an absolute psychological intimacy cannot be attributed to all known
societies.

The substance, as well as the nature and practices of friendship, as a
moral ideal varies historically. For the ancients friendship was 'the crown
of life', the happiest and most human of all forms of love, one of the chief
elements in morality and the essential element in the good life. For Plato
true friendship derived from basic human needs and desires, such as the
need to strive towards goodness, to be affiliated with others and to
achieve self-understanding (Bolotin 1979). The moral emphasis was
strongly established by Aristotle's classification of friendship according
to whether its object is utility, pleasure or goodness (Price 1989). Perfect
friendship is based on goodness: 'it is those who desire the good of their
friends for the friends' sake that are truly friends, because each loves the
other for what he is, and not for any incidental quality' (Aristotle 1976:
263).

Cicero reinforced the devotion of antiquity to friendship by arguing
that without it life does not make sense. According to him, when 'a man
thinks of a true friend, he is looking at himself in the mirror' (quoted in
Porter and Tomaselli 1989: 3). In feudal times, friendship, seen more as
necessary in terms of securing provision of services and resources and
based on inequality of status between lords and vassals, was highly
codified, yet it still involved a voluntaristic component (Silver 1989: 278–
89). Friendship was not centred on intimacy but seen, rather, as a

practical imperative, because in the absence of impersonal means of obtaining resources and incomplete (at least) development of impersonal provision of social order, 'it was risky indeed to do without recourse to persons worthy of trust' (1989: 288). In such conditions, friendship was often institutionalized and was seen as a means of creating durable alliances based upon values of sincerity and honour. Non-institutionalized friendship flourished again in the commercial society of eighteenth-century Europe, where it became a parallel system of relations based on sympathy and affection in contrast to market contacts resting on instrumental exchange. 'The early liberals were concerned to define friendship as intrinsically private. At the conceptual level, they sought to show how personal relations, such as friendship, could not be governed by any formal code, such as provided by religion or honour – nor, indeed by exchange relations similar to that of the market' (1989: 289). While the eighteenth century made religion out of friendship, the next one romanticized it. Much of our contemporary vocabulary connected with friendship finds its origins in the Romantic period. It stressed passion and mutual devotion, and it fostered a belief in deep intimate communion, intrinsic worth and presented friendship as a lifetime commitment.

Modernity has again transformed the nature of friendship. 'Modern man, possibly, has too much to hide to sustain a friendship in the ancient sense' (Simmel 1950: 326). With the growing differentiation and fragmentation of social life, friendship, seen as based 'upon the person in its totality' and aiming at an absolute intimacy, 'becomes probably more and more difficult as differentiation among men increases' (ibid.). However, while friendship in its true sense diminishes under the pressure of modernism, modernity also facilitates it since friendship requires the advanced development of individualized personalities. Consequently, a very specialized type of friendship, a differentiated or fragmented friendship, emerges, which allows us to have different friends for different occasions, for sharing different areas of our interests or activities. This type of arrangement influences the nature of mutual obligation and commitment; however, it does not dismiss the significance and uniqueness of friendship, which still 'may stem from the centre of total personality. It may yet be reached by the sap of the ultimate roots of the personality, even though it feeds only part of the person's periphery. In this idea, it involves the same affective depth and the same readiness for sacrifice, which less differentiated epochs and persons connect only with a common *total* sphere of life, for which reservations and discretions constitute no problem' (ibid.).

With the expansion of another important feature of modernity – that is, abstract systems – friendship is 'often a mode of reembedding, but is not directly involved in abstract systems themselves, which explicitly overcome dependency upon personal ties' (Giddens 1990: 119). As a result of this process of transition, the notion of friendship is no longer contrasted with the concept of 'enemy' or 'stranger' but rather with such categories as 'acquaintance' or 'colleague'.

Paradoxically, today, when time and distance are no longer such serious threats to a relationship, many writers argue that the intensity of friendship has waned because of the development of narcissism, egoism and pure selfishness and because of the growing fragmentation and saturation of social life. Are we losing the capacity for 'genuine friendship'?

According to Giddens, intimate relations informed by loyalty and authencity are a normal part of the social situation of modernity. The nature of friendship has changed, however. Contemporary friendship needs to be worked upon, and it needs to start with a mutual process of self-disclosure, which is the condition of establishing trust relationships. Also according to Gergen (1991), the nature and the very concept of friend undergo change. Gergen, who is less optimistic than Giddens about the fate of friendship, argues that the intensity of friendship has changed to such a degree that now it is too difficult to talk about anything more than fractional relations. 'It is painful to find the old rituals of relationship – deep and enduring friendships, committed intimacy, and the nuclear family – coming apart by the "seams"' (Gergen 1991: 181). Pressure of time, new opportunities for pleasure, job demands, possibilities for many new contacts and so on cause meetings of 'close friends' to become an occasional, compact and short respite rather than a communion of souls (1991: 60–3).

Bellah and his colleagues argue that the classical idea of friendship made sense more in the small face-to-face communities of the past because in modern culture dominated by individualism people are only able to understand the components of pleasure and usefulness in friendship. Today we do not define friendship in terms of shared commitment to the good or solely in terms of utilitarian value. We tend to identify friends as people whose company we enjoy (Bellah et al. 1985: 133–5). Therapists 'propose a different sort of friendship. It offers selffulfilment and a sense of self-worth to basically benign people in a well-coordinated, yet often lonely social world' (1985: 134). Consequently, in this perspective a friend is not someone who protects the emotional wellbeing of another, as in Giddens' definition, but rather someone who improves one's psychological well-being. In the individualistic language of therapy the importance of friendship rests on individuals' self-interest since friendship is seen as contributing to the subjective states of wellbeing that make up a sense of self-worth. The redefinition of individualism in psychological terms and the re-invention of social contacts is also characteristic of the children of the *organizational men* of the 1950s and 1960s.

Leinberger and Tucker's (1993) follow-up study of Whyte's *The Organizational Man* (1956) states that the psychological individualism of this new generation leads them to a continuous pursuit of the ideal of the authentic self. Organizational men of the Golden Age of Fordism, who adapted their personalities to fit the bureaucratic organizational environment, did not see any need for intimate friendship, yet their offspring undertook the task of creating and opening themselves to others. This new, subject-directed type of conformity results in choosing life styles and social relationships as expressions of the self. 'It was the unreality of their parents' style of personal relations that constituted one of the chief experiences of artificiality for organizational offspring' (Leinberger and Tucker 1993: 262). Members of the new generation recall an emptiness in their parents' social contacts. 'These supposedly intimate friendships seemed so repressed, so superficial. They would literally spend their time talking about the weather, as if anything else might be too controversial. It was like they were strangers to each other' (1993: 262). The new generation expresses the need for openness, honesty, full presentation of oneself to others, as one of the interviewees says: ' The thing I most abhor in other people is when they are dishonest. I get very angry with people who don't allow me to trust them. I feel betrayed, but it's really their loss that I'm not going to trust them' (1993: 263).

To pursue authenticity in the interpersonal world is a difficult task because you must not only achieve your own authenticity but also judge its presence in your partner.

> In face-to-face encounters, you can judge the other person's authenticity only on the basis of your own problematic experience of the simultaneous fullness and emptiness of the authentic self, the content of which turns out to be expressiveness itself. In practice, then, honesty in personal relations comes to mean the sending and receiving of signals about expressiveness, rather than the communication of what you authentically are (Leinberger and Tucker 1993: 263).

Therefore, the children of organizational men must resort to expressiveness itself as a means of pointing to their self, which seems to be authenticated by this act of pointing itself. Thus, they employ various personal styles which emphasize expressiveness. Recognizing that their identities reside in their connection with others and seeing creativity as the agency of the authentic self means that they want a new balance in their lives, more equal relationships between work and family or between private and public life. And as they are less loyal and less adaptable than their parents, they often walk out of social arrangements that do not answer their needs.

This individualistic perspective raises several questions. Are friends that one makes in order to improve one's psychological health (the therapeutic model) or prove one's authenticity (the ethic of self) real friends? Are we developing sympathy and expressive communication skills at the expense of loyalty? How is the nature of friendship bonds affected by the fragmentation of this relationship (different friend for different occasions)?

To answer these questions we must, firstly, remember that the historical variations in the meanings of the concept and in the reality of friendship point out that the issue of friendship has always involved such problems as reciprocity of relations, the nature of obligations and the question of discretion. It is all too often forgotten that the mixture of motives is totally normal and natural for all human beings. Even altruistic behaviour can be motivated by self-interest – for example, giving blood in order to boost one's self-image (Wuthnow 1991). The presence of motives other than altruistic ones does not necessarily make such behaviour less valued, although it does not mean that we should value all actions regardless of their motives. Much empirical research shows that people are able to draw a line between acceptable and unacceptable levels of instrumentalism in friendship. 'Friends can quite legitimately make use of one another in instrumental ways without threatening the relationship, provided that it is clear that they are being used because they are friends and not friends because they are useful' (Allan 1979: 43).

Secondly, in order to discover changes in the nature of modern friendship, we must place modern friendship in the context of other contemporary social relationships. Here there are at least two contrasting accounts of the reality of social contacts. According to the first one, technology is 'taking over families and friendships', damaging the ties that bind people together. Not only does television lower our interest in communicating with others but now E-mail and the Internet are replacing personal contacts between people. 'We are becoming so comfortable with taking to a machine that we are losing the ability to communicate with other people,' says Gerry Hanson, the British Polite Society's chairman (*The Economist*, 8 October 1994: 67). How logging for hours on an electronic network can affect social relations is illustrated by a *New Yorker* cartoon showing a dog in front of a computer and talking about his electronic correspondence to his friend standing next to him: 'On the Internet, she doesn't know I'm a dog.' Does the growing use of electronic means really change the nature of our relationships? Many commentators argue that there are serious implications to the increase in depersonalized contacts not only for the individual's well-being but also for the whole society because it threatens the democratic spirit and organization of the nation. Where there is no eye-to-eye contact and where it is impossible to identify a voice, 'how can you guess what lies in their hearts, when you can's see their eyes?' (John Perry Barlow, one of the founders of the electronic revolution, quoted in *The Australian*, 12 October 1994: 37). When people satisfy their creativeness and self-expression alone in front of their computers, it will be very difficult to establish interpersonal trust because these people's willingness to search for more personalized contacts or to join voluntary groups will not be forthcoming.

The second perspective does not accept this stand and questions the apparent social isolation by pointing out that these new means of communication not only modify our behaviour but also enormously expand our opportunity for social contacts. We communicate more and with the growing number of people outside of our immediate surroundings, which probably means that the communications are more specialized or more fitting to our individualized interests. The world-wide community of people using electronic means of communication now includes more than 30 million (numbers of people already connected to the Internet, according to *The Economist*, 15 October 1994: 80). It seems that we do not yet know enough to understand the impact of the 'information society' on our social relations; however, accompanying trends, such as a general increase in social communication, does not allow for too pessimistic a prediction. This increase in communication in more traditional fields can be illustrated many times. For example, in Britain, people are now sending each other 24 per cent more 'special' mail than in 1986 and making 50 per cent more telephone calls than ten years ago (*The Economist*, 8 October 1994: 67). Retail sales of greetings cards in the United Kingdom from 1979 to 1990 tripled (Davis 1992: 51). Although we should be very cautious with the interpretation of all these data, the expansion of social contacts is clearly visible.

Also various theories about the post-industrial society, which place at the heart of its transformation to post-industrial society changes in the character of social roles and interaction, predict the increasing importance of symbolic communication and of social contacts. In post-industrial conditions emotional bonds are expected to deepen since trends towards role relationships characterized by a variety of activities and the uniqueness of the roles requires more personal commitment based on a sense of mutual understanding and acceptance. A role relationship in post-industrial society gains its stability not from the force of conformity to traditional norms but from trust between people in the relationship or from a 'sense of confidence that the relationship as it is presently defined is workable for all concerned, and a sense that the people involved are sufficiently in touch with one another that they will recognize when further change is necessary and will be able to redefine the relationship as called for' (Hage and Powers 1992: 199). Consequently, the post-industrial transformation is increasing the recognition of the importance of emotions and constructing the new reality of more intimate social relations. It 'is creating a society predicated upon *Gemeinschaft*, even more than was the case in pre-industrial times, when emotional bonds were generally based on blood relationships and therefore involved little choice' (1992: 202). Because the new post-industrial conditions provide more leisure time, more choice of activities and better communication systems, they enhance interaction and informal relationships.

Another interesting trend expected to occur in post-industrial society is the growing diversity of contacts. The arrival of post-industrial society means not only an increase in numbers of contacts but also an increase in the diversity of contacts each person experiences. We are increasingly going to interact with people of different cultures, races and ethnicity groups because we will be brought together by globalization. 'Among people with industrial mind-sets, "birds of a feather flock together"; but among more complex selves, opposites attract' (Hage and Powers 1992: 94).

In contrast, much sociological and anthropological writing about modern friendship, focusing on its properties as an interpersonal relationship, concludes that we choose our friends among those who resemble us, who are the same sex, age, occupation and race. There is not much evidence of cross-cultural, cross-occupational or cross-gender friendship. In other words 'birds of a feather flock together'. Not only do friends share many socio-economic characteristics; in general they tend do enjoy the same life style and share some common experiences. Consequently, it is argued that in Western industrialized societies 'friendship patterns do support the wider social order of class, gender and generation; that members of these groups have different patterns of sociability' (Garrett 1989: 132). If friends tend to mirror each other's characteristics, isn't friendship a breeding ground for exclusiveness? Shouldn't we 'welcome the friendless world as the world in which we are open and fair to everyone and not only to some?' (Porter and Tomaselli 1989: 8). Several factors prompt a negative answer to this question. Firstly, we cannot accept the friendless world because of the importance of value of friendship itself, which cannot be so easily dismissed. Secondly, friendship ties, like other 'strong' interpersonal bonds, are less important than 'weak ties' (like shared membership in secondary associations) in sustaining community cohesion and collective action. 'Weak ties are more likely to link members of *different* small groups than are strong ones, which tend to be concentrated within particular groups' (Granovetter 1973: 1376).

Thirdly, because, even if we now are not friends with people different from ourselves, it does not mean that we cannot be friends with them in the future. The on-going transformation of social and economic conditions, which brings people of different backgrounds and cultures together, can demand from us more understanding and more cooperation with the 'other'. This could be a good base for the development of friendship, if supported by policy aiming at securing conditions for a tolerant society (which will be discussed in the next chapter). Moreover, existing examples of mixed friendship, as the experience of the growing numbers of mixed-sex friendships suggest, show that there is no need for friends to be alike and to think alike. Seen in this light, friendship can be something more than a search for security; it can also be seen as an exploration, which can grow into curiosity about others, abolishing, consequently, any thinking in stereotypes. 'Mixed friendship now stands in the avant-garde not just of private life, but of public life too' (Zeldin 1994: 332).

Fourthly, we cannot dismiss friendship, because of its important role in the individual's emotional, psychological and social development. Friendship is an essential step in developing not only self-esteem, but also empathy, trust and understanding of others.

Consequently, on the one hand, the experience of interpersonal trust is essential for the existence of societal trust, which allows us to trust the structure of situations in more complex settings, while, on the other hand, more general societal conditions sustaining societal trust are necessary for friendship relations to be open and not limited to a restricted category of people. The dynamic of these relationships is not without problems. Underlying tensions in modern societies are as follows. They lie between, on the one hand, the necessity for trust in human relations and the impossibility of building social relations without some element of trust, and, on the other hand, the tendency of this informal type of relations to be interwoven with the institutionalized social order, consequently reinforcing their closed structures. It is claimed that post-industrial society will be able to solve this problem by demanding that people and institutions be more complex, flexible, open, cooperative and communicative. If our private and public life is going to rest upon trust relationships, it can be argued that friendship, as an informal, voluntary relationship based on trust, can be seen as the key 'post-industrial' type of relationship. Empirical studies show that friendship entails many characteristics of 'post-industrial' types of social relationships. It allows for flexibility, unpredictability, informality, it is an unhierarchical relationship of equality and thus without any formal power structure, and is a dynamic and imaginative form of relationship. It copes well with uncertainty and risk and is a source of social integration. One more important characteristic of friendship provides it with a particularly 'post-industrial' dimension. As many studies have discovered, friendships play a special role at the times of our life when we are searching for our identity or new social roles (such as teenagers' friendship or the role of friendship after retirement) or when we are in a state of transition or when we try to escape role-playing in the institutional sphere. 'Friendship thus assumes special importance at times of relative rolelessness' (Jerrome 1984: 698). Friendship can be therefore a model for redefining roles in a manner allowing more flexibility, mutual adjustment and understanding. The widespread breakdown of traditional roles, the decline in routine activity and greater personalization of relationships would demand a more imaginative and flexible type of behaviour. 'Role redefinition has become a part of everyday life. . . . In post-industrial society, people periodically redefine roles in creative ways in order to be more adaptive to circumstantial conditions and more responsive to the needs of others' (Hage and Powers 1992: 198).

If our roles are becoming less script-like and based on trust in the same vein as they are in friendship relationships, what do we know about our behaviour in these roleless roles of friends? Not so much, unfortunately. From a sociological point of view the most interesting are the findings which suggest the cultural specificity of friendship relations and which propose to view it not only as an individual phenomenon but also as a social one. Since gender-specific friendship is relatively well researched (For example, Jerrome 1984; Winstead 1986; Moore 1990; Bruckner and Knaup 1993) and since cross-cultural studies show that nation-specific peculiarities seem to affect the general patterns of friendship more strongly than does gender (Bruckner and Knaup 1993; Hollinger and Haller 1990), it would be more interesting to look at less well-known studies on the national difference in friendship patterns. Outcomes of this cross-national research show remarkable differences in the number of friends and in the nature of friendship between various nations. These differences between nations are explained by the different orientations toward the public domain and the private one, the variations in the role and involvement of kin and the family and by the different demands of work and other formal obligations. Recent studies of national differences in the number of friends demonstrate that Americans, with an average 3.5 friends per person, have the most friends among five studied nations. Hungarians, with an average 1.8 friends, were on the other end of spectrum, while the British (3.0), Italians (2.7) and Germans (2.5) were in the middle (Bruckner and Knaup 1993). Cross-national differences in the friendship network need to be interpreted in the context of socio-cultural differences in the meaning of the concept of friendship. For instance, Americans and Australians consider many persons as friends, whom Europeans would at best call acquaintances.

Although attempts to explain these differences in the understanding and practice of friendship are not fully successful, they are able to identify some of the important underlying causal structures. For example, Hungarian small friendship networks are partly explained, firstly, by the societal distrust which existed under the socialist government, consequently limiting the scope for social contacts, and, secondly, by the heavy work-load, which also restricted opportunities for social contacts (Bruckner and Knaup 1993). However, not only does a more democratic and open political system make friendship easier (according to Aristotle, 'in tyranny, there is little or no friendship'); friendship, although of a specific type, is also facilitated where relationships are particularistic and security and stability are not provided by the state (as in Southern and Eastern Europe). Friendship, reciprocity and trust, therefore, provide elements of credit and a guarantee of honesty in a situation where there is no legal contract. The nature of friendship in such cases is less intimate since its task is not only to provide affection and companionship but also to organize production and protection.

This double role of the coalitions of friends as the basic forms of social organization and the source of emotional support and identity is illustrated by Nowak's studies of Polish students in the 1970s – that is, in the period characterized by a policy of intensive socialist industrialization. While people identified themselves first with family in Polish society, 'friends constituted a second type of "important object"; both single friends, ties with whom involved people in a network of interpersonal connection, and whole – as a rule small – groups of friends, if such groups became formed from a network of interpersonal contacts' (Nowak 1989: 136). Economic difficulties and a social vacuum, due to an absence of voluntary associations and suspicions towards the state party, resulted in very strong friendship bonds, which were substitutes for other forms of social organization. Having friends was seen as the main way of achieving some level of social, financial and psychological security. Particularly important, as Nowak stresses, was the role of friendship as a means of social approval and social acceptance because of social discreditation of the official sources of social recognition. Friendship can play an important role in increasing social integration by mitigating some of the societal tensions (Eisenstadt and Roniger 1984: 12). However, friendship as the basic form of social organization not only does not provide a long-term and sound solution for the functioning of any society; it also does not protect these relationships from inevitable transformation into types of relationships more like cliques. Although, in general, friends can expect some instrumental support from one another, when the dynamics of a situation push friends to rely increasingly on each other's help, their new awareness that they are friends because they can use each other could result in a change in the nature of their friendship. In Poland before 1981, the particular role played by a network of personal contacts between people, with friends expected to help in coping with everyday problems, started to degenerate. 'Particularly, an intense increase in the informal economy and some of its aspects, such as corruption, bribery, etc. which were strictly connected with consumer attitudes, had a negative impact on social morality and even decomposed societal life' (Lukasiewicz and Sicinski 1989: 119). Consequently, many social relationships, while on the surface still preserving a language of informal and warm contacts, tended to evolve towards more instrumental ones based on a mutual reciprocity of exchange of goods and services (Nowak 1989).

In Hungary friendship was also seen as being of mainly practical importance – a 'mobility channel for both sexes' (Heinrich, quoted in Porter and Tomaselli 1989: 6). The Polish studies also illustrate that the importance of friendship can be influenced by the changing relationship between the public and private domain. While the role of friendship declined significantly during the Solidarity period (in 1980–1), due to the enormous increase in participation in public life, in the following period (after the declaration of martial law), the role of informal contacts was again growing (Lukasiewicz and Sicinski 1989: 126–7).

Another interesting characteristic of modern friendship is the existence of a variety of types of friends to meet people's various needs and the variation of constellations of types of friends needed over the course of life. Sociological research shows that people are capable of many variations in the practice of friendship. People in modern society require many different types of social contacts. Some they pursue for the pleasure of sociability or the enjoyment of leisure activities, some for the realization of their intellectual aspirations and others to fulfil their emotional needs. Consequently, friends, who share and participate in different aspects of one's personality and life style, are classified into different categories; from close friends to mere acquaintances. For many people the concept of friendship involves a relatively large group of people, including 'old' friends, 'close' friends, and those who could be identified as 'acquaintances' or 'business associates'. Having made this distinction, the most intense friendship, based on openness, mutual trust and understanding, is presented as 'real' and 'true' and specific rights and duties are distributed differently among particular kinds of friends (Jacobson 1975). 'To claim that some friends are allowed to discover the "real self" more than others is to say that some are more trusted than others. This is the major difference between those people labelled "real" or "true" friends and the remainder. "Real" friends appear to be trusted totally and can be relied on to protect their friend's interests' (Allan 1979: 40). In Willmott's (1987) study, the main difference between 'close' friends and other friends was seen as related to the issues of trust and help. A 'close' friend is 'someone you can always turn to for help' (29 per cent of respondents) or 'someone you can trust' (21 per cent) or 'someone you can talk to freely about anything' (21 per cent). Although, we tend to have only a few 'true' friends, they are mostly long-lasting friends, while other types of friendship tend to end with changes in the external situation such as change of job, neighbourhood, city or country. The fact that 'real' friendship, in which trust and solidarity have accumulated through the years, can continue even without frequent face-to-face interactions demonstrates that sociability, although central to friendship, is not the most important factor. (Marcel Proust even thought that true friends are the best *in absentia,* because when they are present they 'steal' your personality.) In contrast, it does not automatically follow that people with whom we spend a lot of time and enjoy ourselves 'will be trusted with the kind of intimate information about the self that is shared with "true" friends' (Allan 1989: 19).

It is debatable to what degree the distinction between 'real' and other friends allows us to predict the durability and type of support which people receive from friends and to account for the dynamism of friendship circles. Both enthusiasm and scepticism about friendship are common; while examples of great friendships and friends' affectionate behaviour in times of crisis are used to support the first stand, sceptics warn that because friendship is open to manipulation and often forged for self-advancement, 'You should never trust people too much' or 'You should never expect too much of people' (Porter and Tomaselli 1989: 5). Among these sceptics we can mention Bernard Russell and Blaise Pascal, both of whom believed that real friendship is an illusion. Pascal demolishes the idea of friendship on the grounds that if we could read each other's thoughts it would disappear.

However, since we are always faced with 'the unknowability of others' (Simmel 1950), acceptance of this pessimistic stand would mean that friendship would be totally impossible. This contradicts the experiences of many people, who, when faced with this problem, commonly accept that intimacy is an optimal strategy in seeking knowledge of the other. Thus, friendship involves risk but – by trusting others' good will – it also resolves uncertainty about others' intentions and permits the taking of this risk.

Kant, who saw true friendship as an important, although a very rare and fragile, opportunity for 'unlocking the prison of the self', also stressed the threatening consequences of the collapse of symmetry and equality on which friendship relationships normally rest. The asymmetry can be brought about by the very act of self-disclosure if one person 'reveals his failings while the other person concealed his own, he would lose something of the other's respect by presenting himself so candidly' (Kant quoted in Singer 1994: 292–3). Since acting as a friend can at the same time demand honesty (you should not lie to your friends) as well as dishonesty (since some honest revelation can a cause of the breakdown of a relationship, which is valued for its own sake), friendship is an art of balancing between one's self-esteem and self-respect, on the one hand, and one's attachment and aspiration to preserve this intimate contact, on the other. When faced with this moral dilemma, especially in some crisis situations seen as having moral implications, many people would try to hide or disguise the problem from their friends. 'Beside a desire to maintain an acceptable self with their friends, this reflects the significance of sustaining equality and structural balance within friendship' (Allan 1989: 128).

In general, empirical studies prove that friends tend to provide each other with some help in times of trouble and crisis. Friends are often better than family members or professionals at helping because they are chosen and share many personal and social characteristics, which means that they are well suited to 'provide services that require precise matching of social statues and values' (Litwak 1989: 85). The help of friends is especially relevant in such situations as identity crisis, emotional problems, need for advice and socializing. When asked to whom they would turn in case of emergency, people from five countries pointed to close kin and friends. Since the frequency of friends being named was inversely proportional to the geographical distance to kin, 20 per cent of Americans and 18 per cent of Australians – both groups living in sparsely populated countries – saw friends as an important source of emotional and instrumental help, in comparison with 9 per cent of Hungarians and 10 per cent of Austrians (Hollinger and Haller 1990: 116–17). It is worth noting that, generally, twice as many people perceived friendship to be more important in providing emotional assistance than instrumental assistance. However, help from friends is not a long-term source of assistance, mainly because our call on friends' resources is of less importance than on kin or family and because the organization of social life makes it difficult to provide help to friends. Moreover, the complexity of many emergency situations, which could, for example, differently affect the social positions of friends, can separate friends (Allan 1989: 104–29). Only exceptional friendship can survive; many people 'whose marriages end, who become chronically infirm or who experience some other long-term change in their circumstances are likely to find that their friendship circles alter in response' (1989: 127).

To summarize, friendship is an intimate relationship which is formed predominantly with individuals other than kin or sexual partners, which is based on trust, reciprocity and equality and which is an important source of solidarity and self-esteem. It seems that although the issue of usefulness is losing its importance in our thinking about the nature of friendship, it is still a significant aspect of being friends, especially among teenagers or women friends. The third component of friendship, as formulated by Aristotle – shared commitment to the good – is not only the least studied but the least verbalized. According to Bellah et al. (1985), this aspect of friendship does not play any role in modern culture, which is dominated by expressive and utilitarian individualism, and which stresses the components of pleasure and usefulness. However, some unique modern features of contemporary friendship, such as the voluntary nature of negotiated networks and shared experiences rather than legal sanctions or ties of blood, by demanding a more prominent role for trust, create conditions for friendship to be founded on a discovery and unconditional acceptance of personalities. Modern friendship takes place in 'a democratized arena of elective affinities, in which persons culturally value each other for their true, that is their unproductive selves' (Silver 1989: 295). Thus, because friendship implies not only respect for but also an opening out to the partner, moral standards need to be upheld by both parties involved. By stressing the element of moral equality between friends, it creates a new potential for the re-activization of the third component of friendship, that one of the main duties of friends is to help one another to be a better person. Although the importance of sharing enjoyment and pleasure of common activities as the main characteristic of friendship will continue to grow, it does not need to mean the abandonment of moral standards. It seems that the importance of mutual commitment, loyalty and trust between friends will increase and may become an essential element of modern friendship, regardless of other changes, which may be expected as the nature of social communication and contacts is transformed.

Friendships can differ not only in their foundation but also in the nature of the parties involved in the relationships. For Aristotle, friendship also includes the relationship between fellow citizens, which take the form of 'concord'; 'a state when citizens agree about their interest, adopt the same policy, and put their common resolves into effect. . . . Thus concord is evidently . . . friendship between the citizens of a state, because it is concerned with their interests and living conditions' (1976: 297). In the next section we will debate whether this type of friendship or 'concord' is necessary for a society to work.

## Trust and society

Societies which rely heavily on the use of force are likely to be
less efficient, more costly, and more unpleasant than those
where trust is maintained by other means.
(Gambetta 1988b: 221)

Sociological research has shown that we tend to trust our fellow countrymen rather than others. On the scale of feelings of confidence and
obligation, which starts with absolute trust in our dearest ones and ends
with less intimate feelings of reliance on others who share some of our
characteristics, trust towards members of one's nation still retains a
relatively high position. The available data from seventeen Western
European nations indicates that in all countries, with the exception of
Italy, people tend to trust those of their own nationality more than they
trust foreigners. For example, in 1980, 91 per cent of West Germans, 90
per cent of people from Luxembourg, 88 per cent of people from the
United Kingdom and 62 per cent of Greeks declared trust in their own
nationality. At the same time only 34 per cent of West Germans, 22 per
cent of people from Luxembourg, 37 per cent from the United Kingdom
and 12 per cent from Greece declared trust in sixteen other nationalities
(Inglehart 1991: 160). A 1990 cross-national survey asking the members
of ten West European states if their fellow citizens were worthy of trust
indicated that in all countries, again with the exception of Italy, 50 per
cent or more of people surveyed trusted their fellow nationals. In contrast, on average only 33 per cent declared that they trust people in
general, with 21 per cent of French and Portuguese, 31 per cent of
Belgians and West Germans declaring distrust towards most people
(Ashford and Timms 1992: 12–13). Figures from the European Value
System Study, which was conducted in more than twenty countries in
1982, show that East Europeans trust their fellow citizens less than West
Europeans, who saw their countrymen as more trustworthy. In the
Netherlands, the United Kingdom, Belgium and Luxembourg, 88 to 90
per cent of respondents stated that 'people can be trusted'; in Czechoslovakia the proportion was only 30 per cent (Musil 1992: 192). In 1982 in
Hungary, only 32 per cent agreed that 'you may trust people', while in
1990 a strong trust in Hungarian individuals was declared at 23 per cent
in comparison with 46 per cent in Denmark and 43 per cent in England
(Seligman 1992: 173). The same study showed that, in response to the
question 'Would you raise your children to have respect for other
people?', only 31 per cent of Hungarians answered positively, while the
corresponding figures of the European average of positive answers was
between 43 and 62 per cent (Hankiss 1990: 207). A 1990 Russian study

also demonstrates how little post-communist conditions are conducive to a feeling of interpersonal trust. In response to the question 'To what extent do the people around you have an irritable, malevolent or even hostile attitude to each other?', 70 per cent of people surveyed answered that almost all or the majority of Russians have such an attitude (Wyman 1994: 52).

Looking at the results of this research we note that there is a clear contrast between, on the one hand, the answers to the question about trust in people in general and the question asking about the trustworthiness of one's own nationals and, on the other hand, a contrast between the answers to two of these questions and the question about trust in the family. For example, on average, 77 per cent of Western Europeans declared complete trust in the family, 74 per cent trust in their nationals (Inglehart 1991: 160) and only 33 per cent trust in 'most people' (Ashford and Timms 1992: 12). Here there is a clear continuum of feeling or commitment, starting with complete trust in one's family's good will to less than complete trust in people in general. The difference between the level of trust in the family and the other two types is self-explanatory; it is connected with lower degrees of uncertainty involved in the relationship with those well-known and members of our family who are committed to us.

The contrast between the last two areas of trust may to some degree be explained by the fact that the enquiry about trust in one's fellow citizens could prompt 'considerations of national prestige, national trustworthiness' (Ashford and Timms 1992: 13). However, even taking into account this inference, the puzzling absence of trust among Eastern Europeans prior to 1989 as well as among Italians still requires explanation.

An argument that Italian society is characterized by a distinctively low level of interpersonal trust has a long history. The absence of trust was exemplified in the 'amoral familism' which Banfield (1958) reported as being the dominant ethos in southern Italy. The absence of feelings of trust or moral obligation towards anyone outside the nuclear family – 'Maximize the material, short-run advantage of the nuclear family: assume that all others will do likewise' (Banfield 1958: 83) – is accompanied by villagers' inability to act together for their common good. 'For private citizens to take a serious interest in a public problem will be regarded as abnormal and even improper' (1958: 85). Banfield attributed this to extreme poverty and backwardness as well as a long history of foreign domination. He argued that centuries of oppression and poverty have left the peasants with a pathological distrust of the state and all authority and without any horizontal bonds of solidarity. Banfield's critics have disagreed with his attribution of this behaviour to a specific cultural heritage, stressing, rather, features of the Italian social structure (Pizzorno 1966; Silverman 1968). However, they have admitted the lack of collaborative bonds in southern Italy.

Almond and Verba in *The Civic Culture*, published on the basis of the survey of 1959 and 1960, also portrayed Italian political culture as having a relatively low level of general trust. In the absence of social trust, more suspicion, distrust, isolation and lower levels of cooperation prevailed.

> The Italians are particularly low in national pride, in moderate and open partisanship, in the acknowledgment of the obligation to take an active part in local community affairs, in the sense of competence to join with others in situations of political stress, in their choice of social forms of leisure activities, and in their confidence in the social environment (Almond and Verba 1963: 402).

Although many changes have taken place in Italy in the last thirty years, there is still a low level of interpersonal trust, which 'seem to be a long-established aspect of the Italian poetical culture which is only gradually disappearing as economic development progresses' (Inglehart 1991: 183). In the 1980 study, 24 per cent of Italians declared a lack of trust in their own nationality. In addition, interpersonal trust was far less low in southern Italy than in the north; with 28 per cent of respondents from the northwest and 45 per cent from the southern region of Italy describing Italians as 'not particularly trustworthy' or 'not at all trustworthy'. Moreover, although Italians do not have trust in their fellow citizens, they place high trust in some other foreign nationalities; for example, 68 per cent of Italians expressed trust in Americans; they also highly valued the Swiss and Dutch (1963: 59–60). Accordingly, in the 1990 survey only 3 per cent of Italians saw their fellow citizens worthy of complete trust (Ashford and Timms 1993: 12).

The debate about the difference in societal trust between north and south Italy has been recently taken up by Putnam (1993) and Gambetta (1993). Putman's comparison of the institutional performance of both regions leads him to suggest that the better performance of northern institutions can be attributed to the existence of a strong civic culture that promotes trust, solidarity and tolerance. Trust within the community is seen as an essential condition for effective, responsive and democratic institutions. The dominant relations of trust among the individuals in the northern region are generalized toward government, and governmental performance reflects the cooperation between institutions and citizens.

Gambetta (1993), like Putnam, argues that 'amoral familism' is not irrational, but the only rational strategy for survival in the specific southern social context. In a situation of a lack of interpersonal trust it is irrational for any individual to seek more collaborative alternatives, except perhaps within the immediate family. Gambetta points out that what was unique about the village studied by Banfield was not lack of trust but rather that it remained 'uncompensated'. Lack of trust in other places in southern Italy resulted in the development of a system of patronage and the Mafia. The emergence of the Mafia takes place when two conditions are met: namely, where there is not only a demand for protection (because of lack of trust) but also where there is the presence of *supply* of it ('of strong, armed men accustomed to dispensing violence') (Gambetta 1993: 3352). Gambetta's view of the Mafia as a possible solution, however perverse, to the problem of distrust, allows us to argue that all the conditions necessary for the development of the Mafia are now present in the former Soviet Union.

This brings us to the other set of societies which showed low levels of trust – namely, to the former Soviet bloc countries. The experience in these societies of fear, suspicion and intolerance – integral to all totalitarian societies – contributed to the low level of trust among their people in comparison with Western countries. The ruling communist parties dismantled the traditional value-generating institutions, disintegrated families and undermined many previous values, such as responsibility, freedom and autonomy. Their attempts to replace these norms with new values failed because 'the almost total inefficiency of their economic system ruined the working morale and generated nation-wide negligence and irresponsibility; because their authoritarian social and political system excluded people from public life and created an alienated, individualistic, consumption-oriented privatizing society' (Hankiss 1990: 207). The centralized power of the party-state undermined a norm of cooperation by eliminating from the public life discourse, negotiation and respect for anything other than official positions.

The main difference between liberal democratic and state socialist systems is a result of the different allowance made for risk-taking behaviour in the political and the economic subsystems. People in communist societies were supposed to trust the system without questioning it, without having a chance to check it, or without even an opportunity to retreat from it. Moreover, there was no official provision for placement elsewhere of the trust that had been withdrawn (for example, there were no legal opposition elites). Hence, to trust or not to trust the system was not the individual responsibility as there was no freedom of choice. The citizen was only called upon to endorse the symbols and decisions of the regime, and emphasis was on pragmatic commitment rather than engagement. Pragmatic acceptance and conformism acted as a cover-up for the system. However, in the long term, it left the system without any mechanism for correction of its distortions and pushed people into other than

officially provided identities and to more particularistic solidarities. The
main structures of trust were the continuation of pre-state socialist
culture and were based on non-market ties of reciprocity and mutuality,
reinforcing pre-modern and primordial types of bonds.

Social solidarity in state socialist societies was defined in a negative
way: *we*, the citizens of the country; and *they*, the party bureaucracy.
With the revolutions of 1989, the process of redefinition of the basic
structures of social solidarity and trust took place. The main problem
now facing post-communist societies is the lack of 'a fixed set of trustworthy or at least uncontested social facts and binding institutional
forces' (Offe 1991b: 882). The new decision-making process requires a
new input of trust. Unfortunately, recent attempts to find reliable foundations for new confidence are often based on ethnic, national or religious identities. Furthermore, the collapse of the communist state has
left, especially in the former Soviet Union, an enormous political and
legal vacuum. It has also resulted in an increased number of property
owners, who, as administrative and financial codes of practices are not
firmly established and the state does not have the means to enforce and
protect them, need to trust somebody able to enforce their property
rights. While in other former communist countries this demand for
protection is not met by supply, in the former Soviet Union there is 'a
plethora of candidates – from disbanded Red Army soldiers to unem-
ployed athletes' and, moreover, 'ethnic groups with a reputation for
private justice acquired in the black market under the communist regime,
as well as muscular former party members, stand to take the lead in
supplying private protection' (Gambetta 1993: 253). Consequently, the
Russian Mafia is already a global phenomenon. In Poland, Hungary, and
the Czech and Slovak republics the likelihood of the establishment of
societal trust and cooperation are fortunately much higher than in the
former, especially southern, republics of the USSR. How successful these
societies will be depends on the nature of trust in new relations since 'a
specific from of generalized trust – rooted in modern individualist norms
– is necessary for the working of civil society' (Seligman 1992: 182).

This call for the establishment of civil society founded on trust, as the
condition of a successful transformation to a democratic polity and
market-orientated economy, is based on the assumption that there is a
correlation between restricted definitions of trust and restricted definitions of membership in the political community as well as the lack of any
universal recognition of individual integrity (Seligman 1992: 177).
Hence, the case of state socialist societies seems to suggest that trust is an
absolutely necessary cultural prerequisite of civil society. The comparison of the former Soviet bloc countries and Italy reinforces the observation that low levels of trust correspond with a lack of civil society.

In both types of societies discussed above what is missing is what Tocqueville describes as civility: the equable treatment of others as fellow citizens, however different their interests and sensibilities (Bryant 1993: 399). Civility, rooted in the mutual recognition of each individual's dignity and membership in the political community, is 'at [the] bottom of the collective consciousness of civil society' (Shils, quoted in Seligman 1992: 172). In civil society, as the preconditions for cooperation, based on universal notions of individual dignity and moral individualism, presumes that others will deal with us in a civil way. It means in a way free of particularistic loyalties and limited solidarities. Consequently, it can be said that the 'civil society calls for the generalization and universalization of trust' (Seligman 1992: 179).

How does this conclusion relate to the thesis of modernization which assumes that there is a correlation between types of trust and society's level of economic development? Various studies in the 1950s and 1960s argued that in pre-modern societies locality and primordial ties set the limits to whom one trusts, but with higher education, technological and economic standards, it becomes possible to know more about distant and different people, so the boundaries of trust are changing, and trust becomes more diffuse and abstract. 'While traditional societies can survive even if one trusts only those one knows personally, modern society can function only if people do not assume that strangers are enemies' (Inglehart 1991: 149). Because Southern Europe as well as Eastern and Central Europe began to industrialize later than Northern and Western Europe, the absence of trust other than that rooted in the solidarity of family or other particular groups can be explained by the more traditional characteristics of these societies. In contrast, in wealthy Western European countries people tend to trust their fellow citizens. On the basis of results of the 1980 survey of ten European countries, Inglehart argues that there are reciprocal causal relations between low levels of trust and economic development, although, he warns, we should not neglect the impact of economic development on societal learning (1991: 160). According to him, economic security is conducive to interpersonal trust, while at the same time, a relatively high level of interpersonal trust, which permits large-scale modern economic enterprises to develop and function effectively, is conducive to economic development.

The argument in the modernization theory is questioned by Putnam's outcomes, which prove that civic traditions are a uniformly powerful predictor of present socio-economic development; 'economics doesn't predict civics, but civics does predict economics, better indeed than economics itself' (Putnam 1993: 157). Arguments of the eighteenth-century philosopher Dorio, recently brought back to the debate about the causes of the backwardness of southern Italy, also connect the lack of trust in this region to non-economic factors – namely, with the deliberate political strategies of the Spanish Habsburgs (Pagden 1988).

The modernization argument also requires closer inspection in the light of two empirical cases; namely, Czechoslovakia and West Germany. As already mentioned, post-war Czechoslovakia, like all other state socialist countries, was characterized by low levels of trust. Before 1939, however, it was a country with a relatively high level of socio-economic development, with an economic and social structure no more traditional than, for example, Austria. Consequently, we need to assume that certain rather drastic changes occurred during the period 1945–89, which destroyed societal trust. This seems to suggests that the link between socio-economic development and trust is mediated by other types of factors, such as the nature of the political system or civil society. Looking at the example of West Germany at the end of the 1950s, Almond and Verba declare that this country was characterized by low levels of trust. The lack of an expression of trust on the broader societal level resulted in a description of post-war German society as anomic and with an undeveloped civic culture. However, further evidence shows a steady increase of interpersonal trust. When asked the general question 'Can most people be trusted?', in 1948 only 9 per cent of those surveyed answered 'yes'. By the end of the 1950s, however, the percentage answering positively increased to 19, and by the mid-1970s to 39 per cent (Conradt 1989: 254). The same optimistic trend has been visible in all other questions measuring civic involvement. The rise in the level of social trust can be seen as being 'related to a growth in system identification and legitimacy, and hence signs of the health and vitality of the postwar democratic order' (1989: 265). The role of post-war socio-economic modernization in fostering civic culture cannot be ignored, but the polity stabilization and the impact of political socialization, resulting in increasing support for liberal democracy, also need to be included.

While Putnam stresses the role of norms of generalized reciprocity and networks of civic engagement as the main factors creating and maintaining trust as social capital, the two examples above reveal that levels of social trust can also be influenced by the credibility of the government. Not only relations among people and the density of their networks but also trustworthy government, having support from and contributing to increasing satisfaction in the functioning of institutions, can play an important role in creating and maintaining trust. In turn, this social capital can enhance institutional performance by lowering the cost of information about the trustworthiness of others, thus enhancing an informal solution to the problem of cooperation. Trust and social solidarity can, moreover, contribute to the constitution and workings of checks on government. This argument was developed by Tocqueville in his emphasis on the role of politics in spreading a general taste for political and social activity, which not only increases individuals' self-esteem but also 'passes then, into civil society' (Tocqueville 1968: 301). The same conclusion is reached by Margaret Levi, when she notes that the different responses of Canadian francophones and anglophones to the introduction of conscription was a result of the differences in the record of promise-keeping of the Canadian federal government. Thus, to ensure a good institutional performance, she says, trust 'among individuals in not enough . . . there must also be trust of governmental actors' (Levi 1993: 378). Without going into the debate about the priority of civil society or that of the state or about their historical order, it can be said that '[b]oth are needed . . . but they each have their own *raison d'être* and their autonomous reality' (Dahrendorf 1990: 96).

To summarize, trust on the general societal level is a by-product of behaviour towards others based on the norm of reciprocity and networks of civic engagements, which can be facilitated by the nature of governmental institutions and the level of socio-economic development. The greater the level of trust within a society, the greater the likelihood of cooperation, which in turn contributes to the establishment of trust relationships. It is assumed that trust towards fellow citizens can be generalized or institutionalized into the political structures, thus becoming a more universal trust, which is seen as the basis for a well-ordered society. At the same time, political institutions can help to maintain or to destroy this generalized trust, while trust within the private realm – that is, trust towards kin and close friends – is seen as people's refuge from high levels of social unpredictability or as a springboard for social activism. The relationship between these types of interpersonal trust – one in relation to family and friends and another towards one's fellow citizens, and between generalized or abstract trust (that is, trust rooted in institutions and their universal norms) – are not clearly specified in the literature. Yet it seems that many writers, from the eighteenth-century writers on classical republicanism, through Toennies, to today's communitarians, assume that there is some interdependence between private and public morality and between private and public institutions. For Italian philosophers, *fede privata*, the private trust, trust in kin and friends, is a necessary condition of *fede pubblica*, the public trust, which is necessary for all political associations; therefore it sustains the state. Doria and Genovesi saw *fede pubblica*, rooted in private trust, as the condition of social stability and economic growth and the basis of the well-ordered republic. The process of decline of any republic starts when 'first private trust [grows] weak and then the public' (Genovesi, quoted in Pagden 1988: 130) and is reversed when people treat 'out-groups' with the same trust as they treat their 'in-groups' (namely, families). This secular ethic of classical republicanism, by stressing the importance of public good over private interest, 'enabled men from different kin groups, and hence from different societies to trust each other', and, consequently, like the Puritan work ethic, encouraged the economic take-off of commercial society (Pagden 1988: 139). Constructive relations between the individual and the community are also at the core of communitarianism. The normative stand of communitarians advocates the regeneration of social solidarity and shared values as a precondition for the integrity of individuals and their ability to be civil members of society (Mulhall and Swift 1992).

Unfortunately, we lack convincing data to evaluate the extent of connections between trust in members of kin and friendship groups and trust towards members of the society at large. A comparison of recently available statistics suggests that there is a tendency for countries that score highly on the 'private trust' scale also to score highly on 'public trust' (Ashford and Timms 1992: 12). This tentative remark is supported by the German data, which show that in the post-war era the growth in interpersonal trust has been accompanied by an increase in declared numbers of friends (in 1957 only 42 per cent said that they had many friends, whereas in 1972 57 per cent said so (Conradt 1989: 254).

On the other hand, we need only to recall Banfield's study as well as Sennett's argument to be warned against any generalization about connections between *la fede pubblica* and *la fede privata*. Both of these writers, although for different reasons and talking about totally different societies, argue that people limited to caring for their families' economic (amoral familism) or psychological well-being (tyranny of intimacy) are not willing to cooperate or enter the public realm. Therefore, the best that can be done is to recognize the interdependence of private and public trust without trying to generalize about its direction and to call for common life to strike 'a rich and balanced mixture' and avoid the extreme of the *Gemeinschaft/Gesellschaft* distinction (Selznick 1992: 509).

So far, we have tried to explain a difference in the level of trust between a model modern society, on the one hand, and state socialist societies and southern Italy, on the other. However, this does not say anything about the current problems with trust within the first category – that is, among Western industrialized liberal democracies. A sense of transition or even of the ending of an era is the dominant feeling, not only among Eastern and Central Europeans. The last decades of this century are commonly characterized as being full of ambiguity, disorganization, dissatisfaction with the existing institutions and distrust of the old authorities. Since the end of the 1960s distrust between the citizen and the state has become a dominant feature in many Western countries. Many surveys have found open distrust of political parties, a clear trend of declining public confidence in the democratic process and the growing alienation among many Westerners towards the bureacratized political system (Dalton 1988: 225–45). The growing social polarization, increased levels of unemployment, the declining ability of the welfare state to meet demands and growing ethnic, racial and religious diversification of modern societies have also been undermining the social consensus of the 1950s and 1960s. The emergence of the extreme right-wing parties, such as the National Front in France, the Republicans in Germany or the British National Party, has provided legitimization for ideas eroding societal solidarity and trust between various social groups. At the same time, the process of globalization, by lowering the state's capacity to steer its economy and increasing the mobility of financial and industrial capitals, creates a new condition for framing identities and loyalties.

Firstly, the process of globalization, by increasing an exit option, reduces the importance of national loyalties founded upon the necessities of economic interdependence. Whereas in state socialist societies exit was not allowed and was treated as treason, today's problems of industrial democracies are connected with an unrestricted right to exit. Hirschman's classic distinction between *exit* (desertion), *voice* (articulation of interest) and *loyalty* points not only to the fact that the nature of the political system matters, but also that loyalty to the system is an important factor in a creative search for solutions. In other words, exit loses its attraction not only when it is possible to have a voice inside the system but also when the system is able to cultivate loyalist behaviour, and, consequently, loyalty 'pushes men into the alternative, creativity-requiring course of action from which they would normally recoil' (Hirschman 1970: 80). Therefore, at least two types of consequences arising from the existence of an unrestricted right to exit can be identified. On the one hand, it reduces public creativity in problem-solving; on the other, it diminishes a general level of solidarity by dismantling the correlation between economic interest and loyalty, both trends leading to a long-term decline in the effectiveness of institutional performance. Numerous examples of corporations and people moving out of their country of origin in search of lower costs, better conditions, lower taxes or cheaper labour can be seen as escaping their obligations towards their own nation. This corrodes the moral obligations of these 'cosmopolitan' people and institutions, consequently making their next move – when profit declines in a new context – even more unproblematic. It also undermines the obligations of the remaining members of society, because for them it becomes too costly and difficult to invest in obligations to others, who can always move out. 'Moreover, obligations in society as a whole are not likely to be taken seriously when migration becomes so dominant a response to tight situations that it is continuously rewarded over staying' (Wolfe 1989: 255).

In a situation where economic bonds no longer attach people to their political and social milieu, there is a danger that global citizens will be without any responsibilities and obligations. 'Without a real political community in which to learn, refine, and practice the ideals of justice and fairness, they may find these ideals to be meaningless abstractions' (Reich 1991: 205). We can only learn to feel responsible for others and construct trust relationships by sharing with others a common fate, culture, rights and duties. Furthermore, cosmopolitianism not only erodes the process of social learning of obligation, it also can enhance resignation by creating a sense of hopelessness *vis-à-vis* difficult, overpowering global problems. In contrast, within smaller units, 'problems may seem soluble; even tiny improvements can seem large on this smaller scale' (1991: 206). However, at the same time, nationalism as a mobilizing force in the global, cosmopolitan world is not relevant because it cannot teach the trust that is needed for a new global order. A focus solely on national well-being is too limited a perspective in relation to new global problems, which require international cooperation.

The second type of factor influencing modern identity and bonds in the global world is the process of integration, as exemplified by the European Union. The emerging supranational frameworks of regional blocs have challenged the sovereignty of national states over social rights. This means that not only are market forces gaining the upper hand but also the states' responsibility for many rights, which are part of the definition of citizenship, and the core of a sense of belonging is reduced and transferred to supranational levels. According to some writers this trend towards integration erodes the nation-state and consequently creates new links and loyalties among citizens and governments, especially increasing regional identities and pride (Horsman and Marshall 1994).

The process of integration is seen as enhancing individual rights by providing people with the means of suing their national authorities for the enactment and enforcement of key rights. Consequently, it can, for example, allow some regions (such as Scotland or Catalonia) to bypass national governments and foster their regional loyalties. According to Huntington (1993) this growing role of economic regionalism accompanied by the declining importance of the nation-state enhances differences and distrust between civilizations, defined by the commonality of history, language, culture, tradition and religion. In this approach, civilization is seen as a broader type of framework for our identities, commitment and trust. However, there is much empirical evidence – for example, the division of the Arab world and the Australian attempt to a create regional bloc with Asian countries – which does not support Huntington's hypothesis about the clash of civilizations and the increasing role of a civilization identity. Moreover, Huntington pays too little attention to the resilience of the nation-state (Milward 1992). The nation-state's existence does not depend only on frontiers. Similarly, the shrinking of the nation-state's economic, political and military functions does not 'automatically destroy its contract with its citizens. For that contract rests on the state remaining the power that people trust most' (Brock 1994: 13). The nation-state is still perceived by the majority of people as the protector and insurance policy of last resort. Fear of losing welfare rights and their own quality of identification were at the core of the low support in Denmark for the Maastricht treaty, and in the low percentage of 'yes' votes in a referendum on joining the European Union in Sweden and the rejection of the EU membership by Norway. The recent difficulties of the European Union in generating loyalty and a sense of common destiny seem to result from its inability to provide real entitlements as well as the absence of any unique political traditions. The trend to integration and to the growth of supranational bodies can also produce a reductive and exclusive effect. 'This is the struggle for the attainment of "prize" citizenship by an enormous mass of people coming from underdeveloped continental areas with high demographic rates' (Zolo 1993: 266). Mass migration from Third World countries puts enormous pressure on the West for equality, protection and fulfilment of citizenship rights. The threat brought by these demands results in many reductive changes to immigration or citizenship laws in Western Europe (for example, in France and Germany).

The issue of exclusion or the denial of legal and social status to migrants points to the third important factor shaping modern solidarities and identities; namely, *entrance rules*. Some people can trust and feel an obligation to all humanity but normally we 'think of ourselves not as human beings first, but as sons, and daughters . . . tribesmen, and neighbors' (Ignatieff 1985: 29). Since borderless idealism and trust lack shape and meaning, we need to define whom we trust and to whom we have any obligation. Thus, there is a need to decide on entrance rules – that is, 'criteria for determination who should belong to the group to which one is presumably obligated' (Wolfe 1989: 247). This dilemma as to who has the right to belong seems bound to be one of the most important issues in liberal democracies. The problem is not only limited to the question of who should be allowed in, although it is a significant problem, particularly for countries with a highly developed welfare state (Wolfe 1989: 247), but it is also connected with the question of what is expected from those who are already in. The recent controversy in France surrounding the ruling not to allow Muslim girls to wear scarves in state high schools can best illustrate this. The non-acceptance of 'ostentatious' signs of religious affiliations in strictly secular state schools is an exemplification of rules of entrance: 'Foreigners arriving in France must understand that henceforth their ancestors are Gauls. They have a new fatherland. Islam has a place in France, provided it is willing to stay as discreet as other religions' (Jean-Claude Barreau, an adviser to the French Minister of the Interior, quoted in *The Economist*, 8 October 1994: 57).

The dilemma over entrance rules applies not only to 'outsiders' but also to rules defining criteria of access, or *voice*, of any group within the nation-state. Wolfe (1989) mentions how the Scandinavian countries' tightly drawn entrance rules exclude from corporatist benefits smaller or unorganized parts of the populace. A much more drastic case of redrawing rules for voice from within is the situation of ethnic minorities in the Baltic republics of Estonia and Latvia. Their attempts to create the polity on the bases of exclusion, distrust of Russians living in these republics (30 and 48 per cent respectively) and an undemocratic lack of recognition of the rights of minorities has been internationally condemned. At the same time, it shows how difficult it is in the post-Yalta order simultaneously to create a new nation, a state and a democracy (Stepan 1994). Yet, sometimes even the sharing of a common nationality and language is not enough to be accepted and fully trusted as a member of the nation-state. Here, of course, one thinks about the failure of the German unification, which has been unable so far to fill the 'psychological gap' between Westerners and citizens of the former East Germany.

According to a 1993 poll, only 22 per cent of West Germans and 11 per cent of East Germans say they have a common identity. Paradoxically, East German identity, which almost disappeared in the first months of the 1989 revolution, re-emerged very quickly; while in 1990, 73 per cent of Easterners declared a single German identity, the percentage dropped to 40 in 1991 (Gloannec 1994: 143). Yet Westerners' identity with West Germany as a liberal democratic state proved to be very stable. The 'psychological gap' between these two groups is connected with the issue of national identity and differences in everything, from their approach to families to different expectations towards the state. Shortly after unification, the East Germans had adopted the achievement principle to the same extent as the West Germans, whereas their expectations regarding the government were significantly higher (Roller 1994: 11). The present determination of Easterners not to be overtaken by the culture and values of the West has led to the re-emergence of many specifically East German rituals and to the electoral revival of the former communists, the Party of Democratic Socialism. They also backed different options for the process of unification. The variant stressing nationalism as a unifying factor seems to be rather more popular in the East, where the *nation* is looked upon 'as a panacea, a cure for all miseries' (Gloannec 1994: 136). The Westerners, who discarded nationalism, rally behind the option emphasizing democracy as a mobilizing factor. The first option suggests the creation of a nation-state as the framework for a political community, in which these two groups are expected to trust each other because they are part of the same German nation. The second option stresses that these two groups are participants in the same democratic political community, which allows for numerous circles of complex identities; regional, national, European and global: 'Germany will be integrated when most Germans are recognized to have access to multiple choices. The task is more daunting than it was a century ago; democracy today is certainly not the mobilizing force nationalism was. The aim – the pursuit of democracy – makes the effort both worthwhile and necessary' (1994: 145).

All of these examples illustrate various recent tensions between the logic of the nation-state and the main current processes of globalization, integration and pluralism. They show that liberal visions of the nation-state, seen as a population of sovereign individual citizens who will rationally combine across the state to negotiate their interests peacefully, is losing its relevance in a more globalized world. The sovereign nation-state ceases to be the sole frame for the political community when people can declare multiple loyalties, when their economic interest no longer bonds them to the nation-state, when their decision can have an impact on people outside their nation-state and when so many problems require a global approach.

At the same time, these examples also problematize the concept of society and reveal the need for a rediscussion of the bases of modern complex multi-national democratic societies. Sociological dictionaries refer to the notion of 'society' as being equivalent to the boundaries of the nation-state, although it is admitted that not all societies always correspond to political boundaries (as in 'Palestinian' society).

There is no need here to review the literature in order to illustrate the changing meaning, boundaries and content attributed to the notion of 'society' through the centuries, for the job has already been done by writers such Touraine (1992) or Bauman (1989). In general terms it can be said that the idea of society has always been intended to include the main bases of social and institutional unity or the main principles of social organization and social order. Before the idea of the nation-state as a unifying principle became synonymous with the concept of society, society meant civilization and later, for Hobbes, Locke, Montesquieu and Rousseau, the polity (Touraine 1992: 56–8). Recently, many writers have declared the end of society as embedded in the nation-state as a result of the process of the decomposition of community, and the growing separation between politics, economics and culture. The modern, more complex social system has separated itself completely from the state, and it no longer derives any principle of unity from it. Modern society 'no longer has any institutional or moral unity, sovereignty, or central principle of legitimacy' (1992: 76).

To sum up, the main characteristic of contemporary modern society, especially in Western Europe, is the extreme separation between the state and social life and the declining importance of conditions facilitating a transition from cultural to political nationalism, because the drive for ethnic homogeneity is no longer so closely connected to economic mercantilism and because of the existence of opportunities for multiple identities. While it may be too much to say that modern Western countries are moving towards a post-national era, this is certainly a period in which nationalism is less valued as the unifying and mobilizing force than democracy, which allows for the existence of differences among the people it seeks to unite. These two observations – firstly, that our life is less and less determined by purely national frameworks, and secondly, that democracy is a prerequisite of a new social unity and international cooperation – still do not provide us with a clear answer to the question of whether 'society' should be vested in nations, smaller groups or wider associations. Emphasis on the significance of trust as a factor shaping a feeling of belonging together in a common undertaking allows us to redefine society as placed within a space best suited to accommodate the multiplication and division of its populace in conditions of economic freedom and with opportunities for voluntary associations and local participation. Trust in the institutional systems, with active involvement within political and economic institutions, and interpersonal trust, with shared acceptance of the values of democratic polity, are thus mechanisms sustaining general trust and maintaining social unity. These mechanisms – trust in and concern for one's fellow citizens – crucially depend upon the nature and amount of information or knowledge each person has. Because in order to cultivate a trusting society there is a need for communication to be open and founded on trust, trust is both the fruit of good communication and its necessary precondition (Vickers 1987: 119–23). Hence, to sustain the level of communication is essential for the existence of mutual trust. Open communication and societal dialogue among autonomous and trustworthy people, yet ones who are different in many aspects, are built up through acts of trust. Trust permits consensus and civil disagreement to occur, without endangering cooperation on matters of common concern.

This idea of society has less to do with formal organization than with a sense of belonging, trust and responsibility and duties towards others who share our values, interests and goals. Its limits are difficult to state with any strict determinacy at a general level. This notion of society as an order of shared knowledge is close to Barnes' definition of society 'as persisting distribution of knowledge', where trust and cooperation presuppose learning (1988: 45). Although society as such is independent of authority, it is informed by its law and policy. Since modernity corrodes many forms of authority, among them nation-states, the question arises of what level of authority is essential for the constitution of such a society? It is rather difficult to provide a general answer, as it seems to be a subject for a more historically and geographically specific enquiry. None the less, it can be said that the combination of democratic pluralism with a continuing role of the nation-state will for many years remain the main framework for society. Although the world becomes an increasingly complex and tightly knit regional and continental system, in which the role of supranational and regional identities and loyalties is expanding, its strategies to cope with many problems will still be state-based. The concept of society, however, must also take account of the nature of modern individualism and consequently that a concept of citizenship relevant for the modern world must accommodate multiple loyalties. It should also extend beyond the territorial boundaries of the nation-state in order to include all levels of indentity and decision-making (from local to the international) which have an effect on people's lives.

To conclude, trust in society is not easy to achieve. In our modern world it needs to be constructed through the active communication of autonomous, albeit different people. Since trust in society can no longer be solely rooted in the common characteristics and similarities of its members, it requires policy able to generate it by enriching and sustaining solidarity, tolerance and legitimacy.

# 6
# Trust as Policy

## Trust and solidarity

> Writing about cooperation and solidarity means writing at the
> same time about rejection and mistrust.... Everyone is af-
> fected directly by the quality of trust around him or her.
> Douglas 1986: 1

Trust, as integral to social order, has been central to sociological
theorizing about solidarity. Solidarity as the commitment which subordinates individual interest to a larger social whole was at the centre
of attention of all classical writers who believed in the progressive
triumph of social and economic integration. They described different
types of solidaristic orders by pointing to different means of reinforcing
trust in pre-modern and modern societies. Industrialization and urbanization, it is argued, had largely destroyed traditional solidarities and
damaged the old social fabric. While for some writers the history of
modernization illustrated only the process of decomposition of
solidaristic communities, others, like Durkheim, believed that growing
economic interdependence improves prospects for social solidarity because it produces greater mutual recognition and sensitivity between the
different sectors of society.

Durkheim, who criticized the utilitarian model, in which a social order
is produced automatically out of the self-interested actions of rational
individuals, saw solidarity – that is, trust, reciprocity and moral obligation – as possible only to the extent that individuals share their values
and norms. Durkheim's 'precontractual' trust was based on 'the governing terms of social solidarity, which in modern, organic society was based
on the ethical valuation of individual personhood' (Seligman 1992: 121).

This stress on individual autonomy as the core principle of social solidarity resulted in Durkheim's search for a mechanism of social organization which would 'subordinate the private interest to social ends' (Durkheim 1962: 48), and consequently to his advocacy of intermediary groups. Durkheim's libertarian solidarism saw the state and corporations as 'public institutions' responsible for enhancing social solidarity and overcoming social conflicts and social tensions. Furthermore, for him solidarity, as a basis for social morality, was necessarily accompanied by liberty and equality. Durkheim recognized 'the primary need for economic life to become more ethical, civilised and humane. . . . Only deeper and more lasting cultural and institutional bonds could effectively moderate conflict and create the basis for people to have mutual confidence and trust, to work together and to find personal dignity and meaning in their lives' (Boswell 1990: 170). The social implications of this were expressed in the development of forms of citizenship that included a social component beyond the purely abstract legal equality of citizenship.

Durkheim's legacy consisted of a recognition that universal solidarity among citizens underpins their very individual and particular existence, and the acceptance of the central role of the social mutuality and solidarity as mediating modern individualism. 'Durkheim and, following him, much of twentieth-century sociology thus attempted to square the circle of modern individualism. They attempted, that is, to posit a theoretical grounding for the solidarity and mutuality of a society comprising "wholes that are self-sufficing"' (Seligman 1992: 123). This emphasis on the social aspect of individual existence, although replacing traditional criteria of solidarity with modern values of individual rights, universal citizenship and the idea of the morally autonomous person, has not, however, resolved tensions between the concepts of 'social' and 'individual' or between rights and solidarity. Furthermore, the Durkheimian vision, while becoming very popular among and beyond scholarly circles, has not provided remedies for the main problems: 'we still feel the lack of solidarity, mutuality and trust in our hospitals, schools, and places of employment. The public space of citizenship still seems to be characterised by abstract legal formulae and not by moral affections' (Seligman 1992: 126). Since Durkheim's strategy for constructing conditions of trust and solidarity showed itself to be insufficient both in theory and in practice, various theoretical and practical proposals have been put forward to foster trust and social solidarity: the most prominent among them being calls for a return to 'community' and later for a reactivization of civil society. The concept of community has experienced an enormous fluctuation in popularity, from being one of the primary notions in sociology before the Second World War, to becoming less relevant in the post-war period (Kymlicka 1993). However, it has kept re-emerging, first within the idea of rebuilding local community in the 1960s and later within the perspective of communitarianism.

The concept of community has multiple meanings. Most often 'community' refers to a locality, to the place in which we live our daily lives. This way of understanding community, stressing social relations with others, marking out bonds of solidarity and identity with people occupying the same space as us, was characteristic of earlier attention given to the concept. In the 1960s the reconstruction of local community was seen as an important part of the political re-invention of the larger society. The assumption behind the project of constructing new solidarity and trust relationships was that 'the very terms of intimate experience would indeed permit people to create a new kind of sociability, based on sharing of their feelings' (Sennett 1974: 298). Attempts to create community in cities were undertaken to introduce face-to-face, close and open social relationships, which would ensure participation, friendliness, trust and attachment into the public realm. Although evaluations of these projects vary, it is generally admitted that the practice of modern community did not meet these high expectations. Sennett argues that this stress on community had only negative consequences as community leads to emotional withdrawal from a larger society. According to him, building a sense of community at local level in the city is not a means by which to revive public space and public life in the city nor in the society as a whole. Furthermore, he notes that 'this struggle for community solidarity serves a stabilizing function in terms of larger political structures of the society . . . the more people are plunged into these passions of community, the more the basic institutions of social order are untouched' (1974: 309).

In the last decade the concept of community has been also playing an important role in the philosophical and political discourse of communitarianism, where it highlights commitment to a common good that transcends individual interests. The communitarian aim, however, is not the traditional one of transcending the self through identification with a class, group or nation. 'On the contrary, the object is to recover strong expressive selves, to make "thin" selves "thick"' (Rosenblum 1989: 218). Scholars writing from this perspective argue that 'community is a structural precondition of human agency (including moral agency)', that communal membership is essential for the possibility of 'attaining any sort of human goods whatever' and that there is no universal theory of justice since 'social justice itself must be understood as embedded within and relative to communal framework' (Mulhall and Swift 1992: 161–2). Their normative call for the politics of solidarity does not demand the sacrifice of tolerance and respect for difference, but stresses the need for liberty and equality as well as for shared deliberation and political legitimacy. Assuming that people are not free-standing but members of social groups that deeply influence their behaviour and that this membership is the precondition of their ability to be civil members of society, communitarianism criticizes the liberal approach for ignoring the fact that individuals are dependent upon society and for unbalanced emphasis on individual autonomy. 'In short, against the liberal's emphasis upon autonomy, the communitarian sets an emphasis upon dependence; against the liberal claim that my life is my own to make of it what I will, the communitarian sets the claim that loci of value in my life are often to be found outside myself' (Mulhall and Swift 1992: 294).

Another concept, which also contributed to the revival of interest in solidarity and trust, is the notion of civil society. This interest has emerged as a result of evidence suggesting that legal formulas of citizenship did not secure solidarity, participation and the expansion of the public sphere. With many symptoms of the decline of solidarity, such as the decrease in popularity of solidaristic parties, the disappearance of class solidarity, the collapse of solidaristic ideology (namely, communism, which proclaims the universal consensus and social harmony and sees a social class as able to act in a solidaristic way upon its own interest) and the growing evidence of depoliticization, privatism and passivity of populace, the renewal of civic institutions and the emergence of new social movements have been perceived as new ways of constructing new identities and social bonds and teaching new responsibilities and obligations. The task of protecting solidarity falls to the institutions of civil society, which offset the commodification, formalism and proceduralism of the state and market spheres. At the same time, civil society presents the opposite of the notion of a homogeneous community because it endorses social diversity, thus making the political system more open, participatory and democratic. In the civil society perspective identity is seen as arising from the solidarity of everyday life based on mutual trust, and new social movements are presented as agents of social re-integration. In a call for the moral reconstitution of civil society as 'realms of intimacy, trust, caring, and autonomy that are different from the larger world of politics and economics', Wolfe (1989: 38) supports the role of civil society as maintaining a social fabric that tempers the operation of the market and the state and anchors them in a normative framework.

Cohen and Arato's (1992) reconstruction of civil society, which is 'a political translation' of Jurgen Habermas' critical theory, also places civil society in a sphere of interaction between society and the state and entails plurality, publicity, legality and privacy. They view the sphere of civil society as the terrain on which both the values of human solidarity as well as an orientation towards individual and collective self-realization might be actualized. Cohen and Arato defend Habermas' discourse ethic by stressing the importance of the values of mutual recognition, solidarity and public criticism to the formation of post-traditional collective identities. They followed Habermas' viewing of solidarity as the complementary concept to justice and consequently, the principle of solidarity 'loses its ethnocentric character when it becomes part of a universal theory of justice and is constructed in light of the idea of discursive formation' (1992: 382). Solidarity is rooted in the experience that each must take responsibility for the other because the concerns for the welfare of others and general welfare are closely connected through the concept of identity, which is reproduced by relations of mutual recognition. Solidarity is defined as 'the ability of individuals to respond to and identify with one another on the basis of mutuality and reciprocity, without calculating individual advantages, and above all without compulsion. Solidarity involves a willingness to share the fate of the other, not as the exemplar of a category to which the self belongs but as a unique and different person' (1992: 472). The positive potentials of modern civil society are actualized by new social movements, which are engaged in 'double politics', focusing around influencing political and economic policy in the direction of greater inclusion and around the affirmation of solidarity and construction of collective identity.

The concept of civil society is now commonly recognized as a basis for democratic legitimacy in the modern world. And while this recent 'discourse of civil society' is 'at the heart of a sea of change in contemporary political culture' (Cohen and Arato 1992: 3), it remains to be identified exactly how and by what mechanisms solidarity is to be ensured. The attainment of a new equilibrium is too often perceived as 'natural', based on the assumption of the existence of self-evident mutual obligations and common purposes, and hence does not provide a clear answer to what the roots of the shared identities that bind people together are. The possibility of a renewal of solidarity through the re-emergence of a plurality of associations is not so obvious since they do not necessarily increase democratic inclusion. Furthermore, it is not very clear whether civil society is merely an association of interest or whether it is based on something more than enlightened self-interest. The concept of civil society, however, allows the new Left to construct a programme of revitalization of the public realm and is the most essential notion in many recent attempts at social reform. It seems that any project of re-invention of active citizenry as the basis of social solidarity needs to include the cultivation of a sphere of autonomous social action.

New solidaristic ideas are also inspired by the rejection of neo-Right projects, that suggest that the problems of modern society can be cured by the extension of individual rights (as formulated in Thatcher's famous expression that 'There is no such a thing as society'). For many commentators, Thatcherism as a political project is synonymous with the abolition of social solidarity. The Thatcherite project is, for instance, defined by Stuart Hall (1993: 14) as the 'only political and moral force that has been in the business of eating away at the cement of social reciprocity'. This policy has undermined the welfare state and has resulted in the breakdown of social solidarity and in a reduction of any possibility of evoking any responsibility that people might have for one another. When consequences of this policy pushing the market principle to its ultimate limit have become visible, with the number of social problems and dislocation drastically increasing, the Right has found it convenient to mobilize political support through such programmes as 'Back to Basics', which addresses the popular themes of crime, family breakdown and social disintegration. Thus, it seems that, on the Right, slogans of community and social cohesion, which are presented as connected with social harmony, stability, partnership, social order and the absence of crime, are used to fill the void by playing on people's increasing feelings of insecurity and nostalgia for the sense of belonging.

On the Left, new solidaristic ideas are aspired to by the recognition of the need for democratization of the state and the public realm, while accepting the demand for choice and individual rights. Tony Blair's recent attempt to redefine the British Labour party by stressing community, solidarity, responsibility and trust; or Delors' formulation of the European Union's main goals as those of cooperation, solidarity and competition; or President Clinton's call for a 'spirit of community' and a politics of the common good – are all examples of more inclusive democratic communitarianism, which is becoming very popular on the Left. This growing recognition of the importance of solidarity raises the question, why does solidarity matter? In many ways it is an expansion of the question about a new interest in trust, which I addressed in the first chapter.

The first and the main reason why such importance is attached to the problem of solidarity is the perception that solidarity is a condition of the good and decent life. Without going into detail, since it is basically the same argument as already present in our discussion of communitarianism, we can note that over the years various political philosophers have stressed that civic participation and solidarity are the cornerstones of the good life. Some writers draw on civic republicanism, and argue for a more genuinely integrated societal community facilitating victory over individualization and separation and in which citizens, educated in civic virtues, take responsibility for the community (Bellah et al. 1985). This way of thinking has found new expression in the writings of Bellah and his colleagues (1985, 1991), which stress the importance of

institutions and associations and the need for more substantial ethical
identities and more active participation in a democratic polity for the
functioning of any decent society. Civic republicanism's emphasis on
politics as depending upon a notion of community and citizenship is
different from the utilitarian, individualist view. The way to develop
public life is to embrace group solidarity – that is, to realize that reciprocity and mutual trust are values in themselves. In this view, the
individual finds fulfilment in relationships with others in a society organized through political dialogue, which can be sustained 'only by communities of memory, whether religious or civic' (Bellah et al. 1985: 218).
Because of the importance of community in civic republicanism it is
argued that '[c]ivic republicanism is communitarianism' (Oldfield 1990:
145). In comparison with liberalism, republicanism argues for a larger
and more active role for citizens and demands identification with the
state as a community, not just as an association with important but
limited functions.

The second reason why such importance is attached to solidarity is the
perception that solidarity increases cooperation by reducing the probability of free riders, hence contributing to societal well-being. Here, for
example, social scientists working on local and international issues show
how trust, or the capacity to make credible commitments, is a very
effective arrangement for enabling participants to cooperate. Many
problems in common-pool resources situations (the so-called 'tragedy of
the commons' which describes the degradation of the environment whenever many individuals are using scarce resources in common) have been
solved thanks to self-monitoring and self-enforcing patterns of human
interaction. All the research on local common-pool resources and public
goods illustrate that 'extensive common knowledge and ease of information provisions facilitate cooperation, while private information and
barriers to communication make it much more difficult' (Keohane and
Ostrom 1994: 423–4). If we realize that some level of trust is the
prerequisite of communication, policy implications become obvious. To
increase the extent of common knowledge and to facilitate information
exchange, which are the condition of negotiation, it is necessary to craft
institutional arrangements, which sustain and re-build trust as social
capital.

Thirdly, it is often, in a more traditional way, argued that social
solidarity is the condition of individual integrity and moral growth. This
type of argument is made from various ideological positions. Apart from
the liberal solidarism of Durkheim, it was the leitmotif of Titmuss'
philosophy of welfare policy. For him solidaristic relations are important
because 'their absence divides people from one another, deprives each of
the other's qualities, creates domination and subordination where they

need not exist, makes each of us less of what he or she can be' (Miller 1987: 7). Thus the condition of solidarity is learning to take responsibility for others, which lifts us to a higher moral level. The fullest form of this argument can be found in the personalized Christian democracy, which started with the *Rerum Novarum* encyclical of 1891. This perspective, 'reaffirmed in a modern form, age-old communitarian ideas of Hebrew, Greek and more particularly Christian provenance, . . . are still important through western culture' (Boswell 1990: 27). To reject liberal individualism and see personal development only along communal routes is crucial, since, for a relationship with others, trust, solidarity and love are necessary for each person's moral and spiritual growth. The moral primacy of communal relationship calls for democracy as the political structure which allows people to take responsibility and participate in communities. Also various forms of pluralistic communalism – that is, beliefs in people's moral development through participation in various natural groupings such as family, local community, welfare associations, religions, organizations, trade unions and so on – stress that these groups help to promote the moral development of human beings. While it is rather difficult to verify this argument (although we can find cases which falsify it), it is one of those social myths whose power is not necessarily related to its truth and which is able to mobilize social energy in its defence. As such this argument for solidarity and trust cannot be totally rejected.

Fourthly, solidarity and trust are important because they make it possible to adopt the long-term solution, which in turn fosters cooperation and therefore general well-being. By enhancing a long-term perspective in the decision-making process, trust allows for planning, for more rational distribution of resources, for the introduction of necessary reforms and for behaviour and decisions to be solely motivated by considerations of immediate profit. Here, apart from Japanese industrial and financial system structures, the best examples come from Germany. German industrial banking, where companies finance investment through long-term loans from banks, which in turn sit on the firms' supervisory boards, is based on lasting and nurturing relationships of trust. Consequently, there is 'an enduring commitment between creditor and company' and this facilitates long-term decision-making, and therefore 'managers have less fear that shareholders will sell out, so they do not face a need to keep dividends high at the expense of training and R&D' (Crouch 1993: 89). This role of trust is not limited to the economic sphere. Its role extends to the political arena as well. It is twice as important because, as Descartes and later Tocqueville argued, democracy, as the system excessively concerned with short-term tuning, is badly adapted to long-term planning:

[d]emocracy does not provide a people with the most skilful of governments, but it does that which the most skiful government often cannot do:
it spreads throughout the body social a restless activity, superbundant force
and energy never found elsewhere, which however little favoured by circumstances, can do wonders. Those are its true advantages (Tocqueville, quoted
in Elster 1988: 97).

Fifthly, a very Tocquevillian argument is developed by John A. Hall,
who argues that solidaristic policies lower social tensions and conflicts.
Looking at historical examples of how Western European democracies
coped with working-class militancy before the First World War, he
explains that where liberal states allowed workers into the political
system by granting them political rights and permitting them to become
reformists, the level of social conflict was low. Therefore, solidaristic
policies of citizenship diffuse conflicts by introducing some kind of social
pact, which confirms some rules and a basic level of trust between classes.
Therefore, the most stable democratic systems are those in which state
and society cooperate and the state is trusted by citizens because they
know they have the capacity to correct its abuses (Hall 1994: 42–8).
Finally, trust as policy is important because it can generate 'high levels of
expectation in its citizens' (Pagden 1988: 130). If a trusting society is a
society 'in which men are prepared to surrender their instinctive habits of
distrust, where they are prepared to have faith in their neighbours'
words' (1988: 130), in such a society there is a lot of energy and
motivation and abilities for improvements and change.

Although it is possible to find even more voices praising solidarity, it
needs to be mentioned that this concept is not without its critics. All
negative evaluations of solidarity question the possibility of rights, freedom, choice, autonomy and diversity in a more cohesive environment. A
politics of belonging to community and 'a politics of solidarity . . . are
threats to personal liberty' (Rosenblum 1989: 209). Social cohesion is
too often achieved 'at the expense of individual autonomy, social pluralism and participatory activity' (Barber 1984: 243). Hence, in solidaristic
policies the central role of pluralism in self-development as well as the
experience of moral conflict are overlooked (Lukes 1989). Furthermore,
groups that are too closely knit are seen as potentially hostile to larger
society (Sennett 1974). Communities that are too integrated can be
undemocratic because of their 'grave risks of monism, conformism and
coercive consensualism' (Barber 1984: 150). The communitarian concept
of community is criticized for being too romantic and regressive since it
sees community as 'designed to repair decentered, disempowered,
narcisstic selves diagnosed as incapable of sustaining either a public or
private life' (Rosenblum 1989: 219). Finally, community does not have a

reference to specific political forms; its character is undefined and its parameters are vague.

While in many instances these critical comments reflect the social reality of communities, it is worth noting that they are describing one specific type of solidaristic arrangement. They refer to communities where '[d]istrust and solidarity, seemingly so opposed, are united' (Sennett 1974: 311). These are collectivities which only reinforce a universal human fear of the unknown by refusing to deal with and absorb the outside world. 'Community feeling formed by the sharing of impulses has the special role of reinforcing the fear of the unknown, converting claustrophobia into an ethical principle' (1974: 310). In such a community it is not only distrust of non-members that is a cementing factor; it is also distrust of other members which imposes conformism and controls members' loyalty. Since the member who changes 'betrays' the community, 'individual devotion threatens the strength of the whole; people have therefore to be watched and tested' (1974: 311). Since I am interested in cases where solidarity and trust are present side by side, I am not going to discuss this type of sectarian solidarity. Our attention will be focused on societal solidarity as rooted in mutual ties of trust, reciprocity and obligation and as guiding autonomous individuals into the practice of citizenship.

I shall not argue that embeddedness and belonging are ultimate values for everybody and as such they should underline societal aims. Following Hirschman (1982), I accept, rather, that the swings from the privately orientated to the public life and back again are a normal part of human history. This shifting involvement enables people to enter and exit various groups and associations, to protect and defend their identities from groups that are too powerful. In modern societies, however, such oscillations have been overdone. 'Western societies appear to be condemned to long periods of privatisation during which they live through an impoverishing "atrophy of public meaning" followed by spasmodic outbursts of "publicness" that are hardly likely to be constructive' (Hirschman 1982: 132). The fragmentation and individualization of modern social structures, the growing differentiation of interest and the absence of the concept of collective interest means that public involvement has lost much of its attractiveness.

Hence, if we accept that the divorce of the private and the public in modern Western societies has gone too far and that – without new attempts to promote solidarity and cooperation – the political consequences can be disturbing, we should accept that a policy of solidarity should be seen as aiming at coming up with 'constructive' proposals for how to overcome this. Consequently, the institutional designs of modern democracy must be based upon the principle of trust and solidarity. Our real starting point for a policy of solidarity is thus a realistic assumption about some characteristic features of modern social life and the modern self, and the recognition of the need for a renewal of public involvement. If we accept that social involvement and solidarity have positive consequences for the practice of democracy, the question arises of how to achieve social mutuality and trust. What policies can increase trust and solidarity, and with whom, and what type of trust and solidarity should we seek?

The minimal project for constructing solidarity and trust should at least answer the question of how to build safeguards against free riders. The answer to this problem is provided by the theory of rational choice, which, however 'has insuperable difficulties with the idea of solidarity' (Douglas 1986: 8). It is the answer which is in sombre contrast to the Durkheimian optimistic and normative vision. There is no doubt that self-interest by itself is not going to ensure the sense and practice of community. Therefore, safeguarding against free riders requires more than what a rational choice proposes; it demands institutions which daily educate and express the common bonds among people and which build interactions as moral transactions, not only as market exchanges. Thus, while the vision of a system in which people decide to cooperate only because of their common values is too idealistic, the vision of one in which cooperation occurs because of self-interest or sanctions cannot be described as a solidaristic one. Somewhere between these two extreme positions there is a perspective arguing that, since modern society shows a tendency to fragmentation, disintegration, alienation and differentiation, because it is the society of the individualistic ethic and autonomy and because society cannot be replaced by community, a change for the better cannot consist of the elimination of the public sphere but must consist of its transformation. This should involve the establishment of structures and procedures securing the openness, reciprocity, stability and predictability of the political environment and the promotion of the spirit of tact, restraint, civilized moderation, negotiation, compromise and flexibility in the public realm.

In short, although trust can be seen as a mechanism for solving the problem of cooperation only when people cooperate irrespective of sanctions and rewards, it does not mean that it should not be based on individual self-interest. The role of trust as policy concerned with solidarity should also include concern with the equal freedom and welfare of unique and self-determining individuals; hence, it should try to create socio-cultural constraints on self-interested behaviour, which is inherent in competitive markets. From this perspective, a solidaristic order or community does not need to rely on emotional bonds; it is based on a rational consensus attained on the basis of convincing others. Thus, when we talk about trust as a policy we stress the issue of solidarity not as necessarily requiring empathy and sameness with others but one based on some mutual understanding, common interest and destiny.

In order to foster and strengthen trust and solidarity, there is a need for policy to create conditions for shared deliberation and construct opportunities for active involvement by people who are trying to sort out their differences themselves via negotiation and deliberation. Three conditions need to be met before one can expect individuals to engage in this practice of negotiation and active participation.

> These conditions are that individuals need resources; they need empowering – in terms of knowledge, skills, information, time, well-being – to become effective agents in the world. They need opportunities – in terms of the decentralization of both political and economic power – in which they can be effective agents, that is citizens. Finally, they need to be provided with the required motivation to take the practice of citizenship seriously, in terms of performing the duties which they owe to the political community of which they are members (Oldfield 1990: 145).

Trust as a policy aiming at the creation of conditions which foster bonds of solidarity requires, thus, a threefold strategy. Firstly, it demands a strategy for facilitating solidarity as dependent on the satisfaction of economic interests; secondly, a strategy for facilitating trust as connected with a culturally embedded view of the relationship between self and society; and, thirdly, a strategy for facilitating trust as connected with the existence of democratic political structures, such as freedom of association and expression, freedom of the press and religion.

This threefold strategy, by providing people with a reason why they should participate, obey and cooperate, increases the likelihood of community, involvement and cooperation. The promotion of trust as a mechanism for creating conditions for economic, social and political solidaristic orders means constructing conditions of equality, participation and commitment which give people a genuine sense of an equal stake in society. Consequently, this strategic shaping of collective life depends on the role attached to trust relationships in the economic, political and cultural spheres. To address these areas means to introduce the theory of citizenship and the state, which discusses the role of the individual citizen, the rights and obligations of government and the rationale of political activity.

Marshall's (1973) theory of citizenship argues that the development of citizenship provides equal status and that a reduction of the social significance of class inequality tends to reduce class conflict and tensions, thereby enhancing social integration. The integrative aspect of Marshall's perspective on citizenship is commonly acknowledged. It is Marshall's principles of equality in citizenship rights which for many 'provides an explanation of the institutional basis for social cohesion and solidarity' (Barbalet 1988: 82–3). Barbalet goes on to show that, for Marshall, citizenship is not merely an equalization of rights but real membership of a real community. 'Marshall's point is that while citizenship in general tends to promote trans-class culture it cannot serve to reduce class inequality while the core of citizenship compromises only civil rights. The significance of social rights in citizenship is precisely that they tend to remove the illegitimate inequalities from the class system, and in doing so perform a key integrative function' (1988: 91). However, Marshall's emphasis on a material civilization, which through mass production leads to a mass culture, also suggests that social integration is attained through well-being within a psychically uniform standard. Marshall argues that not only a normative acceptance of institutions but also a practical expectation that the system will satisfy the material interests of all society diminishes the role of political citizenship as an integrative force. 'Thus Marshall's theory of integration only partly depends on the concept of citizenship, and he belongs to a tradition which does not emphasise normative integration but integration based on satisfaction of material interests' (Barbalet 1988: 92).

Another important point developed by Marshall is that although the social right removes the significance of class inequalities, the contradiction between citizenship and class is fundamental, and therefore integration is never complete. The lesson from Marshall's theory of citizenship is that any policies of constructing solidarity should strive for a realistic level of integration, which can be seen as a balance between normative and instrumental strategies, between conflict and cohesion, between passivity and activity, between inequality and rights. From a policy point of view, the implication is that the institutional arrangements that are devised to foster solidarity should be crafted as not only to increase citizenship rights but also to correct them or adjust their role to changing economic and social conditions. Only by adopting this more flexible and reflexive way of designing strategies can we preserve or create an optimal level of integration. This problem of readjustment is at the present time one of the main difficulties faced by the welfare state, which can be seen as one of the institutional arrangements raising the possibility of solidarity.

In the post-war period social citizenship has played a positive role as 'a personally and existentially real moral trust and political hope for many citizens in modern Western polities' (Roche 1992: 225). Titmuss (1987), who wanted to restore and deepen the sense of community and mutual care in people, in his altruistic perspective envisaged the welfare state as 'a way of building links between persons, providing a common endeavour, a feeling of responsibility for one another' (Miller 1987: 6). He analysed how the upheaval and uncertainty of war contributed to the interest in mutual aid by all classes. Titmuss assumes that the reduction of inequalities, prompted by an awareness of mutual dependence, is central to the task of building solidaristic social relations and developing a web of relationships which fosters concern for other people.

In the solidaristic welfare state as described by Marshall, the possibility of equality and solidaristic policies has been forged, however, as a matter of rights rather than altruism. 'This was the point of Marshall's trinity of rights and the concept of social citizenship. . . . The fully generalized, comprehensive welfare state most closely embodies institutionalized solidarity' (Baldwin 1990: 29). Baldwin tries to explain how such solidarity was possible. He asks why, given a general tendency over the last century for the state to play an increasing role in the provision against risk, only some countries developed a more comprehensive and solidaristic welfare state, covering all equally against risk. For instance, why did the post-war Scandinavian social democratic welfare state provide more to the least advantaged than was necessary to preserve basic stability? Baldwin looks at social solidarity in terms of social justice and rights rather than in terms of charity and gifts. 'Social solidarity is justice in terms of need. Regardless of birth, merit or worth, the citizen in need has a claim to the community's aid' (1990: 31). This mutual aid is possible because of mutual interdependence. However, interdependence alone is not enough; some collective identity is a necessary condition for the interdependence to enhance reciprocal help.

> If the interdependence of the market alone is insufficient to call forth solidarity, a reciprocity of risk at least increases the likelihood of such mutual aid. Only when those, in different circumstances, would have regarded themselves as self-reliant change their minds, only when sufficiently many see themselves as potentially at risk is a distribution according to need acceptable, is solidarity possible (Baldwin 1990: 33).

Assuming that the common dependence and vulnerability foster cooperation and solidarity, Baldwin argues that effective solidaristic policy must affect all people in their roles of recipients and givers. Consequently, it leads him to analyse the risk incidence and the capacity for the self-reliance of all classes as well and the construction of the social insurance system itself as the main variables whose intersection defines each class interest in a redistribution of the costs of uncertainty. Solidaristic reforms are seen as the outcome of a battle of antagonistic interests, which succeeded 'only when sufficiently powerful elements within the bourgeoisie also stood to profit from measures that may have helped the poor, only when a coalition of solidaristic interests that was strong and motivated enough to shift burdens to other groups was negotiated in social insurance's redistributive calculus' (1990: 293).

The recent shrinking of the welfare state can be explained in a similar way. To some degree such an explanation can be found in Galbraith's book *The Culture of Contentment* (1992), and in Reich's (1991) debates on a positive economic nationalism. In general terms, the main causes of change in support for solidaristic social policies are developments in both the welfare system and in society at large. The first issue – problems within the welfare state which result in the limitation of public willingness to be taxed for welfare – escapes Galbraith's attention. He does not consider that the public reject tax increases because they do not support spending on existing forms of bureaucratic state welfare rather than only trying to avoid taxes. The real problem is, Hirst (1994: 165) notes, that 'supporters of the extension of state welfare services have been unable to come up with a clear new strategy that encompasses reforms to both founding and service delivery'. Apart from this new development within the welfare state, there are also new trends within society which are causing changes in support for solidaristic social policies. In general terms, it can be said that social classes formerly in need lost their solidaristic interests once prosperity and the workings of social insurance's reallocative calculus threatened to make them redistributive losers. Consequently, risk categories and classes are disjointed, and we now face the situation where class and risk run too parallel to each other for there to be any common agreement to redistribute burdens without at the same time restructuring the *status quo*. Now the cosmopolitan elites do not stand to gain from the welfare state since there is no longer the possibility of reciprocity, which is a precondition of social insurance.

According to Galbraith (1992), in America and Britain there is now a 'constituency of contentment', made up of those who have been made rich and secure, who need nothing but lower taxes, less state intervention and more opportunities for a quick, short-term profit. This class does not have anything to gain from more public spending, and thus promotes the ideology of *laissez-faire* economics, which by changing the conditions of redistribution suits their objectives. At the same time, on the other extreme of the social spectrum, the number of people experiencing poverty or harsh conditions is growing. For instance, both in Britain and in the United States, income inequalities are now larger than at any time since the 1930s. In Britain the gap between rich and poor has been widening since 1977. While in 1977 the income of the richest 20 per cent of Britons was four times as big as the income of the poorest 20 per cent, by 1991 that multiple had increased to seven. In the United States in 1992, the top 20 per cent of households received eleven times as much income as the bottom 20 per cent (*The Economist*, 5 November 1994: 19).

According to Reich (1991), the fortunes of the most well-off and the least well-off will continue to diverge because of their different positions within the increasingly international economy. Therefore, there is a need for 'a positive economic nationalism, in which each nation's citizens take primary responsibility for enhancing the capacities of their countrymen for full and productive lives, but who also work with other nations to ensure that these improvements do not come at others' expense' (Reich 1991: 207). However, his solution to the problem seems to be cast too much in the republican tradition in which motivation and, thus, education mainly count. Consequently, Reich's position relies too much on 'encouraging new learning' and 'defining who we are', while stopping short of the realization that deregulated markets can destabilize social systems and economies. It seems that a more realistic approach needs to be cast not solely in national terms, and it needs to be admitted that in order to keep borders open and at the same time preserve social solidarity and cohesion, 'western governments need a properly governed international financial environment' (Hutton 1994: 21). Therefore, from a policy standpoint, the implication is that national and international institutional arrangements should be designed in such a way as to establish boundaries to the operation of trade and the financial and labour markets. By putting in place procedures, which, for instance, would ensure that competitive advantage is not won by undermining workers' rights, this strategy could sustain the basic precondition of social cohesion and wealth creation.

Growing disparities in income and the consequences of the globalization of national economies are now being addressed by various scholars who point to the success of capitalism of a non-Anglo-Saxon tradition (such as Japanese or German) capitalism, or to the need for reform in more a collaborative mood. Such debates are proving that the nature of the political system and thinking about new forms of economic and social governance need to include a rethinking of institutional structures. A particular non-solidaristic feature of modern Western politics is its fragmentation due to activities of various interest groups and lobbies. This is *claimant politics* (Madsen 1991), and it means that the notion of a more general national interest is disappearing since politicians, forced to deal with the demands of many powerful interests, with pleas for favours – which economists call 'rent-seeking' – find it impossible to resist their requests. It makes not only acting out of universal principles for the public good more problematic, but it also undermines social solidarity and cohesion since each group increasingly seeks to satisfy its interest 'through the art of acquiring favorable

attention from the state. They do not need to develop a political discourse that makes sense to one another, just one that elicits a response
from the government' (Madsen 1991: 459). In this process of gaining the
attention of the government, social groups insulate themselves from one
another and at the same time they contribute to the problems of the
overloaded government.

One of the most interesting propositions to overcome all of these
problems is Hirst's (1994) project of associative democracy, which advocates transferring political responsibility to self-governing voluntary associations. By increasing citizens' political involvement and empowering
civil society, prompting governmental accountability and democratization of the economy and polity, Hirst steers both political and economic relationships in the direction of cooperation and trust, which
ensures the flow of information and commitment. For instance, as a way
of controlling the economy, he proposes cooperation between self-
governing economic associations and public bodies, based on conditions
which 'are able to create sufficient levels of solidarity and trust between
the members of economic associations, and between those associations,
such trust both overcomes the pressure that are inherent in competitive
markets and by doing so enables the economy to work in a way that
ensures its continued survival at a high level of economic success' (Hirst
1994: 99–100). Hirst recognizes that, especially now, when the structures
of corporatism are weakening, solidarity cannot be taken for granted and
that it has to be constructed through active cooperation in more fragmented and divided environments. However, without attempts to built
and promote solidarity through regional economic regulation, public–
private partnerships, creation of self-governing industrial districts and
democratization of companies, we may face new social conflicts, self-
interested lobbying and poor economic performance. The final result can
be social fragmentation and a collapse of the remaining bases for solidarity as the successful firms and localities pull away from national
commitment and consensus politics becomes impossible (1994: 123).

Hirst also advocates the transfer of the associationalist principle of
social governance to the field of welfare. The promotion of welfare is
only possible by providing new ideas of collective consumption that do
not alienate control and responsibility from the individual and 'not by
schoolteachery social democratic exhortation to be altruistic and pay-up'
(1994: 164). Its aim is to create communities of choice, not of fate. 'The
purpose of the foregoing is not as the preamble to a plea to recreate the
pre-modern pre-industrial face-to-face community in which social life
was simple and spontaneous' (1994: 166). It stresses individual rights
and choice, whereby informed and voluntary participation, not blind
conformity, are the bases of trust and cooperation. Yet associationalism

'allows the citizens to choose the communities he or she will create with others, and demands in return the duties of respect for others' rights to choose' (1994: 202). Thus, the civic culture of an associationalist society will incorporate elements of both liberalism and democratic republicanism. This new way of combining both approaches, emphasizing that these two camps of liberalism and communitarianism have resources to accommodate each other's main claims, seems to be gaining popularity. It is visible in Selznick's (1992) defence of liberal communitarianism, dictated to some degree by the tradition of American pragmatism and the criticism of liberal preoccupation with individual rights. Although the idea of community is at the centre of his approach, because community preserves integrity of persons and institutions and ensures both solidarity and freedom, Selznick stresses that the new solidarity and the new community should incorporate diversity, pluralism and freedom, should strike a balance between justice and democracy, rights and duties, and should combine liberties and rational judgements with autonomy and commitments. In such a community, communication is open and founded on trust, which in turn enhances interaction and reinforces solidarity.

Solidarity policies are not confined to any specific political form; they can, for example, take the form of corporate pluralism or – as in Hirst's case – an associative democracy. While the search for a blueprint for a society in which social cohesion and trust are more easily achieved than is the case today will continue, I shall only point out that any policy of solidarity should take notice of the multiplicity of contexts in which self-formation actually takes place. Any realistic policy of solidarity should avoid a 'romantic' version of 'embeddedness' and 'belonging' and should stress an assumption about the plurality of norms, the prevalence of moral conflicts and the existence of a complex social structure of groups and spheres, which creates conditions for 'shift involvements'. Such policies ought to reject atomistic-holistic models for structuring possibilities for the self or society and be based on more dynamic models of self-construction and self-expression within an open and pluralistic context. While the focusing on a renewal of public life should be its main concern, this type of policy should be realistic in its judgement of people's reasons for such commitments and recognize the possibility of conflicts of values and interests. Therefore it ought to propose a weaker version of a good society and try to nourish not 'strong', interpersonal community-type bonds but rather to enhance 'the strengths of weak ties', which, according to Granovetter (1973), effect societal cohesion. Dense but fragmented ties of local communities sustain cooperation within each group, but 'weak ties' of civic engagement that cut across social cleavages enhance wider cooperation.

The existence of institutional mechanisms – which, while allowing for the expression of a plurality of views, are also able to constrain powerful emotional commitments in the interest of fairness – is the basis of any policy of solidarity. It is enough to mention the consequences of Thatcherism, which constituted a new way of thinking about rules and institutions, in order to realize how important is the culture of institutions, and hence the rules procedures on which institutions are based.

The logic and quality of public discourse is influenced by institutional rules and procedures since they shape the style of arguments that are acceptable and allowed in the public forum. The call for constructing an institutional world in such a way that it can evoke people's willingness to follow norms of 'moral behaviour' (Goodin 1992) should not be based, however, on an introduction of morality, since acting upon moral principles in institutional life does not always work out for the best. As Alan Ryan (1992: 22) notes, it is very difficult to find 'the right path between selfish peace and moral hysteria' and the social and political costs of moral crusades are very high. Hence, maybe we 'should try, insofar as possible, to rely upon mechanisms for motivating moral behaviour that do not work through self-consciously moral agents' (Goodin 1992: 168). We can mention here the rules and procedures which by increasing uncertainty can make people imagine themselves in another's place, hence making them more willing to adopt non-exploitative behaviour and ways of increasing interdependence, which force people to adopt more reciprocal conduct. For instance, if – in order not to lose social support – one needs to perform according to the established and agreed rules, this constraint, when reinforced by public accountability requirements and institutional arrangements that force people to think in the long term, could evoke a willingness to follow norms of reciprocity, non-exploitation and generally moral behaviour (Goodin 1992).

In general terms, the necessary condition for a less fragmented and more solidaristic society is to create a system of institutions which can make people more cooperative by building into their roles such levels of interdependence whereby reciprocity and fairness will become normal behaviour in those roles. In such a system, trust in other people can be defined as the confidence with which we expect others to be constrained by the duties and requirements attached to their roles. This sheds new light on the concept of citizenship rights and duties and points to the need to reconsider citizens' mutual relationships. In order to re-invent common citizenship, which is the most important form of membership and identity in modern societies, we must recognize individual and collective duties which living in a new type of modern, global and complex environment requires.

> The politics of citizenship has for generations formulated its goals, fought its battles and found its voices in the discourse of rights. In the late twentieth century it also needs to be able to speak, to act and to understand itself in the language of citizens' personal responsibility and social obligation, in the discourse of duties as well as rights (Roche 1992: 246).

The idea of citizenship and the discourse of citizens' duties are beginning to emerge as the frames of reference for public policy aiming at engendering conditions in which individual well-being and strong communities go together. In this process of reviving civic institutions the goal is to connect obligations with responsibilities and reconcile the demand of choice, freedom and rights with the requirement of solidarity and reciprocity.

To generate a sense of belonging through the politics of democratization, which avoids liberal individualism and conventional collectivism, stresses duties and rights as well as diversity and interaction of strangers, is to construct conditions in which people learn to deal with one another, however, without making everyone feel the same. However, there is another side to the coin connected with the question of how the system can trust its subjects. Since the contemporary state system, as Wilson (1984: 328) argues, cannot afford to wait for the process of socialization to produce desired attitudes and behaviour, the state 'must impose universalistic principles and must do so not by slow process of socialization, and cultivation, but by political edict'. However, relying solely on technical and legal constraints for the regulation of people's behaviour could in the long term erode feelings of obligation. Hence, there is a need for education and socialization into citizenship rights and duties. Furthermore, since it is mainly a totalitarian regime that cannot trust its subjects after suppressing their freedom of beliefs and opinion, the essential condition for mutual trust, which allows for cooperation and solidarity, is toleration. Any policy which tries to motivate public spirit and self-interest in the same model has to prepare bases from which cooperation can arise. This cooperation should be constructed not as a single solidarity but from out of many different solidarities, which means that it should be rooted in toleration as a way of promoting a sense of citizenship. Consequently, if we want to create a society in which people can identify their good with the good of others and come to feel that they are members of a society but belong on their own terms, it is necessary to enhance the value of toleration through education so that it is accepted as a citizen's responsibility.

## Trust and toleration

The tolerated are increasingly demanding to be appreciated,
not ignored, and becoming more sensitive to suggestions of
contempt lurking behind the condescension. They do not want
to be told that differences do not matter, that they can think
what they like provided they keep to themselves, out of the
way of the majority.

Zeldin 1994: 272

Until recently we have had a tendency to perceive the notion of tolerance
as a historical concept whose importance was mainly relevant to periods
of religious war or the political oppression of minorities. At the core of
such an understanding of toleration is a deliberate choice not to interfere
with conduct which one disapproves of or dislikes, for the sake of civil
peace, harmony or social cohesion. 'Historically, to tolerate was to
permit by law, but not to endorse or encourage members of dissenting
groups, much less to provide them with equal opportunities' (Mendus
1989: 7). The merely pragmatic necessity for tolerance never captured
popular imagination because, as Zeldin notes, toleration is not a passion
but rather 'the reluctant acceptance of a burden, putting up with what
one cannot avoid, is not exciting enough' (1994: 261). It has also not
captured the attention of sociologists, who have devoted themselves to
the issue of equality rather than liberty and tolerance. Tolerance as a
short-term remedy rooted in indifference is no longer, however, an
adequate answer to our modern dilemmas, which are forcing us to ask if
it is enough to 'live and let live', or does toleration require a positive
welcoming of difference?

New importance of the issue of tolerance and the emergence of new
questions about tolerance are the results of social, political and economic
changes occurring around us as well as of theoretical developments,
which have been trying to grasp the meaning of these alterations. Among
the empirical facts, the most essential for our discussion of tolerance are
the consequences of the collapse of communism and dilemmas connected
with the increasing diversity of Western societies; and among the second
type of factors, the post-modernist debate and the dialogue between
communitarianism and liberalism are crucial. Analysing both types of
factors allows us to argue that without broadening the notion of tolerance to include mutual understanding and trust, we will be unable to
resolve our contemporary problems in such a way as to enhance social
cooperation.

The revolution of 1989 not only helped to emphasize the importance
of democracy but also re-invested the notion of toleration with a new
significance. The experience of the former Soviet bloc countries made it

clear that intolerance results in distrust within society and in distrust between the state and its subjects. A denial of pluralism, which is the main feature of a totalitarian system in which there is only a single truth about the best way to live, not only does not allow for individuals' autonomy but also discourages the development of respect for other people and reduces opportunities for communication and mutual understanding between various groups within the society. In response to the state suppression of different opinions, people – Spinoza observed as far back as 1670 – 'would regularly think differently from the way they speak, with the consequence that reliability and loyalty that are so necessary for the preservation of the state would be destroyed; and this would lead to the development of a detestable hypocrisy and perfidy' (quoted in Fetscher 1992: 3).

The results of much empirical research prove that a higher level of intolerance exists among people in former communist countries than among Western Europeans. As described in previous chapters, the outcomes of Polish and Hungarian studies demonstrated the existence in these countries prior to 1989 a social vacuum between the private world and public life, a lack of trust towards others and an unusual importance attached to the intimate circles of families and friends. Other studies show that this societal distrust also extends to people of different nationalities and to strangers generally. For example, a study of students aged between 14 and 17 years from former East Berlin and West Berlin and from Warsaw, conducted in spring 1992, discovered that only 12.0 per cent of students from Warsaw, 18.1 per cent of students from East Berlin but 40.1 per cent of students from West Berlin completely trusted foreigners or people not of their own nationality. Positive opinions about foreigners were expressed by only 14.0 per cent of Poles surveyed, but by 38.5 per cent of East Berliners and 48.7 per cent of West Berlin students. Furthermore, whereas West Berliners are willing to recognize the danger of hostility to foreigners (81.4 per cent), Poles do not worry about its potentially negative consequences (Gesicki 1992: 10). Of course, Poland is a more homogeneous country with a lower level of direct contacts with foreigners, and this – to some degree – explains Polish students' intolerant attitudes, although the absence of any difference in terms of numbers of contacts with foreigners among both groups of German students allows us to suggest that it is not the only factor shaping attitudes towards others. Moreover, other studies illustrate that, in general, 'ethnic tolerance was markedly lower in Eastern Europe than in the Western world' (Ester et al. 1993: 211). For example, according to a study made in 1990–1, in Slovakia, which proved itself to be one of the most intolerant countries in Europe, 23.9 per cent of those surveyed would not have liked to have as neighbours people of a different race; 26.1 per cent would not have liked to have Muslims as neighbours and the same percentage would not have liked to have Jews as neighbours; while for the Western countries, on average, the respective percentages were 9.4, 15.1 and 7.0 (1993: 211).

Eastern European countries also showed quite a low level of confidence in institutions, which is attributed to these countries' autocratic experiences. In comparison with the Western world, Eastern Europeans showed lower levels of confidence in the police (in the Western countries 71.2 per cent, in Poland 31.7 per cent) and parliament (in the Western countries 42.6 per cent, in Slovakia 28.4 per cent) (Ester et al. 1993: 212). It is difficult to interpret these results because, as the researchers themselves admit, it is unclear whether they referred to past experiences under the communists or to contemporary experiences. None the less, it is uncontrovertible that the impact of the previous system, where 'almost everyone . . . was living a double life: systematically saying one thing in public and another in private' (Ash 1990: 137) on people's identities, personalities and concepts of themselves are not going to disappear overnight.

The past forty years of undemocratic rule devalued the importance of law, destroyed in people's minds any connection between law and the behaviour of the authorities and eroded the image of law as the protector of individual rights. Definition of the state as the only source of modernity and progress, while keeping society underdeveloped and backward (Schopflin 1993: 10–16), and an emphasis on the ideology of the strong state rather than on personal freedom and individual emancipation resulted in 'nationalization of the initiative of action in collective life', leading to 'learned hopelessness', a reduction of 'societal ability to act independently in public life' and in the adoption of temporary solutions without considering their long-term effects (Marody 1988: 102). The predominance of a low degree of risk-taking behaviour resulted in people's unwillingness to engage in anything outside their immediate surroundings and reinforced fear of the unknown, which often found its expression in intolerance. Distrust towards others and intolerant attitudes were accompanied by a lack of self-confidence. Studies on authoritarianism conducted in 1978 and 1984 show a very high level of feeling among Poles that social reality is hard to understand and that they lack control over it, and so social life presented itself to them as threatening. This helplessness in the face of an unacceptable system, a high level of anxiety and a low level of self-confidence was particularly felt by the Polish intelligentsia. After comparing the Polish results with the outcome of international studies, Koralewicz writes that it seems that Poland was 'one of few countries, if not the only one, with a negative correlation between the level of education and self-confidence' (1993: 174). Anxiety, frustration and low self-confidence, a cause of authoritarian attitudes, made this group more easily susceptible to manipulation by the centralized power and more willing to approve 'the use of military and paramilitary organizations to constrain opposition to the authority' (1993: 185). In short, in state socialist countries there was an absence of conditions for fostering a tolerant climate and tolerant attitudes.

The 1989 revolution, according to Dahrendorf (1990), brought the victory of modernity, freedom, democracy and openness. And it is true that an image of an all-powerful totalitarian state manipulating alienated, atomized and socially isolated masses no longer describes Eastern European social reality. However, to claim that such a characterization is replaced by one of active citizens and democratic government would involve the concealment of many problems existing on the way to achieving a full democracy. In the process of democratization of Eastern and Central European societies many new dangers have emerged, new spheres of intolerance have surfaced and many violations of human rights have occurred. It is enough to mention the ethnic conflicts in the former Yugoslavia, the former Soviet Union, the problems of Hungarian minorities in Romania and Slovakia, anti-Semitism in Hungary and Poland, the problem of Russian minorities in the Baltic states and so on, in order to realize that in these countries human rights and tolerance are still not part of their civic and legal cultures. Post-communist countries can be seen as laboratories for testing the conditions essential for the emergence of trust between state officials and society and within society. Furthermore, comprehension of both the psychological and sociological inheritance would be helpful in addressing the current problems of intolerance.

A dramatic test of the new democracy and its policy of tolerance is provided by Polish responses to the HIV/AIDS epidemic in the period 1989–92. For policy towards HIV/AIDS several changes which occurred after 1989 have been essential. The most important change is that the process of democratization has created opportunities for marginalized and stigmatized groups to emerge and organize. Secondly, freedom of information and changes in the structure, composition and function of the central AIDS organization allows for less centralized and more democratic policies. To the important positive consequences of liberalization there should be added the new opportunities to scrutinize, criticize and control the activities of health authorities. While these alterations do not necessarily change public opinion, the functioning of various new social movements (of gays, drug addicts, HIV-positive support movements and so on) have made a real difference in practical terms, and the growing information about homosexuality, and the increased openness about issues of sex and drugs, allowed at least for more open and informed debates about the disease. The changes also helped to shape gay consciousness and contributes to their self-esteem, consequently increasing their abilities to organize themselves and to address the intolerant attitudes of society. However, the changes did not automatically make everybody tolerant. The incidences of social intolerance, although certainly deepened and dramatized by the economic crisis and for the first time publicized due to measures for the freedom of information, were increasing at the beginning of the 1990s. It became clear that the state of mind of the majority of the society is behind the institutional changes to the system. The conditions for democracy existed but their meaning was not clear to many. For many democracy meant that you could do what you wanted or that what people wanted was good, and if the majority of the local community did not want seropositive people in their neighbourhood, they had right to evict them. The majority of people refused to learn about the disease and classified the sufferers as belonging to a 'different', not 'their' own reality, thus not deserving equal treatment. Many local communities (for instance, in Konstacin-Jeziorna, Rembrentow, Gloskow, Kaweczyn, Legionow, Muranow, Leszno and Laski) organized protests (such as the blocking of roads, picketing hospitals, intimidation and the beating up of an HIV-positive drug-user, starting fires and so on), and police treatment was extremely mild with no legal action taken (Misztal 1991).

The new democratic openness resulted in new social and economic threats and destroyed many illusions about the national ability to behave collectively in a responsible way. The danger of excessive parochialism has been emerging while the centre has been without much capacity to act and its welfare function has been shrinking since the 1980s. The legacy of the past – a distorted social consciousness, a lack of understanding of the idea of civil rights and a tradition of submission to a political authority – contributed to confusion, disorder and a neglect of the rights of the weakest groups, which, consequently, felt alienated from society.

The lesson from these intolerant political systems demonstrates that, although toleration as the absence of impediment or discrimination is the most important and most necessary element of any democratic regime, in order to create conditions for social cooperation there is a need for a policy of toleration demanding equal respect for all perspectives and all people. At the heart of toleration there should be no indifference to the plight of minorities but an attempt to understand and communicate with them. Toleration as a necessary component of the development of social cooperation and trust within society needs to promote and sustain people's self-confidence, critical reflection and respect for others. People's confidence in their ability to manage and direct their lives and trust in their 'capacity for self-government is necessary to sustain liberty because without self-trust, anxiety-ridden individuals will be all too willing to choose equality in a safe and secure slavery, handing power over to a paternalistic state that promises to manage their interests better than they can themselves' (Macedo 1989: 133). According to this Tocquevillian argument, people without the ability to exercise their freedom actively, will lose self-confidence and trust in others, and will cease to insist on their right to freedom. 'Tocqueville's good form of democracy is characterised by something more ethically substantial than "integration or community"; it is characterised by liberty' (ibid.). In order to be self-confident, able to take risks and to be reflextive, people need to have the autonomy which allows them to be the authors of their own lives. This means that they need to have a plurality of alternatives from which to choose. This argument, that the development of autonomy requires diversity, as expressed in Mill's liberal approach, is a central premise of liberalism (Mendus 1989).

The Eastern European experience, while validating pluralism and individual autonomy as generating a requirement of toleration, also points to the need for a broader rather than a liberal concept of toleration. It not only confirms the importance of commitment to toleration as a necessary condition of diversity and the self-determination, but also suggests that intolerance constitutes a denial of the opportunity for self-confidence, mutual respect and understanding, and thus toleration should promote self-esteem, mutual trust and communication. However, the failure of the system, in which civil society was kept on the verge of extinction, also reinforces to some degree a liberal assumption about the importance of state neutrality as a condition of tolerance. From a liberal perspective the concept of the rights demarcates the area within which government interference may be legitimate. It is assumed that the right has priority over the good, which means that it is the right that specifies the limits within which people may be allowed to pursue their own conception of the good. The principal task of the state – according to Rawls (1972) – is to secure the rights and economic resources that individuals need to lead a freely chosen life. However, as Mendus shows, these assumptions that the right cannot be clearly distinguished from the good and that the right has priority over the good are 'highly debatable' (1989: 119). Thus, the liberal claim to neutrality suffers from an indeterminacy of scope and makes it rather difficult to specify the limits of toleration. Critics of liberalism, especially communitarians, argue that the concept of right is not independent of any conception of the good, and that the universal claims of liberalism neglects the interpretive frameworks within which agents view their world – that is, traditions, habits, practices and institutions, from which people's beliefs originate. Yet, although liberals neglect the fact that our selves are defined and constructed by various communal bonds and commitments, their stand does not necessarily imply that the protection of rights, which puts constraints on the sphere of governmental action, cannot be accompanied by an active state which is devoted to supporting civil society. It is consistent with Tocqueville's argument that a democratic system needs both active and strong political institutions, which are necessary and desirable conditions of democratic freedom and equality, and a strong and active civil society, which provides crucial barriers against state despotism.

Although there is now much evidence of the negative and controversial consequences of state neutrality from Western countries and this prompts an advocacy of the community and the need for belonging and responsibility, examples from the former communist countries, however, reveal that it is even more dangerous to forget about rights and in the name of unity to grant the state too much power. The experience of an authoritarian system and its legacy warn against the danger of starting any political project without securing the right of the individual. The state should not be seen as a means for enforcing universal solidarity because of the danger that people will be not be able to develop their nature and interests free from the arbitrary use of political authority and coercive power. At the same time, state neutrality, while being a necessary condition of plurality, and thus toleration, should not be seen as a sufficient condition for ensuring choice and self-determination. Instead, tolerance should be justified as a way of promoting active citizenship because only through democratization can we hope to increase social cooperation. As we noted in the last chapter, in order to be able to participate in democratic processes individuals need resources enabling them to be autonomous subjects; they need empowering, and political opportunities for participation and motivation (Oldfield 1990: 145). Democracy is linked to a principle of autonomy. 'If people are to be free and equal in the determination of the conditions of their lives, and enjoy equal rights as well as equal obligations in the specification of the framework which generates and limits the opportunities available to them, they must be in a position to enjoy a range of rights not only in principle, but also in practice' (Held 1987: 284).

Because autonomy is promoted by the capacity to represent one's interest and by the possibility of resolving clashes of interest through public dialogue, it demands, at the same time, the development of some particular rights and requests the preservation of more universal rights. Thus, a democratic system which accepts the principle of autonomy needs not only to balance demands for freedom and equality but also to balance simultaneous requests for particularistic and universal rights. This is the most difficult dilemma, which all Western industrialized democracies are now facing due to the increasing diversity of their societies. The best political metaphor for this dilemma is the controversy over the 'Islamic veil', which was brought to public attention in France in 1989 (when three schoolgirls were banned from a school by their headmaster for wearing Islamic headscarves) and again in 1994 (when seventeen schoolgirls were expelled from a school for wearing headscarves to school and when France's Education Minister appeared to be banning girls from wearing Islamic headscarves in school). This issue, which is further confused by many additional factors (such as contradictory signals coming from the Council of State, resulting in several different rulings on the issue, the question to what degree the girls had been under family pressure, and the hysteria of the mass media), is a paradoxical illustration of the values and limitations of democratic liberal principles. On the one hand, it demonstrates how the old liberal value of toleration has now entered deeply into common life and, on the other hand, it exposes its limitations and shows how this principle no longer satisfies the needs of contemporary society. While for some the Islamic headscarf 'symbolises the inequality of the sexes and the confinement of women' (Sole 1994: 14), others stress that it is only the top of the iceberg of more particularistic demands, which will undermine secularism and its universal rights; 'the Islamists are coming as colonisers', says one French official (*The Economist*, 8 October 1994: 57). This last type of statement is generated by a fear that people who do not accept secular, liberal values are able to use the liberal language of equal rights to dismantle the system. The former position expresses the fear that multi-culturalism, by sanctioning oppressive customs and freezing cultural differences between communities, can result in a denial of equal opportunities for everybody.

Both arguments find theoretical grounding in Gray's (1993) 'post-modern liberal conservatism'. He agrees that people are members of many, often conflicting, communities, thus the idea of 'restoring of an organic national community in Britain is vain, chimerical and perhaps harmful' (1993: 56). Although the political culture no longer expresses a common culture, Gray still hopes that 'people have in common enough respect for the ruling idea of a civil society – ideas of toleration, of responsibility and of equality under the rule of law – for diversity in society to be fruitful rather than an occasion for division' (1993: 57). His defence of toleration implies a support of multi-culturalism – 'Cultural minorities, such as the British Muslims, have an undeniable entitlement to government funding of their schools' (1993: 58) – which is limited by the acceptance of common responsibilities and the preservation of equality of opportunity. Despite his acceptance of pluralism as a feature of our modern life, he still advocates limits to it because pluralism not bound by the norms and the common culture of civil society will lead to a Beirut-like tragedy. This limit on toleration, in terms of, for example, school policy, would mean that schools denying equality of opportunity to the sexes should not be supported.

All attempts to define the level of cultural pluralism that is acceptable to a secular and liberal democracy try to grasp the question of how the formal equalities conferred on citizens by law can be transformed into a practical equality. While in the past demands of entry by those excluded from citizenship rights did not undermine the general claim to universal entitlements, the recent dilemma posed by the proliferation of claims for the recognition of religious and cultural differences is seen as having potentials for conflict between universal rights and more particularistic requests. The realization of these potentials depends upon what kind of policy of toleration is practised. Gray is firmly reassuring regarding the undisputable status of universal rights:

> Cultural minorities, whether indigenous or immigrant in origin, cannot expect public subsidy for aspects of their ways of life which flout the central norms of liberal civil society. They are entitled to protection from forms of discrimination which deny them full participation in the common life. They cannot justifiably claim privileges or immunities of the sort enshrined in policies of affirmative action and of group rights, which effectively shield them from the healthy pressures of the larger society (1993: 59).

However, if we accept the multiplicity of cultural identities and if we value autonomy, shouldn't we aim for the construction of diversity in such a way that it would allow us to learn about others and, as well as learning, to become different? This would require tolerance founded in the mutual trust of self-reflective and self-determining individuals. This active trust, writes Giddens (1994: 187), depends on more institutional 'opening up', that is, on less traditional, less rigid and less hierarchical relationships in the economic and the political spheres. Since today, more than ever before, 'we have no choice but to make choices' (Giddens 1994: 187), the significance of the necessary condition of responsible conduct in this post-traditional and diverse context – that is, autonomy – is increasing and, by the same token, the role of tolerance becomes crucial.

In order to learn to act responsibly within the world of multiple identities and standards we need to avoid too rigid stands, and, according to Vickers (1980), shift from principles to practice and through public deliberations try to establish a responsible relationship with others who hold both different ideas of what is right and different standards for determining it. Modern individuals, who have multiple memberships and balance commitments and obligations in a responsible way in these overlapping systems, cannot be coerced to define themselves in a simple way on the basis of single categories of race, nation, religion or gender. Learning how to craft responsible communities is, according to Vickers, the only way to build a sufficient foundation of trust, which – in turn – would foster further communication and mutual understanding. Toleration as flowing from considerations of mutual trust and equal respect does not provide a fixed prescription of why some action but not others should be tolerated, but says that only people being 'sufficiently responsible . . . deserve a corresponding measure of autonomy' (Vickers 1980: 9). Since in modern plural society there is no acceptable alternative to public argumentation, the conditions of dialogue within civil society impose constraints on the way in which the diversity of modern societies can be governed. According to Fitzmaurice (1993), these constraints are incompatible with certain paradigms of justification which do not admit of critical enquiry. However, it does suggest that more particularistic or more traditional positions cannot be defended and that such defence should follow the commonly acceptable norms of a public space based on the discourse and argumentation of autonomous and responsible participants.

In the same vein, Wieviorka (1994) believes that the particular values of a culture are compatible with the universal principles of reason and democracy. The task is, hence, to search and to promote search for the optimal interconnections between the universal and the particular, between the national and the multiplicity of regional, ethnic and individual identities. The main difference between Gray's (1993) more restrictive and less optimistic stand and Wieviorka's and Vickers' (1980) perspectives are that Gray is less committed to the value of public space and the value of a preservation of dialogue within it. Gray assumes that a civil society, such as that in Britain, is 'entitled to assert its identity' against those 'who challenge its central, defining practices of toleration and compromise' (1993: 59). According to him, the limit to pluralism is a necessary condition for the preservation of civil peace, while Vickers questions the universalization of Western liberal democracy and rejects its lineal type of thinking.

Vickers' (1980) argument is underlined by an assumption that to be an autonomous person means both to be entitled and to be responsible in interaction with others, and thus it underlines mutual trust as the basis of the practical learning of how to exercise conscious control over relationships. Results of empirical research appear to confirm that autonomy and individualism may go together with the sense of responsibility. On the bases of outcomes of a 1990–1 survey in twenty-nine countries, the European Values Study team argues that, although individualization is increasing, 'individualism may involve identification with, an action on behalf of, others' (Barker *et al*. 1992: 5). Wieviorka (1994), on the other hand, accepts the possibility of many levels of belonging and incorporates the factor of subjectivity, which allows us to put stronger emphasis on the practical exploration and crafting of reconciliation between various levels. The support for this more open and more imaginative approach is facilitated by the spread of post-modernist ideologies and, in more practical terms, by the successful experiences of some multicultural policies. Post-modern approaches describe contemporary societies as characterized by diversity, discontinuity, contingency, change, incoherence, de-differentiation of the functions of social institutions and a multiplicity of pluralistic and invisible centres of power (Lash and Friedman 1992).

The post-modern understanding of social reality as 'the centrality of differences in a decentered world' (Lemert 1992: 42) places emphasis on the process of the liberation of society from the barriers of the 'nation-state' space and 'the liberation of individuality from the fixity of identity' (Boyne and Rattansi 1990: 39). While stressing the need to recognize differences and particularisms, this perspective argues that the triple-value alliance of post-modernity involves liberty, diversity and tolerance (Bauman 1991). The very foundation of post-modernity, Heller and Feher note, 'consists of viewing the world as a plurality of heterogeneous spaces and temporalities. . . . The postmodern political condition is premissed on the acceptance of the plurality of cultures and discourses. Pluralism is implicit in postmodernity as a project' (1988: 1, 5).

This post-modern emphasis on diversity and tolerance means that no culture should be privileged or dominate any other. Gender, sexual preferences, race, religion, value systems are all to be treated equally, whilst at the same time they are not to be homogenized, standardized or reduced to universal sameness. Everything is 'other' – including one's own values and oneself; the subject is decentred. The post-modernist decentring of the subject is consistent with its rejection of 'grand narratives', its espousal of 'local narratives', language games and genealogies, 'its dread of totalising discourses leading to totalitarianism and its political pluralism' (Boyne and Rattansi 1990: 41). In post-modern practice, self-reflexivity of the subject, pluralism and attempts to grasp the importance of non-class sites of domination are means of the recovery of the discourses of the other and liberating self.

It is difficult to impute a single political meaning to post-modernism. Some writers dismiss it as relativism; others argue against defining post-modernism as relativism; yet others point to its unconstrained pluralism and negative, destructive or even nihilistic side (Wickham 1990; Gellner 1992). None the less, by rejecting the possibility of universal representation, opening our eyes to 'the futility of modern dreams of universalism' (Bauman 1991), post-modern thought has played a crucial role in showing the multiplicity of discourses in the formation subjectivities and social relations. Despite the indeterminacy of the post-modernist project, some 'important developments around the questions of anti-racism and the analysis of the West's "others" . . . which have emerged out of postmodernism concerns and . . . , in fact [it] would be reactionary to ignore or dismiss [them] as irrelevant' (Boyne and Rattansi 1990: 26). Even Gellner (1992: 55), who sees post-modernism as promoting relativism, which is a 'dreadfully inadequate formulation of our problems', acknowledges that maybe this stand performs a public service because the ambiguities of its formulations can 'help ease the situation, and bring forth a compromise between the believers and the others' (1992: 96).

By destroying the grounds for believing in a universal truth, post-modernity does not make our lives more easy but only less constrained by rules and more contingent. It demands new solutions based on the tolerant coexistence of a diversity of cultures. Yet, although post-modernism encourages us to live without an enemy, it stops short of offering constructive bases for mutual understanding and trust. While stressing the need to recognize differences and particularisms, this perspective, however, does not grant the same significance to more universal rights, without which there can be no full respect for difference and, thus, no integration based on communication and trust. Consequently, it sometimes contributes to mistrust of formal rights, propagates guilt-ridden tolerance of political correctness – 'Oppression is what we do in the West. What they do in the Middle East is "their culture" ' – as Hughes (1993: 115) caricatures it – and encourages cultural separatism. It has also intensified the controversy over multi-culturalism, which has been visible in recent years.

The complete social and cultural integration of diverse groups, it is often argued, can only be achieved by redefining the nation in terms of multi-culturalism. A modern multi-cultural society, in which loyalty to the subculture may conflict with loyalty to the overarching state, should adopt a policy of toleration as a way of promoting and sustaining a sense of citizenship (Mendus 1989).

Although a backlash against multi-culturalism has been growing for several years, this policy still offers the only way to reconcile cultures; that is, through discussion and negotiation. Multi-culturalism, like nationalism, takes different forms and needs to take into account particular historical and political conditions, so that the same type of multi-culturalism is not appropriate for all societies. States like the United States and France, with established traditions of incorporation and assimilation of immigrants, or Germany and Britain, which have perceived themselves for over a hundred years as culturally and ethnically homogeneous, are in different situations than Australia. Because Australia has always identified itself as being a nation of migrants, multi-cultural policy can be more radical there than in European countries.

Multi-culturalism in Australia is based on the idea that ethnic communities, which maintain the languages and cultures of their countries of origin, are legitimate and consistent with Australian citizenship, as long as certain principles are adhered to (Castles et al. 1992). Multiculturalism in Australia is based on the recognition of the need for special laws, institutions and social policies to overcome barriers to full participation of various ethnic groups in society. The distribution of migrants with citizenship and cultural rights provides them with the opportunity to safeguard their well-being, while the endorsement of cultural pluralism by the Australian state constructs the bases for mutual dialogue and trust. The redefinition of the nation in terms of cultural pluralism signals, according to Castles and his colleagues, the demise of the nation-state: 'through policies of cultural pluralism the state is now actively supporting forms of cultural identity whose defining boundaries are not those of the nation-state itself' (1992: 128).

Since the late 1970s, with the state tactically moving away from nationalism to multi-culturalism, and with a decline in 'the importance of identification with the nation-state' (Castles et al. 1992: 135), Australia has enjoyed an unprecedented level of tolerance and trust within its multi-cultural populace. These very good results have been achieved primarily through social and political rather than legal processes – 'without the ham-fisted attentions to the law' (Krygier 1994: 24). Social tolerance has been, of course, fostered by legislative protection and governmental regulation, yet the role of the process of education and successful participation of all groups in social, political and economic projects have been also of enormous significance. The experience of all migrant groups contributed to an understanding that the achievement of a tolerant society is a tentative and incremental process of learning democracy and social cooperation together. It also enhanced an understanding that cohesion can be strengthened by acceptance and trust, while intolerance results in rejected groups feeling alienated and isolated. Thus, the Australian policy of multi-culturalism is presented as aiming at the value of equality and the worth and dignity of each human being.

Without forgetting that Australia also has its conflicts and problems, it can be said that the lesson from the Australian example points to the

importance of the deterrent and educative role of legislation and government regulation as well as to the necessity of cultivation of a common
recognition of the importance of democratic structures and procedures. It
is also an argument for the importance in multi-cultural society of
toleration based on trust rather than on indifference. Although the law
protecting people's rights and beliefs is essential for securing the mutual
respect which is required of citizens in democratic systems, the grounding
of tolerance in trust in political practices, trust in institutions and trust
that others will be constrained by the duties attached to their roles,
shapes a feeling of belonging together in a common and democratic
undertaking. This type of tolerance of diversity requires moderation.
Australia has been in this respect a 'lucky country'; passions in the post-
war period never ran very high and the country has remained civil and
peaceful. Ethnic resentments have been negotiated and, while not all of
them have disappeared, they 'have been *moderated* and kept pretty tame'
(Krygier 1994: 24). This moderation, or in Selznick's word 'civility', as
an important means of sustaining integration rooted in respect for persons, governs diversity, protects autonomy and upholds toleration
(Selznick 1992: 387).

   Toleration and fair cooperation requires people to be civil or (to use
Rawls' (1993) expression) reasonable – that is, willing to govern their
conduct on a principle from which they and others can reason in common and to take into account the consequences of their action on other's
well-being. 'Reasonable persons . . . are not moved by the general good
as such but desire for its own sake a social world in which they, as free
and equal, can cooperate with others on terms all can accept. They insist
that reciprocity should hold within that world so that each benefits along
with others' (Rawls 1993: 50). Thus, the ground for toleration is the
ability of reasonable persons to recognize the independent validity of the
claims of others and consensus on the principle of justice as fairness,
which provides a central structure within which people with different
outlooks can share a social life. This seems, however, to be achievable
only under the condition of some moderation. Rawls secures this condition by rejecting from his reasonable republic not only scepticism and
intolerance but also fanaticism. Thus, toleration in his republic is possible because the demands of reasonableness are met since the foundations
for society as a system of ordered and principled cooperation are accepted by all. Williams, who notes that Rawls' state has no way of
including militant Hinduism or Islam, hopes that Rawls 'would help us
to understand better how wide his state could go if he said more about
the frequent condition of mankind, violent and enthusiastic unreason-
ableness' (1994: 7).

It is this type of confrontation or conflict between groups about values which cannot be accommodated, which is the main threat to multi-culturalism. For several years pressing practical problems connected with the increased influence of fundamentalism have raised questions about the limits of toleration. If toleration does not imply any disapproval, does it mean that it requires more than only an assertion of the ultimate values of freedom and individual rights? Should we trust other people's judgements and should we tolerate people acting on those judgements? The issue that brought these problems to public attention was the Salman Rushdie affair. It moved the dilemma of free speech to the centre of the discussion, with various writers wondering whether free speech should be used for promoting truth or to ensure mutual understanding.

According to Jones (1993), we should accept that not everything that is legally permitted is worth promoting from a moral point of view. With the help of the distinction between matter and manners, he argues that although Salman Rushdie had the right to write *The Satanic Verses*, he can be morally deplored for writing it because he used free speech to destroy communication and mutual understanding between two cultures. The similar use of other than legal principles is suggested by Mendus (1993), for whom the value of free speech is directly related to mutual understanding. Her concern with group identity leads her to assume that limits of and justifications for toleration are connected with the possibility of supporting and sustaining people's sense of belonging to a group (Mendus 1993). Defining the value of toleration as connected with the need of individuals to locate themselves within a group is, however, potentially threatening to individual freedom. Therefore, it is not a quest for reconciliation between the universal and particular, but a demand for submission of the universal, and thus it can be said that this stand abandons the liberal concern with reason and rights. Horton (1993: 14–15) rightly notes that Mendus' emphasis on the limits of tolerance rooted in securing a sense of belonging undermines the values of autonomy and individualism. While not to tolerate is to create feelings of separateness and distrust, to tolerate because we are all 'interdependent victims' (Mendus 1989: 162) overlooks and does not allow for the development of a clear understanding of the differences that divide various groups, and consequently, it does not foster mutual understanding and trust. This illiberal communitarianism is based on the assumption that individuals are not able to gain a critical, reflective or detached stand from their community of identity. Macedo (1990), arguing for liberal constitutionalism, thinks that modern pluralist societies ought to demand from us an ability to reflect on our particular attachments and identities. And we, consequently, must be able to 'imagine ourselves without the commit-

ment being reflected upon if we are to test it by a public liberal standard of justice' (Macedo 1990: 274). He assumes that we are capable of detachment and critical reflection on some aspects of our identity because not all aspects of our identities are simultaneously being questioned. This liberal perspective does not aim at isolating the individual from their context or at disembodying the self of all attachments, but rather at meeting the basic impersonal requirements of liberal justice, which demands acting in a manner that can be publicly justified. In order to live up to the demands of citizenship we need to be reflective and able to regard 'our projects and commitments from the perspective of others, from "outside" of ourselves and our narrow circle, but not outside all communities or the human world' (1990: 250).

The justification of tolerance as promoting group identity can also have some unintended practical consequences. Results of a variety of empirical studies suggest that the state should not use the policy of toleration as a means of enforcing solidarity in communities because it can lead to restrictions on their members' individual freedom and outside contacts, it increases free riding on community norms and blocks individual social mobility. This approach stresses that the durability of belonging to migrant groups often may have less 'to do with the long term persistence of outside discrimination than with the ability of these institutions to "compete" effectively with resources and rewards available in the broader society' (Portes and Sensenbrenner 1993: 1336). The ability of these types of solidaristic groups to impose control or demands on their members give rise to many restrictions on individual freedoms and problems with free riders. Reporting on the control and censorship performed by the migrants' organization over the Cuban community in Miami, one Cuban says: 'A million Cubans are blackmailed, totally controlled by three radio stations. I feel sorry for the Cuban community in Miami. Because they have imposed on themselves, by way of the right, the same condition that Castro has imposed in Cuba. Total intolerance' (quoted in Portes and Sensenbrenner 1993: 1340). Anyone who has contacts with migrant communities knows well how often they are intolerant of nonconformists, unwilling to absorb reality outside their parochial scale and able to exercise pressure to keep members in line. However, the most negative consequences of the functioning of these groups based on enforced trust and solidarity is their levelling pressure – that is, lowering the opportunities for social mobility through individual achievement.

Sennett (1974) also notes that when maintaining community becomes an end in itself, intolerance and refusal to negotiate, or even to understand the other side, as well as an actual purge of outsiders often take place.

The growth of this intolerance is not a product of overweening pride, arrogance, or group self-assurance. It is a much more fragile and self-doubting process, in which the community exists only by a continual hyping-up of emotions. The reason for this hysteria is in turn, not a matter of the innate destructiveness of man unleashed in that act of solidarity, but precisely that the terms of culture have come to be so arranged that, without some forcing and prodding, real social bonds seem unnatural (Sennett 1974: 309).

A society which fosters a collective parochial life does not create the conditions for the development of self-confidence or critical, reflective and risk-taking attitudes and, thus, trust towards the other. In order to avoid this type of sectarianism, multi-culturalism should not coerce a sense of group solidarity, and, at the same, it should not permit discrimination of any group or block the group's social and economic opportunities. Such a society should create a policy which is able to take into account the nature and characteristics of a given society (for example, in some countries there may be no need for a racial vilification law, while in others it might be a necessity), and construct a policy of toleration which balances the need for the preservation of autonomous cultures, discourages discrimination and facilitates critical self-consciousness and mutual understanding, but, at the same time, does not foster a group's capacity for monitoring and sanctioning, which would impose restrictions on its members' individual freedom, mobility and outside contacts. This does not mean, however, that minorities should be discouraged from establishing themselves as corporate political actors and that only individual assimilation should be enhanced. As Zeldin, in the quotation on page 228 notes, the tolerated are no longer satisfied with mere indifference:

The tolerated are increasingly demanding to be appreciated, not ignored, and becoming more sensitive to suggestions of contempt lurking behind the condescension. They do not want to be told that differences do not matter, that they can think what they like provided they keep to themselves, out of the way of the majority. Beside, there is no longer a majority to tolerate a minority, because majorities are disintegrating into more and more minorities. Mere tolerance would end up with general indifference (Zeldin 1994: 272).

The search for a viable strategy for a policy of toleration is a very difficult practical task, and although the optimal solution is not so easily achievable, public debates and negotiations can at least rule out some worthless options, and this exploration itself can constitute a significant contribution to mutual understanding and trust. However, in order to participate in public discussions and public life people need to perceive political institutions and basic political guarantees as legitimate.

## Trust and legitimacy

the grounds for trusting rulers are to be found in the sanctions
that punish breaches of trust.

John Locke, *Two Treatises on Government*, 1690

Trust is a salient preoccupation of many theories of legitimacy. Such
theories implicitly assume that the investment of trust in institutions
must be a question of legitimacy and that political trust is associated
with political participation and consent. People who trust that political
power is appropriately exercised, it is argued, have good grounds
for compliance, and if they believe that their government will deal with
their demands fairly and equally, they are more likely to press those
demands on government. In contrast, citizens who do not believe that
their government can be trusted are less likely to participate and express
consent.

No political system enjoys 100 per cent legitimacy and, although some
regimes have even claimed no need for trust (for example, according to
Stalin, there was no room for trust in politics), it is commonly assumed
that trust is essential for a distinctive level and quality of compliance.
While obedience can be sufficiently procured by incentives and sanctions,
social cooperation, however, is unachievable without trust in government. The contemporary state requires legitimation not so much to
function as to be able to make maximal use of all its resources in today's
context of increasing complexity and uncertainty. To achieve this cooperation and the support of its population, the modern state needs to
address new problems of legitimacy deriving from ongoing processes of
globalization, fragmentation and the multiplication of authorities.

Before moving to an examination of these new problems of legitimacy,
the complex concept of legitimacy demands some discussion of various
of its perspectives. In order to obtain a better and more comprehensive
understanding of the problem of legitimacy and its connection with trust,
in what follows I shall, in a very compact way, present the main basis of
the most representative theories of legitimacy. This examination should
start with John Locke's theory since he is one of few who addressed the
issue of trust and legitimacy directly and who thought that the main
problem in any political community is how best to construct, maintain
and repair structures of mutual trust.

The fundamental feature of John Locke's views is the central role of
trust in understanding politics. For Locke, trustworthiness, as the capacity to commit oneself to fulfilling the legitimate expectations of
others, is the main virtue and the basic principle of social order. Locke's
doctrine is based on a general view of man's natural sociability and his

perception of human beings as free agents, responsible for their own
actions. 'To learn how to act responsibly, it is first necessary to learn how
to take full moral responsibility for the content of one's own beliefs'
(Dunn 1984a: 297), which are based on insufficient grounds, thus requiring trust. Men, according to Locke, live upon trust, which enhances their
capacity to cooperate. Since politics is one of the main arenas of cooperation, which links 'free agents, none of whom can know each other's
future actions but all of whom must in some measure rely upon each
other's future actions' (Dunn 1990: 36), it requires a good will and
courage. Although rational political cooperation is hazardous, there is no
rational superior alternative to it (Dunn 1983: 134).

The claim that government is, or ought to be, established or maintained by the free choice and consent of the governed was the basis of
Locke's concept of 'tacit consent', which generally can be seen as an
important element in the legitimacy of authority. Locke's emphasis upon
the personal and moral character of political relations leads him to argue
that governmental power is legitimate when it is 'conceived both by
rulers and ruled as a trust' (Dunn 1988: 83) and that illegitimate power
cannot deserve trust because 'it is no way reciprocal in character' (Dunn
1984a: 295). Thus trust was at the centre of Locke's conception of
government: in the constitutional state political power is only held on
trust and those who govern civil society through the constitutional state
are trustees of the governed. 'Government was a relation between men,
between creatures all of whom were capable of deserving trust and any
of whom could and sometimes would betray it' (Dunn 1984b: 52). A
legitimate authority is essentially the servant of its subjects, because what
gave rulers the right to command was the practical services which they
provided for their people. When rulers betrayed trust and did not fulfil
their obligations towards the ruled, their power became illegitimate and
'the remedy for the betrayal of trust was the right of revolution' (Dunn
1984b: 54).

The centrality of trust in Locke's writing was based, as Dunn (1990)
notes, on the specific concept of the state, on the absence of any differentiation between the public and private spheres of life and on the emphasis
on the personal and moral character of political relations. Consequently,
Locke's optimistic conception of political legitimacy is not well suited for
modern institutionalized and less personal political communities. None
the less there are some important points raised by Locke, which remain
a valued contribution to the discussion of legitimacy. One of the most
interesting of Locke's observations about the nature of trust and politics
itself is his admission that, although trust is an imprecise concept, '[i]ts
imprecision was a necessary imprecision; and the impossibility of escaping from this imprecision was its central point. Politics is still like this'

(Dunn 1984b: 54). Another still relevant and realistic feature of Locke's contribution is his assumption that trust is the sole condition that can make the political division of labour humanly benign (Dunn 1900: 41). Moreover, Locke's general assumption that the only governments that are really legitimate are those that enjoy the consent of the ruled remains a valued contribution to the discussion of legitimacy (Beetham 1991: 12).

In modern societies we need to economize on trust in persons and confine it to political and social institutions. Thus, Locke's personal trust and definition of legitimacy as a normative evaluation of rulers on the basis of meeting their reciprocal obligations have been replaced by the Weberian perspective, which reduces the legitimacy of power to people's belief in its legitimacy. Weber (1948) views rational legitimacy – that is, belief in the proper procedural production of political decision – as the dominant type and unique source of legitimacy of a modern political order. While in the past people complied with authority on the grounds of habits and tradition or charisma, in a modern state they obey by 'virtue of legality', by virtue of the belief in the validity of legal statute and functional competence based on rationally created rules (Weber 1968).

In the Weberian tradition, legitimacy involves the degree to which institutions are valued for themselves and considered proper and right, and it is also used to explain the persistence of stable social and political arrangements. The main interest is in the organization and stability of modern rule – that is, the state and its political and economic performance without invoking normative support. The powerholder issuing commands is seen as 'valid', and for this reason compliance is regarded as binding. Officials of the modern state can claim obedience not because of their personal appeal but because of the authority they hold as a result of their office, which people accept. Consequently, subordination is relatively unconditional and relative to an office; a position rather than a person. 'Legitimacy therefore relies not on trust, but on an impersonal sense of duty on the part of the followers to follow commands of a proper authority, whoever is in authority, and whatever is the content of these commands' (Pakulski 1992: 26).

In the Weberian tradition researchers are reporting on people's belief in legitimacy; thus empirical studies focus on the key elements of entitlement and obligation and test the concept of legitimacy empirically by survey, research on confidence in institutions, trust in leaders and support for the regime. They do not, however, make an assessment of the degree of congruence, or lack of it, between a given system of power and the beliefs that provide its justification. Consequently, trust is not seen as a factor behind people's compliance or cooperation in the specific context but rather as a single quality, that systems of power possess or not. Thus, the legitimacy of political order does not rest upon a shared value system, but upon the organization of the political process and the performance of the state. According to this view, the political-administrative system itself generates general support for its politics through such devices as institutionalized procedures, and symbolic and ideological manipulation of people's loyalty (Muller 1988: 132).

The prevalence in the Weberian scheme of a purely positivist notion of 'rational legitimacy' was widely criticized, and there have been many attempts to introduce a more normative or substantive basis to this conceptualization. Within a wide range of problems encompassed in this tradition, from the point of view of trust, the most relevant criticism is that this perspective misrepresented the relationship between legitimacy and people's beliefs. Such research fails to notice that a given power relationship is not legitimate 'because people believe in its legitimacy, but because it can be justified in terms of their beliefs' (Beetham 1991: 11). Without this distinction no assessment of the legitimacy of a political system would be able to say how far it satisfies people's expectations – in other words, whether they do or do not trust their political system.

The most prominent among attempts to clarify Weber's concept and bring it closer to the historical experiences of the contemporary world has been the school of empirical democratic theorists or pluralists, which combines Weber's concept of the plurality of power with a Parsonian normative stand and devotes itself to empirical studies of the stability and legitimacy of political order. The class compromise and economic growth of the post-war period allowed these researchers to portray the political order as based on genuine consent and legitimacy. Legitimacy is defined in this approach as 'the capacity of the system to engender and maintain the belief that the existing political institutions are the most appropriate for the society' (Lipset 1959: 77), or as 'the belief that in spite of shortcomings and failures, the political institutions are better than any others that might be established, and therefore can demand obedience' (Linz 1988: 65), or as 'a quality attributed to a regime by a population (Merelman 1966: 548). Trust is not identified with legitimacy but treated as one of the aspects of the dynamics of public opinion, helping to explain citizens' attitudes and actions vis-à-vis the regime. 'Trust might be an indicator of legitimacy, be derived from it, and contribute to its reinforcement, but trust should not be confused with legitimacy' (Linz 1988: 66). The feeling of trust is seen as shaping citizens' expectations about other people and their own sense of personal competence in dealing with political forces; consequently trust also influences people's opinion about the performance of governmental institutions.

One of the most interesting studies within the pluralist perspective is Almond and Verba's *The Civic Culture* (1963), which analyses sources of support for Western political systems. They attempted to discover respondents' feelings towards politics; pride in the political system, attitudes towards elections and feelings about the act of voting. Almond and Verba showed that Western democracies of the post-war period enjoyed a highly developed sense of loyalty to the system, a strong sense of deference to political authority and attitudes of trust and confidence. According to them, if a political regime is to survive in the long run 'it must be accepted by citizens as proper form of government per se' (1963: 230). Their idea of legitimacy, understood as political support, failed to distinguish between the different possible meanings of the concepts of pride or support. The research did not focus on the role of elites, power relationships between groups, economic situations or a general system performance – namely, all of the factors which could serve as the basis for an emergence of trust as social capital were not included.

This last point was later developed by Easton (1975) who stressed the role of generalized attitudes towards authorities, which he conceptualized as being built on previous experiences and being a social capital or 'a reserve of good will' which a system accumulates through efficient performance. This distinction between diffused system support and specific evaluation of state performance has been one of the most influential typologies of political support and has led to much empirical research, which established that low trust in institutions does not necessarily lead to rejection of the existing democratic regime. These types of studies show that belief in the legitimacy of democratic government needs to be qualified in such a way as to enable the differentiation between legitimacy beliefs of various groups. They also demonstrate that it is the performance of the democratic institutions over a period of time which gives rise to its legitimacy (Weil 1989).

Luhmann, like Weber, looks for the institutional mechanisms that make a 'legitimacy of legality' possible (Muller 1988: 134). He bases the modern theory of legitimacy upon the complexity of modern societies and the need for reducing the contingency of action. According to him, in complex societies the legitimacy of a political system is not an issue of shared norms and values but the matter of procedural rules and institutional performance which secure acceptance of the system. Luhmann (1979) defines legitimacy as a by-product of effective system functioning. He assumes that general support for political action is produced by the institution itself, thus that democratic institutions and political performance do not need subjective grounds for legitimacy. Once citizens have accepted their own roles within procedural mechanism, Luhmann argued, they no longer possess any opportunity for questioning its results and mobilizing on the basis of values, interests or general principles. He did not admit that procedures can be perceived as illegitimate; for example, in Western societies procedures are held to be legitimate only if they bring about democratic order and if they provide adequate institutional means for realizing group interest (Offe 1984). Luhmann's viewing of legitimation through procedures as a valuable evolutionary development is coherent with his perception of democracy as an evolutionary achievement which enhances political action 'on the level of a higher morality' (Luhmann 1990: 51). Yet, Luhmann (1979), like Locke, argues that trust is central to the maintenance of a society in operation since trust ensures cooperation through the reduction of uncertainty.

A procedural system is only a necessary prerequisite, albeit not a sufficient condition for the stability of a modern political order. According to Luhmann, to 'generate the positive functional consequences, it has to be backed up by more substantive means' (Muller 1988: 136). The working of all complex political or economic institutions, government bureaucracies or monetary systems depends upon trust. It is not, however, the emotional, personal trust of the past but a purely cognitive system of trust predicted on the ways in which institutions and practices present themselves to us. And while this type of trust is sufficient for the functioning of the system, in order to overcome any crisis the system needs more than passive, pragmatic acceptance. In the situations of uncertainty or risk, in order to maximize the utilization of resources, the system requires additional input – that is, trust (Luhmann 1988: 95–9). However, despite viewing trust as a subsidiary mechanism of the procedural system, Luhmann does not investigate the constitutive nature of their relations. Furthermore, he argues that common values are useless in an explanation of the operation of complex and differentiated societies and that an assumption about a normative basis of democracy shows nothing other than the parochialism of European intellectuals. Consequently, as Muller (1988: 135–6) notes, Luhmann does not offer a proper theory of political legitimation. His theory has also been criticized for ignoring economic and social contexts. This prevented him from predicting a legitimacy crisis and thus diagnosing the main problem facing Western societies in the 1970s and 1980s.

The economic and social problems of the 1970s, which undermined the claim of stability and social consensus as being the main basis of legitimacy of a liberal democratic order, contributed to the emergence of theories searching for sources of these new difficulties. The most prominent among them have been various versions of a theory of 'overloaded government' and theories of a crisis in legitimization. Since all of them have been widely discussed (for example, Held 1987), I shall try only to expose their main features which are relevant to our discussion of the concepts of trust and legitimacy.

Offe and Habermas, the theorists of the 'legitimation crisis', argued that the contemporary state is unable to fulfil its required task in relation to the capitalist economy without encountering severe legitimation problems of its own. Both of them see the 'crisis of legitimacy' as a result of the displacement of the basic contradiction of capitalism on to the political sphere. Offe's (1984) neo-Marxist approach explains legitimation problems in terms of the contradictory role of the capitalist state resulting from the interplay between the economic and political performance of the state. The state has to secure and protect the integrity of the market, while simultaneously intervening in it in the social interest. Although state intervention in the economy is unavoidable, it can risk challenging the traditional basis of legitimacy and consequently undermine state authority and its support. While in Offe's (1984) theory there is no place for societal values and attitudes, Habermas' (1976) theory, which connects loss of legitimacy and value crisis, takes a more normative stand.

According to Habermas, crisis depends upon a questioning of the legitimizing principle by political practice. State intervention destroys the legitimizing principles of the private economy, leading to the replacement of demands for material gratifications by symbolic demands. A crisis of legitimacy can be traced to the transparency of the socio-political situation, which allows for a relatively accurate decoding of government aims and failures, consequently leading to a motivation crisis. A deficit of legitimacy is mirrored in the minimal trust granted to the economic and political institutions and doubts about the type of rationality employed by these institutions.

The importance of Habermas' perspective is connected with his emphases on the social significance of legitimacy and the conceptualization of a new source of legitimacy on which belief in legality depends – that is, rationally motivated agreement of the community, effected through discussion, which enacts the law itself and makes this law legal. For Habermas (1985) the moral justification of the modern constitutional state lies in the principle of democratic legitimacy according to which the only norms that can be justified are those that express generalizable interests and thus could rely on the considered agreement of all concerned. Thus, the principle of democratic legitimacy is justified by discourse ethics, which implies that 'the generation of law and power must be referred back to the democratic participation of all concerned' (Cohen and Arato 1992: 395). To some degree Habermas' presentation of the role of agreement or the will generated by the community as the basis of the new type of legal domination is an extension of Weber and an incorporation of Durkheim's normative perspective. However, Habermas, unlike Weber, is a historical optimist, especially when he formulates his hypothesis of the possibility of a reasonable political discourse in which values are explicitly expressed and negotiated. Many commentators criticized Habermas' assumption about the possibility of reconciliation of specific interests with the 'common good'. This, as well as other frequent criticisms of discourse ethics (that is, those of authoritarianism and excessive formalism), are countered by Cohen and Arato, who try to redefine discourse ethics in such a way that it 'can throw light on the dual possibilities of existing democratic institutions, instead of emphasizing only their distance from the normative claims of this form of legitimacy' (1992: 407). Consequently, they view a politics of civil society as an effective revivification of democratic legitimacy, which 'presupposes that democratization is always on the agenda and that acts of civil disobedience in the name of further democratization of representative democracies take the principle of representation seriously and are legitimate' (1992: 602). Their development of Habermas' dualistic approach based on communicative practices results in the introduction of a broad concept of civil society as encompassing a third sphere of social action, independent of the state and the economy, which offsets the commodification, formalism and proceduralism of the other two. A justification of the value-orientation of democratic civil society on the basis of discourse ethics serves as a new ground for democratic legitimacy.

Another version of the normative approach to legitimacy, this time influenced by the American tradition of public philosophy, has been proposed by Bellah and his co-writers (1985 and 1991). Bellah, like Habermas, believes that the crisis of legitimacy is moral in its nature. According to him, the culture of individualism has eroded our institutions and the moral requirements of meaningful citizenship. Bellah also believes that a society is virtue-orientated and that problems of legitimacy will be solved merely by moral reflection and public discussion. Furthermore, in the spirit of Durkheim he argues that values can unite all conflictual interests and solve our social and political problems. Consequently, Bellah's assessment of the role of a modern system of values is totally different from that of Habermas, who, in this regard, accepts Weber's idea that the modern state cannot rely upon a universalistic value system. Bellah, on the other hand, follows Durkheim and 'tries to show how the state's political action can be oriented towards the core of "civil religion", which conveys obligatory meaning' (Muller 1988: 140).

Bellah (1980) believes that the availability of civil religion – that is, a set of religious symbols and practices addressing issues of political legitimacy and political ethics – may help to overcome conflicts and a legitimacy deficit. Diagnosing lost trust in institutions and a credibility crisis as the main American problem, he proposes to transform the culture of individualism by redefining the institutional framework. Since '[d]emocracy requires a degree of trust we often take for granted', the refashioning of institutions should aim at promoting participation, co-operation and democratic accountability, which would be secured, for example, in politics by strengthening political parties, curbing political interest and promoting grass-roots participation (Bellah et al. 1991: 3). This transformation of institutions can be achieved with the help of cultural reforms promoting a viable civil religion, which will re-establish social responsibility, solidarity and trust. In order to widen democratic participation and to increase the accountability of institutions, we need to educate ourselves as citizens. Only then can we really make a difference in the functioning of institutions. By being responsible and concerned with the common good, we can increase our ability to make institutions accountable, and by the same token, stop the erosion of trust in institutions. A good society will be a discursive community capable of thinking about the common good, and its institutions will encourage 'mutual trust and civic responsibility and the practical enactment of good will' (Bellah et al. 1991: 285).

Bellah's belief in a reconciliation of the plurality of interests seems to be too optimistic, and he is also criticized for not paying attention to power. The promise of a coherent pattern of living together based on moral consensus, according to Lukes (1992: 426), is based on an unrealistic vision of consensus since the main characteristic of a democratic society is its diversity. Bellah and his co-writers failed to notice that institutions are also power relations and that, as such, they are closely intertwined in the distribution of material resources. Hence, real changes are connected not with an emergence of new social attitudes but rather with an occurrence of new sources of power. Moreover, since power and consciousness are connected, 'people will not join in discussions about transformation of institutions which they perceive themselves to be helpless to affect' (Fox Piven 1992: 428).

From the point of view of the trust debate, the most interesting observation is that of Bellah's team that we 'have more government but less political and moral capacity to make it accountable' (1991: 26). This loss of ability to think responsibly about institutions leads, in turn, to a loss of trust in institutions. However, Bellah's proposed resolution to this problem is not sufficient. In order to be able to be responsible and to act in a responsible way, we need, apart from civic spirit, resources, procedures and rights which would empower and provide us with interests in the functioning of the institutions.

To sum up, political legitimacy is a complex, multi-level concept, which aggregates systematic and individual properties. The traditional Weberian approach offers a broad theoretical view, guides research towards the context within which political life takes place and facilitates comparative analysis, but, at the same time, it has a tendency to concentrate on formal structures and neglects the political system's subjective aspects (Weatherford 1992). On the other hand, the perspective focusing on attitudes, norms and values does not pay enough attention to power structures and the procedural properties of the system, although it exposes the significance of legitimacy more clearly. In this approach, evidence of a lack of legitimacy demonstrates that 'the normative commitments that derive from legitimacy ensure a distinctive level and quality of compliance and cooperation' (Beetham 1991: 38).

It can be said that, while legality is not by itself a sufficient criterion of legitimacy, although it is a necessary condition of it, normative grounds are not the sole reasons for obedience. Other grounds people have for obedience are connected with the existence of power relations, which

> are almost always constituted by a framework of incentives and sanctions, implicit, if not always explicit, which align the behaviour of the subordinate with the wishes of the powerful. They do it by giving people good reasons of a different kind, those of self-interest or prudence, for not stepping out of line. Obedience is therefore to be explained by a complex of reasons, moral as well as prudential, normative as well as self-interested, that legitimate power provides for those who are subject to it (Beetham 1991: 27).

Thus, any theory building directed at modelling the linkage between these two main approaches needs to define the legitimacy of power as a multi-dimensional concept, including legal properties and performance of the system and people's normative and instrumental expectations as well as their political behaviour. The legitimacy of any political system should be seen as directly linked with its basic organizing principles and rules of power, and as 'the outcome of a complex web of interdependencies between political, economic, social institutions and activities, which divide power centres and which create multiple pressure to comply' (Held 1987: 298). Seeing political legitimacy as compromising legality or conformity to rules, the justifiability of rules in terms of shared beliefs and confirmation through expressed consent, as proposed by Beetham (1991), allows for differentiation between legitimacy, its consequences for social cooperation and the impact of social cooperation on social order.

The complexity of the concept of legitimacy does not allow us to define precisely how much pragmatic interest, normative justification or recognition of legality is involved in a given expression of consensus. However, following Beetham, it can be said that power, in order to be justified, must be delivered from a valid source of authority: 'the rules must provide that those who come to hold power have the qualities appropriate to its exercise; and the structure of power must be seen as to serve a recognisably general interest, rather than simply the interest of the powerful' (1991: 17).

In a liberal democracy, legitimation takes place by the democratic mechanisms of elections and the rotation of ruling parties, and thus legitimacy is closely related to democratic principles and procedures. Since the post-war period legitimacy has begun to hinge more and more on the provision of socio-economic welfare. The modern welfare state has been legitimated by its performance and the consent of the governed as expressed through free and open elections. However, today liberal democracies are experiencing a high level of distrust of their respective political systems and their governments suffer low levels of legitimacy. Although the democratic system appears to survive both distrust and a crisis of legitimacy and although retreat to privacy does not present a threat to the democratic order, it depreciates motivations of consent to merely instrumental interests, and consequently the reduction of opportunities for social cooperation. In order to discover what causes these reduced opportunities for social cooperation, we ought to analyse the relationship between different principles and aspects of legitimacy and their realization in today's political institutions. I would argue that the changing nature of our societies is posing new problems of legitimacy and that the solutions require a new type of trust.

The principles and grounds of justification, consent and legality change with the transformation of societies. The change from the traditional to the modern type of society saw legitimacy evolve from 'the ascriptive to the meritocratic principle of access to the means and positions of power, from paternalistic to the consultative determination of subordinate or common interests; from the expressive to the contractual mode of consent' (Beetham 1991: 98). We witness today the political impact of new types of interest organization and representation, which have been facilitated by the fragmentation of society, the polity and the economy. The gradual withering away of the social class structure of the past, the decentralization of governmental policies, the transformation of economic structures, the declining role of the national centre *vis-à-vis* international and decentralized units are affecting the ability of democratic states to command acceptance and obedience. Today's dilemmas of legitimacy are connected with the changing nature of the representations, the declining ability of national governments to meet citizens' expectations and the growing transparency of the decision-making process. The new strains on legitimacy and the loss of trust result in part from the difficulty of steering a society, from the multiplicity of levels of governing and from the growing ambiguity of criteria for decision making, as modern societies become more decentralized, fragmented, heterogeneous and with strong independent resources and reasoning.

Consequently, today's problem of political legitimacy involves three new concerns. The first is connected with the question of whom we should trust to represent us. This is connected with the challenge faced by conventional politics and the emergence of a new politics. The second concern raises the questions of whose consent should be necessary for a particular decision and how we can trust them to be accountable. It deals with the issue of the appropriate constituency for a given decision and addresses the issue of various levels of governing. The third question asks whom we should trust to make decisions in this world of multiple authorities. It deals with the decline in the legitimating role of experts *vis-à-vis* lay persons and with the emergence of alternative sources of authority. It what follows I will discuss possible connections between each of these three questions and the issue of the quality of social cooperation.

The legitimacy of liberal democracy is based on the principle of popular sovereignty, which implies that the people should have effective choice, that is guaranteed by freedom of expression and association. The classical scheme of democratic legitimation implies representation through political parties, whose task is to facilitate the choice for electors.

> Exercising a choice between them [parties] ensures express consent to the government that is so chosen: on the part of the majority, because they have voted for it; on the part of the minority, because by participating in the election they are assumed to have demonstrated their acceptance of the rules by which the government was chosen (Beetham 1991: 152).

To define legitimation by the democratic mechanisms of elections and the rotation of ruling parties grants the role of securing and maintaining general legitimation to political parties, whose aim is to 'keep alive a public image of the system as open and a general' (Zolo 1992: 120). In an ideal situation, the party system should present voters with clear alternatives; each party should be capable of rotating into office and none likely to destroy democracy. Rational voters, who expect parties to behave as unitary actors who outline their plans before elections and make good on their promises, should be provided with some certainty about the future behaviour of the party so that they could establish a link between their preferences and the act of voting. In such a case, parties act as trustees, and voters trust them to exercise political power in a way accepted by them.

Although 'no party ever approaches the voters' ideals of calculability and complete agreement between individual and party preferences' (Kitschelt 1990: 200), research has shown that some party systems are better than others in ensuring legitimacy. When the party system is less polarized and fractionalized, social support and trust in democratic structures is relatively high. Furthermore, it has been established that citizens judge democracy less by what it 'gives' them than by whether it presents them with real alternatives and responds to their choices (Weil 1989). Hence, it can be said that the creation and maintenance of political trust is one of the main functions of political parties in a democratic regime. 'The party, with its durable structure and public exposure, is a sort of guarantee of political mediation, a kind of "political credit" institution, made possible by continual verification of the available credit, through the electoral process' (Pizzorno 1990: 71).

Until recently, traditional mass parties have been able to secure their credibility through a variety of organizational mechanisms, such as bureaucratization, internal structures and linkages to external constituencies. In this process political parties have become bureaucratic organs of the state, more and more connected with the stability of the state institutions and their capacity to draw voters into their organizational nets, and their links with wider society have been declining, while internal party power has been shifting towards the leadership, further reducing voters' sense of identification. For example, in Sweden between 1986 and 1988, the proportion of voters agreeing with a statement that 'Parties are only interested in people's votes, not their opinion' almost doubled, and this opinion is now endorsed by two-thirds of the electorate (Bergstrom 1991: 22). The growing distrust of political parties, conventional politics, decline in party allegiance, an ageing of the class alignment and growing cynicism about political parties are common occurrences in all Western democracies (Meny 1990). With the Western electorate becoming more fluid and shifting its preferences from one election to the next, the declining faith in the capacity of government and the public's distrust of politicians have been steadily becoming more visible. The weakening of parties' function of social integration, a dispersion of party strength, fractionalization and issue voting replaces the acceptance of a party programme, leading to a decline in the share of the vote taken by the leading parties and to abandonment by parties of their programme's identity and a search for conditional support rather than reliance on voters' sense of identification (Smith 1993). 'If the process of programme convergence approaches the point where all distinctions are cancelled, the electors become unable to choose for want of separate identities, and participation in political life approaches meaninglessness' (Pizzorno 1990: 64). None of the political parties in such a political system could act as a trustee, and consequently the system could not acquire legitimation. Although today's Western democratic systems are not yet in such a desperate situation, the evidence of the distrust in and decline of parties' popularity are posing a challenge for the democratic system of representation.

To ask whom we should trust to represent our interests or who should be our trustees means trying to identify mediators or kinds of 'political credit' institutions, which, thanks to 'durable trust in them will act as a guarantee for the deferral of payments' (Pizzorno 1990: 71). Consequently, an answer to the above question requires a more careful look at the modern pattern of interest intermediation. Although political parties are an essential part of the modern pattern of interest intermediation, they are not the sole element of it. Apart from political parties, 'interest groups and social movements are elements in a closely woven fabric of linkages between civil society and political institutions of the democratic state' (Kitschelt 1990: 179). Furthermore, an understanding of the limits of the representative system – especially acknowledgement of the fact that interests that are not organized and articulated in the political domain can be ignored without any consequence for the legitimacy of the state – should be incorporated into our answer to the above question.

Our first step should be an identification of the relative capabilities of interest groups, political parties and new social movements to produce certainty about their policies and to assume public responsibility for their action. Although interest groups can provide certainty about their future behaviour (always promoting members' interests), their ability to assume public responsibility for their actions – that is, their ability to include in their consideration, when they formulate their policy demands, interests other than those of their members – can be doubted.

In today's new national and international contexts, it is more difficult than during the peak days of corporatism to force special interests to aggregate into a public interest and to assume public responsibility. While corporatist exchange between the state and interest organizations presupposes members' discipline and a similar frame of reference for all political actors, today's citizens, who are better educated and more appreciative of their autonomy, more heterogeneous in their aspirations and less interested in class and union solidarities, do not fit into this scheme any more. They want more control over political leaders, they are more aware of and more willing to use various alternatives and, moreover, they value compromise and consensus less. Hence, the process of decline in support of and trust in conventional parties and the dissolving of corporatist politics has not led to political alienation and apathy. On the contrary, studies reveal an increasing sense of political obligation and preference for expressive participation among many social groups.

Interestingly, the support for and participation in unconventional types of politics have been growing (Ester et al. 1993: 97), and, despite a sense of betrayal of trust by conventional politics, people want to be able actively to influence their own fate. Although the distrust of parties and politicians is growing, the general public is

> more socially active than at any time previously and also more competent than ever to assert their opinions and rights.... At the same time civic virtues are still alive and active.... But the growth of social involvement occurs outside the political parties, through individual strategies or single-issue movements (Bergstrom 1991: 22).

The rise of new social movements, and following it green or movement parties, is one of the most important political developments within Western European societies in the last two decades. This has led to the emergence of new politics, which refers to 'a new issue agenda replacing the alignment of citizens' interests in accord with traditional social cleavages' (Kuechler and Dalton 1990: 288). The new politics proposed by environmental, women's, peace and other social movements and new parties is issue-orientated, and thus it does not provide a fixed guideline for political orientation. Because issues can change easily, they interact in a complicated way with other issues, and because they can be assimilated by other parties or movements, they do not represent a stable partisan orientation. Furthermore, since new social movements neither appeal to nor act on behalf of any given social groups, and at the same time they adopt a 'no-negotiation' strategy, their ability to assume broader public responsibility is not so clear. This ambivalence about their ability to take on interests other than their own main concern can probably explain, at least to some degree, the lack of a wide electoral success among the new movement parties. Another important element contributing to the fact that people do not trust new political parties to such a degree as to guarantee them essential influence over public policy making and implementation, is the ambition of these new parties to maintain a balance between their heritage as a social protest movement and their integration into the established political system, which is a very difficult task. It demands from them the preservation of a balance between the logic of party competition and the logic of constituency representation. Following an internal logic of constituency representation, green parties are

> characterized by a narrower base of voter encapsulation and participation, less centralization of power, and less organizational coherence. In their external behaviour, however, particularly in the choice of electoral candidates, their emphasis on visible leadership, and strategies of alliance build-

ing, they show some sign of moving toward a logic of party competition (Kitschelt 1989: 281).

Acceptance of the logic of constituency representation, on the one hand, does not allow for the emergence of strong leaders. On the other hand, weak organizational structures facilitate unaccountable and unresponsive elites, promote strategic volatility and unreliability *vis-à-vis* potential coalition partners, and make 'their voters especially prone to vote-switching in order to reward or punish parties for their actions' (Kitschelt 1990: 200).

It can be concluded that the new politics of green parties and new social movements is changing the old conventional parties and that it is leaving many legacies. However, by itself it does not offer any new forms or radical solutions to 'political credit' institutions but only points out methods of adjustment and improvement necessary to secure the conventional forms of the further existence of interest representation. The new politics has left a mark on the political arena in restructuring the issue agenda, in pushing for more direct citizen participation and in redefining the boundaries of institutional politics as well as by challenging political parties to undertake a process of change. As Kitschelt (1990) notes, the green parties have introduced a structural differentiation and polarity into the party system. However, the de-alignment that they produced in the established party system has so far not led to a solid re-alignment. New politics, with its explicit rejection of parliamentary elitism and its reliance on extra-parliamentary means, both as a tactic and a form of legitimation, increases our awareness that political parties may well be a necessary condition for modern political legitimacy but that they are not a sufficient condition and that there is a need for more participatory politics. The task of reconstruction of structures of mutual trust have been slowly acknowledged and the established political parties are now in 'a slow evolutionary process of adaptation; producing stability by way of change. . . . The unintended consequences of securing the long-term stability of the political order may turn out to be the most important impact of today's new social mementos' (Kuechler and Dalton 1990: 298).

Although the injection of trust into politics may be accomplished without the destruction of the old conventional politics, it would, however, require a quite considerable change in the nature of the representation and intermediation of interests. According to Dunn (1990: 42), who explicitly proposes rethinking political parties in terms of a project of constructing and reproducing structures of trust, we should opt for trust in leaders' practical capacities instead of trusting their good intentions. This way out from the current impasse would result in a shift from programmes to personalities for the task of representing alternatives. Choice among parties, ideologies and programmes would be then replaced by choice among images of personalities in which the electors are asked to put their trust. This, however, would not necessarily promote a participatory culture, but it could reduce leadership accountability to its constituency; thus it is not a solution capable of sustaining and reproducing trust on a permanent basis.

Looking at the main reason for the survival of the political party in modern pluralist democracies – that is, at its unique role as a kind of 'political credit' institution – Pizzorno (1990: 72) notes that parties flourish when 'citizens are in need of stable structures to which they can trustfully refer to orient themselves not only in their utilization of political machineries but also in their acquisition of new social identities'. Thus, while parties need to restate their separate identities, find their ideological core and ensure continual verification of the available credit through the electoral process, their role is also influenced by external factors such as the structure of the decision-making process or the existence or absence of other alternative structures of identification and trust. Established parties must, consequently, show an adaptive response along two other lines. They ought, firstly, to take account of the changing structures of societies. This means the acceptance of diversity and complexity. Secondly, they have to be able to redefine their positions in terms of new levels of decision making. These two methods are connected, since the best way of approaching the increasing diversity is to disperse the responsibility for problem solving and decision making by means of decentralization and delegation of responsibilities to local, regional, national and supranational levels.

Changing conditions on the international, national and regional levels, which make all political demands more negotiable, and the changing relationships between the main political agents, which reduce the nation-state's stand *vis-à-vis* the other levels of decision making, create new legitimacy problems. A series of overlapping local, national and international structures and processes have been affecting the very nature of relationships between political decision makers and the recipients of political decisions, and consequently democratic theory 'can no longer be elaborated as a theory of the territorially delimited polity alone, nor can the nation-state be displaced as a central point of reference' (Held 1991: 223). Until recently, national consent and cooperation has been needed to legitimize governmental decisions, but 'the very idea of consent, and the particular notion that the relevant constituencies of voluntary agreement are the communities of bounded territory or a state, become deeply problematic as soon as the issue of national, regional and global interconnectedness is considered and the nature of a so-called "relevant community" is contested' (1991: 203).

The new legitimacy problems are the result of the erosion of the efficacy of the system of representative democracy in the face of globalization. When the governance has consequences for citizens within and beyond the territorial boundaries of the nation-state and when decisions affecting people could be taken without their consent by decision-making centres which are not accountable to them, we should be concerned about what are the proper forms of and limits to these various overlapping structures of authority. On which level should decisions affecting various aspects of our everyday lives be taken? To what degree can these decisions be entrusted to local levels of decision making? How we can trust supranational units not to impose on us unwanted solutions? To whom should decision makers of different levels be accountable? The problem of the appropriate constituency for various decisions, or which level's decisions are legitimate decisions, becomes one of the most crucial problems which the process of internationalization is now imposing on us.

In the context of these new problems of legitimacy, three issues can affect the input of trust into the political system. Firstly, there is the issue of a 'democratic deficit', which so often manifests itself in the functioning of supranational organizations. Secondly, there is the question of the different capacities of various political actors to adjust and to act in an international context and under conditions of a multiplicity of authority. And thirdly, there is the problem to what degree decisions of different levels are exclusionary of non-members. These three issues are crucial in determining the fate of legitimacy because their possible resolution might increase or decrease our ability to control and keep decision makers accountable. The optimistic vision of a democratic international order has been constructed by David Held (1991: 234), who, although not believing that this global order will be harmonious, assumes that 'democratic processes and practices have to be articulated with the complex arena of national and international policy'. Looking briefly at some less encouraging evidence, I would like to point out how many difficulties still lie ahead to the construction of a coherent strategy of dealing with globalization.

A good illustration of problems encountered by any supranational body is the widely debated issue of a democratic deficit in connection with the functioning of the European Union (known until November 1993 as the European Community). Public concern with the growing power of the Commission and the Brussels bureaucracy, with its impenetrable maze of procedures, committees and nuclear lines of accountability and the unrepresentativeness of its institutions, was loudly expressed on several occasions. Most recently it occurred during the mid-1994 elections to the European parliament when the public in all members' countries called for more power, accountability and clarity to be given to this institution, 'whose discussions, budgetary deliberations, and "co-decisions" on some matters with the Council are barely comprehensible to the public' (Hoffmann 1993: 29). Although the Maastricht Treaty (December 1991) was an attempt to solve some of the problems of a democratic deficit by increasing the role of parliament and introducing the principle of subsidiarity, it, however, 'does nothing to make the EC more democratic, and could do much to provoke a constant tug of war between the national states and the EC' (1993: 29). Paradoxically, the Maastricht Treaty's ratification itself proved to be the illustration of this very issue. As Hoffmann notes, a low level of support for the Treaty can be attributed to some degree to the fact that the text presented to voters in Denmark and France was 'nearly incomprehensible' (1993: 29). Difficulties in understanding the complex and opaque machinery of the EU contributes to problems in accepting the implications of its decisions. Such decisions are, moreover, often blamed for not only being undemocratic (because they are made not by a representative body but the national executives) but also for being unrepresentative of a particular country's interests (because in many EU institutions, such as, in the Council of Ministers, there is a large disparity between the percentage of votes and percentage of EU population in some cases).

These difficulties with trusting and identifying with a 'Europe' are increasing with the emerging doubts about who really benefits and who loses from the process of integration. As the Norwegian referendum (November 1994) demonstrated, it is the business, urban, mobile and educated classes that are the main supporters of joining the EU. According to Sandholz and Zysman (1989) and Ross (1992), the post-1985 European integration has been pushed by the needs of European capital and supported by European governments; heads of businesses together with national governments and with the Commission can be seen as responsible for the current neo-liberal model of Europe. The fact that organized interests have a considerable impact on European politics is not only evidence of a democratic deficit, it also reflects the problems of democratic representation in general. This is connected with many structural limits which make political parties an inappropriate instrument on the international scene (Pizzorno 1990), while increasing the potential for action of interest groups. Furthermore, not all interests can be equally represented on an international level. Kohler-Koch's (1994: 170) study shows that at the EU level there is a significant imbalance between producer and consumer representations as well as between business and labour organizations; for example, in 1990, among 525 European interest groups registered with the EU Commission in Brussels, 374 of them represented industrial and commercial producers' interests, while only 18 groups represented European trade unions' interests. The distinctive nature of the international decision-making process discourages, even more than at the national level, the participation of less organized, less professional groups as well as those without contacts and resources. The more complex and unstable nature of supranational politics, with its multiplicity of structures, flexibility, unpredictability, many members and different levels of decision making facilitate lobbying by well-connected business interest groups, who, moreover, are always the first to recognize whether their interest is affected by the EU. According to some predictions, the European system of interest intermediation will be experiencing a further process of fragmentation, which will accelerate 'the already considerable degree of complexity of the negotiating system stretching from the regional or even local to the European level' (1994: 177). Similarly, Streeck and Schmitter (1991: 159) argue that the neo-liberal model of the European political economy makes it unlikely that the EU will evolve as a neo-corporatist structure, and they also suggest that fundamental questions concerning the relative status of regions, nations, supranational bodies and interest groups 'will remain unsettled and uncertain' for some time. Consequently, European integration will remain a unique experiment, but 'its very uniqueness has proved a profound doubt and distrust about the relation of the Community to the national states and public' (Hoffman 1993: 30).

Although there will be no clarification of the EU's destiny in the immediate future, its decisions are already influencing many non-members. The existence of a supranational level of governance, as the example of the EU shows, contributes to tensions between citizenship rights, as operating within the sphere of the nation-state, and so-called 'cosmopolitan rights'. According to Held's (1991) optimistic model, the logic of this struggle is expansive and inclusive since it could extend our rights by providing us with the possibility of appealing to higher international authorities in the case of any restriction on liberties on a national or regional level – as changes in British law on the issues of sexual discrimination, equal pay and so on, which have been introduced on the basis of findings of the European Court of Justice, illustrate – and thus a nation-state is no longer unrestricted in its treatment of its own citizens (Held 1991: 219). However, at the same time there are also good reasons to expect that reducive and exclusive effects may occur. According to Zolo (1993) these effects are already produced in terms of growing restrictions on citizenship rights introduced by the EU immigration policy, which is designed to control the influx of global migration.

The reaction of citizenships threatened by this 'cosmopolitan' pressure – in terms both of violent exclusion of immigrants and of practical denial of their legal and social status – seems bound to write in the next decades some of the most tragic pages in the civil and political history of western countries (Zolo 1993: 266).

New problems of legitimacy will not disappear, only become more pressing with the growing process of internationalization. The insufficiency of our mechanisms to cope with problems of more complex, global and fragmented collective decision-making processes demands a rethinking of the nature of relationships between decision makers and the recipients in such a way as to increase the input of trust to the system. Citizens' voices and preferences are already an important part of collective decision making in some areas of public policy such as environmental policy and health policy. In this new type of legitimating negotiations or 'round table' debates, to use Beck's (1994) description, new relationships between participation and legitimacy are proposed and 'the source of legitimacy is not the predetermined will of individuals, but rather the process of its formation, that is, deliberation itself' (Mannin 1987: 351). This process of deliberation not only assumes that there will be a continuous learning process but also that there will be no more experts or 'teachers' telling us in advance what is the proper answer. 'In other words, what is to be learned is a matter that we must settle in the process of learning itself' (Offe and Preuss 1991: 168). The basing of democratic legitimacy on the principle of deliberation is also facilitated by the decline of the supremacy of the model of unambiguous instrumental rationality. Both Beck and Giddens, in their respective projects of reflexive modernity, point out, by showing how science is demystified and knowledge claims are demonopolized, the failure of science as a source of legitimation.

Beck (1992: 184) stresses that until recently the legitimating umbrella of 'progress' and 'rationalization' removed from the political sphere the duty of justifying the direction of technological and scientific development. In the era of a manufactured consensus on progress, decisions in science and business required an effective political content for which the agents possess no legitimation (1992: 187–214). However, this pseudo-political industrial sovereignty in matters of technological development, which possessed only borrowed legitimacy and no responsibility, has been undermined, and the illusion that administrators and experts always know best is slowly being dispelled. Public awareness of the consequences of scientists' errors and their blindness about risks and the growing criticism of the irrational and destructive practices of science have led to the disintegration of the consensus on progress and the monopoly of science. Consequently, 'the coalition of technology and economy becomes shaky because technology can increase productivity but at the same time it puts legitimacy at risk' (Beck 1994: 18). The rationality of technocrats, scientists and administrators is questioned and their concept of 'public good' is rejected. Hence, in the new post-industrial order, with its risk, uncertainty and ambivalence, public dialogue is seen as the best way of solving the conflicts of interest between experts and lay individuals, who are now seen as capable of representing their own interests. 'Anyone who no longer wishes to accept the "fate" of the production of side-effects and hazards, and thus wishes to force the associated loss of legitimation for techno-industrial development, must consider how the "new ambivalence" can be made acceptable and capable of forming consensus' (1994: 28). Good examples of mediating institutions, which Beck presents as the 'round table model' for arriving at consensus, are various ethical and risk commissions. Thus, science can 'revive the Enlightenment' by using its tools in a critical and reflexive way to abolish the model of unambiguous instrumental rationality. In the process of radicalization of modernity the concepts of the political and the non-political become blurred, and sub-politics shapes society from below as more confident people become active in various social movements. This responsibility based on collective reflexivity is a new form of legitimation.

As Beck replaces 'progress' with collective responsibility as a principle of legitimation, so Giddens (1994) replaces the concept of trust in abstract systems (trust invested in expert systems) with the concept of 'active trust' (trust becomes active when expertise is contested by the lay population) as the source of legitimation (Lash 1994: 201). Giddens, like Beck, points out that science has lost in the public eye its previous status of a monolithic source of 'authority'. This consequently changes the nature of trust relations between experts and lay individuals and lowers the significance of trust in abstract systems.

'Trust no longer depends upon a respect for the "causal relation" believed to hold between a guardian and formulatic truth' (Giddens 1994: 89). Because trust is based on the assumption of technical competence, on experts' specialized knowledge, it is available to anyone. Expert knowledge can now be 'reappropriated' and is open to critique and contestation. In the same vein as Beck, Giddens proposes that '[n]orms of discussion and debate relative to change in the domain of 'sub-politics' should be established and guaranteed' (1994: 193). According to Lash (1994: 202), for both Beck and Giddens 'reflexivity entails the dialogical avowal of responsibility by institutions or active mediated trust'.

How realistic is the assumption of these authors about the existence of the trend towards replacing bureaucratic hierarchies with more flexible and decentralized systems of authority? Facilitating a new institutional reflexivity and collaborative methods of enquiry can only be evaluated by a careful monitoring of various instances of collective decision making. The argument that the sheer complexity of many public issues means that ordinary people cannot be entrusted with the decision making is, indeed, no longer popular. The viability of, if not the necessity for, deliberative democracy is now witnessed by various examples of enquiries where there has been collaboration between citizens and experts. Fischer (1993), for example, presents two cases of participatory policy analysis, one in making policy for hazardous waste treatment, and the second in community-based 'popular epidemiology'. These examples demonstrate the suitability of deliberative and participatory democracy for policy problems featuring high levels of technical complexity and political conflict. He also shows that participatory research and cooperative relationships between scientists and citizens, rather than merely providing technical answers designed to resolve or close off political discussion, also aim at assisting 'citizens in their efforts to examine their own interests and to make their own decisions' (Fischer 1993: 171). The role of the expert, as an 'interpretive mediator' between theoretical knowledge and competing practical arguments, is to facilitate public learning and empowerment as well as systematize 'local knowledge'.

This cooperative and participatory enquiry entails an evaluation of alternative solutions applying criteria derived from discursive confrontation of experts and the lay public. This echoes Habermas' idea of communicative rationality with its procedural ethics of discourse and deliberation encompassing questions of both fact and value. From this perspective, as in both Beck and Giddens, a legitimate standard of rationality can be found through reflection and deliberation. Although the radicalization of modernity brings uncertainty, new ambivalence and risk, we are still capable of forming a consensus. This assumption about the availability of and need for struggle for consensus may be criticized from the post-modernist stand, which argues that even this seemingly neutral principle excludes some points of view while espousing some others. Although public policy analysis can benefit from post-modernism's emphasis on how 'discourse' participates in the construction and maintenance of specific identities (Schram 1993), such insight by itself is insufficient. 'No politics can live by questioning alone, for there is also in politics and policy "a responsibility to act", which in turn requires legitimate, institutionalized ways for individuals and groups to make decisions and carry them out' (Dryzek and Torgerson 1993: 135). Hence, democratic deliberation, without abandoning questioning and an 'opening of the monopoly of truth' (Beck 1994: 25), should be orientated to the generation of consensus on criteria for reaching and implementing legitimate policy decisions. Both the formulation of the programme and the decision-making process as well as the enforcement of those decisions should consequently be a participatory process of learning and negotiation.

The aim of such political decision processes should be to ensure the cooperation of all citizens, and thus to create trustworthy relationships between citizens and the state and among citizens themselves. This means that legitimacy as a policy of trust requires not only participatory and deliberative democracy but also the conception of the state as a guide ensuring effective cooperation towards shared goals. Such a vision of public institutions can be found in Vickers' (1973) understanding of the state as being concerned with the regulation of social relationships rather than the pursuit of goals. The state, according to Vickers, needs to create a sufficient foundation for trust to enable the achievement of consensus, and consequently it needs to be seen as a protector and promoter of the public good rather than the agency satisfying the private preferences of interest groups (Blunden 1994). In our pluralistic, complex and inter-dependent society, we need to exercise conscious government and see policy making as a continuous process of adjustment and mutual adaptation rather than as the imposition of an externally generated set of rules. Hence, the effectiveness of democratic government depends on responsible citizenship that is activated through institutions, notably through the appropriate structuring of political action. Any new practice of democracy requires 'free but disciplined dialogue' (Vickers 1973: 86), which could only be ensured by an increase in responsibility. Vickers (1965) argued that a greater degree of individual responsibility, with its associated acceptance of obligations and constraints, can be achieved by the strengthening of our sense of understanding of mutual interdependence. He believed that responsibility requires a pattern of mutual expectations and trust among people and that the art of government consists in maintaining this set of standards, which facilitate a sense of responsibility. Thus, public institutions have both practical and normative justification; they are necessary for the maintenance of order in society and in the relationships between individuals and they are the means of our own moral development (Cook 1994). It is only within the framework of institutions that individuals can learn to appreciate one another and to work together.

If public institutions were to be concerned with more deliberate regulation of human relationships, the level of public confidence they enjoy would need to increase dramatically. The demand for legitimacy, originated in and accelerated by the new role of the state, can only be met by the trust and assurance derived from active involvement in the democratic process. The potential for creating this type of relationship can only be realized by new constitutional procedures improving the quality of citizen participation and membership in cooperative arrangements. This requirement for the creation of deliberative democracy means that public institutions should be designed in such a way as to foster more a deliberative and more reflective formation of motives and to allow for preferences in learning and revision of one's previous stands (Offe and Preuss 1991: 168–71). Havel, who sees his role as an ambassador of trust in a fearful world, while endorsing new principles of democratic participation, defines them in the context of a new role of political governance:

> The state is not something unconnected to society, hovering above or outside it, a necessary and anonymous evil. The state is a product of society, an expression of it, an image of it. It is a structure that a society creates for itself as an instrument of its own self-realisation. If we wish to create a good and humane society, capable of making a contribution to humanity's coming to its senses, we must create a good and humane state (Havel 1992: 13).

While such arguments still largely remain in the domain of Utopian speculation, the fact that they are voiced with increasing frequency and intensity, even by heads of state, suggests that we can be cautiously optimistic about the future of cooperative relations.

The main aim of this book has been to support the belief in the necessity of rethinking social relationships in a more cooperative mood. Evidence of the importance of trust to the well-being and stability of society suggests that to achieve a new quality of compliance – that is, social cooperation – we need to devote more attention to the relationships among people and between people and decisions makers. It can be concluded that if it is our responsible conduct and trust that holds us together, the ongoing process of global interdependency will only increase the demand for trust as an essential condition of cooperation.

# Bibliography

Abercrombie, N., Hill, H. and Turner, B.S. (eds) 1990: *The Dominant Ideologies*. London: Unwin Hyman.

Abrams, P. 1982: *Historical Sociology*. West Compton House, Shepton Mallet, Somerset: Open Books.

Akerlof, G.A. 1984: *An Economic Theorist's Book of Tales*. Cambridge: Cambridge University Press.

Albrow, M. 1990: *Max Weber's Construction of Social Theory*. London: Macmillan.

Alexander, J. 1989: *The Modern Reconstruction of Classical Thought: T. Parsons*. London: Routledge and Kegan Paul, vol. 4.

Alexander, J.C. and Giesen, B. 1989: From reduction to linkage. In J.C. Alexander, B. Giesen, R. Munch and N.J. Smelser (eds), *The Micro-Macro Link*, Berkeley: University of California Press, 1–39.

Allan, G.A. 1979: *A Sociology of Friendship and Kinship*. London: Allen and Unwin.

——. 1989: *Friendship. Developing Sociological Perspective*. Boulder, Colo.: Westview Press.

Almond, G.A. and Verba, S. 1963: *The Civic Culture*. Princeton: Princeton University Press.

Anderlini, L. and Sabourian, H. 1992: Some notes on the economics of barter, money and credit. In C. Humphrey and S. Hugh-Jones (eds), *Barter, Exchange and Value. An Anthropological Approach*, Cambridge: Cambridge University Press, 89–111.

Anderson, D. (ed.) 1993: *The Loss of Virtue. Moral confusion in Britain and America*. London: Social Affairs Unit.

Anderson, E. 1990: *Streetwise. Race, Class, and Change in an Urban Community*. Chicago: University of Chicago Press.

Andersen, H. 1990: Morality in three theories: Parsons, analytical Marxism and Habermas. *Acta Sociologica*, 33, 321–39.

Argyle, M. and Henderson, M. 1985: *The Anatomy of Relationships*. Methuen: London.

Aristotle, 1976: *The Ethics*. Ed. by J. Barnes, Harmondsworth: Penguin Books.

Arrow, K. 1974: *The Limits of Organisation*. New York: Norton.

Ash, T.G. 1990: *We the People: The Revoultion of '89 witnessed in Warsaw, Budapest, Berlin and Prague*. Cambridge: Granta Books.

——. 1993: *In Europe's Name*. London: Jonathan Cape.

Ashford, S. and Timms, N. 1993: *What Europe Thinks*. Aldershot: Dartmouth.

Avineri, S. 1968: *The Social and Political Thought of Karl Marx*. Cambridge: Cambridge University Press.

——. 1970: *The Political Thought of Karl Marx*. Cambridge: Cambridge University Press.

Bach, M. 1990: Individualism and legitimation: paradoxes and perspectives of the political sociology of Emile Durkheim. *Archives Européennes de Sociologie*, 31, 117–40.

Baier, A. 1986: Trust and antitrust. *Ethics*, 96, 231–61.

Baldwin, P. 1990: *The Politics of Social Solidarity*. Cambridge: Cambridge University Press.

Banfield, E.C. 1958: *The Moral Basis of a Backward Society*. New York: Free Press.

Barbalet, J.M. 1988: *Citizenship: Rights, struggle and class inequality*. Milton Keynes: Open University Press.

Barber, B. 1983: *The Logic and Limits of Trust*. New Brunswick, NJ: Rutgers University Press.

Barder, B.R. 1984: *Strong Democracy: Participatory politics for a new age*. Berkeley: University of California Press.

Barker, D.G. et al. 1992: *The European Values Study 1981–1990*. Tilburg: Gordon Cook Foundation of European Values Group.

Barnes, B. 1988: *The Nature of Power*. Cambridge: Polity Press.

——. 1992: Status groups and collective action. *Sociology*, 26, 2, 259–70.

Bartlett, F.C. 1932: *Remembering*. Cambridge: Cambridge University Press.

Bauman, Z. 1989: Sociological responses to postmodernity. *Thesis Eleven*, 23, 35–63.

——. 1991: *Intimation of Post Modernity*. London: Routledge.

——. 1993: *Postmodern Ethics*. Oxford: Basil Blackwell.

Beck, U. 1992: *Risk Society*. London: Sage.

——. 1994: The reinvention of politics: towards a theory of reflexive modernization. In U. Beck, A. Giddens and S. Lash (eds), *Reflexive Modernization*, Cambridge: Polity Press, 1–55.

Beck-Gernsheim, E. 1992: Everything for the child – for better or worse? In U. Bjornberg (ed.), *European Parents in the 1990s*, New Brunswick, NJ: Transaction Publishers, 59–82.

Beer, W.R. 1992: *American Stepfamilies*. New Brunswick, NJ: Transaction Books.

Beetham, D. 1991: *The Legitimation of Power*. London: Macmillan.

Bellah, R.N. 1980: Civil religion: the American case. In R.N. Bellah and P.E. Hammond (eds), *Varieties of Civil Religion*, Cambridge, Mass.: Harper and Row, 3–26.

Bellah, R.N. et al. 1985: *Habits of the Heart*. Berkeley: University of California Press.

——. 1991: *Good Society*. New York: Alfred A. Knopf.

Berg, J.H. 1984: The development of friendship between roommates. *Journal of Personality and Social Psychology*, 46, 346–56.

Berger, P.L. 1978: The problem of multiple realities: Alfred Schultz and Robert Musil. In T. Luckmann (ed.), *Phenomenology and Sociology*, Harmondsworth: Penguin Books, 343–67.

Berger, P.L., Berger, B. and Kellner, H. 1974: *The Homeless Mind*. Harmondsworth: Penguin Books.

Bergstrom, H. 1991: Sweden's politics and party system at the crossroads. *West European Politics*, 14, 8–29.

Birnbaum, N. 1955: Monarchs and sociologists: a reply to Professor Shils and Mr Young. *Sociological Review*, 3, 5–23.

Bjornberg. U. 1992: Parenting in transition: an introduction and summary. In U. Bjornberg (ed.), *European Parents in the 1990s*, New Brunswick, NJ: Transaction Publishers, 1–44.

Black, M. 1961: *The Social Theories of T. Parsons*. Englewood Cliffs, NJ: Prentice-Hall.

Blau, P.M. 1989: *Exchange and Power in Social Life*. New Brunswick, NJ: Transaction Publishers.

Block, F. 1991: Mirrors and metaphors: the United States and its trade rivals. In A. Wolfe (ed.), *America at Century's End*, Berkeley: University of California Press, 93–111.

Blunden, M. 1994: Vickers and postliberalism. *American Behavioral Scientist*, 38, 11–25.

Bocock, R. 1974: *Ritual in Industrial Society. A sociological analysis of ritualism in modern England*. London: Allen and Unwin.

——. 1992: The cultural formation of modern society. In S. Hall and B. Gibben (eds), *Formations of Modernity*. Cambridge: Polity Press, 229–74.

Bok, S. 1979: *Lying: Moral choice in public and private life*. Hassocks: The Harvester Press.

Bolotin, D. 1979: *Plato's Dialogue on Friendship*. Ithaca, NJ: Cornell University Press.

Boswell, J. 1990: *Community and the Economy*. London: Routledge.

Bourdieu, P. 1977: *Outline of a Theory of Practice*. Trans. R. Nice. Cambridge: Cambridge University Press.

Bourdieu, P. and Wacquant, L.J.D. 1992: *An Invitation to Reflexive Sociology*. Cambridge: Polity Press.

Boyne, R. and Rattansi, A. 1990: *Postmodernism and Society*. London: Macmillan.

Bracewell, M. 1993: Civil rites and wrongs. *The Observer*, 21 Nov., 24–5.

Brain, R. 1977: *Friends and Lovers*. Frogmore: Paladin.

Branch, K. 1989: Nicaraguan culture: alive and growing in Dade. *Miami Herald*, 25 May, 20.

Brock, G. 1994: Why we still need the nation-state. *Times Literary Supplement*, 23 Sept., 13.

Bruckner, E. and Knaup, K. 1993: Women's and men's friendships in comparative perspective. *European Sociological Review*, 9, 249–66.

Bryant, C.G.A. 1993: Social self-organisation, civility and sociology. *The British Journal of Sociology*, 44, 397–403.

Burant, S.R. and Zubel, V. 1993: Eastern Europe's old memories and new realities: resurrecting the Polish–Lithuanian union. *East European Politics and Societies*, 7, 370–93.

Burger, T. 1993: Weber's sociology and Weber's personality. *Theory and Society*, 22, 813–36.

Camic, C. 1986: The matter of habit. *American Journal of Sociology*, 91, 1039–87.

Carnevale, D.G. and Wechsler, B. 1992: Trust in the public sector. Individual and organizational determinants. *Administration and Society*, 23, 471–94.

Casson, M. 1991: *The Economics of Business Culture*. Oxford: Clarendon Press.

Castles, S. et al. 1992: *The Challenge to Multiculturalism*. Wollongong: Wollongong University.

Clarke, S. 1992: The crisis of Fordism or the crisis of social democracy. *Telos*, Spring, 83, 71–99.

Coady, C.A.J. 1993: *Testimony: A philosophical study*. Oxford: Clarendon Press.

Cohen, J. and Arato, A. 1992: *Civil Society*. Cambridge, Mass.: MIT Press.

Cole, R.L. 1973: Toward a model of political trust. *American Journal of Political Science*, 17, 809–17.

Coleman, J.S. 1990: *Foundations of Social Theory*. Cambridge, Mass.: The Belknap Press of Harvard University Press.

Collins, R. 1980: *Weberian Sociological Theory*. Cambridge: Cambridge University Press.

——. 1988: The Durkhemian tradition in conflict sociology. In J.C. Alexander (ed.), *Durkheimian Sociology: Cultural Studies*, Cambridge: Cambridge University Press, 107–28.

——. 1992: The romanticism of agency/structure versus the analysis of micro/macro. *Current Sociology*, 40, 77–97.

——. 1993: Heroizing and deheroizing Weber. *Theory and Society*, 22, 861–70.

Conradt, D.P. 1989: Changing German political culture. In G.A. Almond and S. Verba (eds), *The Civic Culture Revisited*, Boston: Little, Brown and Co., 212–66.

Cook, S.D. 1994: Autonomy, interdependence and moral governance. *American Behavioral Scientist*, 38, 153–71.

Coser, L.A. (1977) *Matters of Sociological Thought*. Altlanta, Ga.: Harcourt Brace Jovanovich Inc.

Craib, J. 1984: *Modern Social Theory*. Norfolk: Wheatsheaf Books.

——. 1993: *Anthony Giddens*. London: Routledge.

Crawford, M. 1977: What is friend? *New Society*, 42, 116–17.

Crouch, C. 1993: Co-operation and competition in an institutionalized economy: the case of Germany. In C. Crouch and D. Marquand (eds), *Ethics and Markets*, Oxford: Basil Blackwell, 80–99.

Cushman, P. 1990: Why the self is empty. *American Psychologist*, 45, 599–611.

Dahrendorf. R. 1990: *Reflections on the Revolution in Europe*. London: Chatto and Windus.

Dalton, R. 1988: *Citizens' Politics in Western Democracies*. Chatham, NJ: Chatham House.

Dasgupta, P. 1988: Trust as a commodity. In D. Gambetta (ed.), *Trust: Making and breaking cooperative relations*, Oxford: Basil Blackwell, 49–71.

Davis, J. 1969: *Honour and Politics in Pisticci*. Proceedings of the Royal Anthropological Institute.

——. 1977: *People of the Mediterranean*. London: Routledge and Kegan Paul.

——. 1992: *Exchange*. Buckingham: Open University Press.

Dawe, A. 1978: Theories of social action. In T. Bottomore and R. Nisbet (eds), *A History of Social Analysis*, London: Heinemann, 394–406.

Dertouzos, M. et al. 1989: *Made in America: Regaining of the productivity edge.* Cambridge, Mass.: MIT Press.

Deutsch, M. 1958: Trust and suspicion. *Journal of Conflict Resolution,* 2, 265–79.

Dewey, J. 1910: *How We Think.* Boston: D.C. Heath Co. Publishers.

Dodd, N. 1994: *The Sociology of Money.* Cambridge: Polity Press.

Donhoff, M. 1982: *Foes and Friends. The makers of the new Germany from Konrad Adenauer to Helmut Schmidt.* Trans. G. Annan, London: Weidenfeld and Nicolson.

Dore, R. 1993: What makes the Japanese different? In C. Crouch and D. Marquand (eds), *Ethics and Markets,* Oxford: Basil Blackwell, 66–79.

Douglas, M. 1986: *How Institutions Think.* Syracuse, NJ: Syracuse University Press.

Dowrie, R.S. and Talfer, E. 1962: *Respect for Reasons.* London: Allen and Unwin.

Dryzek, J.S. and Torgerson, D. 1993: Democracy and the policy sciences. *Policy Science,* 26, 127–38.

Duck, S. (ed.) 1990: *Personal Relationships and Social Support.* London: Sage.

——. 1991: *Friends, for Life.* New York: Harvester Wheatsheaf.

Dunn, J. 1983: Social theory, social understanding and political action. In C. Lloyd (ed.), *Social Theory and Political Practice,* Oxford: Clarendon Press, 109–35.

——. 1984b: *Locke.* Oxford: Oxford University Press.

——. 1984a: The concept of 'trust' in the politics of John Locke. In R. Rorty, J.B. Schneewind and Q. Skinner (eds), *Philosophy in History,* Cambridge: Cambridge University Press, 279–301.

——. 1988: Trust and political agency. In D. Gambetta (ed.), *Trust: Making and breaking cooperative relations,* Oxford: Basil Blackwell, 73–93.

——. 1990: Trust and political agency. In: J. Dunn, *Interpreting Political Responsibility,* Cambridge: Polity Press, 45–61.

——. 1993: Trust. In R.E. Goodin and P. Pettit (eds), *A Companion to Contemporary Political Philosophy,* Oxford: Basil Blackwell, 638–45.

Durkheim, E. 1956: *Education and Sociology.* Trans. S.D. Fox, Glencoe, NY: Free Press.

——. 1957: *Professional Ethics and Civic Morals.* Trans. C. Brookfield. London: Routledge.

——. 1962: *Socialism.* Ed. A. Gouldner. New York: Collier Books.

——. 1964: *The Division of Labour in Society.* Trans. G. Simpson. New York: Free Press.

——. 1965: *The Elementary Forms of the Religious Life.* Trans. G. Simpson. New York: Free Press.

——. 1969 *Individualism and the Intellectuals.* Trans. S. and J. Lukes, *Political Studies,* 1, 14–30.

——. 1972: Selection from Leçons de sociologie. In A. Giddens (ed.), *Emile Durkheim: Selected writings,* Cambridge: Cambridge University Press.

——. 1973: *Moral Education: A study in the theory and application of the sociology of education.* Trans. E.K. Wilson and H. Schnurer. New York: Free Press.

——. 1983: *Professional Ethics and Civic Morals.* Trans. C. Brookfield. Westport: Greenwood Press.

Easton, D. 1975: A re-assessment of the concept of political support. *British Journal of Political Science*, 5, 435–57.

Eisenstadt, S.N. and Roniger, L. 1984: *Patrons, Clients and Friends*. Cambridge: Cambridge University Press.

Elias, N. 1978: *The Civilising Process*. Oxford: Basil Blackwell.

Elon, A. 1993a: The politics of memory. *The New York Review of Books*, 7 Oct., 3–5.

——. 1993b; *The Nowhere City*. *The New York Review of Books*, 13 May, 28–33.

Elster, J. 1988: Consequences of constitutional choice: reflection on Tocqueville. In J. Elster and R. Slagstad (eds), *Constitutionalism and Democracy*, Cambridge: Cambridge University Press, 81–101.

——. 1989: *The Cement of Society*. Cambridge: Cambridge University Press.

——. 1990: Selfishness and altruism. In J.J. Manbridge (ed.), *Beyond Self-Interest*, Chicago: University of Chicago Press, 44–53.

——. 1993: *Political Psychology*. Cambridge; Cambridge University Press.

Enright, D.J. and Rawlinson, D. (eds) 1991: *The Oxford Book of Friendship*. Oxford: Oxford University Press.

Ester, P. et al. 1993: *The Individualizing Society*. Tilburg: Tilburg University Press.

Etzioni, A. 1993: *The Parenting Deficit*. London: Demos.

Fentress, J. and Wickham, C. 1992: *Social Memory*. Oxford: Basil Blackwell.

Fetscher, I. 1992: Tolerance. A timely reminder of a 'minor' virtue. *Universitas*, 1, 1–6.

Finch, J. and Mason, J. 1992: *Negotiating Family Responsibilities*. London: Tavistock.

Fischer, F. 1993: Citizen participation and the democratization of policy expertise. *Policy Science*, 26, 165–88.

Fitzmaurice, D. 1993: Liberal neutrality, traditional minorities and education. In J. Horton (ed.), *Liberalism, Multiculturalism and Toleration*, London: Macmillan, 50–69.

Fletcher, R. 1971: *The Making of Sociology*. London: Michael Joseph, vol. 2.

Flood, S. 1994: *Mabo: A symbol of sharing. The High Court judgment examined*. Glebe, NSW: Fink.

Foucault, M. 1984: The means of correct training. In P. Rabinow (ed.), *The Foucault Reader*, Harmondsworth: Penguin Books, 188–205.

Fox, A. 1974: *Beyond Contract: Work, power and trust relations*, London: Faber and Faber.

Fox Piven, F. 1992: Why exhortation is not a strategy. *Contemporary Sociology*, July, 426–7.

Francis, D. 1987: The great transition. In R.J. Anderson, J.A. Hughes and W.W. Sharrock (eds), *Classic Disputes in Sociology*, London: Allen and Unwin.

Frankel, S.H. 1977: *Money: Two philosophies. The conflict of trust and authority*. Oxford: Basil Blackwell.

Frisby, D. 1992: *Sociological Impressionism*. London: Routledge.

Gajek, E. 1990: Christmas under the Third Reich. *Anthropology Today*, 6, 3–9.

Galbraith, J.K. 1992: *The Culture of Contentment*. London: Sinclair-Stevenson.

Gambetta, D. (ed.) 1988a: *Trust: Making and breaking cooperative relations*, Oxford: Basil Blackwell.

——. 1988b: Can we trust trust? In D. Gambetta (ed.), *Trust: Making and breaking cooperative relations*, Oxford: Basil Blackwell, 213–37.

——. 1988c: Mafia: the price of distrust. In D. Gambetta (ed.), *Trust: Making and breaking cooperative relations*, Oxford: Basil Blackwell, 158–75.

——. 1993: *The Sicilian Mafia. The business of private protection*. Cambridge, Mass.: Harvard University Press.

Garfinkel, H. 1963: A conception of, and experiments with 'trust' as a condition of stable, concerted actions. In O.J. Harvey (ed.), *Motivation and Social Interaction*, New York: The Ronald Press Co., 187–238.

——. 1967: *Studies in Ethnomethodology*. Englewood Cliffs, NJ: Prentice-Hall.

Garrett, S. 1989: Friendship and the social order. In R. Porter and S. Tomaselli (eds), The Dialectics of Friendship. London: Routledge, 130–42.

Geertz, C. 1968: Religion as a cultural system. In M. Banton (ed.), *Anthropological Approaches to the Study of Religion*, London: Tavistock, 1–43.

Gellner, E. 1988: Trust, cohesion and the social order. In D. Gambetta (ed.), *Trust: Making and breaking cooperative relations*, Oxford: Basil Blackwell, 142–57.

——. 1992: *Postmodernism, Reason and Religion*. London: Routledge.

Gergen, K.J. 1991: *The Saturated Self: Dilemmas of Identity in Contemporary Life*. New York: Basic Books.

Gesicki, J. 1992: 'Strach przed obcym. *Polityka*, 24 Sept., 10.

Giddens, A. 1977: *Studies in Social and Political Theory*. London: Hutchinson.

——. 1984: *The Constitution of Society*, Cambridge: Polity Press.

——. 1989: *Sociology*. Cambridge: Polity Press.

——. 1990: *The Consequence of Modernity*. Oxford: Polity Press.

——. 1991: *Modernity and Self-Identity*, Oxford: Polity Press.

——. 1992: *The Transformation of Intimacy*. Oxford: Polity Press.

——. 1994: Risk, trust and reflexivity. In U. Beck, A. Lash and A. Giddens (eds), *Reflexive Modernization*, Cambridge: Polity Press, 184–97.

Glenny, M. 1991: *The Rebirth of History. Eastern Europe in the Age of Democracy*. Harmondsworth: Penguin Books.

Gloannec, A.M. le 1994: On German identity. *Daedalus*, 123, 129–45.

Gluckman, M. 1962: Les rites de passage. In M. Gluckman (ed.), *Essays on the Ritual of Social Relations*, Manchester: Manchester University Press, 1–53.

Goffman, E. 1963a: *Behavior in Public Places: Notes on the social organization of gatherings*. New York: Free Press.

——. 1963b: *Stigma*. Englewood Cliffs, NJ: Prentice-Hall.

——. 1970: *Strategic Interaction*. Oxford: Basil Blackwell.

——. 1971: *Relations in Public*. New York: Harper and Row.

——. 1972: *Interaction Rituals: Essays on face to face behaviour*. Harmondsworth: Penguin Books.

Goldfarb, J.C. 1991: *The Cynical Society: The culture of politics and the politics of culture in American life*. Chicago: University of Chicago Press.

Goldsmith, D. and Parks, M.R. 1990: Communicative strategies for managing the risks of seeking social support. In S. Duck (ed.), *Personal Relationships and Social Support*, London: Sage, 104–21.

Good, D. 1988: Individuals, interpersonal relations and trust. In D. Gambetta (ed.), *Trust: Making and breaking cooperative relations*, Oxford: Basil Blackwell, 31–47.

Goodin, R.E. 1992: *Motivating Political Morality*. Oxford: Basil Blackwell.

Gouldner, A. 1970: *The Coming Crisis of Western Sociology*. New York: Basic Books.

Granovetter, M.S. 1973: The strength of weak ties. *American Journal of Sociology*, 78, 1360–80.

——. 1985: Economic action and social structure: the problem of embeddedness. *American Journal of Sociology*, 91, 481–510.

Gray, J. 1991: *Liberalism*. London: Routledge.

——. 1993: *Beyond the New Right*. London: Routledge.

Greif, A. 1989: Reputation and coalitions in medieval trade: evidence on the Maghrabi trades. *The Journal of Economic History*, 69, 4, 857–83.

Habermas, J. 1976: *Legitimation Crisis*. London: Heinemann.

——. 1984: *The Theory of Communicative Action*. Boston: Beacon Press, vol. 1.

——. 1985: Civil disobedience: litmus test for the democratic constitutional state. *Berkeley Journal of Sociology*, 30, 99–112.

——. 1990: *Moral Consciousness and Moral Communicative Action*. Cambridge, Mass.: MIT Press.

——. 1992: *Autonomy and Solidarity*. Interview with J. Habermas. Edited and introduced by Peter Dews. London: Verso.

Hage, J. and Powers, C.H. 1992: *Post-Industrial Lives*. London: Sage.

Halbwachs, M. 1992: *On Collective Memory*. Ed. L.A. Coser, Chicago: University of Chicago Press.

Hall, J.A. 1992: Trust in Tocqueville. *Policy Organisation and Society*, Winter, 16–24.

——. 1994: *Coercion and Consent*. Cambridge: Polity Press.

Hall, S. 1993: Thatcherism today. *New Statesman and Society*, 26 Nov., 14–16.

Hamer, J.H. 1994: Identity, process and reinterpretation, *Anthropos*, 89, 190–1.

Hamilton, P. 1983: *Talcott Parsons*. Chichester: Ellis Horwood Ltd Publisher.

Hankiss, E. 1990: In search of a paradigm. *Daedalus*, 119, 183–215.

Hardin, R. 1993: The street-level epistemology of trust. *Politics and Society*, 21, 505–31.

Harrison, S. 1992: Ritual as intellectual property. *Man*, 27, 2, 225–41.

Hart, K. 1988: Kinship, contract as trust: the economic organisation of migrants in an African city slum. In D. Gambetta (ed.), *Trust: Making and breaking cooperative relations*, Oxford: Basil Blackwell, 176–93.

Havel, V. 1992: A dream for Czechoslovakia. *The New York Review of Books*, 25 June, 8–17.

Hawthorn, G. 1988: Three ironies of trust. In D. Gambetta (ed.), *Trust: Making and breaking cooperative relations*, Oxford: Basil Blackwell, 108–26.

Hechter, M. 1987: *Principles of Group Solidarity*. Berkeley: University of California Press.

——. 1989: Rational choice foundation of social order. In J.H. Turner (ed.), *Theory Building in Sociology*, London: Sage, 66–82.

Held, D. 1987: *Models of Democracy*. Cambridge: Polity Press.

——. 1991: Democracy, the nation-state and the global system. In D. Held (ed.), *Political Theory Today*, Cambridge: Polity Press, 197–235.

Heller, A. and Feher, F. 1988: *The Post-modern Political Condition*. Cambridge: Polity Press.

Heritage, J. 1984: *Garfinkel and Ethnomethodology*. Cambridge: Polity Press.

Herskovits, M.J. 1948: *Man and his Work*. New York: Alfred Knof.

Herzfeld, M. 1980: Honor and shame: problems in comparative analysis of moral systems. *Man*, 15, 339–51.

——. 1992: *The Social Production of Indifference*. Chicago: University of Chicago Press.

Hirsch, F. 1977: *Social Limits to Growth*. London: Routledge.

Hirschman, A.O. 1970: *Exit, Voice, and Loyalty*. Cambridge, Mass.: Harvard University Press.

Hirschman, A. 1976: *Passions and the Interests*. Princeton: Princeton University Press.

——. 1982: *Shifting Involvements: Private interest and public action*. Princeton: Princeton University Press.

——. 1984: Against parsimony: three easy ways of complicating some categories of economic discourse. *American Economic Review Proceedings*, 74, 88–96.

Hirst, P. 1994: *Associative Democracy*. Cambridge: Polity Press.

Hirst, P. and Zetlin, J. 1991: Flexible specialisation verus post-Fordism. *Economy and Society*, 20, 1–57.

Hobsbawm, E. 1993: The new threat to history. *The New York Review of Books*, 16 Dec., 62–4.

Hoffmann, S. 1993: Goodbye to a united Europe? *The New York Review of Books*, 27 May, 27–31.

Hollinger, F. and Haller, M. 1990: Kinship and social networks in modern societies. *European Sociological Review*, 6, 103–24.

Horsman, M. and Marshall, A. 1994: *After the Nation-State*. London: HarperCollins.

Horton, J. 1993: Liberalism, multiculturalism and toleration. In J. Horton (ed.), *Liberalism, Multiculturalism and Toleration*, London: Macmillan, 1–18.

Hughes, R. 1993: *Culture of Complaint*. New York: Oxford University Press.

Hume, D. 1985: *Enquiries Concerning Human Understanding and Concerning the Principles of Morals*. Oxford: Clarendon Press.

Huntington, S.P. 1993: The clash of civilizations? *Foreign Affairs*, Summer, 221–49.

Hutton, W. 1994: Job worries flow from freer trade. *Guardian Weekly*, 20 Nov., 21.

Ignatieff, M. 1985: *The Needs of Strangers*. New York: Viking Press.

——. 1993: *Blood and Belonging: Journeys into the new nationalism*. London: Chatto and Windus/BBC Books.

Inglehart, R. 1991: Trust between nations: primordial ties, societal learning and economic development. In K. Reif and R. Inglehart (eds), *Eurobarometer*, London: Macmillan, 145–85.

Jacobson, D. 1975: Fair weather friend: label and context in middle-class friendship. *Journal of Anthropological Research*, 31, 225–34.

James, W. 1950: *The Principles of Psychology*. New York: Dover.

Jerrome, D. 1984: Good company: the sociological implications of friendship. *Sociological Review*, 32, 696–717.

Jones, D. 1993: Respecting beliefs and rebuking Rushdie. In J. Horton (ed.), *Liberalism, Multiculturalism and Toleration*, London: Macmillan, 114–32.

Jong, E. 1994: *Fear of Fifty*. London: Chatto and Windus.

Judt, T. 1992: The past is another country. *Daedalus*, 121, 83–118.

——. 1994: The inheritors. Post-communist paranoia in Eastern Europe and the dangers of re-opening the past. *Times Literary Supplement*, 11 Feb., 3–4.

Keane, J. 1984: *Public Life and Late Capitalism*. Cambridge: Cambridge University Press.

——. (ed.) 1988: *Civil Society and the State*. London: Verso.

Keohane, R.O. and Ostrom, E. 1994: Introduction. *Journal of Theoretical Politics*, 6, 403–28.

Keshet, J. 1988: The remarried couple: stresses and successes. In W. Beer (ed.), *Relative Strangers: Studies of Stepfamily Process*, Totowa, NJ: Littlefield Adams, 29–53.

Kitschelt, H. 1989: *The Logic of Party Formation*. Ithaca, NY: Cornell University Press.

——. 1990: New social movements and the decline of party organisation. In R.J. Dalton and M. Kuechler (eds), *Challenging the Political Order*, New York: Oxford University Press, 179–208.

Kohler-Koch, B. 1994: Changing patterns of interest intermediation in the European Union. *Government and Opposition*, 29, 166–80.

Kolakowski, L. 1978: *Main Currents of Marxism*, Oxford: Clarendon Press.

Koralewicz, J. 1993: Authoritarianism and confidence in political leaders and institutions. In W. Adamski (ed.), *Societal Conflict and Systematic Change*. Warsaw: IFiS Publishers, 169–92.

Krygier, M. 1994: Does Australia need a racial vilification law? *Quadrant*, Nov., 20–4.

Kuechler, M. and Dalton, R.J. 1990: New social movements and the political order. In R.J. Dalton and M. Kuechler (eds), *Challenging the Political Order*, New York: Oxford University Press, 277–300.

Kymlicka, W. 1989: *Liberalism, Community and Culture*. Oxford: Oxford University Press.

——. 1993: Community. In R.E. Goodin and P. Pettit (eds), *A Companion to Contemporary Political Philosophy*. Oxford: Basil Blackwell, 366–370.

Lafitte, G. 1994: What Mabo makes of us? *Arena Magazine*, Feb.–March, 20.

Lamont, M. 1992: *Money, Morals, and Manners*. Chicago: University of Chicago Press.

Lane, C. 1981: *The Rites and Rules: Rituals in industrial society – the Soviet case*. Cambridge: Cambridge University Press.

Lasch, C. 1977: *Haven in a Heartless World*. New York: Basic Books.

——. 1985: *The Minimal Self*. New York: Norton.

Lash, S. 1994: Reflexivity and its doubles: structure, aesthetics, community. In U. Beck, A. Giddens and S. Lash (eds), *Reflexive Modernization*, Cambridge: Polity Press, 111–73 and 198–215.

Lash, S. and Friedman, J. (eds) 1992: *Modernity and Identity*. Oxford: Basil Blackwell.

Layton, R. 1971: Patterns of informal interaction in Pellaport. In F.G. Bailey (ed.), *Gifts and Poison*. Oxford: Basil Blackwell, 97–118.

Lechner, F.J. 1990: The new utilitarianism. *Current Perspectives in Social Theory*, 10, 93–111.

Leibenstein, H. 1987: On some economic aspects of a fragile input: trust. In G. Feiwel (ed.), *Ascent of Arrow's Economics*. London: Macmillan, 603–11.

Leinberger, P. and Tucker, B. 1993: *The New Individuals*. New York: HarperCollins Publishers.

Lemert, C. 1992: General social theory, irony, post-modernism. In S. Sedman and D.G. Wagner (eds), *Postmodernism and Social Theory*, Oxford: Basil Blackwell, 17–46.

Lever-Tracy, C. 1992: Interpersonal trust in ethnic business – tradition, modern or postmodern? *Policy Organisation and Society*, 5, 50–63.

Levi, M. 1993: Review of Putnam, D. et al. *Marking Democracy Work. Comparative Political Studies*, 26, 375–87.

Lewis, J.D. and Weigert, A. 1985: Trust as a social reality. *Social Forces*, 63, 967–85.

Lieberman, J.K. 1981: *The Litigious Society*. New York: Basic Books.

Light, I. 1972: *Ethnic Enterprise in America*. Berkeley: University of California Press.

Linz, J. 1988: Legitimacy and democracy and the socioeconomic system. In M. Dogan (ed.), *Comparing Pluralist Democracies*, Boulder, Colo.: Westview.

Lippmann, W. 1949: *Public Opinion*. New York: Free Press.

Lipset, S.M. 1959: *Political Man: The social bases of politics*. New York: Doubleday.

Litwak, E. 1989: Forms of friendship among older adults in an industrial society. In R.G. Adams and R. Blieszner (eds), *Older Adults Friendship*, Newbury Park, CA: Sage, 65–88.

Lockwood, D. 1992: *Solidarity and Schism*. Oxford: Clarendon Press.

Lorenz, E.H. 1988: Neither friends nor strangers: informal networks of subcontracting in French industry. In D. Gambetta (ed.), *Trust: Making and breaking cooperative relations*, Oxford: Basil Blackwell, 194–210.

——. 1993: Flexible specialisation systems and the social construction of trust. *Politics and Society*, 21, 307–24.

Lubasz, H. 1992: Adam Smith and the invisible hand of the market? In R. Diley (ed.), *Contesting Markets*, Edinburgh: Edinburgh University Press, 41–63.

Luhmann, N. 1979: *Trust and Power*. Chichester: Wiley.

——. 1988: Familiarity, confidence, trust: problems and alternatives. In D. Gambetta (ed.), *Trust: Making and breaking cooperative relations*, Oxford: Basil Blackwell, 94–107.

——. 1990: The future of democracy. *Thesis Eleven*, 26, 46–53.

Lukasiewicz, P. 1987: Daily life, the social system and the feeling of normality. *The Polish Sociological Bulletin*, 2, 53–68.

Lukasiewicz, P. and Sicinski, A. 1989: Stabilization, crisis, normalization and life-styles. In W. Adamski and E. Wnuk-Lipinski (eds), *Poland in the 1980s*, Warsaw: Polish Scientific Publishers, 115–32.

Lukes, S. 1975: Political rituals and social integration. *Sociology*, 2, 289: 308.

——. 1989: Making sense of moral conflict. In N.N. Rosenblum (ed.), *Liberalism and the Moral Life*. Cambridge, Mass.: Harvard University Press, 127–42.

——. 1991a: Equality and liberty: must they conflict? In D. Held (ed.), *Political Theory Today*. Cambridge: Polity Press, 48–66.

——. 1991b: The rationality of norms. *Archives Européennes de Sociologie*, 32, 142–9.

——. 1992: The rhetoric of thick consensus. *Contemporary Sociology*, July, 425–6.

Macedo S. 1989: Capitalism, citizenship and democracy. In E. Frankel et al. (eds), *Capitalism*, Oxford: Basil Blackwell, 113–39.

——. 1990: *Liberal Virtues*. Oxford: Clarendon Press.

MacIntyre, A. 1981: *After Virtue?* London: Duckworth.

Macpherson, C.B. 1962: *The Political Theory of Possessive Individualism*. Oxford: Oxford University Press.

Macrae, D. 1969: Introduction. In *H. Spencer, the Man Versus the State*, ed. A. Macrae, Harmondsworth: Penguin Books, 7–55.

Madsen, R. 1991: Contentless consensus. In A. Wolfe (ed.), *America at Century's End*. Berkeley: University of California Press, 440–60.

Mannin, B. 1987: On legitimacy and political deliberation. *Political Theory*, 15, 351–62.

Manning, P. 1992: *Erving Goffman and Modern Sociology*. Cambridge: Polity Press.

Mansbridge, J.J. (ed.) 1990: *Beyond Self-Interest*. Chicago: University of Chicago Press.

Marcuse, H. 1964: *One-Dimensional Man*. Boston: Beacon Press.

Margolis, H. 1984: *Selfishness, Altruism and Rationality*. Chicago: University of Chicago Press.

——. 1990: Dual utilities and rational choice. In J.J. Manbridge (ed.), *Beyond Self-Interest*, Chicago: University of Chicago Press, 239–66.

Marody, M. 1988: Antimonies of collective subconsciousness. *Social Research*, 55, 97–110.

Marquand, D. 1991: Civic republicans and liberal individualists: the case of Britain. *Archives Européennes de Sociologie*, 32, 329–44.

Marshall, T.H. 1973: *Class, Citizenship and Social Development*. Westport: Greenwood Press.

Martindale, D. 1960: *The Nature and Types of Sociological Theory*. Boston: Houghton Mifflin.

Matland, R. 1994: Putting Scandinavian equality to the test. *British Journal of Political Sciences*, 24, 273–92.

Mauss, M. 1970: *The Gift: Forms and functions of exchange in archaic societies*. Trans. I. Cunnison, London: Cohen and West.

Mendus, S. 1989: *Toleration and the Limits of Liberalism*. Atlantic Highlands, NJ: Humanities Press International.

——. 1993: The tigers of wrath and the horses of instruction. In J. Horton (ed.), *Liberalism, Multiculturalism and Toleration*, London: Macmillan, 193–206.

Meny, Y. 1990: *Government and Politics in Western Europe*. Oxford: Oxford University Press.

Merelman, R. 1966: Learning and legitimacy. *American Political Science Review*, 60, 548–61.

Merquior J.G. 1991: *Liberalism Old and New*. Boston: Twayne Publisher.

Merton, R. 1957: *Social Theory and Social Structure*. New York: Free Press.

Miller, S.M. 1987: Introduction: The Legacy of Richard Titmuss. In B. Abel-Smith and K. Titmuss (eds), *The Philosophy of Welfare*, London: Allen and Unwin, 1–23.

Mills, C.W. 1970: *The Sociological Imagination*. Harmondsworth: Penguin Books.

Milosz, C. 1993: Swing shift in the Baltics. *The New York Review of Books*, 4 Nov., 3–6.

Milward, A.S. 1992: *The European Rescue of the Nation-State*. London: Routledge.

Misztal, B.A. 1991: HIV/AIDS in Poland: a society in need of the state. *Journal of European Social Policy*, 1, 70–91.

Moore, G. 1990: Structural determinants of men's and women's personal networks. *American Sociological Review*, 55, 726–35.

Morgan D. 1990: Combining the strengths of social networks, social support, and personal relationships. In S. Duck (ed.), *Personal Relationships and Social Support*, London: Sage, 190–217.

Morgan, W. 1912: Trust. In J. Hastings (ed.), *Encyclopedia of Religion and Ethics*, New York: C. Scribner's Sons, 464–5.

Mulhall, S. and Swift, A. 1992: *Liberals and Communitarians*. Oxford: Basil Blackwell.

Muller, H.P. 1988: Social structure and civil religion: legitimation crisis in a late Durkheimian perspective. In J.C. Alexander (ed.), *Durkheimian Sociology: Cultural Studies*, Cambridge: Cambridge University Press, 129–49.

Musil, J. 1992: Czechoslovakia in the middle of transition. *Daedalus*, 121, 175–97.

Nachmias, D. 1985: Determinants of trust within the federal bureaucracy. In D.H. Rosenbloom (ed.), *Public Personnel Policy*, Port Washington, NY: Associated Faculty Press, 133–43.

Nisbet, R.A. 1966: *The Sociological Tradition*. London: Heinemann.

Nowak, S. 1989: The attitudes, values, and aspirations of Polish society. In W. Adamski and E. Wnuk-Lipinski (eds), *Poland in the 1980s*, Warsaw: Polish Scientific Publishers, 133–62.

Oldfield, A. 1990: *Citizenship and Community. Civic Republicanism and the Modern World*. London: Routledge.

Offe, C. 1984: *Contradictions of the Welfare State*. London: Hutchinson.

——. 1991a: Introduction: the puzzling scope of rationality. *Archives Européennes de Sociologie*, 32, 81–4.

——. 1991b: Capitalism by democratic design? *Social Research*, 58, 865–92.

Offe, C. and Preuss, U.K. 1991: Democratic institutions and moral resources. In D. Held (ed.), *Political Theory Today*, Cambridge: Polity Press, 143–71.

Omohundro, J.T. 1981: *Chinese Merchant Families in Iloilo*. Quezon City: Ateneo de Manila University Press.

Ossowski, S. 1962: *O osobliwosciach nauk spolecznych*. Warsaw: PWN.

Ostrom, E. 1990: *Governing Commons: The evolution of institutions for collective action*. Cambridge: Cambridge University Press.

Pagden, A. 1988: The destruction of trust and its economic consequences in the case of eighteenth century Naples. In D. Gambetta (ed.), *Trust: Making and breaking cooperative relations*, Oxford: Basil Blackwell, 127–41.

Pakulski, J. 1992: Trust and legitimacy. *Policy Organisation and Society*, 5, 25–32.

Parental Kidnapping, 1979: *Hearing before the Subcommittee on Child and Human Development*, Ninety-sixth Congress, Washington: US Government Printing Office.

Parsons, T. 1949: *Structure of Social Action*. Glencoe, Ill.: Free Press.

——. 1951: *The Social System*. New York: Free Press.

——. 1963: On the conception of political power. *Public Opinion Quarterly*, 27, 37–62.

——. 1964: *Social Structure and Personality*. Glencoe, Ill.: Free Press.

——. 1966: *Societies: Evolutionary and comparative perspective*. Englewood Cliffs, NJ: Prentice-Hall.

——. 1969a: Research with human subjects and the professional complex. In P. Freund (ed.), *Experimentation with Human Subjects*, New York: Braziller, 116–51.

——. 1969b: *Politics and Social Structure*. Glencoe, Ill.: Free Press.

——. 1971: *The System of Modern Societies*. Englewood Cliffs, NJ: Prentice-Hall.

——. 1975: Social structure and the symbolic media of interaction. In P. Blau (ed.), *Approaches to the Study of Social Action*. London: Open Books.

Peel, J.D.Y. 1971: *Herbert Spencer: The evolution of a sociologist*. London: Heinemann.

Pierson, C. 1993: Democracy, markets and capital: are there necessary economic limits to democracy? In D. Held (ed.), *Prospects for Democracy*, Cambridge: Polity Press, 179–99.

Pizzorno, A. 1966: Amoral familism and historical marginality. *International Review of Community Development*, 15, 55–66.

——. 1990: Parties in pluralism. In P. Mair (ed.), *The West European Party System*, Oxford: Oxford University Press, 61–73.

Poggi, G. 1972: *Images of Society: Essays on sociological theories of Tocqueville, Marx, and Durkheim*. Stanford, Cal.: Stanford University Press.

——. 1983: *Calvinism and the Capitalist Spirit*. London: Macmillan.

Pope, W. 1986: *Alexis de Tocqueville*. London: Sage.

Porter, H. 1992: This sceptic isle. *Guardian Weekly*, 20 Dec., 7.

Porter, R. and Tomaselli, S. 1989: Introduction. In R. Porter and S. Tomaselli (eds), *The Dialectics of Friendship*, London: Routledge, 1–11.

Portes, A. and Sensenbrenner, J. 1993: Embeddedness and immigration: notes on the social determinants of economic action. *American Journal of Sociology*, 98, 1332–50.

Price, A.W. 1989: *Love and Friendship in Plato and Aristotle*. Oxford: Clarendon Press.

Putnam, R.D. 1993: *Making Democracy Work*. Princeton: Princeton University Press.

Rawls J. 1972: *Theory of Justice*. Cambridge, Mass.: Harvard University Press.

——. 1992: Can rationality choice be a foundation for social theory? *Theory and Society*, 21, 219–41.

——. 1993: *Political Liberalism*. New York: Columbia University Press.

Raz, J. 1986: *The Morality of Freedom*. Oxford: Oxford University Press.

Reich, R.B. 1991: What is a nation? *Political Science Quarterly*, 106, 193–209.

Rexheuser, R. 1993: Prusy Wschodnie – dziedzictwo i nowa tozsamosc. *Borussia*, 6, 161–5.

Roche, M. 1992: *Rethinking Citizenship*. Cambridge: Polity Press.

Roller, E. 1994: Ideological basis of the market economy. *European Sociological Review*, 10, 105–18.

Rorty, R. 1994: Why can't a man be more like women, and other problems in moral philosophy. *London Review of Books*, 24 Feb., 3–6.

Rosenblum, N.L. 1989: Pluralism as self-defense. In N.N. Rosenblum (ed.), *Liberalism and the Moral Life*, Cambridge, Mass.: Harvard University Press, 183–226.

Ross, G. 1992: Confronting the new Europe. *New Left Review*, 191, 32–51.

Rousso, H. 1991: The Vichy syndrome. Cambridge, Mass.: Harvard University Press.

Rowse, T. 1993: *After Mabo. Interpreting Indigenous Traditions*. Melbourne: Melbourne University Press.

Rubin, L.B. 1983: *Intimate Strangers: Men and women together*. New York: Harper and Row.

Rumney, J. 1966: *Herbert Spencer's Sociology*. New York: Atherton Press.

Ryan, A. 1992: Some causes for anxiety. *Times Literary Supplement*, 10 Jan., 22.

Sa'adah, A. 1992: Forgiving without forgetting: political reconciliation and democratic citizenship. *French Politics*, 10, 94–113.

Sabel, C. 1989: Flexible specialisation and the re-emergence of regional economies. In P. Hirst et al. (eds), *Revising Industrial Decline*, Oxford: Berg, 215–49.

——. 1992: Studied trust: building new forms of cooperation in a volatile economy. In F. Pyke and W. Sengenberger (eds), *Industrial Districts and Local Economic Regeneration*. Geneva: International Institute for Labour Studies, 215–50.

Samples, J. 1988: Introduction. In F. Toennies: *Community and Society*, New Brunswick, NJ: Transaction Books, xi–xxiii.

Sandel, M. 1982: *Liberalism and Limits of Justice*. Cambridge: Cambridge University Press.

Sandholz, W. and Zysman, W. 1989: Recasting the European bargain. *World Politics*, 62, 95–128.

Schelling, T. 1960: *The Strategy of Conflict*. Cambridge, Mass.: Harvard University Press.

Schopflin, G. 1993: *Politics in Eastern Europe*. Oxford: Basil Blackwell.

Schram, S.F. 1993: Postmodern policy analysis: discourse and identity in welfare policy. *Policy Science*, 26, 249–70.

Seligman, A. 1992: *The Idea of Civil Society*. New York: Free Press.

Selznick, P. 1992: *The Moral Commonwealth: Social theory and the promise of community*. Berkeley: University of California Press.

Sen, A. and Williams, B. (eds) 1982: *Utilitarianism and Beyond*. Cambridge: Cambridge University Press.

Sennett, R. 1973: *The Uses of Disorder*. Harmondsworth: Penguin Books.

——. 1974: *The Fall of Public Man*. Cambridge: Cambridge University Press.

Shalins, M. 1972: *Stone Age Economics*. Chicago: Aldine-Atherton.

Shapin, S. 1994: *A Social History of Truth*. Chicago: University of Chicago Press.

Silver, A. 1985: Trust in social and political theory. In G.D. Suttles and M.N. Zald (eds), *The Challenge of Social Control*, Norwood, NY: Ablex Publishers, 52–65.

——. 1989: Friendship and trust as moral ideals: an historical approach. *Archives Européennes de Sociologie*, 30, 274–97.

Silverman, S.F. 1968: Agricultural organisation, social structure and values in Italy. *American Anthropologist*, 70, 1–19.

Simmel, G. 1950: *The Sociology of Georg Simmel*. Trans. and ed. by K.H. Wolff, New York: Free Press.

——. 1971: *Georg Simmel on Individuality and Social Forms*. Ed. by Donald N. Levine, Chicago: University of Chicago Press.

——. 1978: *The Philosophy of Money*. London: Routledge.

Singer, P. (ed.) 1994: *Ethics*. Oxford: Oxford University Press.

Smith, G. 1993: *Politics in Western Europe*. Aldershot: Dartmouth.

Smith, M.E. 1982: The process of sociocultural continuity. *Current Anthropology*, 23, 127–42.

Sole, R. 1994: Lifting a veil of fear from French schools. *Guardian Weekly*, 25 Sept., 14.

Spencer, H. 1896: *The Principles of Sociology*. New York: Appleton. vol. 1.

——. 1969: *The Man versus the State*, ed. by D. Macrae, Harmondsworth: Penguin Books.

Stacey, J. 1993: *Brave New Families*. New York: Basic Books.

Stasser, H. 1976: *The Normative Structure of Sociology*. London: Routledge and Kegan Paul.

Stepan, A. 1994: When democracy and the nation-state are competing logics. *Archives Européennes de Sociologie*, 35, 127–41.

Stinchcombe, A. 1992: Simmel systematized. *Theory and Society*, 21, 183–202.

Streeck, W. and Schmitter, P.C. 1991: From national corporatism to transnational pluralism, *Politics and Society*, 19, 2, 133–64.

Swidler, A. 1986: Culture in action. *American Sociological Review*, 51, 273–86.

Szacki, J. 1979: *History of Sociological Thought*. Westport, Conn.: Greenwood Press.

Taylor, C. 1992: *Sources of the Self*. Cambridge: Cambridge University Press.

Thompson, D.F. 1987: *Political Ethics and Public Office*. Cambridge, Mass.: Harvard University Press.

Thompson, K. 1992: Religion, values and ideology. In R. Bocock and K. Thomson (eds), *Social and Cultural Forms of Modernity*, Cambridge: Polity Press, 321–66.

Titmuss, R.M. 1969: *The Gift Relationship: From human blood to social policy*. London: Routledge.

——. 1987: *The Philosophy of Welfare*. Ed. by B. Abel-Smith and K. Titmuss, London: Allen and Unwin.

Tocqueville, A. de, 1955: *The Old Regime and the French Revolution*. Trans. S. Gilbert. New York: Anchor.

——. 1968: *Democracy in America*. Trans. G. Lawrence. London: Collins, The Fontana Library.

Toennies, F. 1988: *Community and Society*. New Brunswick, NJ: Transaction Books.

Tonkin, E. 1992: *Narrating our Past: The Social Construction of Oral History*. Cambridge: Cambridge University Press.

Torrance, T. 1993: Or communitarian liberalism? In W.S.R. Pickering and W. Watts Miller (eds), *Individualism and Human Rights in the Durkheimian Tradition*, British Centre for Durkheimian Studies, Oxford Occasional Papers, 1, 105–8.

Touraine, A. 1992: Two interpretations of contemporary social change. In H. Haferkamp and N.J. Smeler (eds), *Social Change and Modernity*, Berkeley: University of California Press, 55–93.

Toynbee, P. 1988: Britain's lost children. *Guardian Weekly*, 24 April, 24.

Turner, R.H. 1989: The paradox of social order. In J.H. Turner (ed.), *Theory Building in Sociology*. London: Sage.

——. 1991: The use and misuse of rational models in collective behaviour and social psychology. *Archives Européennes de Sociologie*, 32, 84–108.

Turner, S. 1994: *The Social Theory of Practice*. Cambridge: Polity Press.

Veblen, T. 1959: *The Theory of the Leisure Class*. New York: Mentor.

Vickers, G. 1965: *The Art of Judgment*. London: Harper and Row.

——. 1973: *Making Institutions Work*. London: Associated Business Programmes.

——. 1980: *Responsibility: Its sources and limits*. Seaside, Cal.: Intersystems.

——. 1987: *Policymaking, Communication and Social Learning*. New Brunswick, NJ: Transaction Books.

Waldinger, R. 1984: *Through the Eye of the Needle: Immigrants and enterprise in New York's garment trades*. New York: New York University Press.

Wallace, W. 1990: Rationality, human nature, and society in Weber's theory. *Theory and Society*, 19, 199–222.

Wallop, M. 1979: Children of divorce and separation. *Trial*, May, 33–8.

Walzer, M. 1983: *Spheres of Justice*. New York: Basic Books.

Ward, R. and Jenkins, R. (eds) 1984: *Ethnic Communities in Business*. Cambridge: Cambridge University Press.

Watts Miller, W. 1993: Durkheim's liberal communitarianism. In W.S.R. Pickering and W. Watts Miller (eds), *Individualism and Human Rights in the*

*Durkheimian Tradition*, British Centre for Durkheimian Studies, Oxford Occasional Papers 1, 82–104.

Weatherford, M.S. 1992: Measuring political legitimacy. *American Political Science Review*, 86, 149–64.

Weber, M. 1948: *From Max Weber: Essays in sociology*. Ed. by H.H. Gerth and C.W. Mills, New York: Oxford University Press.

——. 1958: *The Protestant Ethic and Spirit of Capitalism*. Trans. T. Parsons, New York: Charles Scribner's Sons.

——. 1964: *The Theory of Social and Economic Organisation*. Ed. by T. Parsons, New York: Free Press.

——. 1968: *Economy and Society*, Ed. by G. Roth and C. Wittich, Berkeley: University of California Press.

——. 1978: *Selection in Translation*. Ed. by W.G. Runciman, trans. E. Matthews, Cambridge: Cambridge University Press.

Weil, F.D. 1987: The stranger, prudence, and trust in Hobbes's theory. *Theory and Society*, 15, 759–88.

——. 1989: The sources and structure of legitimation in western democracies. *American Sociological Review*, 54, 682–706.

Weil, S. 1952: *The Need for Roots*. Trans. A. Wills, New York: G.P. Putnam's Sons.

Weiss, R.S. 1974: The provisions of social relationships. In Z. Rubin (ed.), *Doing unto Others*. Englewood Cliffs, NJ: Prentice-Hall. 45–67.

Wejchert, K. 1993: *Przestrzen Wokol Nas*. Katowice: Noma Press.

Welter-Enderlin, R. 1993: Secrets of couples and couples' therapy. In E. Imber-Black (ed.), *Secrets in Families and Family Therapy*, New York: W.W. Norton, 47–65.

White, P. 1993: Trust and toleration: some issues for education in a multicultural democratic society. In J. Horton (ed.), *Liberalism, Multiculturalism and Toleration*, London: Macmillan, 70–83.

Wickham, G. 1990: The possibility of postmodernism. *Economy and Society*, 19, 121–47.

Wieviorka, M. 1994: *La Démocratie a l'epreuve*. Paris: La Découverte.

Wildavsky, A. 1994: Why self-interest means less outside of social context. *Journal of Theoretical Politics*, 62, 131–59.

Williams, B. 1988: Formal structure and social reality. In D. Gambetta (ed.), *Trust: Making and breaking cooperative relations*, Oxford: Basil Blackwell, 3–15.

——. 1994: A fair state. *London Review of Books*, 13 May, 7–8.

Willmott, P. 1987: *Friendship Networks and Social Support*. London: Policy Studies Institute.

Wilson, B.R. 1984: Morality in the evolution of the modern social system. *British Journal of Sociology*, 38, 315–32.

Wilterdink, N. 1992: Images of national character. *The Netherlands' Journal of Social Sciences*, 28, 31–49.

Wiltshire, D. 1978: *The Social and Political Thought of Herbert Spencer*. Oxford: Oxford University Press.

Winstead, B. 1986: Sex differences in same-sex friendships. In B. Winstead and V.G. Derlega (eds), *Friendship and Social Interaction*, New York: Springer, 81–99.

Wolfe, A. 1989: *Whose Keepers? Social Science and Moral Obligation*. Berkeley: University of California Press.

——. (ed.) 1991a: *America at Century's End*. Berkeley: University of California Press.

——. 1991b: Out of the frying pan into . . . what? In A. Wolfe (ed.), *America at Century's End*. Berkeley: University of California Press, 461–72.

Wolfe, R.N. 1976: Trust, anomia, and the locus of control: alienation of US college students in 1964, 1969, 1974: *Journal of Social Psychology*, 100, 151–72.

Wolin, S.S. 1960: *Politics and Vision*. Boston: Little, Brown and Co.

Woollacott, M. 1993: Stop the world while we all get off. *Guardian Weekly*, 7 March, 4.

Wuthnow, R. 1991: *Acts of Compassion. Caring for others and helping ourselves*. Princeton: Princeton University Press.

Wyman, M. 1994: Russian political culture: evidence from public opinion surveys. *Journal of Communist Studies and Transition Politics*, 10, 24–53.

Young, M. 1988: *The Metronomic Society: Natural rhythms and human timetables*. London: Thames and Hudson.

Zarecka-Irwin, I. 1993: In search of usable past. *Society*, 30, 32–6.

Zeitlin, I.M. 1968: *Ideology and the Development of Sociological Theory*. Englewood Cliffs, NJ: Prentice-Hall.

Zeldin, T. 1994: *An Intimate History of Humanity*. London: Sinclair-Stevenson.

Zerubavel, E. 1991: *The Fine Line*. New York: Free Press.

Zetlin, J. 1989: Introduction. *Economy and Society*, 18, 41–61.

Zolo, D. 1992: *Democracy and Complexity*. University Park, Pa: Pennsylvania State University.

——. 1993: Democratic citizenship in a post-communist era. In D. Held (ed.), *Prospects for Democracy*. Cambridge: Polity Press, 254–68.

Zucker, L.G. 1986: Production of trust: institutional sources of economic structure, 1840–1920. *Research in Organisational Behavior*, 8, 53–111.

# Index

trust (*cont.*)
  as social capital, 6, 198
  in traditional societies, 38–9,
    74, 89
  trust in trust, 74, 75, 84, 142
  *see also* civil society family;
    friendship; habit; honour;
    legitimacy; memory
Turner, R. H., 78, 88, 99

utilitarianism, 31, 33–8, 43, 61,
  65, 208; *see also* Spencer, H.

values, 30, 34, 44, 45, 66–8,
  127, 218
Vickers, G., 236–7, 268

Weber, M., 54–60, 61-2, 103,
  110–11, 125, 130, 247, 251,
252
  on legitimacy, 247
  on social action, 54–7
  on trust, 55, 57, 58
  types of relationships, 57–8
welfare state, 4, 48, 202, 203,
  213, 220–1, 222, 224, 255
Western European societies, 159,
  166, 192, 193, 197, 216,
  230, 237, 259
Williams, B., 37, 82, 83, 93, 99
Wolfe, A., 2, 4, 6, 19, 66–7, 69,
  158, 175, 202, 203, 211

Young, M., 103, 105–6, 108,
  109, 140

Zeldin, T., 176, 185, 226, 244